Ed Million

10-19-99

Wrongful Impeachment

Wrongful Impeachment

By
Evan
Mecham

Wrongful Impeachment/Evan Mecham - 1st Edition

ISBN 1-929360-00-2

9 781929 360000

Dedication

I dedicate this book to my wife Florence, our immediate family, and our extended family. They are the foundation of my happiness and accomplishments.

To Florence, who is my one and only true love, my best critic, my strongest supporter and my co-equal partner in everything we do. Her assistance in this book like everything else in our life together has been beyond any price in this world.

To our seven children, Suzanne, Dennis, Christine, Eric, Teresa, Kyle, Lance, their spouses, and our 27 grandchildren, who have been my greatest inspiration in trying to make Arizona and America a better place for them to live.

To my parent, Adelbert and Ina Mecham, and my sibling brothers and sister whose teachings, good examples, and unflagging support has been so important in my life and in whatever I may have done of benefit to others.

Table of Contents

Dedication vii

Table of Contents. ix

Preface. xi

Introduction. xiv

Chapter1
My Crash Course In Politics 1

Chapter 2
Just Missed The Big Leagues - The United States Senate . . 24

Chapter 3
Who Sold Out Arizona On The Central Arizona Project . . . 35

Chapter 4
How The Power Brokers Do Business. 43

Chapter 5
Leading Up To The Watershed Election Of 1986. 67

Chapter 6
The Media Billed It As The Political Upset Of Upsets. 81

Chapter 7
The General Election--The Winner Becomes Governor. 96

Chapter 8
The Starting Lineup Of The Staff. 106

Chapter 9
Then The War Began. 119

Chapter 10
Taking Off. 134

Chapter 11
Law And Disorder. 151

Chapter 12
Their Propaganda Machine At Work. 165

Chapter 13
The October Assault From Four Fronts. 183

Chapter 14
Innocent People Do Not Resign. 200

Chapter 15
The Grand Jury. 217

Chapter 16
French And Eckstein Establish A New Low To
Win At Any Cost. 223

Chapter 17
Staff Changes On The Run. 241

Chapter 18
They Don't Have The Proof But They Have The Votes. . . . 247

Chapter 19
Preparation For The Senate Trial. 256

Chapter 20
The Senate Trial. 265

Chapter 21
The Recall Election. 291

Chapter 22
The Criminal Trial--Corbin's Frivolous Suit. 296

Chapter 23
How The Inaugural Fund Was Stolen. 313

Chapter 24
Arizona A Decade Later. 335

Epilogue. 350

Index. 352

Preface

While I was serving as an executive assistant to Governor Mecham, responsible for 35 state departments and offices, I was frequently asked to speak to various service clubs and other organizations. They all wondered what was going on and what the truth really was about the governor. My answer was, "Governor Evan Mecham is the best friend the taxpayers of Arizona ever had."

I can understand the confusion that the average citizen of this state and even some of the members of the state Legislature had regarding Governor Mecham. Unless you were at his side witnessing this tragic event in Arizona history, you could not possibly comprehend the power of the media and the injustice this man suffered.

Having experienced two United States Congressional campaigns, I gained an understanding of how the media operates; however, I was unprepared for what I observed. For example: I attended most of the governor's press conferences and heard what he said. When I read the newspapers the next day I said, "Where was I?" I couldn't believe the reporters and I were at the same conference. I have never witnessed such distortion of the facts. I believed this could never happen in America!

If I believed for a moment these reports I would have resigned immediately. Working at his side convinced me that he was a man of the highest integrity. I knew his heart was right and he truly wanted to bring about a reform of government.

Governor Mecham's primary fault was he was impatient for results. He wanted to change things immediately and government doesn't respond this quickly. Being from the world of business, he wanted to implement needed changes now! He is also a fighter - a person with more courage than any man I have ever known. His knowledge of the problems was greater than most people because of his service in the Legislature and being a perpetual candidate where constant research is imperative.

I am grateful for this experience because I learned more in a year and a half than I could have possibly learned in 10 years under normal circumstances. People came out of the "woodwork" to give me information that would never have surfaced in normal times. I also learned that there are many dedicated, hard-working state employees and that many things which government is criticized for are incorrect and actually work for the good of its citizens.

I didn't always agree with the governor, but in most instances he was a visionary with programs to add quality to the way government serves the public. He had an uncommon understanding of what needed to be done to revolutionize the efficiency most of us would only dream possible.

As I look back on the Mecham era, I can take pride in the many accomplishments made in such a short period. I witnessed a more responsive government, one that was accountable to the taxpayers. Government waste was identified and changes were initiated to make government more efficient. Foreign trade expanded with the opening of the Taiwan Trade Office. Arizona was ranked the best place in the nation to start a business by Inc. Magazine. It was named the Tourist Destination of the Year by European consumers and on and on. Arizona was pointed in the right direction and the taxpayers were the beneficiaries.

The important thing is for us to learn from this experience and never permit this type of an injustice to happen to a duly elected official again.

Ray Russell

I was privileged to have played a small part in the election and the administration of Governor Evan Mecham of Arizona.
His triumph over the establishment candidates for governor in his fifth try is a profile in American political courage.

I would never have believed subsequent evil and illegal removal of Governor Mecham by the Arizona political machine had I not observed it first hand. It is certainly a stain on the escutcheon of the State of Arizona.

This written account by the man Mecham himself is required reading for all who would understand politics in America. It makes me proud to have been with Ev during both the triumph and the tragedy.

Max Hawkins

September 2, 1998

As one intimately knowledgeable of the facts, 10 years hasn't lessened my belief that a miscarriage of justice occurred when the Arizona Senate convicted Governor Evan Mecham of Articles of Impeachment and removed him from office. Mecham's suffering the highest political penalty for his conduct in the Office of Governor, should concern all of us, for if trumped up charges can be sustained to reverse the will of the electorate in Arizona, it can happen anywhere in these United States.

President Clinton now potentially faces an impeachment and trial by the United States Senate. While allegations of misconduct, especially the character issues, aren't anywhere comparable, nevertheless the political impeachment mechanism is. My hope is that "we the people" will have learned from the Mecham experience. This timely book helps. It clearly reminds us that our political institutions are not infallible and that justice cannot prevail if the majority of those responsible for the proceedings serve their own narrow parochial political interests over the interest of the nation and at the expense of the truth. For the sake of the people, lets pray the United States Congress comports itself better than its Arizona equivalent.

Fred Craft

Introduction

"Power corrupts and absolute power corrupts absolutely"
                                                          Lord Acton

One of the reasons that I won the 1986 election to become the 17th Governor of Arizona was my promise to take the power in government back from the Phoenix 40 and govern in behalf of all of the people. That promise made me a lot of powerful secret enemies.

Soon after taking office I was warned by several sources that I would not be allowed to complete my elected term. I was concerned by these warnings but not alarmed. I knew that I had no "skeletons" in my closet nor would I allow myself to participate in anything illegal or unethical that would form a basis for my removal from office. Also, I thought that I would gain the support of most everyone when they could see the benefits from an efficiently run government that would be a smaller burden on its taxpayers and treated everyone fairly.

I was to find out that it is control, not fairness, that is the bedrock foundation of government by power brokers. I underestimated both their determination to remove me, and their commitment to use any means, legal or not, foul or fair, to succeed.

For almost four decades I have observed with concern, a number of corrupt activities being used to gain and maintain control of government in Arizona. Webster's defines corruption as: "(l) Originally, changed from a sound condition to an unsound one; spoiled; contaminated; (2) Deteriorated from the normal or standard; specifically, a) morally unsound or debased; perverted; evil; depraved. b) taking bribes."

A lot of corruption has been brought about in Arizona by a powerful semi-secret group operating behind the scenes, who has maintained control of government in Arizona through key elected officials. The members of this group have enjoyed it so long that they seemed to think it is their right to continue as Arizona's unelected rulers. Very early on in my term as governor I felt their shadowy control through harassment by the Attorney General's office on several issues. They also brought down an unprecedented avalanche of negative press led by the Phoenix 40 propaganda machine *The Arizona Republic*, which coordinated daily attacks on mostly phantom issues. The power brokers' errand boy, Burton Barr, met regularly with House Speaker Joe Lane, House Majority Whip Jane Hull, and the core of Barr hero worshippers in the House and spewed statements criticizing my every word which were in every morning paper. Anything productive that anyone said was seldom reported in the *Republic*. When House Majority Leader Jim Ratliff said in a Sun City speech that I had accomplished more in the first seven months than previous governors he had worked with had in a full term, it was only reported in the *Sun City Sun*.

The power brokers' task to remove me was not easy and they just barely made it work. It was brilliantly planned and they had the power to get it executed. We were told that they were trying to find where I had broken some law. My staff and I, plus two separate law firms checked everything to see if, inadvertently, some law had been broken. No infractions were found. When Corbin started his "secret" grand jury investigation (highly publicized through "leaks" to the press), we were not surprised they could get indictments because the jurors are told it is only an accusation.

The power brokers knew the indictment accusations had to stand up in Superior Court, and that they had no proof. So they could not remove me from office that way. But impeachment was

---

Introduction

their secret weapon. It requires no legal proof of wrongdoing, just a majority vote in the House and 20 of 30 votes in the Senate. It is an entirely political action restricted to the removal of elected officials from office. The accusers make the rules, hold the hearings, do the prosecuting, judge the proceedings, and then vote the decision. The accused has no civil rights, and there is no due process—in other words, no constitutional rights. There also is no court of appeals except going to the voters in the next election. In the 1988 election following my impeachment, voters did respond, removing from office the highest number of members of the legislature in any state election before or since.

Few people realize what was at stake and why the power brokers would use such extreme, and sometimes illegal measures, to remove me from the Office of the Governor. I was surprised at the ends to which they were willing to go and I understood better than most what was at stake. They had me indicted in criminal court, facing impeachment by the legislature, and if that wasn't enough, I was also the target of a recall petition drive generously financed by the power brokers that wanted me out. No office holder in the history of the United States has ever been attacked simultaneously on those three fronts.

The state of Arizona is a $12 billion business and the governor is the chief executive officer of that business of government. To those who had enjoyed enough control over the governor to get what they wanted out of government, my presence in the ninth floor office of the governor meant they had lost that control. To those who wanted a government that is fair to all, I was good news. To those who want inside influence to get the special benefits they were used to having, it translated into the loss of a lot of power and money. I can show where my administration in just 15 short months saved the state several hundred million dollars. Having a governor who will veto a bad special interest bill can mean the difference between gaining and losing a fortune to some powerful big companies. One such bill I vetoed because it was bad public policy may have affected a few hundred million dollars of a particular company's revenue. That earned me a phone call from an angry lobbyist who began our conversation with the greeting "Just who in the hell do you think you are to veto our bill." Apparently he made a much happier call to my successor when virtually the same bill that I vetoed was passed in the next session of the legislature and signed by the governor.

It pains me to say that Arizona is one of the most corrupt states in the Union. Part of the "tame" side of this corruption, let's call it "white collar" corruption generally involves the political establishment, and will be much of the sum total of this offering. The violent, criminal side of Arizona will not be covered specifically even though it is connected to white collar corruption. While the two appear divorced from each other, the violent, criminal side could not prosper without corrupt politicians controlling key parts of our government. This record is not the entire story, but it is all that needs to be told to get thinking people to become aware of what all too often happens in modern-day government.

I wrote the first draft of this book in 1988-89 to record for my family, the actual facts of what happened to me and my administration as governor of Arizona in 1987-88 and how I was wrongfully impeached.

Now, after 10 more years of corrupt, inefficient government at rapidly increasing costs to the taxpayers, I have concluded that this record should be available to everyone who is interested in the future of self government in the states and the nation. Thinking people everywhere need to know that what is happening in Arizona can happen in their state unless the public is awakened to the danger of a government under the control of unelected power brokers.

Chapter **1**

MY CRASH COURSE IN POLITICS

"No government is respectable which is not just—without
unspotted purity of public faith, without sacred public
principle, fidelity, and honor, no mere forms of government,
no machinery of laws can give dignity to political society."
Daniel Webster

It is 2:00 p.m., June 16, 1988, and here I am in courtroom 402 of the Maricopa County Courthouse in Phoenix, Arizona. It has been two hours since I received the phone call at my Glendale office telling me the jury would be announcing their verdict at 2:00 p.m.

After receiving the phone call, I called my wife, Florence, to say I would be home soon, and we would leave the house at 1:00 p.m. I called my brother, Willard, to say I would pick up him and his wife, May, at 1:15 for the twenty-five minute drive to the courthouse. There we were to face the jury and receive the verdict that would either acquit us of the felony charges brought against us by state Attorney General Robert Corbin, or, as the newspapers had been stating daily for almost five months, I would go to prison for as many as twenty-two years. Willard could be sentenced for possibly eight years. This whole thing is a shock to both of us. We have never been accused before of anything more serious than a traffic ticket.

This two-hour wait is the culmination of a ten-day trial that has been publicized nationwide. It is the only criminal trial to date in Arizona that has ever been broadcast live on statewide television from start to finish.

There have been no fireworks in the trial. No big surprises to justify the type. No millions of dollars had been stolen or taken by fraud. No drug kings standing trial for their heinous crimes against the people. No other gripping accusation that would justify the notoriety of this trial. This was a politically motivated trial in a criminal court. And, it was designed to remove me from the Office of Governor of Arizona by getting a jury to convict me on at least one felony count. That one conviction would automatically remove me from office, break me financially, send me to prison, and destroy me so totally and completely that I could never be involved in the political arena of Arizona again.

Attorney General Bob Corbin, an effective puppet of Arizona's power brokers, had originally spread the word that he had me "cold" on the commission of at least twelve felony counts. With nothing more to go on, though, Corbin settled for a six-count accusation instead. The actual charges centered around the failure to report $350,000, loaned to my successful campaign efforts for governor of Arizona in 1986. The law I was accused of breaking had been designed to make all candidates properly report their sources of campaign money. Many candidates, including several in the 1986 election, had submitted reports with what the Attorney General's Office or the secretary of state had pointed out were possible mistakes. In every case but mine, the candidates had been graciously invited to simply correct the mistake and re-file. When we were made aware of what might be considered technically wrong on our report, we did what all of the others did: made the suggested changes and re-filed. As my campaign treasurer, Willard was indicted for preparing the reports that I signed and filed with the secretary of state. He was the only campaign treasurer in the state's history to be so accused.

When I became aware of the attorney general's grand jury investigation of me, I paid two law firms a total of $25,000 from my own funds to verify the accuracy of our records. Never did I dream that what we had done could be perceived as breaking the law. We knew of no intentional wrongdoing, but, as I said before, we wanted to know if some law had been inadvertently broken. None was found!

Waiting for the jury, my thoughts raced. While it was true that I had been under some pretty severe pressure at times, nothing could compare to this fiasco. In all the other instances, my opponent was something or someone I could see, feel or take corrective action against. If I surrendered, at least I knew I had done my part. As a military flyer, I had bailed out of two burning P-51 fighters and crash-landed another. I had survived other close calls that often come with military flying. As a prisoner of war in Germany, I was ordered by an angry Luftwaffe interrogator to talk. I held fast, following the orders of a higher source, refusing to tell anything except my name, rank, and serial number. The interrogator screamed that by morning the Gestapo would take great pleasure in executing me as a spy if I still refused information. I did not sleep well that night, but deep in my heart I felt secure with the inner peace that they were delivering meaningless threats.

The two-hour wait I endure this afternoon in June is altogether different, though. These power brokers are serious. This accusation is the final move by the powerful, unelected rulers of Arizona to attempt to remove me from the political arena. Under these conditions, they would be assured of no more challenges to their dictatorial, shadowy back-room rulings. It was the last direct move on their part to end a war that they initiated in June of '86, when I successfully challenged their "robot for governor," Burton Barr.

On April 4, 1988, the power brokers had already reclaimed "their" governor's office. They now owned enough legislators to guarantee the necessary votes for impeachment. During that "kangaroo court," I was repeatedly told the votes were there, even before any evidence was presented. I wasn't so worried then; all they could do was remove me from office. However, I was alarmed at their illegal activities and, worse yet, the fact that they had worked because they had complete control of the government. What they did prove by their actions was that they had the power to "crucify the little
b———-d,," as *Arizona Republic* publisher, Pat Murphy, had said they would.

I have little confidence in the judge assigned to this case and am glad that it will be a jury of (I hope) my peers, not the judge who will decide what the rest of my life will be like. My attorney, Mike Scott, told me early on that there was absolutely no evidence to back up the prosecution's charges. When he filed to have the case dismissed for lack of evidence, he said that it would be granted if I were an ordinary garden variety criminal, but he was afraid I would get different treatment. He was right. Of the first twenty-four motions he made, the judge ruled against us twenty-three times.

Our hope is that even corrupt Arizona is not so far gone that the power brokers can fix juries as they can so many other things. We will soon know. The prosecutors had such a lack of evidence, and their case was so weak that half of the time they had spent presenting their case was in meaningless moves to use more time.

After the prosecution had finished presenting its case, we were recessed. It was at this time that our attorneys introduced the possibility of resting our case. What would happen if we relied on the jury's ability to see the prosecution's strategy for what it was— a desperate attempt to emotionally persuade instead of systematically prove their accusation? Good or bad, we decided against the idea to rest, with so much riding on the outcome of this case.

Willard and I feel our defense has done a good job, and if the jury is fair minded we will be acquitted. But now it is crunch time, and the worries won't go away. We had been offered a plea agreement the evening before the start of the trail. They had offered to drop the felony charges if I would plead guilty to two misdemeanors and Willard would plead guilty to one. We had refused, but now everything is rushing through my thoughts as I struggle for some peace of mind. I know we were innocent, but will the jury also know?

Still waiting! In my rush of recollections, I have had to restrain my feelings of anger at all the powerful people and their minions who were subjecting us to this gross injustice. Had it been just me, it would not have been so overwhelming. But, it didn't work that way. My wife, Florence, had suffered in silence for two years as I was viciously attacked every day by the monopoly press in Phoenix. My children and grandchildren were also caught in some of the vitriol aimed at me. Willard had done nothing to justify being singled out for such harsh treatment, except to volunteer to help me by keeping accounts of the money and records of the finance committee. None of our family or extended family had given me one word of complaint, but I knew that both my political friends and enemies had an affect on them. One day, in the thick of things, one of my nieces told me she had never been more proud to be a Mecham, which I think is a wide spread feeling among the family.

Two o'clock! We slowly make our way behind security officers through the sea of reporters that extend from the elevators to the courtroom door. The barrage of questions—"How do you feel? Are you confident? How do you think your lawyers did? Why didn't you testify?"—blends into a low roar and goes unanswered.

Everyone is finally seated and the judge signals to bring in the jury. These eight strangers selected from a jury pool of 100 people would decide our fate. One by one, I searched their faces as they filed in and were seated, hoping to find encouragement in their expressions. Finally a quick glance from one man who looked to be in his 60s. I wanted to believe it was a friendly gesture meant to put my mind at rest.

The judge asks the foreman of the jury, "Do you have a verdict?"

The foreman answers, "Yes."

* * *

Ah, but before I continue, let me give you a more complete picture of what led up to this fateful day.

I had been a close observer of what was happening in state government, since getting a crash course on Arizona politics as a member of the Arizona State Senate in 1961-62. I was shocked to find a handful of powerful people, never elected by the people, controlling Arizona state government through their manipulating influence of key members of the state legislature and, most usually, the governor.

Bills were debated on the floor of the legislative chambers. The actual decisions on important issues were made behind the closed doors of back-room power brokers. To give you an appreciation of how I felt and what it took to bring me up to speed on how government operated, let's shift back momentarily for a thumbnail sketch of what first attracted me to the legislature.

I was, for the most part, politically self-taught. It wasn't any wheeling-and-dealing background or particular admiration for any political figures that motivated me to run for office. It was simply an acute desire to correct what was wrong with government.

I grew up on a farm in mountainous, northeast Utah. My father and mother were excellent teachers and role models for their five sons and one daughter. The discipline learned from tilling the soil and tending to the animals built in me a solid foundation for knowing right from wrong, and a lifelong joy and satisfaction in my work that has proved invaluable.

During my first year of college, at age 18, I enlisted with the U.S. Army Air Corps for pilot training during World War II. The following three years in training and combat flying quickly matured me and added to the family values taught since boyhood. Getting through the high pressure of both training and combat was almost without equal when it came to bringing out the will to win. It offered a young man such as myself a feeling of invincibility that was second to none, but it would also severely challenge him when that invincibility was shattered.

My most shattering experience took place on March 7, 1945. I was flying one of four P-51 fighters, escorting a photo version of a P-38 on a mission over East Germany. Suddenly, there was an explosion in the belly of my plane. That one event ended the war for me in a most unexpected way. The Germans had developed a sleek new jet fighter called an ME262. It could climb faster than we in our propeller-driven P-51s could fly straight and level. One of the Germans attacked me from below, destroying my plane with bursts from the four 30-millimeter cannons in his nose. The armor plate built into the seat of my P-51 kept me from being physically destroyed as well.

Miraculously, I got out of the wreckage. My parachute worked, and I became a P.O.W. with no injuries more serious than a fractured knee. Being face to face with the Germans in that camp made me realize that our enemies were simply people like us, with many of the same needs and aspirations. The world's problems usually arose with its leaders. It was not the soldiers who started wars; it was the leaders who created wars, knowing they themselves would never have to risk their lives in battle.

This belief was proven true when forty-three years later, Rudolf Sinner, a former Luftwaffe pilot, sent me a Christmas letter from his home in Austria. It was he who had shot me down. For all these years, Sinner had thought I had been killed in the explosion. He was genuinely happy to learn I had survived. We were connected through the work of Lorenz Rasse. He had spent the majority of his life researching WWII air battles and then linking the two sides. I was pleased to receive his letter; the last part of which I have quoted here:

After the bizarre explosion through which I accelerated at 850 km/hr (528 mph) following my cannon burst (4 barrel cannons – 30 mm) (by which my ME262 shot down your P-51), I was convinced that there could be very little remaining of the pilot.

Happily, I now learn that was in error. I would like to hear from you. How do you remember the incident? What happened thereafter (were you wounded, taken prisoner, any permanent disabilities)?

Until then I wish you and your family a Merry Christmas and for the coming year, happiness, health, and contentment.

Your former Enemy,
R. Sinner

As a P.O.W., traveling through what was left of the beautiful countryside that I'd helped to devastate from the air, I had been forever changed. I never again was able to ignore the regrettable consequences of any act, no matter how unavoidable it might seem. At the same time, the line between good and evil seemed very clearly drawn by the events of World War II, and I knew I could not allow anyone or anything to blur that distinction. So it is with my feelings about today's politics. There is within me that invisible line of distinction between right and wrong, and I do believe that someday the power brokers must face the regrettable consequences of their actions against the people of Arizona!

When I returned from the war in 1945, I married my high school sweetheart, Florence Lambert. We moved to Logan, Utah, where I became district manager for The Commercial Life Insurance Company. We worked hard and prospered, but after eighteen months, we looked to build a better future in Arizona. Soon, we were the proud owners of a little tract home in Phoenix, and I enrolled at Arizona State College (now Arizona State University) under the G. I. Bill. I'd had an agricultural scholarship at Utah State before going into the service, but now my farming days were over unless I made enough money to buy a farm. I made business management and economics my majors. As we built our future, we also began to build a family, beginning with our daughter Suzanne, born in Phoenix, in February, 1948, and our son, Dennis Evan, soon followed, in December, 1949.

To support us during this time, I started selling cars for Ed Spear's Dodge-Plymouth, and later went into a partnership on a small used car lot on East Van Buren. In those days, East Van Buren was "Automobile Row" in Phoenix. Because the trade in that city of (at that time) less than 100,000, was so centralized, it was an ideal place for a young salesman to learn the trade and test his skills. I found I liked selling cars. Cars were solid things that people needed and wanted. If you gave people an honest deal, they came to trust you, helping build your business by referring all their friends and relatives who were looking to buy a car, too. At that point, my dream was to make enough money to go into business for myself.

Besides Florence, I had another love—flying. I joined the Arizona Air National Guard 197th Fighter Squadron at Luke Field, and, I must admit, it was great to get back to flying P-51s again. We had a crack fighter squadron that was a joy to be a part of. Sometimes, however, the joy was questionable. On summer maneuvers at Victorville, California, in 1949, over a four day span I crash-landed one P-51 and bailed out of another when it caught on fire with no place to land. But, that's the way of love; when you're thunderstruck, you pursue it relentlessly!

In 1950, I was at the end of another pursuit. I had approximately a semester to go to graduate from ASU, when Bob Burns, who ran a new car dealership in Buckeye, recommended me for a Pontiac franchise in Ajo, Arizona. He had received the franchise but didn't have the money to open the business. It was just the sort of combined opportunity and challenge that intrigued me. With the $6,500 I had saved and another $6,500 invested by my mother, I became the nation's youngest Pontiac Dealer.

Moving our young family was tough on Florence, though she was as excited by our new life as I was. In 1950, Ajo was a small community of about 7,000, built around a copper mine and smelter. Ajo had a strong Hispanic population, and I found them to be great people—hard working, with a healthy outlook on life! A real pleasure to be with. Mining towns aren't known for their luxury accommodations, though, and the best we could do was rent a broken down old shack. It rented for $35 per month, and Florence and I joked that after three months the landlord should have given us the deed and five dollars change. When I bolted our Kenmore automatic washer to the floor, it nearly tore the house down on the spin dry cycle. Thereafter, Florence always had to stop it and wring out the clothes by hand before drying them on the line in the backyard.

The only building available for the new dealership was a two-stall garage attached to a service station in north Ajo. Mortgage money was almost as unavailable as a decent house in this little mining town, so I hired two men to help me build the permanent dealership facility out of the profits from car sales as we went along. The next year we built a new house for the family. In fact, ours was the second house in Ajo to boast refrigeration. It was quite a move from our $35 per month shack.

Our third child, Christine, was born while we were living in Ajo. Between family and business, we quickly established ties in the community. I worked hard to establish my business, was a member of Rotary, active in my church, and soon knew half of the people in town by their first names. We sure were a happy family, Florence and I and the children.

The political composition of Arizona back then was considerably different from what it is today. The population of

Arizona was less than 20 percent of what it is today, and about half of that population lived in small rural communities on farms and ranches. Phoenix had a population of about 100,000. Arizona's famous economic hegemony was comprised of the five C's, "cattle, copper, cotton, citrus, and climate." Climate translated to tourism and, unlike today, it was dead last. Manufacturing was even less important; at least two-thirds of the voters were registered Democrats. Outside of Maricopa County, most elections were settled in the Democratic primaries. To all but the most idealistic, being a Republican seemed like an exercise in futility.

In Ajo, Republicans were out-numbered eight to one. However, new constituencies were beginning to develop, and civic involvement generated by my budding business and other ties to the community urged my attentions toward local politics. In 1950, for the first time in decades, Howard Pyle was elected as Arizona's Republican governor. Voters apparently decided they weren't quite ready for their first female governor—Democratic nominee, Anna Frohmiller. Pyle was re-elected in 1952; thanks in part to the Eisenhower landslide, while Republican, John Rhodes, won in the 1st Congressional District and Barry Goldwater became a U.S. Senator.

I knew Goldwater as a pilot in the service squadron of the Arizona Air National Guard while I was a P-51 pilot in the fighter squadron. I hadn't seen Barry in about two years, when he suddenly showed up toting a copy of the U.S. budget. He complained about how big and wasteful it was. It was quite a change from the playboy I'd known who'd spent most of his time flying, taking pictures, floating down the Colorado River and collecting Kachina dolls while his brother, Bob, ran the family department store. His upset victory over Democratic incumbent, Senator Ernest McFarland, was a real boost to the Republicans, who were just beginning to build a competitive party in Arizona.

McFarland, in turn, defeated Pyle and returned the governorship to the Democrats in 1954, and in 1958, decided to reclaim his senate seat from Goldwater. Attorney General Robert Morrison planned to step into the governor's office right behind him. The 1958 election was hotly contested, but the Democrats were expected to take both key offices. These were the expectations, that is, until the Phoenix newspapers suddenly unearthed scandals about both Democratic candidates.

Cartoon pictures of Joseph Stalin mouthing the slogan "Why Not Vote For Goldwater?" were apparently brought in from out of state and dumped in the desert. It was as if someone had planned to distribute them and then changed his mind. Word was leaked to the press, tying them to a labor union that was supporting McFarland. Despite his death a few years earlier, Stalin was still one of the most despised figures in American political iconography. The slur against Goldwater was so obvious that most voters couldn't help but be offended. McFarland claimed the whole thing was a dirty trick by Goldwater's campaign manager, Steve Shadegg. Shadegg, of course, denied the charge, but the story printed in the Phoenix papers on election morning revealed that indeed Shadegg had mailed hundreds of copies of the cartoon statewide in unmarked plain envelopes. The news was too late to do McFarland any good. While the jumble of associations in the cartoon may have made no sense politically, the backlash against McFarland swept Goldwater to another surprise victory.

The one and only time I met Eugene Pulliam, Publisher of the Phoenix papers, he told me McFarland had the election won until that cartoon appeared. It was Pulliam's big issue response in his newspapers that turned the tide, he said, obviously relishing his "star is born" capabilities. Pulliam's money and power had accustomed him to making public policy by shaping and paternalistically "speaking his mind" through the printed word directly to politicians. Politicians could either broadly grin and mend their ways while bearing the pressure, or be forever disowned and punished by Pulliam. He always protected Goldwater in this way, and Goldwater could always be counted on to do the will of Pulliam and attorney, Frank Snell. Pulliam and Snell were two of the three master-minds of the current power brokers union.

In the last spring of 1954, Pontiac awarded me their franchise for Glendale. I had worked hard and sold enough cars to get the total support of the zone manager in Los Angeles. He chose me over a lot of applicants who had much more money than I, feeling I would do the best job! I rewarded his confidence in me by out-selling the Phoenix and Mesa Pontiac dealers by the second year we were in Glendale.

The Pulliam press had a hand in making the 1958 gubernatorial election another shocker. Paul Fannin, a well-respected businessman with no political experience, was the only Republican challenger on the horizon. So, Bob Morrison, the Democrat nominee, was expected to be a shoe-in. During the general election campaign, however, the Phoenix papers reported that Morrison had abandoned a wife and child in the San Francisco Bay area. He had allegedly left some bad checks behind as well, before moving to Tucson. There he reportedly had changed his name, assumed a new identity, graduated from law school and remarried. Having established his new life, he went on to become Pima County attorney and state attorney general. The timely release of these news stories gave Fannin what had seemed like an impossible upset victory over Morrison for the governorship.

Morrison later acknowledged having divorced his first wife, but apparently had adequate explanations for his behavior, since no actions of any sort were ever taken against him. Morrison was so furious with the Pulliam newspapers that he raised over $2 million in a public stock issue in 1962, to start a Democratic newspaper in Phoenix—the short-lived *Arizona Journal*.

The seemingly charmed life of the Republican Party in the 1958 election finally broke the Democratic stranglehold on state government. As a citizen, I was elated; I hoped, in particular, that we'd finally get some action on property taxation and government spending.

Arizona's property tax structure was a real shambles. Instead of the full cash value assessment prescribed by law, new economy and middle class homes were being assessed at thirty-five percent of their value while more expensive homes were being assessed at an average of ten percent. Commercial property was being assessed at anywhere from two to ten percent, with the percentage often based on who owned the land.

For the last forty-five years, land tax assessment scandals have been legion in Arizona and are still being uncovered. Bluntly put, some of the wealthy folks who own thousands of acres of property in this state have been able to save millions of tax dollars by sending campaign contributions to the right people.

By 1959, I could see that part of the problem was that Governor Fannin was getting little help enacting constructive legislation from a Democratic legislature. The friends I spoke to seemed to believe as I did about the issues, but none of them felt capable of doing much about it. Like today, one of the biggest mistakes we made back then was to think that politics was better off left to the professionals.

As the 1960 election season approached, I began to talk with Bill Pyper about the state legislature and politics in general. Pyper had been a state senator in 1953-54, and he explained to me the mechanics of getting on the ticket and running for office. I could see no reason why I shouldn't be one of the people to help Fannin help Arizona.

I called Republican County Chairman Ralph Staggs to ask for nominating petitions for state senator. He seemed interested to meet with me about it, and invited me to lunch. When I showed up for my lunch with Staggs, there were a half-dozen other men there. "We don't need you to run," one of them said. "We've already got a candidate." "Well, now, Ev," someone else said, "What else did you want to talk about?"

I replied that I didn't want to talk about anything else in particular. I had some issues on my mind and felt like running to get something done about them. "Where did the other candidate stand on those issues?" I asked. Then I went on to question what else they had on their minds besides asking me to back off?

Ralph Burbacher was their candidate. He was a wealthy man and willing to run. They were both vague and reassuring about the issues. "There are two slots on the ballot," I said. At the time, the state Senate was made up of two senators from each county, elected on a countywide basis. "Help both of us get in. We'll probably make a good team."

"You don't understand," they said. "Why don't you run for the House seat from your district?"

I replied that Bill Barkley was my representative and that he was doing a good job.

"But he is a Democrat," they said.

I shrugged, already having told them I believed Barkley was doing a good job.

My Crash Course In Politics

"Why don't you run for county supervisor?" was the next offer.

I said it so happened I didn't want or need to be a county supervisor. And so the discussion continued.

By the time I got back to my office at the dealership, I was thoroughly disgusted. I got on the phone, individually, with the two people I knew best at that lunch and asked them why they didn't want to try to win both seats. When they agreed with me privately that we ought to try, I concluded that they'd been afraid to speak up in front of County Chairman Staggs. My next call was to the county Republican committee office. I asked them to circulate my nominating petitions. I was going to run for the Arizona State Senate.

Burbacher and I both ran. The Democratic incumbent, (and former Phoenix mayor), Frank Murphy, ran with Joe Haldiman Jr. In those days, the Senate was composed of two senators from each county. The House was composed of representatives of legislative districts in each county, with the smallest counties having one representative. Maricopa, with over half of the population of the state, had the majority of representatives in the House, but all counties had equal representation in the Senate—the same principle as the U.S. Senate.

My two primary issues were:
1. To equalize the percentage of cash value all property was appraised for in assessing property taxes as called for in the state constitution.
2. To get stronger leadership in the state legislature to stop the creeping socialism from Washington that was steadily engulfing the states.

I spent $6,500 of my own money to try to get elected to a position that paid $1,800 per year. It did not make financial sense, but I looked at it as a sacrifice for better government. When the votes were counted, Haldiman had won easily, but Murphy and I were locked in a close race. It took two days to count all the ballots, but I had finally won the other Senate seat for Maricopa County.

I took my seat in the state Senate, in January, 1961, one of only four Republicans in the 28-member chamber. I didn't have anyone to fill me in about how the Senate worked, but it didn't take me long to learn the ropes. I was shocked to learn that the operation of the state senate was directed from the downtown law office of Snell and Wilmer. The Senate president, the majority leader, and the chairman of the all-powerful Appropriations Committee were all confirmed without either opposition or discussion. Years before, they had been "appointed" by the "establishment boss," Frank Snell, and the Senate vote was merely a ratification of Snell's choices. The real boss was Senate Majority Leader Harold Giss from Yuma County. He got his orders from Snell, and everyone in the operations of the Senate got their orders from Giss. The House appeared to be semi-independent, but they almost always followed the Senate lead.

Shortly after the election, Governor Fannin's chief of staff, John McGowan, called we four Republicans into his office for some indoctrination and friendly advice. He said that the powers that be had promised us the privilege of caucusing with the Democrats, and they would give us good committee assignments if we didn't challenge the re-election of the "chosen three." They knew that we couldn't stop their election, but political bosses like to avoid controversial noises that might stir up the peaceful natives.

In those days, Frank Snell, in addition to heading up the state's most prestigious law firm, Snell and Wilmer, was also chairman of the board of Arizona Public Service. Snell and Wilmer represented many of the largest economic interests in Arizona, while most of the rest were represented in part by Jennings, Salmon, and Trask. The Bimson family, operators and controlling shareholders of Arizona's largest financial institution, the Valley National Bank, and Eugene Pulliam, Publisher of both *The Arizona Republic* and *Phoenix Gazette*, helped Snell cover all the bases. Fifteen years later, these men officially organized the Phoenix 40, for the stated purpose of promoting civic values and to fight public corruption. Nothing of real importance went through the Senate without the literal approval of this group.

I noted quite early in my Senate service, that only a few of us carried actual copies of the bills under consideration to their committee meetings for reference purposes. Instead, most of the senators carried smaller notebooks containing summaries of the bills, instructions as to how they should vote, with the reasons they should give for so voting. I was told that the two major law firms usually wrote the summaries. On occasion, the lawyers and accountants who worked for the mining and other "establishment" companies also wrote summaries. While the legislature was in session, a number of these companies maintained suites on the top floor of the old Adams Hotel—for this work and for entertaining. Much of the real legislating was done there rather than at the Capitol.

Needless to say, their summary of my tax equalization bill was negative. The status quo meant too much to the big property owners for it to be anything else. I struggled with it for two years. Each year, I managed to get the bill through only one committee to which it had been assigned. Everyone professed to want a tax equalization program that would be fair to all Arizonans, but everyone knew such a program would not be considered seriously for a long time to come.

I did have a few successes to justify my $1,800 per year Senate salary. We resurrected a Time Sales Finance Disclosure Act, an early consumer protection bill that had lain dormant for years without action in the Senate. It was designed by the Arizona Auto Dealers Associations to protect the public against dishonest auto financing tactics of unscrupulous dealers and finance companies. With the help of Charlie Goff, a retired Chevrolet dealer, and a few other senators, we made this proposal into law before the federal government forced other states to adopt similar protective measures.

I also stopped a gasoline tax increase in Maricopa County, in what almost became an amusing event. Senator Giss had been asked to enter an enabling bill to allow Maricopa County to vote to increase the gasoline tax on sales within the county. Giss had declined to enter it himself and passed it to Senator Glen Blansett from Navajo County. Blansett asked me if I would sign it, and I said "No, I'll oppose it in the floor. Why are you taking the lead on it when it does not affect your county?" I continued to question. Inasmuch as it only affected my county, I guessed the reason I had not been contacted by the county officials behind the bill was because they believed I had no power to prevent its passing.

One of the committees to which the gas tax bill was assigned was chaired by Senator Ray Thompson from Yuma County. I told him of my desire to stop the bill because I believed we should straighten out our unfair property assessment values before we added any new taxes. He said he had to bring it up, but if there were a tie he would vote against it. I then asked enough friendly senators on the committee to vote against it, to kill it, which they did. Suddenly, I received calls from Phoenix Mayor Sam Mardian, County Supervisor Barney Burns, Contractor Maurice Tanner, and *Arizona Republic* Managing Editor, J. Edward Murray. They all wanted to take me to lunch and show me why I should quit opposing the bill. My answer was the same as stated above. We should straighten up our highly unequal property taxes before adding any other tax. I suggested to each of them to help me get my property tax equalization bill through and then I would support their enabling bill and let the voters decide on the gas tax increase. They all turned me down, flat.

The most enlightening exchange on this bill was with Murray of the *Republic*. We went to the Arizona Club for lunch. He brought two of his staff members with him. One was Ben Avery, the *Republic* reporter who covered the state Legislature. I chided Ben on his extensive editorializing of my press release announcing my candidacy for the U.S. Senate. I did not yet realize that they viewed this as their journalistic right. The lunch talk was pleasant until we got down to the business at hand. Mr. Murray surmised that I did not seem to realize that the enabling act by the Legislature was to allow the voter to make the decision. I assured him I understood the process equally as well as he. Murray then suggested that since I was always championing the cause of the people, this was a perfect way to show I supported their right to choose. After all, he questioned, "Who do you think you are to make such a decision—God Himself?" My answer was equally as pointed. "Neither you nor I are God. I merely want the people to have all of the facts before making such a decision. I am willing to support the bill if you will give me, in writing, your guarantee of the same amount of space and the same position for the opponents of the gas tax as you put in as a proponent." I assured him that I had seen the *Republic* put over many such issues by overpowering the public with only one side of the issue reported. His quick refusal was laced with anger, which proved to me that he had no interest in fairness on the matter. He then threatened to take it out on me in the Senate race if I did not go along on this issue, and that's where the discussion ended. The enabling act never got out of the committee, and he did take it out on me in the U.S. Senate race that fall. In fact, they have opposed me in every race I have run since.

The leadership of a legislative body exercises absolute control over which bills move through the committee system and reach the floor for a full vote. First, the leadership makes all the committee appointments. Then, they assign the bills to go through various committees—sometimes only one committee, but sometimes as many as four. If a bill doesn't pass through every committee it's assigned to, it dies without ever having been voted upon by the full House or Senate. Since a committee chairman decides if and when his committee will hear a bill, the leadership can prevent any bill from passing simply by appointing their most loyal henchmen to the key committee chairs. The chairmanships themselves provide plenty of incentive for loyalty, since they give these selected senators great leverage in log rolling and horse trading for their own pet legislation.

In the Senate, Majority Leader Giss was also the Judiciary Committee Chairman. This was highly unusual, but it allowed him hands-on control of any bill he wanted because all bills had to pass through the "Jude" to make sure they were legally correct. Without ever publicly acknowledging his opposition, Giss could kill any particular legislation just by postponing it for protracted legal considerations.

The legislation that got the most public attention that session included the new narcotics bill, the outlawing of the Communist Party in Arizona, and a bill amending the loyalty oath to require that every public official deny membership in the Communist Party while holding office. The House of Representatives sent over the tough new narcotics bill and the two anti-communism bills as a package they had unanimously passed. Despite this kind of support from the Democrat controlled House, Giss decided to prevent the bills from becoming law.

As a member of the Judiciary Committee, for twenty-eight days in a row, I tried to move the bills for committee consideration. Each time, Giss announced vaguely that there were "legal problems" with the bills, and no one seconded my motions. I didn't think Arizona could outlaw communism all by itself, but Joe Haldiman (the other Maricopa County Senator) and I were getting sacks of mail every day from our constituents in support of these two bills. If people wanted them, I didn't see why we shouldn't pass them. It was the narcotics bill, however, that was really fueling my sense of urgency. Arizona had one of the worst and most ineffective narcotics policies in the country, and change was sorely needed.

On the 28th day, I got tired of Giss' refusal to even hear the three bills in the Judiciary committee, so I decided to take another route of action. I told Senate President Clarence Carpenter that I was going to make a motion in the Committee of the Whole Senate to bypass the committees and report the three bills to the floor for the full Senate vote. I didn't really believe I could get the 15 votes needed to pull this off, but it seemed to be my only chance. I knew Giss couldn't afford the embarrassment of not being able to hold his majority together, and opposing a popular measure in public might be more of a challenge than he wanted to face. Since what I was doing was in the Senate Rule Book, I knew Carpenter had to recognize me to make my motion on the floor of the Senate in the Committee of the Whole Senate. In an attempt to avoid this, Giss came to me and asked if I would agree to let them complete the floor action on all of the bills scheduled on the debate calendar that day. Then he suggested we recess and go up to the third-floor caucus room to talk it over. If I still wanted to make my motion after the discussion, we would come back to the Senate chamber and I could make my motion. He hoped to get away from the media and talk me out of it in the caucus room.

Once in the caucus room, the sweetness changed. Giss proclaimed he would not tolerate any ultimatums on the handling of bills and that I must back off. Several other senators took a much more conciliatory tone but said about the same thing. I knew I had struck a tender nerve and had a chance to win. After they all got through lecturing me, they turned to me as if expecting me to cave

20

in. Instead, I reviewed my twenty-eight day frustration with the majority leader, whose excuse had been that the bills were not properly written. This excuse was no longer valid. Plenty of time had passed to correct any flaws in the bills. As a conciliatory move, however, I agreed to wait until the next debate calendar on the following Wednesday to make my motion. This would give him time to correct any flaws and report the bills to the Committee of the Whole Senate to act on them in open session. I then excused myself and left the room.

The press was waiting outside the door and had already heard a lot of the caucus, so a lot of news reports of this eruption in the Senate went out to the public. It caused a lot of people to call their senators and put pressure on them to pass these bills. It was working better than I could have hoped, and the senators were putting pressure on Giss to meet my offer. On Wednesday, he asked me to give him three more days to get the work completed on the bills. They came to the floor and passed with flying colors, without me ever having to make my motion.

Another time, Giss tried to ram through a pet deal to spend $65,000 in tax money on a TV show subsidy. The show was supposed to celebrate the 50th anniversary of Arizona's statehood, but it was really a puff-piece for some major Democrats who were running for re-election. Some of the more fair-minded Democrats concurred with that assessment. I was able to get enough votes to put an amendment on his bill on the floor that had the effect of killing it. After that upset, Giss was apparently afraid the "leadership" was losing control, so he suspended all business for three days while they replaced committee chairmen they thought were getting too friendly with Prescott Senator, Sam Steiger, and myself. He also took Steiger and me, along with six Democrats, off all our important committees.

During this three-day hiatus, the rumor mills were speculating that Steiger and I were trying to overthrow the leadership. That may have come about because it was the reason Giss was giving for his reorganization. As a result, a number of the senators quietly came to us in agreement. They said they would join us when we could guarantee them we already had fifteen on board. With three days of official inaction, what would be the harm in seeing just what we could come up with?

Of the fifteen votes for the majority needed to reorganize the Senate, we found we had a basic core of eight old-time Democrats who were being deposed as chairmen of committees, plus myself and Steiger. We felt that the other two Republicans would be split. Anderson would go with us and Corbett would stay with Giss. Frank Bennett from Santa Cruz and the three other Democrats we needed would go with us, but each required, before they would come into the reorganization caucus, a guarantee they would be the fifteenth man. We could never overcome this obstacle, so Giss' reorganization went forward.

Despite my misgivings about who really controlled them, I never opposed the Senate leadership, when I could avoid doing so without violating my principles. I voted "no" if I didn't agree, but only arose to give battle where winning was at least possible or my principles were at stake. I voted against the appropriations bill each year because I felt they were at least ten percent too high. I spoke my mind when I had a point to make. If I opposed a majority bill, I did it on the provisions of the bill and not the senators who were pushing it. As a result, I built many good friendships in the Senate and got along well with almost everyone.

One of these friendships was with Sam Steiger, a fellow Republican, who later went to Congress. He enjoyed being a maverick, and he'd been an ally in fighting the leadership on bills like Giss' pork barreling. Albert Anderson, the other freshman Republican that year, was one of the finest men to walk the earth. All in all, I liked nearly all the members. I had a particular respect for at least eight of the rural Democrats, who were very solid conservatives.

During a Special Session called in 1961 to reform the liquor laws, I invited Steiger to accompany me to Governor Fannin's office to discuss the governor's position on the proposed bill. The leadership, through Senator Wine, asked me to find out what the governor would settle for, so they and their special interests could have their way with the rest of the bill. We told Fannin of the opposition's confusion and suggested that he could name whatever he wanted in the bill.

A public scandal had developed over the operation of the state Liquor Department. The formula in the law that controlled the number of liquor licenses issued kept them far scarcer than the market demanded. Corruption had become rampant because the licenses were issued to individuals and not the businesses that used them. This made it possible for a license owner to lease out a license issued by the state for a few dollars, for as much as $800 or even $1,000 a month. Some were reportedly being sold for as high as $50,000 a piece. Certain lawyers were charging clients a $10,000 fee to acquire the few new licenses, as they became available. No one ever found out with whom those lawyers shared their $10,000 fees.

What neither the public nor I knew at the time was that a judge had already ruled that, under the existing law, corporations couldn't own licenses. This meant that many local establishments were operating illegally. The whole big emergency reform push was being engineered in order to quietly correct this problem while leading the public to believe that they were actually seeing liquor law reform.

Fannin hesitated when we asked him what he wanted in the bill. He seemed afraid to act. He would only say we had to get a bill out and he didn't want to cause trouble or disrupt the Legislature.

I called him back at the end of that day and again the following morning with no better results. The governor simply refused to commit himself. We became exasperated with each other, and our final words went something like, "Look Ev, you mind your business and I'll mind mine!"

When I walked into the Senate chambers the next morning, Wine was waiting for me. "Have you seen the governor?"

"Yes." But, surely he couldn't expect me to divulge what the governor had confided in private!

"Quit playing games," Wine told me, "this is a serious situation!"

I said I couldn't really give them an official message, but that, well, if I were on the Conference Committee, I would suggest the following provisions on the reform bill. After I detailed them, he seemed satisfied that I was talking for the governor and left. I was not too surprised to see the bill come out for a final vote with exactly the provisions I had recommended. Arizona ended up with some liquor law reforms that year after all.

Some significant education bills were also passed. One brought the existing junior colleges under a state community college umbrella, with state funding to assist in establishing community colleges throughout the state. It has turned out to be an excellent investment and has brought vocational and associate degree levels of education to many people who would not otherwise have had the opportunity to achieve a degree. The other education bill was the first small step toward state subsidy of kindergarten through grade 12 schools.

And, I passed my crash course in Arizona state politics.

Chapter 2

JUST MISSED THE BIG LEAGUES-
THE UNITED STATES SENATE

"The proper function of a government is to make it easy for the people to do good and difficult for them to do evil."
Gladstone

In 1962, toward the end of my term as a state senator, almost accidentally, I broke into the "big leagues" of politics. United States Senator Carl Hayden, who had been in Washington as long as Arizona had been a state, was coming up for re-election. Hayden, a Democrat, had the longest tenure in office of anyone in the history of the Senate. Because of this seniority, he was the chairman of the Senate Appropriations Committee. In the eyes of those who know where the political power lies, this is the most powerful position in the United States Senate. Inasmuch as spending the taxpayers' money is the "mother's milk of politics," this made Senator Hayden the man with whom everyone wanted to be on good terms. He seemed like a genteel, elderly gentleman statesman of 83 years, but, in reality, his administrative assistant, Roy Elson, was "the power behind the throne," the real senator in everything but name.

For decades, Arizona Republicans had been offering opposing candidates as sacrificial lambs to Hayden in the general election. Little money was spent on their campaigns; they just went through the motions to fill the spot on the ticket. In fact, when a huge fund-raiser was held for Hayden in Phoenix, during the fall of 1961, it was promoted by Democrats but publicized as if it were a bipartisan event. President Kennedy was flying out from Washington to serve as guest speaker and deliver the coup de grace to any potential Republican candidate at the same time.

I thought the time had come to challenge Hayden on his long history of tolerating Washington's big spenders, and allowing Elson to usurp his authority—in effect, making Elson acting senator without voter approval. Also, if Arizona retired Hayden in the 1962 election, Senator Richard Russell from Georgia would replace him as Appropriations Committee Chairman. Although he was a Democrat, he was a conservative Democrat, and that was the great advantage to having Senator Russell controlling the spending. Surely, I thought, we Arizona Republicans at least ought to challenge the bipartisan "hype" of the upcoming fund raising event.

Even though I was only a freshman state senator, someone should do something. I called a number of party people, including State GOP Chairman Steve Shadegg, but none of the senior party people seemed the least bit interested.

Some grass-roots partisans, in particular some Young Republicans, I spoke with seemed miffed about the fundraiser. They thought, as I did, that challenging Hayden was a worthwhile cause, no matter how high the odds. I contacted the chairman of the event, Tom Chauncey, owner of KOOL-TV and Radio stations, stating our objections and in a press release that created quite a stir.

The state Young Republican Convention, where I was a speaker, passed a resolution calling for a strong challenge to Hayden. However, we had no success finding a candidate. I felt I wasn't ready for such a major campaign myself, yet the more I thought about it, the more I doubted there was any other course to take. When Barry Goldwater returned to Arizona during December, 1961, we talked about my running against Hayden. He said he thought it was a good idea and offered his full support. He promised to raise at least $50,000 out-of-state, and frequently make himself available in-state to help me campaign. I quickly began to put an organization together and then announced my candidacy.

Since I had already talked to Barry, I didn't bother to check with state GOP Chairman Shadegg, who was basically Barry's boy.

Shadegg had gained his reputation and position by managing campaigns, including both Goldwater's and Hayden's, and he had changed his political registration from Democrat to Republican only just before Barry had installed him as party chairman. Shortly after my announcement to run, Steiger and I went to visit Shadegg. To our surprise, Shadegg said I wasn't going to get a free ride. While he hadn't been able to come up with an opponent to Hayden before I threw my hat in the ring, Shadegg suddenly felt he had to fill the air with Stetsons. Perhaps he was trying to scare me off. Although he had never run for office before, the other primary candidate Shadegg finally came up with turned out to be himself.

One of the things that helped us win in the primary, and almost win in the general, was getting Mac Matheson as campaign manager. Living in Tucson, Mac had given Stewart Udall a close race for the U.S. House in the fall of 1960. District 2 then comprised all of the state, except Maricopa County, which was District 1. When Udall was chosen by President Kennedy to join his Cabinet as Secretary of the Interior, his brother, Morris, ran in the special election for the vacated congressional seat. Matheson then became the Republican challenger again and narrowly lost to Mo.

Mac had a good organization, and most of his people came on board with us in the 1962 race. Mac was a very fine man, a good conservative. Had he won, he would have written a much different history by his service in Washington.

In many ways, Shadegg's campaign managing pioneered the abuses that mar so many of today's political campaigns. He had already been well paid to write a manuscript for the Republican Senatorial Campaign Committee. In it, Shadegg described the key to winning any election was to attack weaknesses in the opposing candidate's reputation. Forget whether or not they were politically relevant. He believed that a winning campaign was to thoroughly investigate your opponent, then, at the worst conceivable moment, haul his dirty laundry out for public examination. In our race, the bankruptcy of this approach should have become evident to him after our primary contest. Because there were no skeletons in my closet, Shadegg tried to invent a few of his own. Although his campaign strategy was completely inappropriate, he never did change tactics and attempt to discuss the issues. Perhaps the old adage: "A lawyer who represents himself has a fool for a client," ought to have been extended to campaign managers as well.

One of the most satisfying happenings in the whole primary campaign with Shadegg was over an article in *Time* magazine about our race. The article had a picture of Steve and a good puff article about this nationally known political expert who would easily beat the little known state senator, Mecham. Shadegg almost papered Arizona with reprints. When the votes were counted, I won by a good margin. I maintained that margin even in the Phoenix precinct where he kept his full-time residence and in Prescott, where his summer home was located. The next issue of *Time* had a good action shot of me taken the night of the primary election with a caption reading: "He beat the expert!"

As written in his book *What Happened to Goldwater,* Shadegg's account of that primary race is wildly different from mine. He blames his loss to me on the fact that Goldwater privately begged him to run against me but publicly stayed neutral. Shadegg claims he had to get into the race because my "campaign tactics" were hurting the whole party. Yet, well before I'd started campaigning, Shadegg told me I wasn't going to run unchallenged. He announced his own candidacy in March while I was still busy in the state Senate and had little time to say anything, let alone stage any dirty tactics. Shadegg even went so far as to report a completely imaginary conference we supposedly had. He said he'd tried to explain the "subtleties of the problem" to me. The problem being me.

After the general election was over, Bernie Wynn, political columnist for *The Arizona Republic,* told me that party leaders had already made a deal in 1960 to run only a token candidate against Hayden in 1962. He was in the meeting that included Goldwater, Fannin, Rhodes, and Shadegg. As with most deals made in "smoke filled rooms," there were no plans to go public with their decisions. Bernie did not think he was breaking their confidence by telling me, after the fact. I didn't know at the time that, in effect, my entrance into the race threw a monkey wrench into their plans. Barry certainly did not give me any hint of any deal being made in December of 1961.

The scenario was simply this: Shadegg had failed in his bid to become the Republican National Committeeman from Arizona at the April 1960 State Republican Convention. After that, Richard Kleindienst, then State Chairman, agreed to step down as Chairman of the State Republican Party in September to open up that spot for Steve Shadegg. In exchange for this, Kleindienst, who had backed Paul Fannin in his successful race to become governor of Arizona, and who, by his own admission, had a lifetime ambition of becoming a United States senator from Arizona, was to become the hand-picked Republican nominee to oppose Hayden in 1962. The tacit understanding was that if Hayden, who at the time was 83 years old, was alive and well by election time, Kleindienst would run only a token campaign. If Hayden were to die in office, Fannin would appoint Kleindienst to complete his term.

My announcement drastically changed the scenario. I was told that in early 1962, Kleindienst conducted a political poll and determined that he could not beat me in the Republican primary, thereby deciding to bow out of contention. It was after that decision that Shadegg, who had held the post of state chairman for only 18 months, decided he would enter the primary because I "didn't understand the subtleties of the problem."

Shadegg voiced his "party unity" line numerous times throughout the campaign. Of course, he vouched support to the winner of our primary in the general election. The more important implication he rarely left to anyone's imagination was that, since he had only resigned as GOP state chairman to run against me, a vote for Steve Shadegg was a vote for party unity.

This one-sided interpretation of the concept of party unity will always be a favorite ploy when bosses control party leadership. Years later, when I lost the 1974 gubernatorial primary to Russ Williams, I did everything I could to help him win the general election. When Shadegg lost to me, he not only failed to support me, but he had many of his people actively work against me. He continued to oppose me until his death.

Just after I'd announced my Senate candidacy in December, 1961, I had begun to get rather peculiar phone calls from a man named George Fowler. He identified himself as a detective who had done a lot of work for Goldwater and was going to help me. Fowler told me that he was the person who discovered where the labor unions had cached the Stalin cartoons. He said he delivered them to

Shadegg's business office, where hundreds had been mailed in unmarked envelopes throughout the state during Goldwater's 1958 campaign. Fowler pointed out that was a clear violation of federal statutes, but Shadegg was never charged. Generally, Fowler would offer little tidbits of information and then ask me questions.

One day Fowler called to tell me I was going to be contacted by a member of the "downtown establishment." The members of this group, whom he only referred to as "they," didn't want me to run against Hayden. "They" were going to offer me an alternative. He informed me that I would be offered plenty of money to run for re-election to the state Senate in 1962—maybe more than I would need for that purpose. I would be given a lot of publicity. I would co-sponsor all the right bills. I would be making a lot of speeches. I would often represent the governor and generally get an all-around great build up, so that in 1964 when Fannin didn't seek re-election, I would be his heir apparent. With their help, of course, I would be a shoe-in as governor in 1964.

At first, I really didn't take him seriously. But in a few days, Fowler called again and repeated the proposal in such detail that I finally told Steiger and ask him what he believed was happening. He said that if it were a real proposition, it would come again until I gave them some kind of reaction. He was right! Two days later, Fowler showed up in my office with the same bag of groceries.

My experience in the Senate made me believe that Fowler was telling the truth, and that, in fact, the downtown establishment people could deliver what he had promised. It concerned me that I was receiving mixed signals. If the party leadership did not want me to run, Barry could have easily taken care of that back in December, when we had talked and urged me to run with the promise of help. Had Barry told me in December, before I had announced that the downtown power brokers did not want anyone running against Hayden, I would have understood. If he did not want to tell me about the downtown bosses, he could at least have told me about the meeting which Bernie Wynn told me about, after the general election. But, in February, when the mixed signals were coming through, I did not know what to think. I still trusted Goldwater but I did not trust the secrecy of the power brokers, so I really unloaded on Fowler. The message he took back to his employers was that, whether or not I ever held any high political office, I'd never try to get there by making "deals."

A few years later Fowler came to see me at my office at the *Evening American*. He was really angry with Senator Goldwater and Harry Rosenzweig over some things they had said and done. I jokingly said he should not get too worked up over anything his "bosses" were doing. He said they were not his bosses, to which I countered that they were his bosses in late 1961 and early 1962, when he brought me the "offer" to be governor in 1964 by getting out of the 1962 Senate race. He was momentarily startled and then grinned and asked me how I knew. I told him how I deducted he was the mysterious messenger who he told me was going to contact me. He then verified the whole story and signed an affidavit that it was true.

During the 1962 Senate campaign, I was *persona non grata* at GOP headquarters. Even state Chairman Richard Kleindienst quietly worked against me in support of Democrat Hayden. He told this to one of the newscasters at KPHO Channel 5 TV in what he must have thought was a private conversation. A friend of mine was in the room and overheard the whole story.

Right after the primary, Barry and I were billed together at the Westward Ho Hotel to address the state convention of the Young Americans for Freedom in downtown Phoenix. The event was broadcast live on television, so we each had a limited amount of time to speak. My campaign was based on a trip to Washington to help Barry advance a common, conservative agenda, and I certainly knew enough not to do anything to upstage him. As I was introduced, the young people, many of whom were involved in my campaign, gave me a rousing standing ovation. I used only half of my allotted 15 minutes so that Barry could have additional time for his talk, but when I sat down I received another standing ovation. Unfortunately, Barry's address did not go over as well. He had reversed his position of advocating that the United States withdraw from the United Nations, and many in the audience were unhappy with that.

On the way home, I was feeling pretty good about things. But my wife, who had been in the front row of the audience, said to me, "Well, you've got some trouble that you didn't anticipate."

"What's that?" I asked.

She replied, "You think Barry is your friend, but he isn't." She'd seen Barry's face when I'd been applauded by the Y.A.F. There had been only a grimace of a smile on his face " He doesn't want to share the limelight. Trust me when I tell you, he'll stab you in the back at the first opportunity."

I was stunned and concerned by her observations. Although Florence's observations were not to be ignored, often having proven to be a better judge of character than I am, so I didn't dismiss it lightly. "No, Barry is my friend," I assured her. "He will do everything he said he would to help me."

Actually I received less than $20,000 in financial help from the party, and Barry's pledge to raise $50,000 was reduced to a belated $5,000. His campaigning on my behalf amounted to being the master of ceremonies at a few political meetings and dinners, where, at best, he gave me a neutral introduction. He finally consented to briefly appear with me on election eve in a live television appearance. His endorsement of my candidacy amounted to a lot of damnation with a bit of faint praise.

With the support of an excellent grass-roots organization throughout the state, I was gaining rapidly on Hayden. Toward the end, I had appealed to the director of the National Republican Senate Campaign Committee for help in offsetting the barrage of commercials saying how important it was to keep Hayden in office. After conferring with Barry, who was chairman of the committee that year, the director promised only that he would turn over some research they had on Hayden's record. I never even got that help.

After his early promises, Barry's lack of follow-through was more than disappointing. When his voice was used on a campaign commercial in support of Hayden, he told me he hadn't authorized it and didn't think it was proper, but he did nothing to stop or disavow the commercial. I didn't press further.

After the Senate adjourned for the fall, we kept asking when Senator Hayden would be home to answer some questions. We were not surprised to have received no answer. Their very professionally managed campaign was designed to keep him in absentia.

The first reason given for Senator Hayden to stay in Washington came from a White House press release. The Bay of Pigs confrontation was heating up between the United States and

Russia over the installation of Soviet nuclear missiles in Cuba. The president wanted Hayden there for advice and counsel, or so the story went. This proved to be stall tactics, but we said nothing.

The missile crisis subsided and again we asked when Senator Hayden would be home. Our answer came through in quite an unexpected manner. An Associated Press reporter in Washington D.C tracked me to Yuma by phone while I was on a campaign trip. He said he had just learned that Senator Hayden had been taken to the Bethesda Naval Hospital for a yet-unknown ailment and wanted my comment. I said only that I hoped it was not serious and wished him a speedy recovery so he could come home and see the people of Arizona before the election. We could not tell if he was really ill, or just a ruse to get me to publicly make some disrespectful comment that his campaign could use against me.

The Arizona Republic started printing daily stories that the Senator had a light case of influenza. None of the news wire services were allowed to see him or talk to anyone who knew what was happening. Then a friend of ours who had contacts was able to get into the hospital to inquire. Word came back that no one was allowed to get near the Senator except a key assistant and the Washington reporter for *The Arizona Republic*. The one thing we learned was that they were not keeping a daily temperature chart on him. Our informant said that meant either he was not ill or that he had died. We concluded that he was not ill but was put in the hospital under complete security, providing a good excuse for his lack of presence in Arizona. Jack Karie, a senior reporter for the *Republic* in 1962, later verified that Senator Hayden was not ill but was kept in the naval hospital so no one could get to him. Jack was given the assignment to take the daily telephone report from the *Republic's* Washington reporter and write a front page story how the senator was battling back and hoped to be home to vote in the election.*

*Whether Hayden was willingly hiding out or being detained against his will, it was obvious that the campaign management would not let him return to Arizona. They knew we would then get an up-to-date picture and insist he answer some questions before the people went to the polls to vote. At age 83, his appearance and demeanor were quite different than the images being used in the campaign.

This is one of the many shocking things I have seen and heard that do not seem possible in our grand land of America. Karie said he got so sick of such deception that he came to my headquarters and got my bumper sticker to put on his car.

As the election returns started coming in, first from the heavy Republican parts of northeast Phoenix and Scottsdale, they indicated that I was losing. To win a statewide race, a Republican has to win Maricopa County, which comprises 60 percent of the state's population and has a Republican majority. As the returns came in from highly Democratic Pima County, we were pleasantly surprised to be very close. The 12 rural counties were overall Democratic, but they were mostly conservative. Surprisingly, I won the overall majority of the rural counties. It was Republican Maricopa County that gave Hayden the narrow victory. The front-page editorials in the Pulliam newspapers, once again, made all the difference. They warned that Hayden must be re-elected so he could get the Central Arizona Project bill passed in Congress, and that is what made the difference.

Indeed, I didn't beat Hayden for the U. S. Senate, but I gave him the closest race of his entire political career, losing by 48 percent to 52 percent. I'd scared the establishment badly enough to cause them to pull out all the stops in his campaign.

It was a tremendously exciting experience for me. As a bunch of neophytes with a bit of grass-roots support, we nearly knocked off one of the most powerful, Madison Avenue-imaged politicians in the country. I think that we would have won if the power brokers hadn't been able to trick voters into believing that without Hayden in the Senate, we might not get funding for the Central Arizona Project.

Eugene Pulliam had personally assured me of fair treatment in his newspapers when it looked like I had no chance to beat Hayden. As the contest became more viable, he was quick to show me the kind of integrity I found I could expect from his newspapers over the following decades. While Hayden's massively financed campaign was blitzing Arizona with newspaper, television and radio ads, the Pulliam papers began to run their own unprecedented front-page editorials screaming of Arizona's need to keep Hayden in office because he was head of the all-powerful Senate

Appropriations Committee. Never mind his faults or his politics, Pulliam proclaimed, if Hayden were not re-elected, Arizona would dry up and blow away from lack of water. Ironically, of course, Hayden's victory put him in perfect position to kill the private funding of the CAP, crippling the state's best chance for an adequate and cheap water and electrical energy supply.

In the closing weeks of the campaign, I was getting such a positive response everywhere I went that I had real hopes of winning. My experience in the state Senate made me feel that I could be effective in the U. S. Senate. My concern for the federal government's rapid swing to the left, its centralization of power fueled by massive spending and tax increases, made me know I could have made a difference in Washington.

But, for me, the greatest part of the '62 campaign was the love and appreciation that I developed for the people. I covered every nook and corner of the state. I shook at least 50,000 hands and worked myself to exhaustion. And, I learned what made the heart of Arizona beat. I vowed never to forget any of it.

Senator Hayden paid me a visit at my office in our Pontiac dealership in December. We had never seen each other in person, and I appreciated his thoughtfulness. We had a very pleasant visit. He said he wanted to meet me in person and thank me for running such a clean campaign. I complimented him in return. His organization had the money and had overpowered me in the campaign, without ever making our differences a personal issue.

Chapter 3

WHO SOLD OUT ARIZONA ON THE CENTRAL ARIZONA PROJECT

"No man can for any considerable time wear one face to himself and another to the multitude without finally getting bewildered as to which is the true one."

Hawthorne

The deciding factor in the 1962 U.S. Senate race was the perception that only Senator Carl Hayden could deliver the funds to build the Central Arizona Project and that the only source for those funds was Congress. Even today, few people realize the tremendous opportunity that Arizona lost by allowing the Federal Bureau of Reclamation to build the CAP with tax dollars instead of the State of Arizona building the CAP and the Marble Canyon and Bridge Canyon dams with private funds.

The Central Arizona Project is the enormous reclamation project, which brings Arizona's share of Colorado River water into the central and southern part of the state. The project, a series of pumping stations and a 325-mile long canal, was discussed for nearly half a century before, finally, being placed on the drawing board at the end of World War II. Every politician who wanted to win an election made a habit of declaring their almost religious devotion to the project, and pledged their undying efforts to secure its passage. For decades in Arizona politics, passing the CAP bill was almost akin to finding the Holy Grail. The story was told of one candidate for sheriff of Pinal County who put a sign on top of his car telling people to vote for him so he could get the CAP passed. He was elected!

By election time, 1962, the protracted lawsuit between California and Arizona to decide the legal rights to the river's water had finally concluded in Arizona's favor. The U.S. Supreme Court had decided to award Arizona undisputed ownership of 2.8 million acre feet of water per year, and the details were being finalized. The State of Arizona, through the Arizona Power Authority,* secured commitment from a consortium of five large financial houses in New York and Boston, to sell low interest, tax-exempt revenue bonds for the private funding of what was then to be a $1.15 billion project. The bonds were to be paid off over 50 years from revenues produced by the sale of water and electricity, generated by the project's two hydroelectric dams. These dams were located on the Colorado River—one at Bridge Canyon in the middle of the Grand Canyon, the other at Marble Canyon, upstream from the Grand Canyon.

No person of sound mind, armed with the facts about both the state plan to finance CAP and the Federal Bureau of Reclamation plan, could possibly choose the federal plan on it's merits. If there was some secret reason for using the federal plan, it was never shared with the people of this state by the political leadership and the news media of that day. Compare these facts.

1. The cost of the state plan was $1.15 billion, including the two hydroelectric dams. The cost of the federal plan has been estimated at more than $3 billion for the canal alone. Even in 1998, the final cost of the project and the final amount to be repaid to the federal government have not been settled. Whatever the end amount, it will be a mortgage on all of the land under the project. In the state plan, the bonds were based on the revenue from the dams and the lower-priced water.

2. The cost of the hydroelectric power from the dams of the state plan would have given the homes and business

*Footnote: (The Arizona Power Authority (APA) was originally created by the Arizona State Legislature to receive and market Arizona's share of the power from the Hoover Dam.)

---

customers of Arizona electricity at one of the lowest costs anywhere, for a tremendous economic advantage. Nuclear power plants generate the next lowest cost electrical energy, which is conservatively estimated at 20 percent more than hydroelectric. Coal and gas-fired generating plants cost even more.

3. The cost of the water from the state plan would have been low enough to allow it to be used for farming, which was in the original plan. Under the federal plan, in most cases, the water cost is too high for agricultural use. Farmers who were planning to use CAP water for agriculture have had to turn land back to the desert because of the costs. The high water costs have been passed on to the city dwellers.

4. With the state plan, construction was to begin in the early 1960s, with completion expected by 1972. The federal plan started much later and was not completed until 20 years after the state plan would have been giving citizens its lower cost benefits.

5. The Palo Verde Nuclear Plant would not have been needed. Instead we would have had totally clean power into perpetuity from the state plan dams.

6. One of the most important advantages for the state plan was that the people of Arizona would have owned, controlled, and had the profits from the CAP after paying off the bonds. We did not need another arm of the federal government running another part of our lives, as they are now doing under the Bureau of Reclamation in control of the CAP.

I could list many more advantages to the state plan, but cannot list even one advantage for the federal plan. Even more unbelievable is the fact that our senators and representatives in Washington had no assurances that they could get the CAP built with federal tax money, whereas the state plan was a certainty, until they killed the license to build the dams.

The feasibility studies of the two hydroelectric dams were finished. The initial engineering studies were complete, including the drilling of test holes in preparation for the construction of the dams. In total, it was a state project, needing only the Federal Power Commission license to proceed because the Colorado River is an interstate stream.

I knew this was a viable plan to build the dams and the canal system with private financing, but could not use it to counter the federally financed project in my campaign for the U.S. Senate; the feds had not yet issued the license for Arizona. I also knew that most of the efforts for the project were being directed toward getting Congress to appropriate tax money for a federally funded Bureau of Reclamation project. That was Hayden's position and, generally speaking, the Democrats' position as well. I did not have the benefit of any information from our Republican congressmen, Senator Goldwater and Representative Rhodes. My information came from the Arizona Power Authority, the arm of Arizona state government responsible for obtaining the license and getting the project built.

The biggest and perhaps the only club that the Hayden campaign was able to use against me in the election was that his presence in Congress, especially on the Appropriations Committee, was absolutely essential to the legislative success of the CAP as a federal reclamation project. Without the certainty of Arizona being able to secure the license from the Federal Power Commission to build the project, I could not counter that we had a state plan that was far superior to the federal plan.

It was after the November election in 1962, that the FPC voted four to one to give Arizona the license. FPC Chairman Joe Swindler then had the license issued and was within two hours of mailing it to Arizona, when President Lyndon Johnson, at the urging of the Secretary of the Department of the Interior Stewart Udall and Senator Hayden, ordered the license to be stopped. Although there is no known constitutional authority for the president to be able to interfere in such a regulatory judicial action, from the practical side, who is going to ignore a presidential order? Again the federalists had won, at the expense of states rights.

The Johnson intervention was followed by Hayden and Rhodes introducing identical bills in the Senate and House, forbidding the FPC from issuing Arizona the license to build the dam. Hayden's bill, S502, passed both houses with a limited term provision to give proponents of the federally funded CAP time to get it passed by Congress. If the federally funded CAP did not pass, then Arizona could still go back to the FPC for the license to build the project itself, financed with private money. FPC Chairman Swindler urged Representative Rhodes to add to S502 the provision that if the CAP had not passed Congress by it's sunset date, Arizona would automatically receive the license from the Federal Power Commission. Rhodes refused and voted for S502, without that saving clause for Arizona. After Rhodes retired from Congress, he joined a prominent Washington D.C. law firm to lobby principally to public utility firms at a salary several times his salary as a congressman. Goldwater held out for some time but ended up joining the others.

When I asked some members of Congress why they voted for a federal project when a better state plan was available without federal money, their answer was simple. Although they thought it set a bad precedent, they went along with it because the Arizona delegation wanted them to, and it only directly affected Arizona.

State funding of the Central Arizona Project with private, tax-exempt revenue bonds was obviously the best plan. To say that our political leaders never convincingly articulated their reasons for opposing it, is an understatement. The public simply was never told what was really happening. After running a multitude of puff pieces about how Arizona's political heavyweights were working so hard to push the CAP through Congress, the Pulliam press never made the public aware that the dams were being torpedoed by our own senators and representatives in Washington. The opposition of Senator Hayden and of Representatives Rhodes and Udall to the state plan resulted in a disaster to Arizona that is yet to be fully realized and has certainly never been fully explained. The information given to the public was so one-sided that few people ever knew there was a more viable alternative plan to counter that of the federally financed Bureau of Reclamation.

The dams were the key to the plan. The head of the Arizona Power Authority, John Smith, had promoted the dams after carefully researching all the alternative plans. He was led to believe he had the backing for them from Governor Fannin, and at least the support of Rhodes and Goldwater. The Federal Power Commission was ready to issue the licenses after extensive investigations. Wall Street had decided the dams would act as the cornerstones of a financially sound project. Then suddenly, without any sort of public debate, the dams were gone from the plan. Water sales alone were not enough to pay for the project. Without the sale of electricity generated by the dams, the project would not produce enough revenue to retire the bonds. Without the revenue from the bond sales the state plan was gone, along with any hope of getting the project under construction in the near future.

My biggest disappointment about the 1962 campaign was in not being able to get a debate in front of the public on whether the Central Arizona Project was to be federally funded and controlled, or privately funded and owned by the people of Arizona. In addition to all the other reasons that favor the state plan, the monetary loss to the people of Arizona from the federally funded CAP has amounted to billions of dollars. Unfortunately, the higher costs of the federal plan will continue for many generations to come.

Had I been in the Senate in place of Hayden in that crucial period, I would have insisted that the FPC mail the license to Arizona. This would have enabled the privately financed state plan to move forward. Since President Johnson did not really have the constitutional power to stop the FTC, it is doubtful he would have tried to do so over the opposition of the state's senators. Without Hayden's lead, Goldwater's true sympathies appear to have been in favor of the state plan.

The only thing I can say for certain is that I would have done my best to see that the voters of Arizona were given the truth. Had the people known the truth, they would never have allowed the theft of their assets, which is a direct result of the federally financed project. This is a clear-cut case of political corruption. It was corrupt because it was not what was best for the people of Arizona, and the truth was hidden from Arizona voters. It was a complete breach of the public trust that elective office bestows on its office holders.

When our congressional delegation went back to Congress for federal funding of the CAP, they had to horse-trade with

California to assure the bill's passage. To finally get the California votes they needed, they gave back to California much of what we'd won in the decade-long Supreme Court case (for which state taxpayers had paid law firms such as Snell & Wilmer more than $7 million). California was guaranteed 4.4 million- acre feet of water per year from the river, regardless of the size of the flow. Thus, in a drought year, Arizona has to absorb the whole shortage of the 7.5 million-acre feet of lower basin water allocated. In such years, there's a good chance we could end up with dust instead of water. The concession significantly affects Arizona's future economic health.

Furthermore, the introduction of federal bureaucratic delays and legislative haggling has more than tripled the project's price tag while reducing the project itself to exclude the energy producing dams, which would have been such revenue producers in perpetuity on the state plan. I again remind the reader, the increased costs have greatly increased the price of the water, making it too costly for most of the agricultural uses for which it was originally intended. Instead of both the dams and the canal delivery system being completed by 1972, as scheduled by the privately financed state plan, the federally funded CAP, consisting only of a canal and pumping stations system, was finally completed in the early 1990s. The bloated cost of the federally financed project has now become a mortgage of $2.5 to $3.5 billion on all of the land it serves. As of 1998, the final figure and the settling of the financial details are still ongoing.

With CAP electricity, there would never have been a need to build the $6 billion Palo Verde Nuclear Power Plant with its resulting higher electricity bills to consumers. The state plan guaranteed supplies of water and cheap electric power to central Arizona, which undoubtedly would have helped attract major industries with long-term plans. Due to the intervening energy crisis of the early 1970s, and the subsequent rise in energy costs, these dams would have been an even better investment than anticipated. Not only would the bonds have been easily paid off, but, as the need for more electricity arose, the surplus revenues from the hydroelectric dams could be helping to alleviate current fiscal pressure on Arizona's taxpayers.

Were all of our leaders simply unable to see the consequences of their actions? It is hard to believe that a Senate veteran like Hayden would not have foreseen the legislative price that California, with 40 votes in the House of Representatives, would force Arizona to pay in return for federal funds for the project. Think of the unbelievable precedent it would have set, if the largest reclamation project ever built had been funded with private money under state control. The only explanation I've ever been given as to why Arizona's own people in Washington moved so dramatically against their own professed political philosophy, is that they wanted to keep the Federal Bureau of Reclamation in control of Arizona's electric power. In itself, this hardly amounts to persuasive logic.

Chapter 4

HOW THE POWER
BROKERS DO BUSINESS

"You may deceive all of the people part of the time, and part of the people all of the time, but not all the people all the time."
Lincoln

My first six weeks in the Arizona State Senate had been the most enlightening in my life. I had been so full of idealism and the desire to be of service, that the thought of outside people controlling what elected representatives did, never seriously crossed my mind. Then I saw them in action.

Frank Snell was virtually the uncrowned king of Arizona. He used an Arizona Public Service employee named Jack Gilbert to furnish campaign funds and otherwise be of service to the senators, as well as to keep track of them. The mining company, Phelps Dodge, controlled the two senators from Greenlee County. The Cattle Growers Association still had plenty of clout with rural senators in those days. The public utilities, railroads and banks all packed a wallop, with Snell acting as director of operations for all of them. A call from Snell to Senate Majority Leader Harold Giss could absolutely guarantee 19 of the total 28 votes on any issue in the state Senate. Most often it would command 24 of the votes.

They said in those days that it only took $250,000 a year to control Arizona. At first, I wondered how they spent that much money, since campaigns were relatively inexpensive back then. But then I've never had a taste for fringe benefits.

Players have changed over the years and new organizations have sprung up to accommodate the greater numbers involved in the decision-making process, but the game is essentially the same as it was nearly 30 years ago. Here in Arizona, power politics is much more important than party politics. The parties are often treated as teams, among which the owners are free to shuffle the lineup, make trades, and buy and sell players. If the player knows on which side his bread is buttered, his first loyalty is not to the team but to the owners.

In fact, the two party system works well for the power brokers. If any politician gets too big for his britches, the big boys can always threaten to support his opposite number in the next election. One solid indication of their control is the source of revenues for state campaigns. Most of the money does not come from the Republican or Democratic parties, but, rather, from the political action committees that front for the special interest groups. To circumvent legal limits on campaign donations, the money is often routed through the employees of the businesses controlled by the power brokers. Sometimes the employees have been coerced into donating to promote their own job security. Sometimes they are not even aware their names are being used. One of the clumsier examples of this tactic was Conley Wolfswinkel's brazen $27,000 "donation" to Jay Rhodes' campaign for Congress in 1986. The contribution was made in the names of more than 20 of Wolfswinkel's employees who were not even notified of their donations. The law was badly violated, but no criminal charges were filed against those who broke it.

For nearly 40 years, the power brokers have been Arizona's "other governors." Their control of the governorship was never more sure than with Bruce Babbitt in office. They also expected the same kind of obedience from Burton Barr, their choice to be Babbitt's successor. Politicians with personal aspirations are very easy to handle because they can be persuaded to negotiate away the public interest on any position, in exchange for favors that will advance their own careers.

I never felt that Republican Jack Williams, governor from 1967 through 1974, was one of their boys. Neither was Democrat Raul Castro, a fiercely independent and rather conservative Democrat. No, Castro had pulled himself up by his own bootstraps from the humblest of beginnings to be elected in 1974. The power brokers, including the Pulliam press, made life so miserable for him that after less than three years he essentially abdicated, disappearing from Arizona politics to take an ambassadorship under the Carter Administration. That resulted in Wesley Bolin moving from secretary of state into the governorship, until his untimely death. Bruce Babbitt then moved from attorney general to governor.

The people who run Arizona would like you to believe that my perspective on the state's recent political history is the result of paranoia or willful perversity. But you can only be fooled for so long before you start to question. Can you forget that most of these events have been documented over and over again by parties of diverse political stripe? Can you overlook the fact that even the power brokers' own media inevitably have had to record many of these events as news? Doesn't it seem odd that while the media have scrupulously avoided drawing any kind of conclusions about these events, they seemed anxious to draw editorial conclusions about me and others who have opposed them?

After a while, it just becomes impossible to forget, overlook or ignore the bias of these power brokers; then you have to start a little investigating of your own. Perhaps the most dramatic instance of the power brokers selective blindness came with their attempt to cover up the massive report exposing the ugly interface of business and politics in Arizona, produced by the Investigative Reporters and Editors Association (IRE). The IRE, a national organization of investigative reporters came into Arizona from across the nation to investigate the Bolles murder. What really happened? Why had it not been solved? It was published in major newspapers nationwide. Why not in Phoenix—the setting of most of the articles? Some would call that censorship of the news.

Ironically, the report was written to document the causes they found behind the 1976 car-bomb murder of Don Bolles, an investigative reporter for *The Arizona Republic*. For nearly a

---

decade, Bolles had been writing about the alleged links between the state's racing interests and organized crime. In his articles, Bolles made reference to tie-ins of both to some of the leading names in metropolitan Phoenix—members of the power brokers.

The team of IRE investigative reporters that descended on Arizona from all across the country to continue Bolles' work, unearthed a swarm of criminals. These criminals were apparently in collusion with corrupt politicians, businessmen, lawyers, and judges. They found a transplanted East Coast Mafia contingent that not only flourished in the acquiescence or neglect of the state's politically and economically powerful, but may also have been involved in active partnerships with these leading citizens.

Michael Wendland's book *The Arizona Project* provides a tour through the dark alleys of Arizona, which most of us have managed to avoid for too long. Those of you who are skeptical of my objectivity in these matters ought to find Wendland's account significant. It's an insider's description of the investigation by an award-winning reporter. His Detroit beat and political affiliations certainly distance him considerably from me.

Wendland's book shows the objectivity of someone from out of state who has no backs to scratch or stab. It also stumbles on the contradictions that arise when an author, without a solid knowledge base, analyzes a situation. In spite of the gloomy picture they painted of Arizona politics in 1976, the IRE reporters saw reason for hope. At first they were "taken in" by what the "reform-minded" Phoenix 40 with "spark plugs" such as influential attorney Dick Mallery, aided by such "white knights" as Attorney General Bruce Babbitt, were mounting up. The Phoenix 40 consisted of a group of influential civic and business leaders who banded together just months before the Bolles murder. They stated their purpose was to give their community "a constructive sense of direction and purpose," which decried the inefficiency of Arizona's law enforcement and criminal justice system, and established their own Task Force on Crime. The IRE reporters themselves, by thoroughly investigating and broadly publicizing outside of Arizona the deeds of those who might be responsible for Bolles' murder, would hope to insure that none of their kin was ever again silenced for trying to report the truth. Wendland himself notes in his new epilogue in *The Arizona Project*, that the IRE Report seems to have been naive, if not occasionally schizophrenic. The very same report which begins by praising the Phoenix 40, ends by discussing the indictment of "40" member Herman Chanen for allegedly defrauding the government on a construction contract. Likewise, then state Senate Majority Leader Alfredo Gutierrez is spoken of in a favorable light, less than 40 pages before the Report discusses Gutierrez's association with known drug smugglers. The IRE lambasted Harry Rosenzweig as one of the kingpins of local corruption and, the direct link between organized crime and the state's leading politicians, calling him the father of prostitution and gambling in the Valley of the Sun.

The Bolles murder they came here to "avenge" is no closer to being solved today than it was when the IRE reporters landed more than two decades ago. Many of the commentators believe this just may have something to do with the fact that the same forces that controlled this state in Bolles' day control it now.

Two local men, writer Tony Amigone and attorney Barry Wolfson, present some theories and some facts in their essay, "The Arizona Conspiracy," published as the prologue in *The Arizona Project* and separately as a pamphlet in 1988.

"The botched investigation of the Bolles murder could actually have been a cover up of the very matters Bolles was trying to unearth."

They ask, "Does Attorney General Corbin's stated desire to see convicted Bolles murderer, John Harvey Adamson, executed as soon as possible reflect an honest passion for justice, or cold appreciation that when Adamson is buried the secrets about conspirators in high places will be buried with him?"

Not coincidentally, they also asked about the claims of my supporters that elitist power brokers conspired to bring down the one man (Ev Mecham) who threatened the established order.

The following extensive excerpt from the "Arizona Conspiracy" documents a number of their questions:

> Those who occupy positions of power in Arizona are quick to point out that the various unofficial theories of powerful conspirators controlling the media, the police, the government and the financial networks of the State remain

vague and essentially unsubstantiated. But . . . is this so surprising if the very people we rely on to provide us information, the media, the police, and the rest of the government, if these same people are themselves the conspirators?

Picture this: after hearing the Maricopa County Attorney proclaim on national television that "country club types did Bolles in," the State Attorney General Babbitt quickly invokes a never before used law to snatch the Bolles murder investigation from the County Attorney's jurisdiction just before the prosecutor can impanel a grand jury. Shouldn't a rational person at least wonder whether the AG's primary concern is not to catch the murderer but to prevent an investigation into "the country-club set?" Is considering this possibility an exercise in paranoia, or is it just common sense?

Who can say? When key players are given immunity before they even hint to prosecutors at what they might know; when police records are altered or vanish; when public prosecutors act like Keystone Cops, what hope does the public ever have of finding out why Don Bolles was really murdered and who directed the hands that planted the bomb? Probably none, at least not to a legal certainty. And if the Phoenix 40 conspires with the Attorney General or other officials to run the state for their own profit, is it really likely we'll ever know? But later, Attorney General Corbin declares that the Attorney General's Office can't impanel a grand jury itself because it doesn't have the authority to do so in homicide cases.

Shouldn't a rational person at least wonder whether the AG's primary concern is not to catch the murderer but to prevent an investigation into "the country club set?"

Amigone and Wolfson first create a plausible scenario showing how power brokering might work in Arizona. They target the group known as the Phoenix 40 for this purpose, but their analysis might just as well have included several other similar Arizona power groups.

In 1976, the reporters investigating the Bolles story devoted the bulk of their articles to documenting the activities of "known organized crime figures" who had moved to Arizona and their relationships with prominent local figures in government and business. Their apparent allies, the Phoenix 40, had announced that "organized crime in Arizona involves intricate conspiracies against the people of this state carried on over many years and aimed at controlling whole fields of activity in order to amass huge profits . . . much of it locally controlled." Today, Evan Mecham and his supporters charge the Phoenix 40 with virtually the same conspiracy. Their reasoning is grounded in a belief that Mecham's administration was threatening to end either the graft and self-enrichment or the legalized strangle hold on political and economic developments that Arizona's "power-brokers" are said to have enjoyed for decades.

The 40 is now (1988) actually composed of 52 active and 28 emeritus (non-voting) members who meet in private, supposedly to discuss matters of civic importance. While there has always been at least one clergyman on board and the president of Arizona State University is an emeritus member, the membership is comprised almost entirely of the business leadership in the community, particularly of the top management from the city's banks, major news media and utilities.

Though the group does meet in private, notions of its secrecy are somewhat exaggerated. The rumor that its membership list was a closely guarded secret, ironically spread in a 1988 article by *The Arizona Republic*, whose staff includes five members of the group, is unfounded.

While administrative officers of the "40," when contacted almost never seem able to find the list, it was nevertheless published at their inception in 1976 and again this year. Nor is the group always unanimous in its opinion, as witnessed by the 1986 gubernatorial election, in which the two favored candidates, one a "40" member and the other the wife of a member, split their potential voting block, allowing Evan Mecham to win the governorship with 40% of the popular vote.

To show the methods used by the power brokers, note the similarity of the actual handling of the America West Arena and the

Bank One Ballpark developments in recent years, to the *theoretical* scenario written by Amigone and Wolfson a decade ago.

> The meetings to discuss promoting a domed stadium are vague and laudatory. A special committee is appointed to look into it. The people on the committee hire a consulting firm to prepare a report, the conclusion to which is already well known to those concerned. One committee member owns the consulting firm, or has a friend who does. Another one is a real estate investor who can suggest site selections to the consulting firm that will increase the value of his own adjacent property. A third is a developer who can begin working on a bid for the project, knowing that other Phoenix 40 members will be on the city's selection committee, or will draft the bid specifications so as to favor their friends, or have pull in the right government office when the time comes for sorting out the "competitive bids" for the project. And so on.
>
> The committee reports that the domed stadium will be a boon to the city. The Phoenix 40 members who run *The Arizona Republic* start to crank out editorials and soft news stories in support of the project. Influential "Supporters of Major League Sports" lobby the zoning board for the necessary changes that ultimately will electrify local land values. Since the "40" is by definition composed of many of the Valley's civic and business leaders, it is only natural that they assume or are chosen for precisely the leadership positions the paranoid has imagined . . .
>
> "As long as no one gets more than moderately greedy, there is nothing illegal about any of this. Enormous profits can be made just by allowing local economic gravity to exert its pull. And anyone who thinks the fact that a half-dozen members of the Phoenix 40 happen to be numbered among the dozen businessmen who have made those enormous profits is a Certifiable Paranoid.
> ——"Where Incest and Charity Both Begin"

Perhaps the subtlety of this colossal (hypothetical) con job is behind *The Arizona Republic's* consistent failure to report on its existence or the paper's professed failure even to see any pattern in Conspiracy Theory data. Responsible reporters don't peddle rumors they can't substantiate, and unspoken agreements of the "you scratch my back and I'll scratch yours" variety simply can't be substantiated. At the same time, readers might be wary to note that the late Eugene Pulliam, publisher of both *The Republic* and its sister paper the Phoenix Gazette, and Pat Murphy, their current publisher, [at the time this was published but replaced in 1988] were founding members of the '40,' and four others of the newspapers' executives are currently Phoenix 40 members. In any event, the would-be paranoid is left with raw data, often no more than inconclusive strands from newspaper stories, to assimilate and spin into webs.

Conspiratorial opportunities of the domed stadium variety abound within the Phoenix 40 even without assuming hypothetical connections, because some individual members of the group seem to be networks unto themselves. John R. Norton III, for a short time the number two man in the U. S. Department of Agriculture, was at a single time president of his own agricultural company, director of the United Fresh Fruit and Vegetable Association, a director and chairman of the executive committee of Ramada Inns, Inc. (headed by Dick Snell, another Phoenix 40 member [and son of Frank Snell]), a director of United Bancorp of Arizona (formerly headed by Phoenix 40 member James Simmons), a director of Turf Paradise, Inc., director and vice president of Calcot Ltd., a director of the Central Arizona Project Association, a director of the Western Growers Association, and a director of the Arizona Public Service Company (on whose board a number of other Phoenix 40 members also sit). In other words, Norton has significant influence in agriculture and in the supply of water to agriculture, in banking, in utilities and high-use utility industries, and in government. Well, there's no law against making a living, and as a member of the Phoenix 40 you can bet he's civic minded, can't you? Within its limits, perhaps: Norton admitted quitting the Department of Agriculture, purely for profit motives, when he was told that accepting $3.5 million dollars in federal payment-in-kind price supports would be a conflict of interest.

This kind of inter-locking board membership is the rule rather than the exception among Phoenix 40 members. Phoenix 40 Chairman Frank Snell, senior partner of the prestigious law firm of Snell & Wilmer, is also past chairman of APS, chairman of Arizona Bancorporation, board member of Combined Communications Corporation, Allison Steel Manufacturing, Bagdad Copper Corp., Arizona Equities and Camelback Inn. He was counsel for APS and Valley National Bank (on both of whose boards his son, head of Ramada Inns, Inc., also sits), Goodyear Farms, Anderson-Clayton Cotton Company, Allison Steel Manufacturing and Reynolds Metals.

Past "40" president Herman Chanen, a Babbitt-appointed member and soon-to-be president of the Board of Regents, which grants millions of dollars in construction contracts each year, is head of Chanen Construction Co. Chanen Construction was granted a lucrative contract under Governor Babbitt to "oversee" the State's prison construction projects, giving him not only a 3% 'management' fee with no responsibility, but also a good deal of power to do favors for other contractors and developers. All these appointments came long after Chanen's National Housing Industries, Inc. was accused of conspiracy and making false statements in bidding on military housing units. (In 1976, Judge Walter Craig, who figured repeatedly in the IRE investigations, dismissed the charges against Chanen. Chanen was represented by the law firm of '40' founder Frank Snell.) Chanen is also a member of the board of directors of Valley National Corporation, parent company to Valley National Bank, one of the State's largest lenders, and a board member of Samaritan Health Service."

A closer look at the 3% management contract reveals that not only did Chanen get a 3% management fee, but also provisions by which if money was saved on any of the given projects, he got a commission on what was saved and if it took more money to build a project and was caught with overruns, he got a percentage of the cost overruns. The end result was that he received over three million dollars on 72 million dollars worth of construction. He had no liability whatsoever. The architect was still responsible for all of his duties on a normal job, as was the contractor. Since no other fees were saved by having the project manager, one can only assume the job was created to pass government money out to Chanen that could have been spent to build over three million dollars more prison beds. The Legislature approved this contract, and the Attorney General drew it up, so it could not be classed a secret in any form.

Perhaps the most controversial one man conspiracy among the Phoenix 40 is one of the group's original founders and the IRE's "spark plug of reform" Richard Mallery. (A main reason Mallery probably wasn't made Chairman of the Phoenix 40 was his previous involvement with Arizona's Charter Government group. The "40" didn't want to look too much like the old Charter Government group from which many of these same people had run Arizona's political machinery for the previous 30 years, because the Phoenix 40, after all, was ostensibly founded to create a "new force" to clean up corruption caused by the old state power-brokers.) While a senior partner at one of the Valley's most powerful law firms, he constructed a private corporate empire for himself that spanned real estate development, construction, investment, tax shelters, and even a foreign trade "think tank."

In January 1980, Mallery was head of the committee appointed by the mayor of Phoenix to select a site for a proposed municipal arts center. Three years later, the committee chose the southeast corner of Van Buren and Second streets for the theater, though it was not the first choice of the consulting firm that looked into the proposal. When questioned about the site selection, Mallery admitted that he owned substantial property in the neighborhood, but denied any conflict of interest.

In 1982, Mallery was appointed to a committee by Governor Bruce Babbitt to set up an international trade "think tank" called the Pacific Basin Institute near Pinnacle Peak and Pima Roads. At the same time, a Mallery partnership known as PB Investors was set up to buy land near the site. Mallery again denied any conflict of interest. (After all, when APS, whose president was Phoenix 40 member Keith Turley, paid almost $2 million for land on which to build the Palo Verde Nuclear Power Plant to one of

Turley's relatives, there had been barely a whisper of impropriety. Even the knowledge that this land previously had not been the primary site—because it was in the middle of nowhere, had no water supply, and puts Phoenix in jeopardy from even a minor accident because of prevailing easterly winds—had failed to generate any serious ethical questions.

But at least two cases emerged where even many of Mallery's friends believed he stepped over the fat grey line of legal ethics. In 1980, two developers came to Mallery, their attorney, for advice on putting together financing for what is now the $325 million Phoenix Gateway Center at Van Buren and 44th streets, where the East Papago Freeway and the Hohokam Expressway are expected to meet. After several meetings, Mallery was apparently unable to come up with investors, but offered to help sell the land, on which one of the developers now owed a $50,000 mortgage payment. He told Mallery what he wanted to get for the land as well as what his rock-bottom price would have to be, and his faithful attorney promised to do his best for him.

Only as the land sale was about to close did the developer learn that Mallery himself was one of the purchasers who, incidentally, seemed to have little trouble funding the project once he'd taken it over. The value of the property jumped from the purchase price of $3 a square foot to more than $20 a square foot—about a $20 million profit for Mallery's investment group. This time rumors started that the Arizona Bar Association might actually investigate one of its most influential members. But it was only a rumor. Power Brokers take care of their own.

The deal that finally seems to have undone Mallery, though it may be a bit of anti-paranoid optimism to think his power has been shattered, was one in which he embarrassed other Phoenix 40 members with whom he had founded an organization called the Phoenix Community Alliance. In concert with a group called Chicanos Por La Causa, the Alliance was promoting downtown redevelopment, particularly the taxpayers' purchase of an abandoned school lot. It was to be turned into a showpiece recreational and cultural center and perhaps even a domed football stadium to attract an NFL team. Mallery promoted the project as

"good for the city," but forgot to tell even the other Phoenix
40 members that it would be particularly good for him,
since he had gone ahead and purchased much of the
adjacent land. Furthermore, it was learned that Mallery was
also an officer and director of HuntCor, the construction
company that probably had the best chance of building the
domed stadium. When this information emerged, the
reputation of the Alliance was badly damaged and the
citizens of Phoenix voted down the bond proposal to
purchase the site. Mallery was forced to resign from the
Alliance, for the first time admitting to an "error in
judgment."

Mallery was never found guilty, or even accused of any
crime, but then the power brokering game has little to do
with the letter of the law. The city's leaders began to
distance themselves from Mallery, and he's been asked to
head fewer site selection committees lately. Later on he was
used quietly by Governor Symington on his problems.

In themselves, individual scandals such as these aren't
proof that the Phoenix 40 is a secret power brokerage that
controls the fate of Arizona, but they do show the propensity
of group members with power to abuse that power for
personal gain.

Next, Amigone and Wolfson describe how "all real
conspiracies end up being political conspiracies in one way or
another."

The Phoenix 40 originally declared it would not endorse
political candidates or "tell an elected official how to run his
office or what to do." Political candidates representing the
group were generally well known, however. In the 1986
gubernatorial election, for instance, all the major candidates
but one shared ties to the Phoenix 40. Democratic primary
contender Tony Mason is a Phoenix 40 member, as is the
husband of eventual Democratic nominee Carolyn Warner.
The original front runner for the Republican nomination,
Burton Barr, was supported financially by at least a dozen
of the group's members. Bill Schulz, who ran as an
independent candidate and for a while led in the
gubernatorial election polls, is a Phoenix 40 member. (U. S.

Representative John Rhodes had planned to run as the Republican candidate in the Mecham recall election with the announced support of over a dozen Phoenix 40 members, despite the group's supposedly apolitical posture. Rhodes is himself an emeritus member of the group and a lobbyist for the group's most powerful constituency, the utilities. With this kind of representation in the state's politics, the group hardly needs to tell office holders its wishes. What the group wants is well known to the candidates to begin with.

Not so with Evan Mecham. Only Mecham, the surprise winner in the three-way gubernatorial election, was not only unsupported by the group but antagonistic to it.

Of course it's hardly surprising that a group comprised of the capitol city's leading citizens would be active in state politics. Is this really a Conspiracy Theory, or just a squinty-eyed way of looking at things? A conspiracy against Mecham had to be motivated by more than the group's mere distaste for the governor's unbending attitude and conservative ideology. What real (profit) motive would millionaire businessmen have to go to the trouble and expose themselves to the resultant public scrutiny to remove an elected governor from office?

A substantial conspiracy theory would have to show that the privileged position of Phoenix 40 members, engendered by insider information and special considerations from friends in state government and regulatory agencies, was being threatened by Mecham. A Theory worth its capital "T" must detail a reasonable threat to those privileges:

Motive One: Legislation

The governor doesn't pass legislation that can restrict big business, though a chief executive with a better legislative rapport could have gotten legislative sponsors for pet legislation. That's the job of the Arizona legislature, which is usually quite accommodating to local businessmen. In 1987, when Phoenix 40 member John Teets, chairman and CEO of Greyhound Corp., felt his company threatened by a hostile takeover bid, the legislature promptly passed a law to prevent it. The following year, when Phoenix 40's Karl Eller wanted his

---

Circle K Corp. to be able to take over another chain of stores, the legislature passed House Bill 2253 reversing the earlier law.

But the Governor can veto such sweetheart legislation and try to break up this kind of love affair between the legislature and powerful lobbyists. What bills did Mecham veto during his brief tenure that might have angered the Valley's power brokers?

A Mecham veto was responsible for stopping what appears to be one of the more awesome displays of local political power brokering in recent history. In this ongoing case, Phoenix 40 members appear about to accomplish what two of America's leading corporations without 40 representation couldn't: to induce the Arizona State Legislature to allow corporate entities to set up their own little kingdoms in Arizona.

The effort began when Goodyear Tire and Rubber bought up 12,000 acres of farmland near the town of Goodyear (named for the company's plant there). When it decided it wanted to develop the land, Goodyear Tire went into partnership with Westinghouse Electric's property division. In 1985, Westinghouse-Goodyear quietly began to lobby the state legislature, and early in 1986 Hal Runyan, State Senator from Litchfield Park, the only portion of the acreage already developed, introduced Senate Bill 1263. This nifty bit of legislation proposed basically that Westinghouse-Goodyear be allowed to assume the rights and privileges of an elected city government. Without holding any sort of election among the inhabitants of its holdings, or of nearby municipalities and the county who might be affected, the developer would be allowed to determine its own zoning and master-plan requirements, exercise the right of eminent domain even on private property not owned by the corporation, and bypass most of the state's rigid water planning and use regulations. The corporation would be allowed to borrow money and issue tax exempt bonds, and then literally tax its citizenry to repay those debts without notice or election.

Needless to say, with hundreds of millions of dollars in profits at stake, Westinghouse-Goodyear ran a pretty extensive lobbying campaign. The bill seemed about to slide through the state legislature when the mayor of the town of Goodyear, who didn't like his power being usurped, alerted the other mayors of the League of Arizona Cities and Towns to the potential danger. These local politicians promptly marched en masse down to the State Capitol (not to mention to the office *of The Arizona Republic* and the *Phoenix Gazette*) and blew so many whistles that the legislators tripped over themselves reversing field. The bill was tabled and never came to a vote.

But the bill's sponsors, Runyan, Jim Ratliff (from Del Webb's Sun City), Bob Denny (also from Litchfield Park), Greg Lunn, and Chris Herstam, weren't letting the bill die, just rest a little. A few minor revisions were made giving the mayors of adjacent towns the right "to approve and annex" these special, company run districts. The corporations owning these special districts would still retain all the powers previously enumerated, but now the local mayors could be sure of at least a small cut of the action when they added their own land taxes onto those already to be imposed by the corporation.

A year later the bill was back on the floor of the legislature, this time with the League of Arizona Cities and Towns as a backer. This about-face seemed slightly remarkable, since the major features of the bill that had so horrified everyone before, waiving the water regulations and granting a corporation the right to issue tax exempt bonds and to tax citizens for repayment were unchanged. Jack DeBolske, head of the League, said sure he was still against the idea, but, given the lobbying power of Westinghouse-Goodyear, he knew that mere Arizonans didn't have a chance in the long run. The current bill, he said, was the best compromise anyone could hope for.

What DeBolske didn't mention was that Westinghouse wasn't even in the center of the picture any more. In December 1986, SunCor, the definitely for-profit real estate subsidiary of Pinnacle West Capital Corp holding company of the Arizona Public Service Company and MeraBank had purchased nearly all of that Westinghouse-Goodyear land west of Phoenix. Pinnacle West's Keith Turley and other Phoenix 40 members were now the real force behind the bill.

The bill passed. Governor Evan Mecham vetoed it on the legitimate grounds that, unlike any other bill granting bonding authority, this one imposed virtually no limits or controls on the amount of debt that could be incurred by the developer and transferred to the taxpayers for repayment.

Guess what? Now that Evan Mecham has been removed from office, the bill has already sailed through the Senate and is now in the House. The Arizona Tax Research Foundation, which opposes the bill, calls the revisions "purely cosmetic." A debt ceiling that has been written in for the developers is proportionally 20 to 30 times higher than we allow our own school boards and cities when they issue bonds in the name of their taxpayers. New Governor Mofford graciously approved the bill after its passage.

Motive Two: The AG and The Law

The Arizona Project suggests how convenient it can be to control the local judiciary. The Bolles murder is one obvious case where the state's justice department may have blocked an investigation into the dealing of the state's most influential people. Recall for a moment the IRE scrutiny of some of Judge Walter T. Craig's judicial actions, by which Arizona's most prominent jurist seemed to act favorably for friends and acquaintances in trials that were often felt to be conflicts of interest. What might go on in less well publicized cases can only result in paranoid eye rolling. Imagine the advantage to developers or businesses that could influence the prosecution of competitors or assure their own non investigation or be forewarned of a pending investigation. Mecham's supporters have already accused Attorney General Bob Corbin with "selective prosecution" for pursuing Mecham's alleged campaign violations but no one else's, for alleging Mecham interfered in an investigation while white-washing the Department of Public Safety for its interference in Mecham's own impeachment trial. Even Moise Berger, Corbin's hand-picked successor to the Maricopa County Attorney's office, claimed in a tape-recorded phone conversation with a Phoenix policeman that his attempts to investigate white-collar crime in the state had continually been thwarted by pressures and developments "all the way from the very top."

The tentacles of the Attorney General's office are felt in virtually every other state office and a great many private ones. The AG can trade favors with state legislators at will, bartering favorable legal opinions on pending legislation for budget boosts and increased prosecutorial power. State agencies are paralyzed without the AG's official nod on dozens of legal technicalities, and Corbin's enemies sometime have to wait a very long time for answers because of the AG's tremendous backlog, of course. When Mecham suggested the use of outside lawyers to clear some of these things up, Corbin quashed the move. Yet on a regular basis he farms out lucrative liability cases from the state's Risk Management program, security and land fraud cases, and other matters to private law firms of his own choosing.

Corbin has always effected a tough and impartial anti crime stance. During his 1978 campaign for attorney general, he suggested that the only way to stop drug-running planes was to shoot them down. (And ask questions later?) He called the court system "Too damned lenient," and suggested that child molesters could only be stopped if the bad parts of their brains were cut out with lasers. Yet when he was Maricopa County Attorney, Corbin was frequently berated in the press for his failure to prosecute white-collar crime. Corbin had been backed in his campaign for county attorney by Harry Rosenzweig who raised a sizeable amount of money for the occasion. (Rosenzweig and pal Robert Goldwater blasted in the IRE report for their ties to organized crime figures and gambling interest and several of their associates have been contributors to Corbin campaigns.) In November 1965, Corbin made Moise Berger his chief assistant and, in 1968, when Corbin decided to return to private practice, he backed Berger's election to county attorney. Berger repaid the favor by appointing Corbin a part time special deputy at fully 2/3 of his previous salary. Corbin's hand-picked man eventually resigned in disgrace amid allegations that he'd accepted bribes for scuttling the state's crucial investigation against land fraud czar Ned Warren.

A connection between Warren and Corbin himself surfaced later, when Corbin was hired by the state attorney general's office to investigate allegations that Arizona's former real estate commissioner had accepted bribes from Warren and others. Only after the investigation was completed, was it learned that Corbin's law firm had performed a substantial amount of work for a peculiar shell company with virtually no assets, including work on its merger with Great Southwest Land and Cattle Corp, a Warren entity that was later shown to be one of the state's worst land fraud operations. Among that corporation's functions was the collection and distribution of the very bribe money that Corbin was supposed to be investigating. Perhaps Corbin was still impartial. But it's interesting to consider the fact that, at the time of the investigation, Corbin's law firm was still owed considerable money by the shell company.

Since the mid-1970s, first Bruce Babbitt and then Bob Corbin moved to strengthen the Attorney General's Office by designing legislation providing themselves with broader prosecutorial powers, tough but sometimes open-ended laws, and often special oversight provisions. Embarrassed by Arizona's reputation as the Land Fraud Capital of the United States, by the obvious abuse of lax regulation of trust and corporate structures that allowed criminal gains to be masked by "blind trusts," and by its growing popularity with the Eastern crime families as documented by the IRE reports, the Legislature was quick to adopt virtually every one of the AG's requests.

From the time Corbin took office, the AG's staff has doubled and his budget quadrupled. When Corbin had decided not to run for the Republican nomination for governor against then House Majority Leader Burton Barr, presumably making Barr a shoe in over Mecham, Pat Murphy ran an editorial praising Corbin as the greatest thing to happen to the law since Moses brought down the Ten Commandments but somehow managed to include in this puff piece the information that Barr would show his gratitude by engineering even more money for the Attorney General's office. Since the Arizona Attorney General's office already had the highest per capita spending rate of any AG's office in the country while Arizona had one of the nation's highest per capita crime rates, Corbin must have seen his office as particularly vulnerable to a budget-balancing ax.

So Corbin had motive to help remove the Governor. That he had opportunity is obvious, but was his investigation and prosecution of Mecham anything but a legitimate exercise of the authority he was elected to uphold?

Mecham's supporters point to charges of Corbin's use of "selective prosecution" to help his friends and to hurt his enemies as evidence that Corbin was in fact "out to get" Mecham. For example, they say, Mecham's alleged campaign disclosure violation was a minor matter and normally would have been dismissed or forgiven by the Attorney General's Office.

And after all, virtually every candidate involved in recent gubernatorial politics in this state made similar financial disclosure violations, but none of the others was even investigated by the AG's office. Although Arizona's new Governor, Rose Mofford, spent ten years as Secretary of State in charge of the office that handles the financial disclosure forms, she says she failed to report several loans and partnership interests on her own forms because she didn't understand the "confusing" requirements. (Mecham was publicly ridiculed for calling the requirements confusing.) Corbin claims he can't investigate Governor Rose Mofford because of a conflict of interest: he'd be governor if she were impeached. Carolyn Warner, the Democratic candidate in the 1986 gubernatorial election failed to report a $200,000 loan from Pinnacle West subsidiary MeraBank. Because of MeraBank's affiliation with APS and the Phoenix 40, hiding such a loan has precisely the same implications that Mecham's alleged non disclosure had, yet the AG's office had no trouble believing hubby Ron Warner's excuse for the oversight; his secretary must have made a mistake. After all, is Phoenix 40 member Ron's word is better than Willard Mecham's. Bill Schulz, the Phoenix 40 member who ran against Mecham as an independent candidate, may have been saved from a similar legal infraction when news leaked from his campaign before the due date for disclosure filings, that he was hiding large contributions from two large developers, Schulz denied any knowledge of the matter.

Corbin's opponents have frequently claimed he uses "selective prosecution" and times the release of his legal opinions often needed by businessmen or other state agencies before they can proceed with essential matters of business to further his own ends. Such a charge was made by State Representative Reid Ewing, author of the tough new campaign finance law. Ewing voted in favor of the Resolution of Impeachment against Evan Mecham but later voted against the Articles of Impeachment after hearing the evidence.

Last But Not Least: Appointments

The governor certainly does control various regulatory agencies through his power to make appointments to head those agencies. Not only did some of them turn out to be major headaches for the defenders of the state's status quo, but, if Mecham had remained in office, he would have eventually uprooted Phoenix 40 majorities in a variety of important boards.

Few Arizonans are probably aware of the immense fortunes that depend upon mundane-sounding state agencies for their health and continued growth. The state's electric company, Arizona Public Service, is a perfect example.

Because APS is a regulated monopoly, its rate increases have to be approved by the Corporation Commission and it requests a variety of legislative measures annually from the state legislature. Normally APS has a leg up in the legislature thanks to generous campaign contributions to a variety of legislators, not to mention the fact that Senator Majority Leader Bob Usdane is a vice-president at MeraBank, an APS affiliate.

An on-going $12 million audit of the Palo Verde Nuclear Power Plant is expected to uncover hundreds of millions of dollars of waste by the project's managers, but public access to the audit, now nearly a year overdue, has been postponed twice. Because of continuing financial disaster on Palo Verde, regardless of it's cause, early in 1988, APS received one of its biggest rate increases ever— 9 %—costing local consumers about $91 million.

This ought to be an indication that the governor's office had cooperated with APS pretty darn well, but APS didn't see it that way. The utilities initial enthusiasm for Mecham

appointee Ted Humes to head RUCO, the Residential
Utilities Consumer Office, died when Humes, a previously
pro-utility spokesman whom many believed would gut the
watch-dog organization, turned on APS to fight their
original 19.6% rate hike request. Humes also sponsored
legislation that greatly expanded RUCO's powers on behalf
of the rate-paying public. The loss of those seven
percentage points meant over a $100 million to APS.
Humes himself speculates that his action against the APS
rate hike was a key factor in turning the utility's legislative
power supply against the governor. Seven of the top APS
executives sit on the Phoenix 40, and they can't have been
pleased.   There are endless examples of key appointments
that affect various industries and businesses more directly
and obviously than does RUCO. Some of these
appointments, such as the State Liquor Authority, could be
made immediately, while others were a matter of waiting
for vacancies on the Board of Regents or the Arizona
Department of Transportation. Thus Mecham became an
increasing threat to anyone worried about control of these
agencies. Since there were soon to be vacancies on the
Board of Regents and ADOT, both of which control
hundreds of millions of dollars in construction and supply
funds, getting rid of Mecham even before the projected
recall election may have been a matter of concern to special
interest groups. Appointments on the State Racing
Commission, Lottery Commission, Liquor Commission,
and the Land Department were also to come.

   If the AG and state law enforcement officials can
steadfastly proclaim and expect us to believe that Don
Bolles was killed because he helped to deprive Kemper
Marley of a seat on the Racing Commission, how much
more important must all of these appointments be when
taken together? Arizona state agencies pay out about $300
million annually to private contractors for state construction
projects. They award millions of dollars more in supply
contracts for everything from office furniture to Fritos. The
State Land Commissioner recommends sales of State lands
providing developers with potential profits of billions of
dollars. Liquor, real estate and other licenses, all worth big

bucks, and saleable commodities for those who can influence enough agency heads or board members.

But, . . . State contracts are awarded on the basis of competitive bidding, not nepotism. The competitive bids are first narrowed down by the state agency according to what the agency feels is the credibility of the bidder. And if inside information of the final bids can be supplied to a favored bidder, his success is assured. And this is only the beginning: cost overruns far in excess of the original bid, tripling or quadrupling the contractor's or supplier's profits, can later be approved by the friendly state legislature. Among the cost-overrun investigations aborted by Mecham's impeachment were matters pertaining to both the construction of Palo Verde and Chanen's involvement with State prison construction.

OK, so there's data suggesting opportunity and motive for a conspiracy against Mecham. But wasn't the evidence against the ex-Governor so overwhelming that even a legislature dominated by his own party voted more than two-to-one on his guilt?

The *Wall Street Journal* summed up the two charges on which Mecham was eventually impeached in the following way:

Even Corbin's grand jury had failed to indict Mecham for either of these "crimes." Yet the legislature had no doubt they warranted conviction.

The *Journal* described Mecham's impeachment trial this way:

"The coup that deposed him was mounted by local mandarins offended by precisely the policies and rhetoric that won him election, and they installed a regent who promptly moved to reverse his most controversial appointments and actions."

Anti-paranoids, those people who find it easy to ignore the possibility of conspiracies for conventional complacency, can be as big a problem as paranoids who see manifestations of heinous plots in every aspect of daily life. The point of this argument is that one ought to at least bear all the possibilities in mind.

> From "Arizona Conspiracy" by Barry Wolfson;
> used by permission

One of the things I like best about this explanation of power brokering in Arizona, is that it avoids the hysterics that usually attend accusations about how some group "plots" to get someone else. Power brokers don't see themselves as maniacal thieves of public wealth. They see themselves as businessmen protecting their own legitimate interests. But, when a man diverts the stream of public funds to water his own garden at the expense of other users, he is a thief. When he joins with a few powerful friends to beat back public protests to this effect, he is a conspirator. And, when he becomes willing to do anything within his now considerable power to protect that wealth, including using it to deprive the state of its duly elected leadership, that man is a threat to our republic.

When you read the following story of my campaign for governor, my struggle to clean up Arizona's government, and my impeachment, try to keep the open mind that Amigone and Wolfson suggest. Arguments can't be conclusively made to everyone's satisfaction; if they could, we wouldn't have politics, we'd have Plato's philosopher kings. But I am in a unique position to offer first-hand information about what went on in those days, and you cannot honestly make an informed judgment without it.

Chapter 5

LEADING UP TO THE WATERSHED
ELECTION OF 1986

"A government for the people must depend for its success on the intelligence, the morality, the justice, and the interest of the people themselves."
President Grover Cleveland

The opposition to my administration began before the administration itself. My deeds in office were not to be the cause of my impeachment. In the eyes of the back room power brokers, my crime was winning the Republican gubernatorial primary. Then, as if that wasn't bad enough, I compounded my sin in their eyes by winning the general election.

To a group that had always taken the voting population of the state for granted, my victories must have been inconceivable. The Arizona establishment had important plans that depended on retaining control of the governor's office. Losing a piece so vital to their long-range strategy, on what seemed to them a quirk, was very infuriating.

When Jack Williams decided to retire in 1974, I felt drawn out of my decade-long political hibernation by the dearth of good candidates. However, getting my campaign geared up was difficult because I'd lost contact with most of my supporters from the early 1960s. I placed second out of five Republicans in the gubernatorial primary. When the 1978 race came around, I was better prepared and beat Jack Londen in a friendly, but highly contested, primary.

Having recently stepped into the governor's office after the death of his predecessor, Bruce Babbitt had all the sentimental advantages that Johnson had over Goldwater in the 1964 presidential elections. He also had the complete backing of the Pulliam press and the financial support of the establishment, affording him not only a torrent of free publicity but also more than twice the funding I had. In the end, Babbitt took 52 percent of the vote. This was still about eight points less than the papers had predicted that very election morning, in their attempt to start a stampede.

While Bruce Babbitt and I have always treated each other cordially, our politics are radically opposed. I felt his policies, particularly those of rapid spending and corresponding tax increases, would be absolutely ruinous to Arizona. Therefore, I decided to run against him again in 1982. I thought I would have a better chance of being elected, now that the voters would have his track record to look at.

Perhaps anticipating my candidacy, the Republican Party leadership made an unprecedented pre-primary endorsement of their own candidate—Senate President Leo Corbet. As a member of the establishment, Corbet had usually voted for Babbitt's spending and tax bills, so I felt he wouldn't be able to effectively oppose the Democrat on his record. (This is, of course, what did happen in the general election.) Although my legs had been cut out from under me by the endorsement, I felt I had to run against Corbet in the primary, if the Republicans were going to have a decent chance against Babbitt in the general election.

For the second time in my political career, I couldn't get my campaign off the ground. Many of my potential supporters were party loyalists and worked for Corbet because their leaders had endorsed him. The papers roundly condemned me for not abiding by the party leadership's pre-primary endorsement. I always thought that the reason for a primary election was to let the whole party choose their candidates, instead of just the leadership. Because party loyalists felt obliged to support him, I was never able to raise the money to respond.

My defeat in the 1982 primary was so thorough, I decided never to run again. I felt that no matter how hard I tried, I'd never be able to beat the establishment. I gave the Evan Mecham version of Nixon's "You're not gonna have me to kick around anymore" press conference and thoroughly enjoyed it. While I was really sorry for my supporters, it was a relief to go home and feel I'd never have to put up with that kind of punishment again, to feel I could forget about politics for good. I did, until May of 1986.

In 1986, Democrat Bruce Babbitt departed the state for his ill-timed shot at the presidency (and, as Johnny Carson put it, quietly dropped from obscurity into oblivion). With the increasingly conservative leaning of Arizona's voters, the Republicans were naturally expected to win back the governor's office.

The first meeting regarding the 1986 election for governor was held at the University Club of Phoenix, in 1983. It was a committee of five Phoenix 40 members who were there to offer a sixth member, Bill Schultz, a guarantee of a $2 million campaign for governor if he would switch his affiliation from Democrat to Republican. Schulz, formerly a Republican, had registered as a Democrat and had come within a whisker of beating Barry Goldwater in his last race for the U.S. Senate, in 1980. The five committee members were Keith Turley of APS, William Franke of Southwest Forest, Richard Mallery of Snell & Wilmer, Carl Eller of Circle K, and Duke Tully of *The Arizona Republic*.

Schulz had recently sold his vast apartment holdings, so the $2 million did not convince him to become a Republican again. Inasmuch as allegiance to the power brokers' goals of control of government for their own purposes, party affiliation appeared to be no big holdback. Besides, no one would ever have known of the meeting had not Schulz publicly revealed it later on. Pat Murphy then reported it in *The Arizona Republic*.

Armed with plenty of money and his record of nearly defeating Goldwater, Schulz became the front runner for governor of Arizona in the upcoming 1986 election. He made trips across the country talking to officials of other states and got good publicity for his efforts.

He hired Bill Jameson to consult and assist, as he put his book *The Arizona Governor* together as a campaign platform. With his money, intelligence, successful business record, good appearance, good family, and high energy, Bill Schulz was destined to become the governor with no meaningful opposition. Then disaster struck his family in a health matter relating to one of his daughters. He dropped everything regarding politics to devote himself totally to her recovery. That changed the lives of several people, including my own.

Power brokers care only about power; party lines are drawn in the dust, to be stepped over at will. Barr became the power brokers' Republican option, and Schulz's withdrawal opened up the race for the Democratic nomination. A number of well-positioned candidates were anxious to represent their interests, and the biggest problem that the brokers thought they'd have for the 1986 gubernatorial election was their own wealth of talent

Having so many Phoenix 40 members running for the office didn't seem to matter, since one of them was bound to win. Democrats Tony Mason and Caroline Warner, Republican Burton Barr, and even Bob Corbin had acceptable ties to the power brokers.

Barr was the most obvious heir apparent to the governorship. House majority leader and long-time associate of all the state's top wheelers and dealers, he had the most political clout and possibly the biggest war chest of any candidate. He also had the biggest ego and the unquestioned backing of the Pulliam press, who had referred to him for years as the most powerful political figure in Arizona. Power brokers love to put the spotlight on their front man as the one with the power because they want to stay out of view. Both the front man and the back room power know that without them, he is a hollow shell.

Burton Barr represented everything I despised about Arizona politics. He'd wielded his authority in the state legislature to enrich himself and his friends, while giving lip service to the needs of the state.

In furthering his own ends, Barr was a complete pragmatist, voting in whatever direction was convenient, with complete disdain for political ideology. Barr paid little attention to party activities, seeming to be above it all. If his district had been Democratic instead of heavily Republican, he, no doubt, would have been registered as a Democrat. In the Senate, he acted in partnership with Democratic Minority Leader Alfredo Gutierrez to insure passage of his pet legislation—not caring if he had to trade away votes on good bills and support bad ones. He worked with Babbitt to please the downtown establishment, thereby assuring himself of the election-year money to buy back the support of even those conservative Republicans he'd sold out, time after time.

Barr was a consummate politician with notable wit and charm. However, he also allegedly owed part of his favorable press image to personal influence with the *Republic* and *Gazette* publisher, Duke Tully. It was Barr's arrogance, in particular, that bothered me, being an indication of how little he thought he actually owed to the people he represented. After a speech at the Phoenix Rotary Club, he was asked how he could have ensured the passage of a one percent sales tax in 1983, by promising it would only exist for one year; and then turn around in 1984, and pass a new bill to make it permanent. Barr's response: "I lied. Next question." This remark is not made bizarre by being taken out of context. Its flippancy is typical of Barr, who always felt free to treat the people of Arizona in an arrogant manner. The remark says that voters don't deserve the truth, that however you get your own way is the right way, and that everyone should be satisfied because he is. I felt that this attitude made Burton Barr an extremely dangerous candidate for governor.

Initially, I decided to back Ray Rottas for governor. He'd been a good state treasurer and, before that, a state senator. However, Ray became discouraged when it was apparent that the "downtown boys" were going to shut him out of any funding. He'd heard that Bob Corbin was going to run.

I gave Corbin a call. I wasn't convinced that he was a big enough man for the governor's office, but next to Barr he looked 15 feet tall. (Unfortunately I didn't realize at the time that he was the chief viper in a nest of vipers that was a key part of the power broker control of Arizona.) Corbin told me he wasn't really sure if he wanted to be governor. He loved the AG's office, and thought it was more important and powerful than the governor's was. "If I do become governor," he told me, "the first thing I'll do every morning is stop by the AG's office to find out what's really going on in the state government." His statement showed me that he either did not understand how state government was set up, or he was covering the fact that his power broker bosses had told him not to run. He said that beating Barr would be a piece of cake because he had enough on him to blow him out of the water any time he so desired.

Of course, such statements by AG personnel were far from rare. I was soon to personally find out that an unscrupulous attorney general could often demolish an opponent without evidence of wrongdoing. How he abused the power of his office to get me out of office will be handled in detail later.

At least one reporter at every major paper owes his job to liaison work with the AG's office, and he always can be counted on to print a damaging disclosure from "highly placed sources in the Attorney General's Office." Assistant AG Bernard Lotstein, who played a part in prosecuting me, once said that the AG's office had a standing agreement with reporter Al Sitter of the *Republic*. All Lotstein had to do was drop him a name, and Sitter would write a torpedo piece based either on what Lotstein could "leak" to him or whatever speculative allegations could be manufactured from the paper's general files.

They had a similar arrangement with Sam Stanton, the *Republic* reporter assigned to shadow me. The AG's assistants would sneak information out the back door to Stanton, who would then come around the front to check on the "rumors." Corbin, Steve Twist, and John Shadegg would then pretend to be obliged to tell him just what he needed, to conjure up a certain picture for his readers and supply nothing that would clarify what was really going on. If they had nothing on a particular victim, they would simply "verify" that an investigation was being made. If they had the faintest hint of an allegation from anywhere, they would report that the victim was being investigated for "fraud" or "murder." No retractions were ever printed of course. After all, Corbin would say, he wasn't responsible for the newspapers. He only answered their questions.

Of course, if reporters questioned Corbin about an establishment figure, he was quick to announce that there had been "no signs of wrong doing." When pressed in one of his investigations concerning an obvious campaign violation cover-up by a group called TOYS, Corbin pointed out that "wrong-doing" was what he said it was. By definition, there wasn't any wrong doing if he said there wasn't.

People are only human, of course, and an occasional abuse of power by the AG's office is hardly enough to condemn the entire staff. However, this sort of character assassination seemed to be the rule rather than the exception, and it had been practiced by more than a few people, including Corbin himself. Consider the embarrassing flap during the 1988 presidential primary race, when the *Republic* announced sources had leaked to them that Corbin was about to launch a grand jury investigation of Bruce Babbitt's campaign funding. When a furious Babbitt turned on them, the *Republic* announced that the source had been no less than Corbin himself, though Corbin denied it. There was never an investigation.

I don't know how seriously Corbin ever really considered running for governor. On February 19, 1986, a Friday afternoon, he reportedly told Pat Murphy that he was almost certain to run. At 10:00 a.m. the following day, he called back to announce that he'd changed his mind. What really happened during Bob Corbin's dark night of deliberation is anybody's guess.

Corbin's only expressed reason for changing his mind was that he liked being attorney general too much to give the job up. It's obvious from his conversation with me that this wasn't a sudden revelation to him, however. The most intriguing question was whether Corbin had ever actually intended to run in the first place. Had he been bought off by Barr's promises of additional legislative funding concessions for the AG's office? Pat Murphy suggested this in a somehow approving editorial. Or had Corbin simply been planning all along to use the possibility of his candidacy to leverage those concessions from Barr? Other political insiders claim that John McCain, already considered a shoe-in to replace Goldwater in the Senate, had promised Corbin a federal judgeship. That is how things work in the realm where power brokers and their office-holding minions control the system.

The Arizona Republic led the way in generating publicity for Barr. Their poster boy, soon-to-be Senator John McCain, arranged a photo opportunity with President Reagan in the Oval Office. No reporters had been present, so it was easy for the *Republic* to build up this occasion as a major happening. They quoted McCain on how thrilled President Reagan was that an unselfish and noble person like Burton Barr was ready and willing

74

to accept the governorship of Arizona. The *Republic* turned this quickie photo session into a pre-primary endorsement for Barr, implying that the president had practically begged Barr to make this terrible sacrifice.

What President Reagan actually did was emphasize how important it was to get more Republican governors into office before the 1991, redistricting for congressional and legislative seats occurred in the state legislatures. With only 16 GOP governors in office, Republicans stood little chance to gain representation in the U.S. House, through redistricting after the 1990 election. When I entered the governor's race, President Reagan made the same photo opportunity offer to me, but I didn't want to drag him into the primary, so I waited until the general election to visit him.

With the retirement of Goldwater, McCain and Barr were poised to take over Republican Party leadership in Arizona. It seemed strange, though, that McCain, rather than Barr, was already acting like the party's leader. The governor is the titular head of the party. He can have the biggest impact on it through the many appointments he makes and his daily dealings with local and statewide issues.

Furthermore, McCain himself was a virtual outsider to any grass-roots movement in the state, and many residents familiar with his story viewed him as something of a carpetbagger. After checking out Florida and Texas, he had moved to Arizona in 1980. His last primary duty with the U.S. Navy was as liaison officer to the U.S. Senate, which molded his decision to become a professional politician. Arizona was the easiest state in which to make a political career for himself. He married Cindy Hensley, and was immediately made a vice president in public relations for her father's beer distributing company. From the start, McCain used that position—primarily to meet the right people who could advance his political career.

He met me quite overtly for that purpose just a few months after his arrival in Arizona, unabashedly announcing Congress as his first goal. I suggested that he might want to work his way into the party on a local level for starters, and get acquainted with the political scene in Arizona by running for a seat in the state legislature. In order to introduce him to some of my conservative friends and to see what he had to offer, I invited him to be the guest speaker at our monthly Freeman Institute Century Club dinner.

McCain's story of his war exploits and patriotism was certainly a safe subject at the conservative Century Club. He was a Vietnam War hero, a Navy pilot who had been a POW after he was shot down over North Vietnam. The injuries suffered during this ordeal apparently made it impossible for him to follow his father's and grandfather's Naval careers as Admirals. His stint in Washington as Navy Liaison to the Senate had apparently afflicted him with an incurable political virus. The speech was long on platitudes and short on substance, but it was still a credible performance for a newcomer.

When John Rhodes announced his retirement in 1982, McCain moved into District 1 so that he could run for that seat in the U. S. House of Representatives. Initially, I supported him against a former legislator named Donna Carlson West, and guided my friends at local conservative groups such as the Eagle Forum in his direction. But it soon became apparent that McCain's concern with conservative issues could only be measured in votes. While vocally appreciative of the Eagle Forum in their Mesa stronghold, he heartily denounced them in front of a more liberal Scottsdale audience.

Just as telling was McCain's rapidly developing friendship with Duke Tully, publisher of *The Arizona Republic*. McCain had quickly decided that the easiest way to step into Rhodes' shoes was to don the mantle of the Pulliam Press that Rhodes had worn so comfortably for years. Despite his proud Navy tradition, McCain seemed to find it surprisingly easy to befriend Tully, who built a public career on the notorious fiction that he had been a decorated Air Force fighter pilot in the Korean War. Telling the story of his war heroics, Tully always seemed to look down from some lofty moral podium that sanctioned the judgments his newspaper passed on other people. A real bombshell exploded when Maricopa County Attorney Tom Collins, acting on a tip, found that Tully's military record was a complete deception. His medals and uniforms were fakes. He had never even been in the Air Force, although he had gradually promoted himself from a lieutenant, when he first started the hoax, up to a lieutenant colonel by the time he was exposed. Tully resigned in disgrace from the *Republic*, but McCain was untroubled. He admitted that the he had known about the deception for some time, as did Bill Shover, the number three man at the *Republic*.

Ralph Watkins, my campaign finance chairman and well-known businessman, told me his experience when McCain was making his getting acquainted rounds. Ralph and his friend Lanny Cope were visiting with McCain about his future in Arizona. When he told them of his plans to run for Congress, both Watkins and Cope suggested that, as a newcomer to the state, his desire for a political career might be more successful if he first won a seat in the Arizona House of Representatives. This would give him the time and opportunity to learn a lot more about the people and the state, before trying to represent them in Washington. They added that he would have to have the full support of *The Arizona Republic* to become known and win a seat in Congress on his first attempt. To their surprise, McCain said he had that support already locked up. He said that he and Duke Tully were very good friends, dating back to the times they flew combat together in Vietnam.

When it was revealed that Tully's military career was a complete falsehood, where did that leave McCain with his claim that they flew together in Vietnam? The legal term for Tully's deception is impersonating an officer, which I am told is a federal felony. Tully left town without being prosecuted and continued to retain McCain's friendship.

Not surprisingly, perhaps, in those days McCain had been a protege of liberal Democratic Senator Gary Hart, and apparently was born again as a conservative only when he found Arizona's climate particularly kind to that political skin.

Ray Russell, a man who stood behind the issues he felt were important, whatever political labels were applied to them, decided to enter the congressional race against McCain. I shifted my support to him, and urged my friends to do the same. Some felt committed to McCain by now, and it's hard to fault people for loyalty. In the end, McCain beat Russell by 2,700 votes in the four-candidate race.

As expected, when Goldwater announced his retirement, McCain was ready and waiting for the 1986 election. The party's logical choice for Goldwater's Senate seat was Bob Stump. He was Arizona's senior GOP Representative in the United States Congress and a sorely needed conservative voice in the U. S. Senate. But McCain showed considerable political acumen, and cut Stump's legs out from under him before he could start to run. Flashing a major bankroll and the full support of the Pulliam press, McCain made it obvious to Stump that contesting Goldwater's Senate seat would be at best an uphill battle, and at worst could cost him his seat in the House and end his political career. Stump opted to stay in the House. With the backing of the Phoenix establishment, McCain rolled to an easy general election victory over under-funded Democrat Richard Kimball, a former state senator and corporation commissioner, with comparatively few resources.

Less than six years after his arrival in Arizona, John McCain had married an attractive heiress, spent four years in Congress, and now captured the Senate seat held by Barry Goldwater for 30 years. He'd had the kind of success normally reserved for leading men on television soap operas.

Like his approach in moving to Arizona to become a senator, his presidential scenario was simple and practical. The 1988 GOP presidential primary featured so many prospective candidates that it looked like it would be a battle royal. After gaining control of Arizona's Republican Party, and thereby its delegation to the GOP convention, McCain planned to parlay the state's votes into a vice presidential nomination for himself. Following two terms of loyal service to the successful bidder, McCain would be ready to step into the Oval Office in 1997. If the Democrats won in 1988, McCain, having gained national exposure in the general election, would be ready to rescue the GOP in 1992. No one could accuse him of thinking small.

If the plan seems incredible to most of us, stop and consider George Bush's selection of little-known Dan Quayle as a running mate. McCain's meteoric rise in this state suggests he had a shot at the same kind of promotion. If only he'd been able to make it in Florida or Texas, McCain might have been chosen. The plan did not really depend on that many unpredictable or improbable events. But in the Arizona gubernatorial primary of 1986, I inadvertently collided with McCain's machinations, and one of its few moving parts ground to a halt.

Since our initial contacts and my early support for McCain in his bid for Congress, I hadn't heard much from him. After I'd backed Russell in the campaign, McCain surmised that he'd gotten all the free help he could from me, and apparently decided that would be the extent of our relationship. Still, when we bumped into each other at public functions, he was always pleasant, and I had no reason to believe he harbored any animosity toward me. Initially, he and Barr hadn't gotten along all that well, probably because each saw himself as the king of Arizona's political hill. But when the establishment decided on their line-up for the 1986 election, the two were ordered to kiss and make up. McCain began working with Barr and the power brokers quite openly; and I wasn't surprised when he teamed up with Barr in the Republican primary in 1986. They campaigned together, with McCain usually acting as spokesman for the two. Once my candidacy became a serious threat to Barr, McCain's animosity surfaced and he began to balk at even shaking my hand in public.

When Corbin and Rottas stepped aside in the governor's race, Barr seemed poised for a virtually uncontested primary victory. I had to accept the fact that as things stood, we would have no other choice. The Democrats' choices of Carolyn Warner and Tony Mason were no better, from my standpoint.

The days from mid-May to mid-June were among the most miserable of my life. I didn't want or intend to get involved in politics again. Since my exit in 1982, I'd enjoyed being on the sidelines. But I couldn't help seeing how badly things were going in Arizona. I'd usually laugh at Max Hawkins and a number of other friends who kept telling me I had to get back in, but the suggestion began to linger in my mind. I'd consciously change my thoughts to another subject, but the idea of running for office was omnipresent. When Max Hawkins held a press conference and announced that he was going to draft me, even the mild interest it aroused was enough to push me into confronting the challenge of a political campaign once more.

All my life I have approached decisions, big or small, by asking God to help me make the right choices. Some members of the press have attempted to distort my religion as they have everything else, turning my simple belief that God will guide the person who asks, into some self-aggrandizing proclamation of messianic leadership. All I can say is that people who make decisions without asking for God's inspiration think they are a lot smarter than I think I am. I believe the same avenue of inspiration is open to all. We have a loving Father in Heaven who wants to help us; but we need to ask His guidance in prayer to open up the channel of communication. After asking, we need to have faith that He will guide us and then listen for the impressions He will give in answer. My faith in this process is a personal thing about which I'm usually not vocal, but for which I am deeply grateful. When a reporter once asked me to respond to a statement attributed to Barry Goldwater that, "Ev thinks he has an 800 number to God." I answered that I did, and so did everyone else—including Barry, if he would use it.

After my month of prayerful inquiry and reflection, I knew I ought to enter the race for governor, but also that I could not do so without the complete support of my family. We are a close family with a lot of love for each other, and we have to be united to be happy. Having seen the amount of money I'd spent, and the bashing I'd taken at the hands of the press in the past, the family had been solidly opposed to my re-entering politics. I called them together, including the spouses of my children, with the exception of our oldest daughter, Suzanne, and her husband, who were living in Virginia. We consulted with them by phone. I explained what I'd been going through for the past month and told them that I felt I should run, but that if a single one of them opposed it, I wouldn't.

It was an amazing thing for me to watch their transformations over the next two hours. My family, including my wife, Florence, is made up of strong-willed people. None of them are any too bashful about expressing their opinions. I answered their questions, but the discussion was otherwise entirely theirs. In the end, the children all turned to Florence and said, "Well, Mom. It's up to you." They knew that politics was always harder on the spouse than on the participant. The one in the arena can fight back. The spouse has to suffer in silence.

Florence is a very sensitive, loving, quiet, and private person, certainly not one to favor the public glare of politics. For these reasons in particular, the decision to allow me to go ahead was a very difficult one for her. She thought about the matter for another day before telling me she no longer opposed me entering the race.

I certainly didn't need the job. I also knew that, considering the state of the state following Babbitt's spending binge, being governor would be no picnic. But I felt Arizona's problems were reaching a critical mass, demanding immediate attention. Next to the presidency, a governorship offers the greatest opportunity to effect changes through governmental action. For someone like myself, with an agenda for correcting the wrongs in government, it is a very desirable leadership position. I believed I had the right motives, the right plans, and the right experience to be an effective governor. I also knew that I could bring to the office one ingredient that had usually been lacking in establishment candidates: a love for the people.

I'd always resented the attitude typified by Harry Hopkins, who advised FDR to "tax, tax, spend, spend, elect, elect—people are too damn dumb to know the difference." People may be uninformed. After all, there is little done in politics or through the media to actively inform them. The information that is dispersed is not designed to allow people to make an intelligent decision, but to direct their thinking to accommodate the political goals of the establishment operators. The only correct way was that suggested by Thomas Jefferson, when he wrote: " I know no safe depository of the ultimate powers of the society but the people themselves; and if we think them not enlightened enough to exercise their control with a wholesome discretion, the remedy is not to take it from them, but to inform their discretion by education."

After my June conference with my family, I told Max Hawkins to go ahead if he thought he could get the necessary signatures on the nominating petitions in the brief time we had left. He did it in just two weeks, and on July 1, 1986, I entered the primary, quietly confident I would win.

Chapter 6

THE MEDIA BILLED IT AS THE POLITICAL UPSET OF UPSETS

"If ever this free people, if this government itself is ever utterly demoralized, it will come from this incessant human wriggle and struggle for office which is but a way to live without work."
Lincoln

When reporters repeatedly asked me if I really thought that I had a chance to win, and I replied that I did, I saw nothing but disbelief in their eyes. Barr had been running for well over a year by that time; experienced political observers probably thought I was too late to have a chance against him. All but two of the Republican legislators and a variety of key people all over the state had already promised to support Barr. He had filled a huge war chest for the occasion. By calling in every chip pledged to him during his 20 years of political wheeling and dealing, Barr appeared to have amassed an unstoppable political Juggernaut. His overconfidence, based on the establishment's decades of success at controlling Arizona politics, was my greatest ally at this point.

Perhaps the single most effective element of my primary campaign was the tabloid newspaper we mailed directly to the homes of registered Republicans. The majority of the space was devoted to what I planned to do to get the state government working properly. I invited people to save this tabloid and make sure I did what I promised I would do. We also detailed important parts of Barr's record in the legislature. Max Hawkins had gathered quite a bit of information about Barr's dealings, and he and I took that information to Maricopa County Attorney Tom Collins and to Attorney General Corbin to see if an investigation into a conflict of interest was in order. Corbin told us that there was no basis for an investigation because the legislature, under Barr's leadership, had repealed the part of the law dealing with conflict of interest as it applied to state legislators. Their rationale for subjecting everyone but themselves to the law was that the legislature, with its own House and Senate Ethics committees, didn't need to be subjected to the same law that applied to everyone else. Since the establishment leadership controlled these committees, not only was there never any danger of embarrassing investigations, but the leadership gained one more club to hold over the heads of recalcitrant legislators who might fall out of step with their parade. And needless to say, when we took our charges to the House of Representatives Ethics Committee, we were turned away without a hearing.

The voters, however, weren't too busy to listen. After having controlled the media so successfully, Barr seemed astounded that anyone had the temerity to print anything about his record that he did not want known.

Much of what we printed was a compilation of articles from his own dear *Arizona Republic*, the *Mesa Tribune,* and the *New Times* framed with some pointed questions that, given this information, we thought the press and the government ought to have asked.

We mailed the 12-page tabloid that included five pages of news clips and facts about Barr along with my own record and platform to Republican households. After it was mailed, I was accused of dirty campaigning. All I had done was publish clips of news articles, legislative actions, a map showing places along the freeway where Barr had shares of real estate partnerships, and then I asked if some of the things he was engaged in constituted a conflict of interest? I pointed out that if we had handled anything dirty about Barr it was his own record. The biggest damage to Barr was what local newspaper columnists, feature writers, and news reporters had said about him. *Republic* columnist, Tom Fitzpatrick, wrote in his Sunday column of March 20, 1983:

The accumulation of power is a fascinating thing. Power feeds on itself. It changes the atmosphere around a man perceived to possess it.

This is the way it is for Burton Barr, the House Majority Leader, whom many call the most powerful man in the state.

Republican legislators find it easy to do what Barr tells them to do. They learn swiftly that Barr has the power to reward or punish them. Barr can intimidate them merely by ignoring them or by refusing to give them campaign contributions from money donated to his campaign fund by the moneyed.

Newcomers perceive that everyone does Barr's bidding, and if they want to become part of the team, they fall quickly into line . . . .

When it comes time for Burton Barr to run for re-election, the campaign contributions pour in. Smart money flows toward power . . . .

Roger Garrett, a liquor lobbyist, is a first-rate example. Garrett worked for Barr as a young legislative lawyer for several years. Barr thought highly of him.

Garrett opened a law firm. Suddenly, he turned up as representative of the Arizona Licensed Beverage Association, the group that represents virtually every tavern and liquor store in the state.

Garrett entered his name in the liquor lottery and won licenses in two years out of three. Garrett's incorporation papers for a proposed bar, the Westbridge Cocktail Lounge, show that Barr's wife, Louise, is listed as vice president and secretary of the corporation.

Barr says this means nothing. He treats questions about the matter as being beneath contempt.

Barr has held power for so long that he doesn't understand that others will perceive there is a connection between his own opposition to raising the legal drinking age to 21 years of age and his relationship with the liquor lobby's lucky Roger Garrett.

Holding power for a long time makes a man think strange things.

The Greyhound Good Government PAC contributed $2,000, and Fred Hervey, chairman of the board of Circle K, chipped in with $500.

The list goes on and on for pages. It is mind boggling to read down the list and see all that money coming in.

As you read down the list, the questions hit you in the eye.

Here's one from a man named Charles Fritz of Chicago. He donated $1,500, and it isn't until you look it up that Fritz turns out to be on the board of directors at Turf Paradise.

You look at a donation of $750 attributed to George Gillett in care of his attorney Jack LaSota and wonder what that could possibly mean.

And then you remember that Gillett owns Tucson Greyhound Park and that he nearly lost his license last August in a hearing before the state Racing Commission.

Gillett got off with a $250 fine, and LaSota was his attorney. You have to assume that Gillett was just so pleased with the quality of justice in Arizona that he wanted to take part in the political process.

And what better way to get involved in the political process than to become a friend of Burton Barr?" (From *The Arizona Republic*, Mar. 20, 1983)

A summary of Barr's horse and dog racing involvement were reported in my tabloid as follows:

In three successive Barr-backed bills the State's share of Pari-Mutuel Revenues at Turf Paradise has been cut from 7% to 1% and has more than tripled the commissions going to the track owners. Annual reports of the State Racing Commission show that House Bill 2175 supported by Barr in 1978, together with House Bill 2470 sponsored by Barr in 1982 have reduced the State's share of Revenues by $14,500,000 and increased the commissions paid to the track by $50,000,000. During this same period of time, records filed with the Arizona Corporation Commission show that the asset value of Turf Paradise property has increased 10 fold, from $2,896,865 in 1978 to $22,663,915 in 1985. This does not include the appreciated value of land owned by Turf Paradise, estimated by a research analyst of the Arizona House of Representatives to be in excess of $40,000,000.

Originally introduced by Rep. Akers (by request) HB 2175 was intended to provide some relief to horse breeders at the smaller tracks in Arizona. However, in committee it was completely gutted and made into a vehicle to transfer to Arizona taxpayers the burden of picking up the tab for "capital improvements" that were already in progress on the privately owned facilities of Turf Paradise.

Wide spread abuse and misuse of capital outlay funds at all three commercial horse tracks in the state; Turf Paradise, Prescott Downs (in Prescott), and Rillito Downs in Tucson, prompted a full scale investigation leading to the Legislature's attempt to plug some of the loopholes left open in the 1978 racing bill. This was supposed to clean up some of the racing scandals in Arizona by creating a Department of Racing, and establish some guidelines as to what could or could not be considered as "capital improvements." Sponsored by Barr, it again increased commissions going to the horse tracks, made further decreases in the state's share of Pari-Mutuel Revenues, and gave the dog track owners the same right as the horse tracks to dip into state revenues to pay for improvements to their privately owned dog tracks.

The 1982 House Bill 2379 is the ultimate insult and injury to the taxpayers of Arizona. It is a gross abuse of legislative power for the benefit of a few and to the detriment of the general public. It demands an immediate and full scale investigation of the corrupting influence of those in the racing industry upon the legislative process.

The State's share of Pari-Mutuel Revenues has been effectively reduced from 7% to 1% of the (Pari-Mutuel) Handle; the Track's share increased from 11% to 20%; assets paid for with State Revenues are depreciated to show a paper loss on its income statements, making it possible for the track to avoid paying any State or Federal Income Taxes; and the book value of Turf Paradise Assets have been increased 10 fold from $2,896,865 to $22, 663,915.

The way in which millions of dollars of State Pari-Mutuel Revenues have been diverted from the State's treasury into the coffers of the race track owners, is nothing short of scandalous. No one is more to blame than Burton Barr who used his position of leadership in the Arizona

Legislature to enrich the owners of the Horse and Dog Tracks at the expense of the Arizona taxpayers.

About six weeks after I became governor, I personally asked Attorney General Bob Corbin to conduct a full scale investigation into the fraud and abuses that had been going on in the racing industry in Arizona. He promised faithfully to do so and assigned two special investigators from his office to meet with one of my special assistants, Mac Matheson, who had been accumulating and documenting evidence of fraud and abuse as early as 1982.

Matheson met with these two special investigators, Terry Chapman and Janice Lamparter, and turned over to them numerous files of Photostat copies of state documents. He took the two investigators to interview witnesses who had personal knowledge concerning evidence of bribery involved in the passage of the three legislative bills. Corbin soon pulled the investigators off the case and summarily quashed the investigation with no explanation to me.

The tabloid printed another classic example of Barr's abuse of power in the Legislature – his efforts to destroy Arizona's control of the Department of Weights and Measures:

In 1974, Ray Helmick, the new Director of the Arizona State Department of Weights and Measures, was making good on his desire to make that department work properly.

Helmick came from another state that ran a good department and knew that Arizona was a dumping ground for shoddy and under weighted produce that couldn't be sold in states where there were good standards enforced.

The House of Representatives had responded and passed a bill for some added enforcement powers and sent it over to the Senate. Helmick's field people and Phoenix City Weights and Measures Inspectors had found thousands of packages of short weighted meats in some markets. They are responsible for furnishing the data to the state Attorney General for his indictment of two grocery chains and three milk companies on shortages.

One of the grocery chain owners, a customer of Burton Barr's food store equipment company, was irate over the indictment. His complaint to Barr brought instant action from the Majority Leader. An assistant Attorney General reported that when Barr called him to complain about the indictment that he was angry almost to the point of incoherence.

Barr proved he had the power to get things done. He got the Senate to return the House Bill previously passed and sent over to them. He then changed it to take away the separate departmental status of Weights & Measures and put it in the Department of Administration. That put an enforcement agency in an administration agency, which was organizationally improper.

Helmick was demoted and two years later was fired. The enforcement teeth of the agency were pulled. They are supposed to be an enforcement agency but couldn't even issue citations to repeated offenders.

The charges against the five companies for short weight and measures were dropped by the Attorney General, accompanied by an explanation that he didn't think they meant to cheat the public. A short time later the Attorney General resigned to accept an appointment from Governor Babbitt to become a Superior Court Judge.

The consumers of Arizona lost millions of dollars annually from short weights, low measures and shoddy merchandise, until 1987 when the Arizona Legislature acted on my request to restore to the Weights & Measures Department the power to protect our consumers.

On August 3, 1986, the *Mesa Tribune* printed an editorial that put the freeway land questions in the proper perspective. It read as follows:

Barr Should Answer Allegations Promptly

Five-time Republican gubernatorial hopeful Evan Mecham is used to ruffling political feathers, even with his own party. The outspoken Glendale car dealer last week did it again.

Mecham has called for a "full, fair, deep, unbiased investigation" into land purchases by his rival in the primary election, House Majority Leader Burton Barr.

Mecham claims Barr, who helped draw up the program to promote a $2.5 billion Valley Freeway construction program last year, may have profited personally from "inside information" about the Freeway routes.

Barr has vigorously denied he ever has used his legislative post for personal gain.

That very well may be true. Barr has a reputation for high personal integrity.

But with billions of tax dollars earmarked for the most expensive public works program in the state's history, any suspicions of official impropriety must be answered quickly and completely – regardless of where they originated.

Mecham, in claiming Barr should have declared a conflict of interest, perhaps inadvertently pointed up a serious gap in Arizona's conflict of interest law. Legislators passed the law only after exempting themselves from key provisions.

There also are no requirements in Arizona for political candidates to make detailed disclosures of their financial holdings. Tony Mason, another gubernatorial candidate, has made that a campaign issue by disclosing his own finances. He has challenged other candidates to do the same.

At the very least, Mecham's questions deserve fast and complete answers from Barr. In addition, a balanced legislative committee should review the matter.

The taxpayers of Arizona also deserve better laws dealing with conflict of interest disclosures and financial disclosure by their public officials and candidates for public office.

Such requirements do more than protect the taxpayers. They also protect honest public officials.

We also reprinted the following article from the May 14, 1986, *NewTimes*, written by Doug MacEachern:

"Where Go the Freeways, So Goes Burton Barr"

Barr owns interest in a variety of properties, including a few adjoining planned Freeway routes. According to his financial disclosure statement filed with the Secretary of State's office, Barr owns:

1. An interest in a limited partnership that purchased 146 acres at Pecos and Kyrene roads in Chandler in September 1983. The property is at an intersection planned for the southern extension of the Outer Loop.

2. Nineteen acres purchased by his wife for his three children at 51st Avenue and Beardsley Road in north Phoenix in January 1985. Beardsley Road forms part of the northern extension of the Outer Loop.

3. Part of 41 acres north of Ray Road and west of Dobson Road in Chandler. Like the Pecos and Kyrene property, this land was purchased through a syndicate that sells limited partnerships in blocks of real estate. This piece is less than a mile from the Price Road extension for the eastern leg of the Outer Loop.

Burton Barr has a reputation for exploding on strangers, particularly reporters who dare ask him prying questions about his personal life. He doesn't explode anymore, though. He is running for governor. "For once in my life," he says quite calmly, "I'm not mad that you're asking. I feel you're entitled to ask."

And he responds. "Yes," he says, "Burton Barr has worked on that Freeway deal harder than anybody in America." But never, he adds, for his own personal benefit: "Let me say this first off: never in my 22 years in public office have I ever earned a cent as a result of any information I've ever had. It's that simple. That's a flat statement of truth. I want you to know that."

The parcels, he says, were purchased either by his wife as an investment for their children, or through a syndicate for Maverick Profit Sharing Plan, an investment group formed for employees of his restaurant equipment firm. "There are syndicates everywhere," Barr explains. 'Syndicators go buy land. I assume they buy land where it's going to be profitable. Profitable land is near where there's a Freeway."

Barr explains his dealing with the innocence of a man whose mind is busy with matters of greater import than personal finance. "I know you're going to laugh at this," he says, "but these [investments] are like profit sharing [plans]. I give them to my partner and say, 'Here, look at them. You like 'em? Then go buy 'em.' I don't ever pick them up and say 'Hey, it's near a Freeway!' I didn't relate it to anything," he says, "or think about it."

As much as Barr allows that I am "entitled to ask" about his personal property, I do not believe he is at all pleased that I exercised that right. But I think we should have known about Barr's freeway side land long ago. It wouldn't have hurt him to tell us. He should have, and, because he did not, he's created his own restive nest of doubt. (*New Times*, May 14-20, 1986)

Another excerpt from the *Republic* tags Barr as "The PAC Bag Man":

Barr attracted more in contributions than any other legislator in Arizona history.

Most of the money came from political action committees. As usual, Barr doled nearly all of it out to GOP candidates.

"Here are a whole bunch of people, who, when they were first running, Burt Barr walked up and handed them a check for $5,000," explains Andy Hurwitz, Babbitt's astute former chief of staff, "He said, 'I don't want anything from you. Just be the best legislator you can.' The next thing, they've got elected, and he's coming around and asking for their vote."

Does it buy votes?

Adds Sen. Peter Kay, a Republican who prides himself on never taking any of Barr's money: "Do you think those people are going to say no?"

Some people say so much PAC money makes Barr beholden to certain industries. They say money buys them access to Barr's office. Bob Fannin, a lawyer and lobbyist who has represented such interests as the Arizona Association of Realtors and American Greyhound Racing, says he would "feel guilty" about lobbying for a bill if he hadn't contributed to Barr.

Perhaps the best balanced political commentary in the campaign was written early in the primary race by Bob Schuster, editorial page editor of the *Mesa Tribune*.

State Republican leaders have every reason to be deeply concerned about Evan Mecham's last-minute entry into the GOP gubernatorial primary.

Majority Leader Barr indeed has some baggage from 20 years as the consummate legislative compromiser.

And Mecham is lean and mean on the campaign trail. Democrat Carolyn Warner could end up finishing in the general election what Mecham starts in the primary.

No wonder state GOP Chairman Burt Kruglick took the unprecedented step of endorsing Barr when rumors surfaced early this summer that Mecham might run.

Depending on how the issues and candidates line up, a primary contest can either strengthen or weaken the winning candidate.

Assuming the polls hold and Warner, who now is state superintendent of public instruction, beats businessman Tony Mason in the Democratic primary, Warner should go into the general election a formidable contender.

The Barr-Mecham race will be much different. Mecham is the only main party candidate who is clearly separated from the pack on issues. And if Barr represents compromise, Mecham clearly represents non-compromise.

By far the most conservative, Mecham touts a strict free-enterprise, limited-government platform. It hasn't changed one iota from the 1978 election when he ran a respectable race against Bruce Babbitt, losing by less than 8 percent of the votes cast.

His candidacy can't be written off as merely an ego trip by an off-the-wall perennial candidate. Mecham was drafted by strong forces within the right wing of Arizona's GOP who see Barr as the guy who has sold them down the river in two decades of wheeling and dealing with Democrats and the state's fattest special interests.

Mecham also differs in style from Barr. Although Barr is responding remarkably to coaching to improve his delivery in front of crowds, he still has trouble focusing succinctly on specific issues and selling his points.

Mecham, on the other hand, cuts like a knife directly to his point.

For instance, Mecham maintains that Barr, as power broker between big business and Democrats, has caused taxes to soar and special interests to benefit at the expense of the average citizen.

He cites as examples the temporary sales tax increase of 1983.

Mecham charges Barr knew all along the sales tax increase would become permanent even though it was touted as a way to compensate for a revenue dip caused by a sagging economy.

If elected, Mecham said he would work to immediately repeal the tax.

In both cases, the average Arizonan is getting fleeced by the state's "establishment government" that has catered to the Phoenix 40, says Mecham, who characterizes himself as a "small businessman."

"I want to see this state develop, but not so we mortgage our future. The free enterprise system works best where government doesn't give a monopoly benefit to a favored few."

Mesa Tribune editorial commentary

Ironically, in spite of the information available, every daily newspaper in Arizona editorially recommended Barr's selection over me.

When Barr realized that people were listening to us, he railed against our "smear tactics" – apparently meaning that we weren't allowed to ask questions before the public that his Ethics Committee was refusing to answer. After years of keeping the voters in the dark on so many of the things being done under the Barr leadership, our truthful tabloid was a devastating blow to his campaign. His only answer was to go on a smear campaign accusing me of dirty campaigning. I never called Barr any names or accused him of anything that was not a matter of public record. If there was anything dirty in our campaign, it was his record that we revealed. I carefully confined my own utterances relating to Barr to asking questions. When Barr did not answer the questions, the majority of the voters made up their own minds in my favor.

The primary campaign came together quite well. My basic program describing how Arizonans needed to throw off the establishment yoke and elect a governor more responsive to them, was well received. I pointed out the rapid increase in spending and taxation during the Babbitt years was a result of this marriage between special interests, the House majority leader, and the governor. I pointed out the low priority given to solving the real problems, such as the rapid increase in the sale and use of drugs and the deterioration of our educational system. The people were interested in what I had to say.

As primary election day approached, it was interesting to see how the news media in general, and *The Arizona Republic* in particular, were trying to manipulate the results. They kept reporting polls that showed Barr leading me by 15 percent and that I did not have a chance to win. My camp felt differently but knew it was in the hands of the voters. There had not been any real debates between us in the campaign. We appeared at many of the same events and each made our own time to make our points. We were very civil to each other, but Barr didn't really discuss issues, preferring to spend more time being entertaining and talking in generalities on the issues. When I mailed out the tabloid with several pages of the plans and programs I had in mind to solve Arizona's problems and included the pages of reprints from newspapers about Barr's record, I expected him to respond. He didn't. His attitude was almost condescending, and he appeared to be above it all.

Conversely, I spoke very clearly of my plans to stop the big annual increases in the state budget, and I guaranteed the people that there would be no tax increases in my term. I had quite a number of issues I talked about, including a pledge to get rid of the sale and use of drugs. I felt good about the reception I was getting everywhere.

For candidates, election days are the longest days of the year. The TV stations want to tape the candidates to fill in a little action while waiting for the returns to start coming in. You try to stay busy making sure all of the assignments are being done, but mostly you just wait as the hours pass very slowly.

Barr prepared for his expected victory celebration at the ballroom of one of the downtown Phoenix hotels. He followed the practice of well-financed campaigns, where the candidate takes a few rooms in the hotel for himself and his close supporters to wait for the results. When there is enough lead in the vote count to assure victory, the candidate goes down to make an anticipation of victory speech to the many supporters and wannabes that have gathered, and the celebration goes on in earnest. It usually ends with the defeated candidate phoning the victor his concession announcement, wishing the victor well, and pledging his support for the upcoming general election.

We prepared for our election-eve vigil at the campaign headquarters, in the west showroom of our Pontiac dealership on Glendale Avenue. Our refreshments consisted of punch and cookies made by our workers and supporters. Some came out of loyalty—not really expecting a victory. All of the press was in downtown Phoenix where the action was expected. They felt my concession speech could be handled by phone because the victor is the one who makes the news, and that is where they wanted to be.

As the returns started to come in, I was in front. I was told, but never saw any proof, that *The Arizona Republic* started their early edition with a headline of Barr winning. They soon corrected that because I led from the very first reports and never trailed. As my lead built, so did the crowd. Then the news reporters and TV cameras began to arrive to report what they were broadcasting as a major upset. By 11:00 p.m., my lead was ample enough to guarantee victory, but there was no word from Barr. Burt Kruglick, the state GOP chairman, called his congratulations. He and almost every other Republican official had endorsed Barr in the primary, so he was not sure what my attitude would be. We both agreed to let the past be forgotten and go forward to win the general election.

Barr never observed the usual courtesies by making a concession speech and offering congratulations. Instead, he finally came down to a less than full ballroom to make an attack on me, and complain about the dirty campaign he said I had run. I could understand his disappointment. He felt he had been sent the crown by the power brokers and I had stopped its delivery.

As expected, I was elated but I knew we were only halfway to our goal. We had run a good, issues-oriented campaign and the voters had understood it. My promise to liberate the government from the Phoenix 40 and restore it to the people was being heard and believed.

Every daily newspaper in the state had endorsed Barr and opposed me. In spite of the bias of the news media, the people had heard, understood, and voted to support the changes we needed to make in state government. I was anxious to get started on the campaign for the general election. It would be an even bigger challenge.

Chapter 7

THE GENERAL ELECTION--
THE WINNER BECOMES GOVERNOR

"Laws will be wisely formed and honestly administered in proportion as those who form and administer them are wise and honest"
Jefferson

During the primary election, Barr and I had both promised to support the Republican candidate in the general election. At one point he said if they put a gun to his head it wouldn't keep him from supporting the Republican ticket. Well, it took a lot less than a gun to make Barr actively work for the downfall of the duly elected Republican candidate for governor. Instead of supporting me as the nominee, he swore his undying hatred for me and pledged to get even. On the night of the primary, he was plotting to carry out his pledge. After the primary, his wife worked for Bill Schulz, who came into the general election race as an independent. Barr himself refused even to return my phone calls. I later learned that he was downtown working for Democratic Mayor Terry Goddard, presumably helping Goddard put together a 1990 gubernatorial bid. Of course, it was also a convenient place for someone with Barr's financial interests to keep tabs on proposed construction projects and highway developments.

Needless to say, most of the party leadership, with their ties to the establishment was chagrined at my primary victory. All of them, from McCain to Republican State Chairman Burt Kruglick, had publicly endorsed Barr. Fortunately, most of them realized that the best way to serve their own interests was to serve the party's, and this meant accepting me, just as I was willing to accept the other Republican victors.

Some of them showed they could be real team players. From 11:00 p.m., on the night of the primary election, when Burt Kruglick called me to concede that I had beaten the candidate that he had endorsed, he did his very best to see that I won the general election in November. We got together the next morning to plan a campaign strategy, and he often traveled with me around the state. It was at Kruglick's urging that Goldwater endorsed me publicly and consented to do some television commercials supporting my candidacy.

On the other hand, Barr and the liberal Republican members of the legislature (the ones who call themselves "moderates") couldn't have cared less about party unity, when it no longer served their personal ends. I was not surprised that Barr did not keep his pledge to support me when I won. I had hoped that, as a key player in the party, he would at least care enough about his brethren to accept defeat in a gentlemanly fashion and stay out of our way in the general election. Instead, Barr helped launch the Bill Schulz "Independent" campaign for governor. The strategy seemed to be that Schulz, a wealthy businessman, could put enough of his own money into his campaign to win outright. If that did not succeed, he would take enough of the moderate to conservative votes away from me to give Democrat Carolyn Warner the victory.

When Bill Schulz came into the general election race as an Independent, it created quite a stir. The usual candidate money shortage problems would not worry him. He had enough to finance his race completely without missing a dime. He would be the biggest spender of the three of us, and I obviously would be spending the least. The very close race Schulz had run for the U.S. Senate against Goldwater had been very impressive. Before the illness of his daughter caused him to withdraw from the race in 1985, he had looked like he would go into the office almost without opposition. He had gone to a lot of states to see how they did things, and then he hired political consultant Bill Jameson, well known and respected in Arizona state government circles, to help put his plans for Arizona together.

The General Election--The Winner Becomes Governor

I looked forward to the general election contest between Caroline Warner and myself as a classic contest between two distinct ideologies and management plans. She was a forceful and engaging speaker and presented her points of view very well. I felt I could match her in ability to present my views, so it would be a contest of who had the best plans for Arizona's future. I was sure that more voters favored my Constitutional conservatism over her liberalism.

The entrance of Schulz changed everything. Like me, he was a successful businessman, and I was sure his views would be much closer to mine than to Warner's. I felt that he would take more votes from me than from her. He had been a Republican who changed to Democrat when the legislature failed to perform to his liking on some issues important to his apartment business. But now the Democrats, who had been so happy with him as their standard bearer before his withdrawal the previous year, now looked at him as a spoiler that would dilute Warner's vote. This helped Warner hold a lot of the Democrats who might otherwise have gone to Schulz.

I quite enjoyed both of the other candidates. Aside from some friendly minor jabs, we got along very well. One of Mrs. Warner's favorite sayings she jokingly used was that I drove down the road always looking in the rear view mirror. That was one straight out of the liberal handbook to convince voters that those who want to stop further advancement into the welfare state are locked into looking backward all the time. Warner and Schulz got in each other's hair somewhat, but I remained friendly to both, which was reciprocated. Mrs. Warner was so courteous that she even straightened my tie on occasion, so I would look my best.

I believe we worked together to make our presentations to the same audience better than in any other election I have seen. This was good because it gave the voters the opportunity to see the contrast between our plans for how Arizona should be governed. It also proved the old adage that you can disagree without being disagreeable.

Bill Schulz's sudden re-entrance into the gubernatorial race in September, as an Independent candidate, put an unexpected financial crunch on us. He spent over $2 million on advertising within a six-week period, and we knew we had to respond somehow. My election committee had managed to tie up some excellent time-slots for television advertising, including some exclusive World Series coverage, but in order to hang onto them, we needed to make a substantial and immediate down payment.

The finance committee was holding promotional meetings with every potential big donor they could think of. Lee Watkins, who was working with finance chairman Ralph Watkins (no relation), brought in lawyer-developer, Barry Wolfson, and his partner, Hugh Gregan.

Although I wasn't aware of it at the time, the two arrived at my headquarters by a strange route. Gregan was a former NASA engineer with a knack for real estate, and Wolfson was a tax exempt bond specialist who had left a major Phoenix law firm to strike out on his own. They had teamed up to create a series of innovative bond-financed housing projects in 1984, which had netted them a small fortune.

Used to making millions simply by monopolizing the normal avenues of financing major business transactions, the financiers and lawyers who traditionally controlled such bond issues were furious with Wolfson and Gregan. While apparently well within the letter of the law, these deals were controversial enough to be exploited by an envious financial community that wanted to ostracize the two outsiders. The established institutions began a publicity campaign against the two upstarts at the same time that they themselves began to exploit the strategies that Wolfson and Gregan had pioneered. *Fortune Magazine* dubbed them "Country Slickers." Letters and phone calls from influential people in banking and finance flooded government offices at both the federal and state levels, suggesting that the pair be investigated.

I knew none of this at the time, and very little hit the press until well after the election. The news reporters had made a detailed inspection of my campaign finance reports, and nothing was mentioned about Wolfson and Gregan being plainly listed as the largest two contributors at $15,000 each. It was well into 1987, before headline after headline proclaimed their "abuse of public funds"—though the articles themselves could usually assert no more than that the pair had donated $1,000 from their development fund to the YMCA. The Corporation Commission and then the Attorney General's Office began an investigation that went on for years, without ever asserting a criminal charge. None of these civil court charges have ever been proven, and most of them were thrown out of court without a trial.

Clearly, Gregan and Wolfson thought Arizona could do with a change in leadership—and hoped to benefit from that change. Their attitude is pretty easy to understand.

In September, 1986, I knew nothing about them. When Lee Watkins, a mutual acquaintance of the two, had first approached them for campaign contributions, they likewise knew little about me or my politics. What was important to them was that both Schulz and Warner represented the powers that had been persecuting them. When Watkins convinced them that I didn't run with the power broker pack, each man donated $15,000 to my campaign.

While my opponents were aligned with the financial establishment, I was not; and I had to be particularly skeptical of anyone supporting me who was even capable of making that kind of contribution. To put it bluntly, I wanted to know what a stranger, willing to put up so much money, expected to get out of it. So, on October 3rd, Watkins brought Wolfson and Gregan to the campaign headquarters for a brief meeting. Our entire conversation, which took place in front of my campaign headquarters, lasted about three minutes. When I learned later that Wolfson was willing to loan a substantial sum of money to the campaign, I asked him point blank what he expected in return for the loan. He said he expected nothing but better government, and 10 percent interest on his money. I said, "That's exactly what you'll have, nothing more and nothing less."

Following this brief introduction and hand shaking, I left for a speaking engagement, and Wolfson and Gregan then went with Lee Watkins into the headquarters building, where a meeting of my finance committee was being held. Every potential donor we could think of was there, though I didn't attend myself. After listening to Jim Colter and Vern Gasser explain our immediate financial dilemma and propose a complicated letter-of-credit plan to the group, Wolfson and Gregan excused themselves for a few minutes for a private conference. When they came back, Wolfson said he knew from experience that we'd never be able to get bank financing, as we had hoped, in the time we had left. He had a much simpler idea. He said he had a bit of money gathering about seven percent interest in a junk bond mutual fund. He'd lend the committee up to $650,000 of it, the full amount we needed, at 10 percent interest. It was good business for both of us.

When Jim Colter told me about the offer, I told him to set up all the paper work and take care of the legal end of the transaction. Eventually we drew $350,000 against the $650,000 line of credit Wolfson had offered. I signed a standard promissory note and a letter written by Wolfson that, among other things, assured him we wouldn't broadcast the news of his loan. It was the usual confidentiality clause expected in a business transaction, and I assumed that Wolfson wanted it there so that he wouldn't be deluged with calls from other political candidates and end up making a lot of enemies from politicians he had to turn down. At Wolfson's request, Colter also arranged for a number of my campaign supporters, including Donna Carlson and Tom Pappas, to make guarantee notes to me and for me to sign them over to Wolfson. A straight note to Wolfson from me or from Mecham Pontiac would have been simpler, but it was already arranged and we were in a hurry, so I signed the papers as they were drawn. With these guarantors in place, clearly this wasn't what is sometimes called a "slow note," that is a campaign contribution disguised as a loan that somehow never gets repaid. I was personally guaranteed on each note, and I paid all notes that the campaign could not pay.

That was the full extent of our relationship, until more than a year later the attorney general and the press tried to make the loan become a public scandal. It was first charged that Wolfson had bought favors from my administration. No one was able to point to a single benefit received by Wolfson, other than the agreed-upon loan interest. Neither his law firm nor any other business he was associated with ever received a cent of state business. The only newspaper reporter that ever even bothered to investigate the charge was Dave Becker for the Cox chain. Becker, a long-time Wolfson watcher, concluded that there was not a single piece of evidence to indicate that there was any impropriety to the loan.

With the strong financial backing of her fellow Democrats and her husband's Phoenix 40 connections, Warner spent over $2 million. Schulz spent approximately $2.25 million in six weeks. I spent $1.25 million combined primary and general election totals. If money alone could have won that election, Schulz would have been the victor. If the newspaper's editorial endorsements had carried the day, Warner would have won. Inasmuch as I won with a comfortable margin, it must be concluded that my programs were more impressive to more of the voters than the others.

The day of the general election is like the primary, but worse. There is little to do but wait, and, unless you can keep busy, it is the longest day of your life. You fall back on routine, following your normal physical activities, except that, instead of going to the office or to speak to a breakfast meeting, you go to vote. The news people have already asked your scheduling secretary the time and place, and you try to accommodate them by showing up as predicted.

You get to the campaign headquarters by mid-morning and make sure everything is going according to plan. All of those months of planning and work are for this one big day. Have we correctly identified our voters, and are we getting them to the polls to cast their ballots? Did we get all of our signs up at the polling places? (I got my assignment done, so I can only hope everyone else did his or her.) Are there any last minute surprises, any late-breaking news? There are many questions being asked, and, thankfully, for most there are satisfactory answers.

No campaign works its plan perfectly, but ours had so many faithful volunteers that it worked better than most. There was a confident feeling at our headquarters, an unused showroom and offices at my Pontiac agency in Glendale. The polls published throughout the campaign by *The Arizona Republic* didn't give us room for the optimism we really felt. Given their track record for inaccuracy, we felt we had reason for optimism. They had practiced overkill in their attempts to belittle my campaign, calling me "a four-time loser, a perennial candidate, and a car dealer," as though that in itself was reason not to vote for me. They called my campaign staff "a bunch of amateurs," etc. I was less worried about actual voters' sympathies than I was about the impact of these loaded polls on my supporter turnout and on the "bandwagon" factor among undecided voters, who were simply in the practice of backing a winner.

People came in and out of headquarters with good wishes. Sometimes the optimism they voiced sounded only expressive of their hopes, but I was always glad to have it anyway. A few of us were discussing the start-up of a transition team for our new administration, and I suggested that we call Governor Babbitt to set up an initial appointment with him for the next day. Sam Steiger made the call, perhaps eager to hear Babbitt's surprise at our confidence about the turnout of the election. His cautious answer was that he would meet with the victor at 11:00 a.m.

In the afternoon, Florence and I flew down to Tucson in our Aerostar to thank the campaign workers and staff there. Flying time is only about 30 minutes, so we planned to be back in Phoenix for Republican election parties in Mesa and at the Phoenix Hilton. As we approached Sky Harbor Airport, we were asked to circle Apache Junction while some other planes landed. Fearing our coordinates had become as lost as those of the Lost Dutchman gold mine, we called the tower back to remind them we were out there. They gave me clearance to land.

As we taxied into the executive terminal parking, Jim Ferguson, a part-time volunteer, came running out to the plane to tell us about Dan Rather's announcement: "Hold onto your hats. The CBS exit poll projects Evan Mecham winning the governorship of Arizona!"

The percentages Dan Rather predicted at 7:00 p.m.—40 percent for Mecham, 34 percent for Warner, and 26 percent for Schulz—were not verified until later in the evening. CBS's exit polling of Schulz voters also revealed that, had he not run I would have beaten Warner 55% to 45%. Our only scare came during an interview with Channel 12, when the wire service for the local station suddenly transposed my 85,000-vote lead to Warner. My son, Eric, who was at the computer center, called to ease our minds.

The Republican election headquarters at the Hilton Hotel in downtown Phoenix was packed with all the TV station crews. I went from one radio and TV interview to another, and, except for shaking a few outstretched hands, I barely got to see anyone except reporters. Mrs. Warner came by around 11:30 p.m. to wish me well, which I appreciated. She kept her chin up and tried to hide the extreme disappointment she must have felt. By 1:00 a.m., it was all over, and I was glad to exchange the tumultuous excitement of the crowds for the quiet peace of home.

McCain's response to my victory lacked the forthrightness I might have hoped for. We arranged for a show of unity, which he treated primarily as a media event. I urged my campaign workers to help McCain, and he at least did nothing overt to dispel the appearance of harmony between us. But behind the scenes, McCain and Jim Kolbe, who had stumped together in the southern part of the state, were furious at Kruglick for diverting energies to me that might have been used to their benefit. This was in spite of the fact that both of them had easy races against opponents with much less media support, or money than either of them.

Reflecting on all this, I'm able to nudge a number of pieces of the puzzle, big and small, into place. A few days after the general election, McCain called me for a breakfast get-together with our newly elected Washington Congressional delegation. Supposedly, it was to discuss the ways in which the five of them in Washington and I, back in Arizona, could best work together for the good of the state. But when I arrived at the breakfast, Kolbe was in a hurry to catch a plane, and the only matter of business they wanted to discuss was the replacement of Burt Kruglick as GOP State Chairman. When I asked McCain who he had in mind for the job, he was reluctant to tell me, and finally mentioned someone I'd never heard a thing about. When I asked why they were unhappy with Kruglick, McCain and Kolbe said, among other things, that he wasn't "cooperative." Trying to puzzle this out, I asked the other three congressmen what they thought about all this. Bob Stump was a strong supporter for Kruglick. Jon Kyl said he was happy with Burt and saw no reason to dump him. In his typical fashion, Jay Rhodes was suspended in indecision like fruit in Jell-O. He knew there was no real reason to replace Kruglick, but he didn't want to cross McCain. He said he'd just go along with whatever the rest wanted.

I told them I'd talked to Kruglick about his future as party chairman. He wanted to stay on two more years, through the 1988

National Convention and presidential election, but he'd told me that he recognized that the chairman was usually the choice of the governor. He'd do whatever I thought was best. I'd told him I thought he'd earned the right to stay, and that he'd have my support. I explained to our Washington delegation that I thought the party was reasonably well united at the moment. That leaving Burt in office would lend some credibility to that unity in the face of an ongoing publicity campaign by the *Republic* to create the impression that my election had caused irreparable damage to party unity. I told McCain that if he felt strongly enough to run his own candidate against Kruglick to do so. I suggested honesty to be the best policy, asking him to lay his cards on the table so we'd all know where we stood. I intended to stay behind Kruglick, and I thought we would beat any challengers in the January party elections.

This apparently ended our discussion of Arizona's best interests. We agreed to meet periodically and to work together, and McCain and Kolbe hurried away.

When I returned to my office, I called Kruglick to warn him about the threat to his future. To my surprise, he told me that McCain had just left. Apparently McCain had gone straight from the breakfast meeting to tell Kruglick that he had his full support. There had been no mention of what had actually transpired at the meeting.

At the January meeting of the Republican State Executive Committee, I was enthusiastically received and Kruglick was re-elected chairman, without opposition. Although McCain had lost this battle, it didn't take long to see that he would continue to be one of the most important players in the on-going effort to remove me from office—and from the Arizona political scene.

Chapter 8

THE STARTING
LINEUP OF THE STAFF

"O say what is truth? Tis the fairest gem that the richest of worlds can produce"
John Jacques

Every politician, when running for his political life, accepts help from people without first dipping them in an acid bath of scrutiny to see what lies under their skin. As long as it's understood that they're not promising political favors in return for private help and have the courage to stick by that understanding, the worst that can result under normal circumstances is bad publicity. On the other hand, it is natural that many of these people will stay on to work in the administration of a successful candidate. Candidates get to know these people through their campaign work. Furthermore, a political campaign is an intense and emotionally bonding affair. It's not unusual to feel you know some fellow worker quite well, when, objectively, you may only have been acquainted with him or her for a few months and only in the single context of the campaign. It's natural, both for the candidate and the worker to feel gratitude toward one another. For those who really believed in the candidate's cause, their goal is to stay on and see the administration he or she has helped create carry out its mission. No matter how honest and sincere a candidate's pronouncements that he is not simply rewarding campaign workers with political plums, many of his campaign people will inevitably end up on his administrative staff.

I think that such "spoilage" occurred less during the transition of my campaign into an administration than it has in most others. Unfortunately, not all of the people I chose for my staff were as motivated as I thought they were. Because I tend to articulate my position on political issues quite plainly, it's rather easy for someone to express agreement on issues, simply because that's what they think I want to hear.

To coordinate the job of filling the hundreds of positions for which the governor's office is responsible, I appointed Sam Udall as one of my ninth floor assistants. During the campaign, Sam had specialized in liaison work with the smaller counties, so I knew he'd do something about the chronic under-representation of these Arizonans in the state's government. By appointing rural Arizonans to about a third of the positions on boards and commissions, we were keeping a campaign promise to remedy the serious under-representation of rural people in state government. Maricopa County, which is essentially the Phoenix metropolitan area, and Pima County, which is basically Tucson, have about 80 percent of Arizona's population. They control 23 legislative districts, leaving only seven for the other 13 counties in the state. The governor is the only equalizing force to protect the rights of the rural counties; in the past, the governor was usually one of the Phoenix power elite, and the smaller counties were virtually not represented in state government. Because they recognized my commitment to give them a greater voice in the Capitol and to assure them fairer treatment, these rural areas had strongly supported me in the elections.

We disappointed a lot of people who wanted to work on the transition team and some who would have liked to work in the administration itself. There wasn't room for all of them. We set about to replace Babbitt appointees with our own. I appointed a screening committee to go over the mass of resumes of applicants for positions and jobs. All executive positions were handled directly by the screening committee, while the others were passed on to the appropriate departments or to the personnel office of the Department of Administration.

No one was promised anything during the campaign. After winning, everyone was open to apply for a position just like the many who hadn't been directly involved. Most of those who worked on the campaign were volunteers who wanted better government, not jobs. No one got a job unless we thought they were qualified for it. Some were disappointed when we didn't have a spot for them.

A lot of armchair strategizing is read into governmental appointments. When I nominated Ted Humes to take over as director of the Residential Utilities Consumer Office, there were two immediate assumptions made by the media. First, Humes' appointment was seen as a move on my part to placate APS chief Keith Turley and the Phoenix 40. Humes was perceived to be highly pro-utility. His appointment to head the committee that was supposed to be the state's watchdog over the powerful utilities was widely touted as a peace offering to the political potentates who traditionally sit on the boards of the Arizona Public Service and the Salt River Project. Second, the appointment was perceived as an attempt to gut RUCO. I was loudly assailed for being anti-consumer and mindlessly pro big business.

The truth is that Ted Humes had the experience for the job and, as a hearing officer, had shown his fair mindedness in dealing with utilities and consumers alike. A few months later, when he helped bring about a drastic cut back on an APS rate hike request, Humes vindicated my faith and silenced at least those critics willing to entertain the facts. This, of course, was not everyone. Instead, some of the same pundits who had originally claimed my appointment of Humes was kowtowing to Turley, now read it as just the opposite. Now it was viewed as a slap in the face of the APS chief. Actually, it was simply an appointment of a qualified man to do a good job for the public. Naturally that was not the "'spin" the media put on it. Certainly, I appointed people I knew to posts, but at the risk of sounding naively self-serving, I have to repeat that my only goal in doing so was to fill positions with people who I thought would do the jobs I wanted done. After working long hours over the resumes, the screening committee interviewed the best candidates, and then usually presented me with a list of three people for each position. This not only saved me time, but seven interviewers can see a lot more in an interview than I could have alone.

I used Arizona's Republican Party organization, more than had previous governors, in finding good people for these positions. In addition, before I made a final decision on hiring anyone, Sam Udall checked with the County and District GOP Chairmen to make sure the people we were thinking about hiring were of good standing and reputation in their own communities. The name of the single candidate I then chose was given to the Department of Public Safety for a thorough background check. Any brush with the law, including DWI's, that came out in the DPS checks was enough to reject a person as an appointee.

Only two of the 143 Senate-approved appointments made in my first year of office were considered technically unqualified by the Senate. Senate Majority Leader Usdane said they had fewer problems with my appointees in the Senate confirmation process than any other he had worked with.

Two of the key department heads we choose were Ted Williams for the Department of Health and Dr. Eddie Brown for the Department of Economic Security. They were the best qualified of the lists the selection committee gave me for these two departments. Williams was a Democrat and was the first black man to be appointed as a department head in Arizona state government. Dr. Brown was the first Native American to be appointed a major department head. Both were very professional and served with distinction. I singled them out here because the same media that was so intent on painting me as a racist had a hard time with those high-profile posts going to minorities, for the first time in the state's history.

I did break with tradition by filling all my positions with Arizonans. My predecessors in general, and Bruce Babbitt in particular, had frequently given his highest-paying positions to people from out of state.

The people I appointed weren't perfect; but they were, by and large, superior to the ones they replaced, and these men and women were investigated more thoroughly and more intensely than any other governor's appointments ever have been. I have always been pleased with the record compiled by the appointments we made to the state agencies, boards, and commissions. Most governors are embarrassed by the scandals that develop out of the actions of some of their appointees. I was not. Not one of our appointees was ever reported for illegal, unethical, or self-serving activities that are quite common in governmental appointees.

While detractors were busy spreading rumors that I was hiring mostly member of my own particular church (The Church of Jesus Christ of Latter-day Saints), and unqualified political cronies, the *Mesa Tribune* began a full-scale investigation of my appointees. I'm not aware of any other instance, where appointees at any level of government anywhere in the nation, were investigated in this way. Considering the treatment I was receiving from the press, I wasn't the least surprised they tried to use it as the basis of an exposé on my administration. Reporters were calling my appointees and asking them a variety of personal questions, usually beginning with their religious affiliation.

Finally, in the late spring of 1987, the *Tribune* reporter who'd been heading up their investigation called and asked me if I knew what I had done.

I said, go ahead and tell me!

"Do you know you've appointed almost five times as many Protestants and twice as many Catholics as you have Mormons?"

I told him that there were probably a few Jews and other non-Christians in the ranks as well, but that I couldn't give him any figures or verify this because we'd never asked, nor kept track of religious affiliations. His report showed that our appointees were on the average better educated and more experienced in the fields in which they were appointed than were workers in the previous administration. It debunked the "political cronyism" charge by reporting that the majority of my appointments had not been personally acquainted with me before their interviews. Only a small number of them had contributed to my campaign, and even fewer had assisted in the campaign in any direct way.

There were approximately 38,000 state employees. Approximately 600 of them were exempt from civil service rules. These 600 make up most of the governor's policy making and management team through which the state is actually run; and so most of them are changed by each new administration. In addition, there are 2,200 governor appointees, some full-time managers, and others who serve on various boards and commissions without pay (except per diem and travel reimbursement). These board members are replaced gradually as their terms expire over several-year cycles.

Much of the friction that was supposedly occurring within my administration was actually initiated by lame-duck Babbitt appointees, bitter that they were soon to be replaced by men and women with different goals and agendas. And it was the continuing loss of these appointees, through whom the power brokers had controlled so much of the $4 billion a year business of the state, that may have occasioned the greatest panic among the power brokers. By installing people not beholden to the elite, I could have cost them untold millions of dollars in previously guaranteed business over the four years of my administration.

Their attack on Ted Humes was typical of the style of their opposition. Under Babbitt, the legislature had created a "temporary" Residential Utility Consumer Office, supposedly to watchdog the utility rates that were constantly being manipulated by the state's energy monopolies. In actuality, Babbitt had used the agency as a publicity agency to attack nuclear power. Susan Williams, a Babbitt appointee, wanted to remain as head of RUCO, but it was clear that our views didn't coincide and that, if RUCO were really going to promote what I felt was good energy policy, I needed someone else in there. Williams persisted and asked to stay on for an additional six months through the budget hearings. RUCO itself was due to expire around that time, and if the legislature was going to let it die, there didn't seem much point in making a new appointment.

I met with the leaders of the legislature. Carl Kunasek, Bob Usdane, Hal Runyan, Joe Lane, Jim Ratliff and Jane Hull, and asked if they wanted to continue the agency past the current fiscal year. Because of some items on the agenda, Senator Bob Lunn, Chairman of the Senate Health Committee, was also present at that meeting, and he was very vocal about keeping RUCO. Most of them wanted to let it die and save the $4 million per year it took to operate, but at the same time they thought it would be political suicide to do so. I decided, therefore, that if they were going to spend taxpayers' money on RUCO, it ought, at least, to be used to watchdog energy rates for consumers. At that point, I nominated Ted Humes, a man with a law degree and inside knowledge of the utilities industry, to replace Susan Williams.

Senator Lunn later said, in one of his frequent attacks on me, that I told them I would appoint Humes as head and he would kill the agency. That was only one of many things that Lunn said that was not true. No one else at the meeting remembered it because in never happened. After that, I refused to ever discuss anything with Lunn, unless he was accompanied by the Senate Leadership.

When his nomination was approved, Humes took over the agency just in time to strangle a huge rate-hike that had been requested by APS. The media quietly forgot everything they had said about him. By that time, Lunn had imagined other upsetting things I was planning to do to the state, and so he never had to explain or retract his false accusations.

After nine years of the liberal, high-spending Babbitt administration, I knew we were going to need a massive housecleaning effort in state management positions. One administrator can accomplish very little by himself. The team that a leader can put together and direct effectively is far more important than the hands-on work he accomplishes himself. Building such a team from the ground up, in the few weeks that we had, was therefore an extremely important challenge.

Because of the complete overhaul I planned for the executive branch, I knew there would be far more work with various department heads than I could manage myself. Therefore, I decided to handle the situation by dividing all the departments into three groups and appointing Ray Russell, Edith Richardson and Sam Steiger as special assistants responsible for these groups. They moved into the three remaining corner offices of the ninth floor suite (corner offices usually being the most desirable in executive suites because of the views they afford), and their positions became known as the Three Corners.

Dr. Ray Russell had never been involved in government before, although he had run twice for Congress, narrowly losing to John McCain in the 1982 primary and to Jay Rhodes in 1986. He had acquired a good deal of administrative experience as executive director of the National Veterinarians Association, as president of the Theodore Roosevelt Council of the Boy Scouts of America, and in developing his own business. I also knew, personally, of his leadership abilities from important church activities. These civic activities had earned Russell the respect and appreciation of a great many people. They are often shrugged off by politicians, but I felt they showed the kind of leadership abilities and concern for positive social results that I wanted in my administration. I asked Ray to oversee the boards and commissions dealing with health and health insurance, environmental quality, community colleges, real estate, banking, tourism, building and fire safety, and contracts.

Both Edith Richardson and Sam Steiger had extensive government experience. Richardson had been active in party politics for a long time, helping John Conlan become congressman from the 4th District when it was created, and then becoming his chief assistant. She had spent considerable time in the Faith America Group, a political conscience-raising organization financed by conservative Christian businessmen. She had also served as the executive director of the Republican Party under Jim Colter. She was assigned the Departments of Revenue, Economic Security, Racing, Affirmative Action, and the Office of Women.

Richardson didn't get along particularly well with Steiger, at least in part, because of a bitter political dispute during the 1976 primary. After serving in the U. S. House of Representatives for 10 years, Steiger had run against Conlan for the seat of retiring U. S. Senator Paul Fannin, in 1976. Sam narrowly won the primary against Conlan, and the bad feelings created there allowed Dennis DeConcini to win the seat in the general election.

While my political association with Sam went back a long way to our days in the Arizona State Senate, I hadn't really been close to him since helping in his first congressional victory. His lifestyle was completely different from mine, so we were never social friends. The first time I had ever met Steiger was during our indoctrination session at the governor's office when we were both freshmen in the legislature. Round-faced and pleasant looking, he'd stuck out his hand and said, "My name is Sam Steiger. I'm the only Jewish horse trader in Arizona." I caught a good deal of flak for appointing him one of my special assistants. On the other hand, he was a bridge to a lot of people who were certainly not vintage Mecham supporters, and I felt we needed to be able to bring together diverse elements if our administration was going to accomplish its goals.

As soon as I'd won the primary, Sam had called me and volunteered his services for the general election campaign. He'd told me he would do whatever I asked of him. As was the case with everyone who worked with me, we didn't discuss the possibility of any job or appointment for him if we won. After the election, I realized that Sam really wanted to be chief of staff, if not actually de facto governor. It didn't really bother me that Sam felt he could do a better job at it than I could. Many people who haven't held executive positions fail to realize what it takes to be a successful C.E.O. Although I had never run an organization as large as the state government, my whole life had been spent in building business organizations from scratch. Recruiting, training, and directing people in the competitive business world, so that your organization is profitable and successful, is the best training anyone can have for an executive management position in government. Many of the organizational problems in government today have been created, and continue to exist, because elected officials often do not have management skills and experience. I felt sure of my own abilities and wanted strong people to help me achieve my objectives. Unfortunately, as things unfolded, I gradually became aware that Steiger was using his office in pursuit of his own agenda.

This first came to light when he was working on the selection committee. When we began discussing members for the Racing Commission, Steiger tried to sell everyone on agreeing to give him a seat on the Commission. It was reported to me that he got very emotional and ended up telling the group, that was the reason he was there. This concerned several of the key staff because the Racing Commission was one of our first targets to clean up. I didn't consider Sam for that spot.

When I had first decided to run for governor in June, one of the first people I had contacted had been my long-time friend Jim Colter. I'd first met him in 1962, when he'd helped me in my campaign for the U. S. Senate. Jim was then a small cattle rancher and the school principal in the little town of Eagar, Arizona, near the New Mexico border. He later moved to Tucson and attended law school at the University of Arizona and then moved to Phoenix to set up his private law practice. I sold him automobiles and he handled legal work for me whenever I needed a lawyer. When the conservatives overthrew the establishment wing of the Republican Party in 1976, Jim did a short stint as state chairman before the Goldwater-Rosenzweig people were able to push him out with Tom Pappas, in 1978.

Jim helped me in every race I ran after 1962. In 1986, he virtually dropped his legal practice and volunteered to work full-time as my campaign manager in the general election. I knew he shared my goals, believed in the principles I espoused, was completely loyal and honest, and knew the political scene and the players in Arizona as well as anyone. I felt that his legal skills would also be very beneficial. After my election, I offered Jim the position of chief of staff.

Another natural appointment was Max Hawkins, the man who urged me to run again in 1986. Max knew state government very well. He had served as finance director for three previous governors, had been head of the Department of Administration, and had a reputation on both sides of the political fence as a good administrator. It was Hawkins who persuaded Wesley Bolin to appoint Rose Mofford as secretary of state when he became governor. When Babbitt became governor, upon the death of Wesley Bolin, he fired Max because he didn't fit the Babbitt liberal mold. Max had worked hard to manage the government effectively. But by nature, he was quite different from the cadre of pragmatic politicians who surrounded Babbitt. Hawkins, agreeing that he didn't fit in with the political insiders then in power, re-registered as a Republican. He volunteered to help me in my 1982 race against Leo Corbet. He was convinced that I really wanted to clean up this mess and run the government effectively. We quickly became good friends.

Hawkins' inside knowledge of the operations of state government was an excellent compliment to my own, and he was an invaluable aid to me. When it came time for me to appoint him head of my Department of Administration, however, I was told by a number of legislative touts to keep him privately on my staff, but not to risk a Senate confirmation. They said Max just had too many enemies.

I took a careful look at what the critics were saying, to see if they had any significant reasons why Max wouldn't be an effective administrator. Behind all the grumbling, the only clearly articulated complaint I heard was that Max had been behind the primary election tabloid that revealed Burton Barr's record. Barr still had substantial influence in the legislature and planned to do everything he could to oppose Hawkins' appointment. Since Max and I had actually done the tabloid work together, I could hardly fault him for that. Max and I saw eye to eye on most issues, and I thought he had some excellent ideas to streamline the state's government. I went ahead with the nomination. He was confirmed with 22 out of 30 possible votes.

I was the first elected governor in the state to have served in the Arizona legislature. I had campaigned on my ability to use the knowledge gained there to work effectively with the legislature. I was particularly anxious to have a legislative liaison that also understood the legislature, and who would be acceptable to its members. Early in the general election campaign, Steiger had secured the volunteer services of Donna Carlson and her assistant to handle our public relations. Donna had been an effective member of the House for several terms and had solid conservative credentials. When Sam told me he thought she would be an extremely effective legislative liaison and that she had good rapport with the Republican legislators, she appeared to be a natural fit for our administration. The few legislators I talked to about it seemed to agree, so I went ahead and hired her. It was one of the biggest mistakes of my political life.

I was surprised by the number of people who became interested in leaving the private sector to work in the government. For instance, I'd known Ron Bellus for a few years. He had a secure job in the advertising industry and had volunteered his services to help with the media and advertising in the election. Suddenly, after the election, he wanted the job as my press secretary very badly. Because of Ron's enthusiasm, and because I felt I could trust him completely, I allowed myself to be convinced that he had sufficient experience in press work to take this on.

Another person who surprised me by his appetite for office was Bill Heuisler. Bill, a private investigator, had been a political activist for many years. He had accepted the job as my campaign coordinator for the Tucson area early in the primary when supporters were few, and he was one of the few workers I'd paid over the past several months.

About a week after the election, I flew down to Tucson to make a speech and Bill picked me up at the airport. I knew Bill's business had suffered from the time he'd taken away from it for my campaign. I asked him if business was picking up again now that the campaign was over. He told me he wasn't doing anything about his business now because he was waiting for an appointment. He suggested he would make an excellent investigator into the corruption we knew existed in state government. He told me that he had already made a lot of contacts that would help him "blow the lid off" what was happening in Arizona. To my surprise, he had already done a good deal of talking about this "appointment" to other people, telling them he was going to be a sort of "inspector general." After he broke the news to me at the airport, he kept pushing for an appointment through Steiger and others.

I had some serious problems with this. First of all, there was no such office as the one Bill had been describing. Second, while I didn't know every detail in Bill's background, I knew that he'd been involved in some disorderly conduct as a young marine and with the Tucson police before he quit drinking. My plan was to find him some low profile position in the Department of Administration, where his talents could be used effectively. However, Bill continued to talk about his imminent appointment, this time to the press. They responded by blackening his reputation to make him look like a drunken thug and convicted criminal. When he saw this happening, he realized what he'd done to himself, backed off, and announced publicly that he did not want me to consider him for any position in my administration.

Mac Matheson, on the other hand, I practically had to drag into the administration. He had helped me in every statewide election in which I had run. He was my original campaign manager in 1962, when I ran against Hayden. Mac had always done everything we asked of him, asking for nothing in return. When he told me he didn't want a key executive position, I convinced him to come and join the staff to see that our correspondence was handled properly. He would be a great help to me in some of my speech and letter writing.

Lee Watkins, who had been the strong right arm of Ralph Watkins in the fund raising for my campaign, had been in insurance before deciding he wanted a ninth floor position. I had known him slightly for a number of years, and didn't really have anything up there that would fit his capabilities. But, with the organizational skills he'd shown and the contacts he'd made during the campaign, I thought he would do a good job of heading up my special committee on drug abuse problems.

That is how my team was put together. My players weren't chosen from a roster of campaign debts. These people weren't army ants, unleashed to blindly follow hormonally coded messages that leaked out from some nest in the Capitol building. In the months to come, many of them suffered as only human beings can suffer. They never quite understood why their best efforts were being spurned and their actions willfully misrepresented by opponents. Later, I was to discover to my sorrow, that a small few were working with my political foes for my political demise.

Chapter 9

THEN THE WAR BEGAN

"No man has a more perfect reliance on the all-wise and powerful dispensations of the Supreme being than I have, nor thinks His aid more necessary."
General Washington

My campaign manager and long-time friend, Jim Colter, accompanied me to the meeting with Babbitt the day after the election as scheduled. I had never been to the "ninth floor," as the governor's suite of offices in the west wing of the Capitol building is called. I had my first look at it while we were waiting in the protocol room, a large chamber adjacent to the governor's working office. It had sofas and a large, clean-topped desk, used principally for the ceremonial signing of bills and proclamations. There are sliding glass doors that open onto a balcony, providing a beautiful view overlooking Phoenix, and beyond to the mountains that ring the eastern side of the Salt River Valley.

Our November 5th visit was brief, but cordial. Colter, who was to be my chief of staff, was asked to work out most of the details with Babbitt's chief of staff, Ronnie Lopez. Everyone pledged mutual cooperation. We were given some office space on the second floor of the Capitol tower for Colter, some secretaries, and myself. The rest of the transition team, with Edith Richardson, Ray Russell, and Sam Steiger as special assistants, was to work in the basement of the Senate building, courtesy of the Senate leadership.

120

Governor Babbitt and I had known each other for several years, from the campaign trail and through some mutual friends. (One for whom we both served as pallbearers at his funeral.) On this day, Governor Babbitt offered me some advice, rather unexpectedly. It was to the effect that I should guard myself with the press. Stay at arm's length and control the news emanating from my office, principally through press releases. Later I was to realize the wisdom of that advice. I wanted to be completely open and honest with the press, which was right to do, but I should have been far less exposed to them.

In addition to preparing our budget and several key pieces of legislation, I also got busy on some practical political issues that had concerned me. My goal was to settle them by negotiation even before I assumed office.

The state and the Pima-Maricopa Indian community had been stalemated over the purchase of Indian land to complete one leg of the outer loop, which was part of a master planned freeway. The tribe clearly had a bargaining edge, since the state's only alternative was to demolish miles of middle class housing that would cost $150 to $200 million more than the Pimas were asking. Bad feelings had developed between the City of Scottsdale and the Indians, resulting in the tribe barricading the northbound lanes of Pima Road which encroaches on reservation land. It looked as if the continuing delays from litigation over questions of right of way might ultimately result in the cancellation of the freeway leg.

Washington Attorney Fred Craft, who had been helping me with some things in the nation's capital knew of negotiations under way by the U.S Department of The Interior, which would allow us to help put together a plan beneficial to all concerned. I had met Interior Secretary Don Hodel in Washington, and he had made a campaign visit to Arizona on my behalf in October.

On November 18th, I was able to call a press conference to announce that we had helped the Arizona Department of Transportation (ADOT) reach an agreement with the Indian community, effectively ending the six-month stalemate. Part of our solution was to bring the Indians in as a partner in the development of what was known as the Indian School Property in north-central Phoenix. The government decided to close down this 97-year-old, outmoded federal boarding school in 1985, but had no concrete plans on what to do with the property. The land escalated dramatically in value while Phoenix grew around it, so that it is now 106 acres of prime real estate. The Collier Company from Florida was negotiating with the U.S. Department of the Interior to trade $50 million, plus a piece of ecologically important property in the Florida Everglades, valued at $45 million, for the right to develop the 106 acres of Indian School property.

Out of the money the Pima Indians were to receive from the State of Arizona for the freeway right of way, they were to put up $50 million and purchase a partnership interest with Collier in the development of the Phoenix Indian School property. In this win-win trade, the feds would get the land they wanted in Florida. The Pima-Maricopas would get a valuable financial stake in Arizona's economic future. The Collier's would get their development. The state would end up with a freeway right of way across the Pima reservation that would cost hundreds of millions of dollars less than would have been paid for land in the developed part of Scottsdale. Additionally, we would have had enough Indian School land, adjacent to the existing VA Hospital, to expand that overcrowded facility and build an Old Soldiers Home. The feds wouldn't have to pay out $50 million to the Colliers for the marshland preserve, and the balance of the money the government received for the Indian School land could be used for educational purposes for Indian children.

The Pima-Maricopa Indians were happy. Arizonans in general should have been happy—not just because we had the freeway land at a savings to the taxpayers, but because the deal would provide a boon to the Pima-Maricopa economy that would have a multiplier effect, pumping money into other local economies. The new freeway was expected to increase the value of the bordering tribal lands by $500 million.

Phoenix Mayor Terry Goddard and the downtown establishment were not pleased at all. The U. S. Department of the Interior had offered to sell the Indian School land to the City of Phoenix, but Goddard wanted it as a gift. He had hoped to use Representative Mo Udall and Senator Dennis DeConcini to leverage The U.S Dept of the Interior into giving the 106 acres to the City of Phoenix, as a park. Such a deal would have enhanced Goddard's own political career.

At that time, I'd already heard that the city had no chance of receiving more than 15 or 20 acres. But the improbability of Goddard's hopes aside, the greater good of our proposal to the average person in the city and the county, should have been persuasive.

I invited Mayor Goddard to the press conference, to join President Anton of the Pima-Maricopa Tribe, the Department of Transportation officials, Scottsdale officials, and me in making the announcement. He refused, and, instead, held his own press conference to blast what he perceived to be the theft of his park fantasy.

The compromise we reached with the Pima-Maricopa Tribe ended the deadlock between the tribe and Scottsdale, and these original negotiations were eventually concluded by the Arizona Department of Transportation, in April of 1989.

In November of 1986, I was fairly confident that this agreement would be well received, even by honest critics of my election victory, as a sign that I was capable of working with others to accomplish concrete benefits for the state.

Imagine my astonishment when I received the following report: While we were having the press conference on the second floor of the Capitol tower, publisher Pat Murphy, just then leaving a ninth floor visit with Governor Babbitt, had been overheard fuming about me, "We'll get the snide little S.O.B." Sure enough, the next morning, while our plan was greeted with approval by most of the cities in the Valley and the initial news reports from across the state were generally favorable, the *Republic* nit-picked away at our solution, completely ignoring the stalemate it had replaced.

Frankly, I didn't quite understand. Pat Murphy was just one of a number of leaders who had formerly opposed me, but who'd recently written me letters expressing their hope that we would all be able to work together constructively over the next four years. I'd assumed that, the election over, everyone would forget their differences and work for the common good. I asked Ralph Watkins to arrange a meeting with Murphy for noon that day, December 19th.

Ralph, Jim Colter, and I met Murphy, his operations manager, his managing editors and his editorial page editors from both *The Arizona Republic* and *the Phoenix Gazette* at their downtown plant. I couldn't help chiding the *Republic* editor over a number of factual errors they had made. It wasn't just that newspapers are supposed to get the facts right; I wanted to know if they'd gotten them wrong on purpose, so that truth wouldn't interfere with their attack.

They seemed to accept my complaints with good grace. What concerned me most, I said, was the utterly negative attitude of the papers. I'd formerly assumed this was part of their campaign preferences, but it appeared to be continuing now that the election was over. They seemed to be gearing up for an all-out, four-year war. I asked Mr. Murphy straight out, man to man, what we were looking at. Murphy disavowed any intention other than working harmoniously with the administration for the good of the state. He assured me that, if I had any question about this or thought anything the papers did was out of line, all I had to do was call him to discuss the problem. Any factual errors, he promised, would be corrected immediately.

I left with the feeling that we'd done the right thing by coming down to Murphy's turf to show him we were as eager to cooperate in a constructive relationship as anybody could be. The remark overheard in the elevator, I decided, had been made at an ill-tempered moment, having no real significance. Shortly thereafter, however, another source reported to me that Murphy had now told some of his staffers, "We'll crucify the little bastard." And in confirmation, the nasty editorials began to roll in on a daily basis.

Murphy even threw his editorial cartoonist onto the pile-up. Steve Benson, a talented young man, had been lampooning me almost daily in the *Republic*. Steve had chased me down just prior to the general election to tell me he supported me. He also told me I'd get a fair shake from the paper, and I think Steve really believed it at the time. Murphy seemed to have an almost hypnotic control over him.

One of Murphy's early schemes to swing the general election had been to lure me to a "debate" with Warner and Schulz. It was to be officiated and judged by the *Republic*. After the debate, they planned to announce their official endorsement, obviously of Warner, and create the appearance of an objective selection. When I refused to step into the trap and called a press conference for the same time, I think they saw I wasn't coming to their "staged party." They must have anticipated I was going to announce that I would not accept their endorsement, even if they would give it to me because Murphy had Benson called me repeatedly that day. I didn't return his calls, but I did accidentally meet him at Sawyer Aviation, where he and another R&G staffer were chartering a small plane. I happened to be there at the same time to pick up my own plane, which I was flying to Tucson for a speaking engagement. Apparently, Murphy had singled out Steve to talk to me because of my personal relationship with Steve's grandfather, Ezra Taft Benson. He seemed really frustrated when I told him that, considering what the paper had been printing about me, I didn't trust them to be objective about a debate.

When I got back to the Tucson executive terminal later that night to fly back to Phoenix, Steve was waiting for me. This time he had a message he claimed was from his grandfather, Ezra Taft Benson, in Salt Lake City, telling me that I should go to the debate. I laughed and told him I knew his grandfather better than that, and if his grandfather wanted to give me a message, he would call me direct. Steve acted like it had all been a joke and walked away laughing. But in retrospect, I think that his inability to deliver me may have humiliated him so badly that day that forever after he felt justified in throwing everything he could against me, hoping I would be destroyed and forgotten.

When the *Philadelphia Inquirer* came to Phoenix about six months later to examine the controversy that was by then in full furor, they counted over 750 *Republic* articles about me, and the recall movement in my first six months in office. Certainly, an attempt to recall a governor is an unusual event and the occasion for press coverage. But an average of more than three articles a day, every day of the week, for six months? No political figure in the history of the state or the nation had ever been subjected to that kind of overkill. Any vague references to anything positive I might have accomplished was completely buried in this avalanche of bad news.

But then, I'd been elected in the face of media opposition and that of the Phoenix establishment. I'd campaigned on basic issues and won with grass-roots support because the people agreed with me, not because I was the media's darling. When Murphy's onslaught started, I just took a deep breath and dug in, figuring that if I followed through on my campaign promises and accomplished what I'd set out to do, public sentiment would eventually force Murphy to reconsider. Apparently, however, the Pulliam papers had set the standards among the Capitol press corps for too long. Whenever I made a speech, news coverage was seldom about the topic of that speech, but of totally unrelated questions asked and reported completely out of context. The people never did hear about what was happening to my program in the Legislature, the bills that were passing, the programs we were getting under way. Almost all of the comments used by the Phoenix papers were those of my critics.

Perhaps the most dramatic example of such a controversy mushroomed into the consciousness of Arizonans on November 5, 1986, following my very first press conference since winning the election. Countless stories have pointed out that my troubles began when I rescinded the Martin Luther King Day as a paid holiday for state workers. The truth is that I never rescinded that, or any other holiday. As governor, I did not have the authority. Only a vote of the Legislature or a vote of the people can establish or remove a paid holiday for state workers.

In the 1986 legislative session, the MLK holiday was considered, but failed in the House on a 29 to 31 vote. After the Legislature adjourned, Governor Babbitt went to a black church on Sunday and read to the congregation a proclamation to establish a paid holiday for state workers on the third Monday of January. Irate legislators blasted this act as illegal, and the state attorney general published his opinion that the governor did not have the authority to create a paid worker holiday.

Babbitt had previously entered the race for the Democratic nomination for President and was accused of using this MLK proclamation to try to gain favor with the black Democrats across the nation. Most knowledgeable people felt sure Babbitt, as a former state attorney general, knew his proclamation was not legal.

When Attorney General Corbin challenged Babbitt, he flippantly said to go ahead and sue him. Babbitt's term as governor was to end on the following January 5th, so he knew he did not have to face the results of his illegal act.

During the primary and general election campaigns, the MLK holiday was never an issue. The only mention of it was during the primary, when each candidate was asked what he or she would do about the proclamation, if elected. The Democrats said they would recognize the proclamation as legal and allow the paid worker holiday. The two Republican candidates, Barr and myself, both said the proclamation was not legal, there was no holiday, and we would rescind the proclamation. Attorney General Corbin told each candidate that the next governor would have to rescind the illegal proclamation or be sued personally for spending between $3 million and $4 million that was not authorized by the Legislature.

I had so many requests for interviews on November 5th that I couldn't possibly have granted them all, so I called a general press conference to answer everybody's questions at once. I described how we were going to carry out the campaign platform, particularly how we planned to reduce spending, deal with drug abuse, and promote trade with the Pacific Rim nations. There were quite a few questions about details and some apparent surprise that I still had the same plans that I'd had when campaigning for election. After about 45 minutes, we concluded the press conference, and most of the press began to leave. The King holiday had not even been mentioned. But as everyone was leaving, one reporter, apparently as an afterthought, asked if I had changed my mind about "rescinding the King Holiday." Rather than explain again that there wasn't one, I answered in one simple word; "no." I didn't elaborate, and there was no follow up question.

Imagine my surprise the next day when I learned in the pages of *The Arizona Republic* that the number one priority of the Mecham administration was to rescind Arizona's Martin Luther King Holiday. In spite of all of the things we covered in the press conference, very little was said about anything except my answer that I would rescind Babbitt's illegal proclamation.

In the media, which didn't seem to care one whit about the legal consequences of allowing an illegal declaration to stand,

Babbitt was portrayed as a hero. He got credit from the blacks, who wanted this recognition for Dr. King. He got credit from state employees who wanted a day off with pay. He got credit from other minorities who bought the story that this man was sensitive to the needs of minorities. He got credit from some Democrats, as a governor who had the courage to act where the Legislature would not venture. He certainly got credit from Pat Murphy, ever on the alert for an opportunity to pat his favorite-son candidate on the back. And, as the new governor who had to explain that there actually was never a legal holiday created, I got the shaft.

Having established this "truth" for themselves, the newspapers quickly called a variety of public leaders they supposed would be critical of my position. Since the media was telling them what I had said, few of them bothered to ask me or find out what really had transpired. Predictably, remarks from people such as House Minority Leader Art Hamilton, carried extra weight because he was one of two black Representatives in the Arizona House. He responded as if he had expected no better of me, but at the same time as if he were shocked: "It comes as no surprise, but the manner in which he did it, the first thing out of his mouth, and the gratuitous way he said it, suggests a blind spot and a gross insensitivity that I find frightening."

Hamilton's response in the press was expected. It also was hypocritical in his attack on me. If those who opposed the King holiday were racists, then Majority Leader Jane Hull and Barr's errand boy, Chris Herstam, should have been painted with that brush as well. Those two cast the "no" votes, by which the MLK Holiday had failed to pass the House in the spring of 1986. Had they voted for it, the holiday would have been passed by the Legislature, Babbitt would never have had reason to make his illegal proclamation, and I would not have had to undo his illegal act. But, of course, there is no record of Hamilton ever publicly calling any of his fellow legislators racists and bigots for the many times the MLK Holiday was considered and turned down by the majority of the legislators.

Hamilton and Barr were very good friends; we were told that they often met. What Hamilton had said about me was completely without any basis in truth. We could only deduct that

Hamilton was playing his part in the well-orchestrated plans to brand me as a racist in the public eye.

Everyone involved—the press, the legislators, most of the people, and the conspirators who wanted me out—all knew that the attorney general had given the opinion to the legislators that Babbitt's King Day proclamation was illegal and that there was no legal King Day in Arizona. That is what made this whole charade reek of hypocrisy.

The reporters quickly came back to me to ask if I'd veto a King holiday bill if it passed the Legislature. I repeated my standard statement that I would never say in advance what I would do on any bill, until it reached my desk. Having served in the state Senate, I knew that it was impossible to tell in advance what would be in any bill until its final passage.

Naturally, my words didn't appear this way. Instead, my "failure to deny, without any reservation," that I would not veto a King holiday, was framed by a continuing diatribe quoted verbatim from Hamilton: "I think he missed the message of the 60's, and that is that King and what he stood for is for people of all colors and religious belief. Instead of trying to heal this state after a very divisive campaign, he has begun his administration with a message that some people just don't count."

This was two days after the election and two months before I would take office. All I had done was hold one 45-minute press conference. My need to "heal this state after a very divisive campaign" came as a bit of a surprise, too. Although Warner and Schulz, the other two candidates in the general election, had gone after each other a bit toward the end of October, my relationship with both of them was very pleasant. It was one of the most civil campaigns I was ever in.

If anyone had cared to do a little news analysis, they would have realized that the people who were really worried about my insensitivity to their needs were members of the Phoenix 40.

As time would show, the most divisive thing to happen in the whole history of Arizona was the actions taken by Arizona's backroom "establishment" through their minions in the Legislature, the attorney general, part of the judiciary, and the press, to remove the people's choice from the office of governor.

The media wasn't interested in what anyone actually said, but only in the evolving "story." Various public voices announced that "the holiday is not Evan Mecham's to give, it is ours to take," and that "the day he rescinds it, the people of Arizona will start an initiative to put it on the ballot in 1988."

I agreed that the holiday wasn't mine to give, nor was it Babbitt's to give. Only the Legislature could pass a law to establish a paid holiday, and they had refused to do so. They can also refer it to the people for the voters to decide. When Babbitt proclaimed it without having the authority to do so, he broke the state law. Even worse, his hoax caused a lot of people to believe they had a King holiday.

In my opening address to the Legislature, I asked them to refer the question of having a MLK holiday in a referendum to the people, so that the voters could decide in 1988. The press and my critics ignored what I said and went right on with their constant attacks.

I have never passed a value judgement on Dr. King, I feel we are all equal before God, and I agree that one of the proper roles of government is to see that the rights of all people are protected from the predatory acts of others. I was badgered constantly to say whether or not I thought Martin Luther King deserved a holiday. What I said in response was that of all the great individuals in our national history, white and black, male and female, only two, Washington and Lincoln, have been honored individually with holidays. The logic seems to be that without these two, our nation would never have survived. Even Thomas Jefferson, our greatest statesman and probably the single most important intellectual force in the shaping of this nation, has not been honored this way.

There are those who maintain that not Dr. King himself, but his significance as a symbol of our commitment to civil rights, requires our observation of his birthday. In that case, we ought to be observing paid holidays for a number of significant other symbolic personages, such as Susan B. Anthony, who worked so valiantly for women's suffrage. Claiming that the problem was one of public financing, Congress chose to downgrade the two existing birthday holidays for Washington and Lincoln into one generic "Presidents Day," in order to create a King Day. I opposed downgrading Washington and Lincoln into a President's day in order to elevate King above them in Arizona.

Not wanting to disappoint those who were planning on what they thought was to be a holiday, I instructed the department heads to allow everyone who wished to take King's birthday off as one day of their vacation time. I heard of only two state employees out of 38,000 who did that. When the Legislature failed to act again, I proclaimed the third Sunday of January as Martin Luther King, Jr. Civil Rights Day. Such an unpaid holiday was within my power to accomplish. Although no one has ever suggested that there was any other legal course of action open to me, the attacks intensified. There is no record in 1987 of any other state in the union setting up a holiday except by legislative action. This included the 24 states that did have separate paid holidays honoring Martin Luther King, as well as the 26 that don't. None of the governors of the other 25 states that did not have a King holiday were branded as racists, nor were their states the target of convention boycotts. It might be added that in none of them was their state's dominant newspaper part of an alliance that was determined to remove their governor.

The issue of whether or not there should be a paid King holiday was never the issue in my trial by media. Bob Corbin refused to sue Babbitt but said that he would sue me, personally, for $3 million, if I did not rescind Babbitt's illegal proclamation. I asked the Legislature, which had the power to pass the King holiday, to refer it to the people and let the voters decide the issue once and for all. They refused to act, but some were very vocal publicly about how "insensitive" I was.

I repeat, when the House voted on the King holiday in the 1986 regular session, it failed by one vote. One of those who could have turned the tide was Representative, now Governor Jane Hull.

I never heard of Art Hamilton calling Hull or his fellow Legislators insensitive racists, when they voted against the bill to create a King Holiday in 1986. Nor did Hamilton castigate them publicly, when they failed to pass a referendum to let the people vote on it, as I suggested they do in 1987.

A point that seems to have escaped everyone was that Babbitt may have committed an impeachable offense. His proclamation establishing a state worker paid holiday had the effect of spending $3 million to pay state workers for a day they were given off with pay. Only the Legislature, not the Governor, can appropriate the state funds. Corbin said it was illegal, but he took no action against Babbitt, who had six more months in his term. No one in the legislature, including Art Hamilton, suggested having the House start hearings by the judiciary committee to see if articles of impeachment should be considered against Babbitt. It would appear that his action was far closer to being a serious crime, than anything of which I was accused. By comparison, it made their accusations against me look pretty silly.

Goldwater's opinion of my handling of the MLK holiday by declaring the third Sunday in January as Martin Luther King Day in Arizona appeared in an article by Henry Stover in *Spotlight*, the Washington weekly with national circulation. "The more I see of Governor Mecham, the more I like him. He had the courage to rescind a paid holiday, which the former governor had no authority to declare. He then had the courage to ask the state Legislature to vote on the holiday, and put it on the next general election ballot. And when that wasn't done, he had the courage to proclaim Dr. Martin Luther King Jr. Civil Rights Day, which is as far as the state constitution will let him go. Dr. King was a leader at a critical time in American history, and he had the guts to stand up for what he believed. I think he would have respected that same quality in Governor Mecham, as I do. Charging the governor with bigotry is nonsense. Either you believe in the (state) constitution or you don't. Our governor took an oath to uphold the law and the constitution."

Before moving on, I should clarify the Art Hamilton issue further. When he was being so vocal to the press about what I was thinking and how I was responding to the happenings, he was never present nor had I personally met him. I recall three times I saw him where we could talk directly. The first was when I asked the Democrat minority caucus in the House to allow me to visit with them. Hamilton, as the Minority Leader was in charge. I would call his demeanor as polite, nervous, and cold. They never invited me back, although I offered to come anytime and discuss anything with them.

The second meeting with Hamilton was when he requested to see me. I made time immediately. He brought another person along as a witness, whom I assumed was a House staffer. I was surprised how nervous he was.

The third time I met Hamilton was when I invited the House Minority Leadership to be my guests for lunch in the conference room on the ninth floor. Lunch with the Governor on the ninth floor was deemed to be high on the pecking order of things at the Capitol. I wanted them at ease so we could have a relaxed chat about anything they wanted to bring up. To my amazement, Minority Leader Hamilton refused to eat with the rest of us. He sat down in a position so he could look at me quite directly. He literally stared at me during the entire time and made no comment at all. I had a delightful conversation with the others. Within an hour, I received a phone call from Reid Ewing, from Tucson. He was a Democratic member of the House and was very bright and able. He talked to me anytime he had something to discuss. He told me that Hamilton had returned from the lunch and told some of the Democrats that I was not the buffoon my critics were trying to make me out to be, and that they had troubles. He said that I was smart, had an agenda of what I wanted to accomplish, and how to get it done.

A favorite Martin Luther King holiday attack strategy by the newspapers was to count the revenue that Arizona was projected to lose because of my obstinacy in not inventing the constitutional power to pay for the King Day. Again the *Republic* and *Gazette* reporters would call people who had merely made preliminary inquiries about holding a meeting in Phoenix, and ask them if they'd heard the terrible news and what were they going to do about it. Suddenly put on the spot, these convention organizers no doubt sometimes were influenced to pick another locale. Since, in many cases they had never made their final choice of a city, it's impossible to know how many conventions actually were lost. It's equally impossible to know how many were lost only because the newspaper reporters were basically threatening to expose these conventioneers as racially insensitive if they showed up in Arizona that year. Later in the year, when the actual figures were available, the real convention business, measured in hotel rooms occupied, was up 10 percent in the Phoenix area. In Tucson, beyond the roar of the *Republic*, it was up 42 percent. These statistics never made it into the news columns of *The Arizona Republic*.

One thing we belatedly discovered was that the Phoenix Convention Center had been having a decline in its business for several years. Apparently, blaming me for this decline made it easier for the operators to explain their own failure to keep a huge facility in use, thus creating a great expense to Phoenix taxpayers. Despite blaming me for their shortfalls and the posting of these negative figures at least weekly in the *Republic* and *Gazette*, the Phoenix convention business, in 1987, showed an increase over 1986.

At the December 19th meeting with Murphy and his staff at *The Arizona Republic*, I had tried to see if, short of capitulating to his every policy whim, I could do anything to assure coverage of the real issues. It seemed to me that his editorial policies were bound to hurt the state by obscuring the actual "news" of state government. In discussing issues, he pointedly told me that I shouldn't even think of rescinding Babbitt's order on the King Holiday. I pointed out that Corbin had promised to sue me, but Murphy merely replied, "So let the courts decide it." This was the same newspaper that had refused to print the Investigative Reporters and Editors series on corruption in Arizona. His excuse then was that he was afraid the paper might be sued—even though not a single successful lawsuit on the series was launched anywhere in the country.

I could see then that law and public responsibility would not be big concerns of the Phoenix newspapers. In the final weeks before my inauguration, Murphy's attacks intensified. I had my answer.

It seems fitting to mention here that GOP National Committeeman Jack Londen came to my office in the early spring of 1987, with word that if I would agree to get the MLK holiday passed, the *Republic* and *Gazette* would support me instead of oppose me. Was it a legitimate offer? I'll never know because making secret deals is not my way of doing things.

Chapter **10**

TAKING OFF

"Those who hesitate to get into this fight because it is controversial fail to realize that life's decision should be based on principles, not public opinion polls."
E. T. Benson

I assumed that most of the problems I was having with the press and with recalcitrant politicians were of a transitory nature and, for this reason, I looked forward to my inauguration all the more.

Traditionally the governor had been sworn in on an open portico at the second floor level of the Executive building, with the audience looking up from their chairs on the eastern approach to the old Capitol building. It seemed less pretentious to me for the governor to be outside with the people. Because I wanted things to be more comfortable for the officials and honored guests who were attending, the inaugural committee had a large platform constructed outside the east entrance to the old Territorial Capitol building (now used primarily as a museum). I'd also invited the other elected officials, who normally took the oath afterward, in private, to have equal recognition by being publicly sworn in at the governor's inaugural.

Just before 10:00 a.m., on January 5, 1987, with the sound of drum rolls in our ears and honor guards lining both sides of the walk, Florence and I were escorted from the street to the platform.

Toward the back of the crowd of on-lookers a single protester marched about nervously with a sign calling for my recall. When a 19-gun salute followed my oath, the protester threw down his sign in terror, thinking he was done for.

The inaugural ball had been arranged partly to help generate funds to pay off some of the outstanding campaign debts of $350,000. This had been the route taken by most of Arizona's governors before me. However, a new campaign finance law had been passed by initiative measure on the November 4th ballot, and there was confusion about the applicability of the new law to debts contracted prior to that election. Ralph Watkins asked the Attorney General's Office for an opinion. The thrust of the advice received from assistant AGs Steve Twist and John Shadegg (the son of Steve Shadegg, my old opponent in the 1962 U. S. Senate primary), was that there would be no problem if funds from corporate contributors and others, which were to be used only to defray expenses of the inauguration and the inaugural ball, were kept separate from funds raised by the sale of tickets. Based on that advice, Bill Long and Joyce Downey, acting for my inaugural committee, set up two separate bank accounts to keep funds separate—one for proceeds from the sale of tickets, another for contributions by corporations and others.

The inaugural committee sold tickets for $25 to attend the ball itself, and $250 to attend a special preliminary reception. As printed on each ticket, proceeds were for the express purpose to "Defray expenses and retire campaign obligations." The amount raised from ticket sales totaled approximately $103,000. Funds contributed by corporations and others to put on the inaugural celebrations paid all but $15,000 of the expenses, leaving $92,000 in the bank account in which the ticket sales money was deposited. These funds were always kept in accounts of the Mecham Inaugural Committee. Never at anytime were they ever transferred to the State of Arizona or to the Office of the Governor.

I had always assumed that, while opinions coming from the Attorney General's Office were of course only "opinion," the office was more or less bound by its word unless the courts contradicted it. I had acted on the King holiday issue under that assumption, and while I was being flayed alive for his opinion, Corbin had never once said, "Uh, hold on there, Ev, maybe we should take a second look at this." Legal opinion outside of the AG's office seemed to be that the new campaign finance laws did not apply to my campaign, which ended before the new laws became effective. It did not really matter because the $250 ticket contributions were well below the per person limit for the new law as well. Completely wrapped up in my preparations to take office, I left the details of this to Colter and to my campaign finance committees and accepted their reports as correct.

After all, there was work to be done. In both my inaugural address and the state of the state message to the Legislature, I had outlined what I hoped to accomplish under the program I've called "the New Beginning." The basic principles of this plan had evolved over the 27 years I'd been involved in politics, though they'd only recently seemed to come into vogue with many politicians across the country. I wanted to see the power that had been illegally usurped by the federal government returned to the states, as called for in the Constitution. I wanted to see more caution used in government spending, so that it would not outstrip population and economic growth and contribute to inflation. I wanted to see tax increases stopped. I wanted to see the federal tax structure overhauled so that everyone was treated fairly. And, I wanted to strengthen Arizona's efforts to prevent drug sales and use. Because I had been opposed so vehemently by most of the power brokers, I was convinced that the only reason I'd been elected was because most of the citizens of Arizona wanted to see these things happen, too.

During the time I was planning my legislative strategy, Bill Stulls, with Channel 12 television, interviewed me and asked what epitaph I wanted on my tombstone when I passed from this world? I was caught completely by surprise; I told him I really had never thought about it before because I didn't plan to go for a while yet. "But when I do, I think I would like it to say: 'He did what he said he would do.'"

Immediately following our November 4th victory, we set to work six days a week preparing to put our programs into action. The week's vacation I'd promised Florence was postponed indefinitely. Besides physically assembling and organizing my administration, we had to put two state budgets together, plan our legislative needs with newly elected leaders, and meet with representatives of a multitude of political, business and social organizations, many of them quite sincere, who insisted their immediate input was crucial to our proper understanding of the state's needs. I had to thank business leaders who had belatedly decided they wanted to help reduce my campaign debt, and wanted to be sure I personally knew of their assistance. I never asked any of them for contributions, and I gave them no assurance of anything but good government for all.

The budget problem was worrisome because the Executive Budget Office (EBO) was still under the control of the outgoing governor. By constitutional directive, he had to prepare a budget, even though everyone knew it would not be used because it was a list of "wants" compiled by his agencies rather than a list of our actual "needs." The $2.75 billion he budgeted was $200 million more than was really needed. The state fiscal year is July 1 through the following June 30th. We were approaching the fiscal mid-year that comes in January, and the projected income that Babbitt and the Legislature had used to produce what they had pretended was a balanced budget was nearly $160 million short of his spending appropriations. Because Arizona's constitution does not allow deficit financing, our only choices were to increase taxes or immediately reduce spending. In the past, Babbitt, Barr, and Gutierrez corrected mid-year budget overdraft with "emergency" tax increases. My commitment to no tax increases dictated that we reduce spending.

We concluded that the necessary cutbacks could be best accomplished by calling a special legislative session to reduce the budget to the amount of income expected. Between December 15th, when I was finally able to use the Executive Budget Office, and January 12th, we pounded out a budget revision with the legislative leadership. Not only did we trim the necessary $157 million for the first half of 1987, but for the first time in memory the result was a joint recommendation from both the governor and the legislative leadership.

Preparing the budget for the following fiscal year was an even bigger job and entailed a lot of overtime by the budget analysts and some of my staff. The manager of the EBO informed me that his staff wasn't used to having the governor spend any time with them in its preparations. I could see no other way to make informed decisions about all the various budget requests than by reviewing all the available information with the analysts who worked on these matters in the agency year around.

My college and business experience was a great asset in the budget process. My major field was business management, economics, and accounting. This included a good education in money and banking, and in personal management.

My special assistants and I had to meet with the department heads affected by all these decisions and make sure we could explain and, when necessary, defend, the budget figures we were coming up with. The Democratic governors who'd been in office for the 12 years since Jack Williams' term expired, had literally doubled the number of government departments, and Babbitt's terms had increased spending by 340 percent.

The week after my election, I'd met with all of the department heads to try to allay their fears about me that the press was already busy stirring up. I knew, if they'd been reading the same newspapers I had, they must be assuming they were about to experience the greatest devastation visited upon any group since Attila the Hun swept across Asia. At the meeting, I assured them, while I expected to be offered the traditional courtesy resignations of all the people who served at the pleasure of the governor, I had no intention of replacing everyone simply because I had that privilege. I wanted to make sure all of them received fair consideration and evaluation. While I believed that many of them would not want to serve under me because my philosophy differed so much from Governor Babbitt's, I had not yet made many decisions about personnel. I was open to suggestions. I told them I knew they were still working for the Babbitt administration until January 5th, but would appreciate their cooperation in furnishing information to my transition staff in the meantime.

In the weeks following the meeting, I received several resumes and exactly one courteous letter of resignation. The press took the unprecedented position that I ought not to replace Babbitt's people, and, at the same time, that their failure to resign was an indication of my inability to manage. By December 10th, our own organization was fairly well established, and, since we had still not heard from a majority of the outgoing administration, it seemed time to make our position as clear as possible. The notices we sent to the top executives said that, unless they heard otherwise from us in the interim, they should expect to be replaced on January 5th. The blast from the *Phoenix Gazette* was much as we'd expected:

"Some of the worst fears about governor Evan Mecham's administration are being realized. His termination Thursday, a week before Christmas, of 15 top department directors spoke volumes about his transition operation: clumsy, mean-spirited, and amateurish. The governor didn't even have the courtesy and savvy to inform those Babbitt administration officials he wanted to keep. The incumbents were phoning the Capitol press corps for information. The form letter itself, delivered to some of the state's most qualified, respected executives, was perfunctory and callous. Indeed the whole episode smacks of vindictiveness. It is as if Mecham and his staff just wanted the satisfaction of firing Babbitt appointees. This governor, like any other governor, has the right to select his top assistants and cabinet. But there was absolutely no need for the 'Pink Thursday Massacre.'"

Apparently the *Gazette* forgot they had reporters at the press conference in November where we covered everything as described a few paragraphs back. As so often happens, the party (the *Gazette*) that is trying to make someone they do not like (Mecham) look bad, ends up describing its own faults.

The saddest part of all this was, as always, the media steadfastly refused to play a part in disseminating information about the real issues that were bubbling with a fresh vitality in those days. Could we bring crime rates down? Could we stop the sale and use of drugs? Could we make government more responsive to the people? Could we plan our water use and transportation strategies more intelligently and effectively? Could Arizona play a part in America's rapidly expanding trade relationship with the Pacific Rim countries? Could we bring our education programs up to an acceptable standard without bankrupting the state? Could we promote more economic development in our rural communities to combat the escalating unemployment rate there? I thought these were vital questions, but the media never seemed to find them of much interest.

The way in which my appointments were being manhandled had made me uneasy, not only about the press and the Legislature, but about the attorney general as well.

Two days after I nominated Al Rodriguez to be my director of the Liquor Department, Corbin called my office. There'd been a huge ruckus in the Senate about the nomination, at least partly because the man who he'd be replacing was the son-in-law, or son-in law to be, of one of the Senators, and perhaps partly because the liquor industry is enormously sensitive to honest scrutiny. Rodriguez was a retired U. S. Army Colonel, a veteran of the Vietnam War, one of the most highly decorated U.S. Army officers, with 65 decorations, five of which are from foreign countries. His last five years of duty was as the Defense Attaché at the U.S. Embassy in El Salvador. Before his career in the U.S. Army, he was a policeman in his hometown of Douglas, Arizona, where he also was elected to a term as mayor after his retirement from the Army. His qualifications were too good to be effectively attacked. Therefore, the papers had to resign themselves to attacking me personally for putting another Babbitt appointee out of a job.

Corbin found an unbelievable way to rewrite this scenario and attack Rodriguez as well. He said I was in big trouble with this nomination, that in fact I ought to be clearing all my nominations with him before I ever moved on any of them. He said the press knew that he had been investigating a homicide involving Rodriguez.

I didn't bother to ask him how the papers had heard, since only the AG's office itself could have the information to tell them about such an investigation. Instead, I pressed him for more details. He said the "Rodriguez Affair" concerned the shooting death of a Mexican national at the border nearly three and a half decades ago.

It turned out that Al Rodriguez had been one of seven police officers on a surveillance team assigned to intercept a burglar suspected in more than 25 robberies in the Douglas area. The burglar had injured two Douglas police officers in making a previous escape back across the border to Agua Prieta, Mexico, so violence was expected. Al and another officer spotted the suspect near the border and a pursuit onto Mexican soil ensued. Al ended up shooting the suspect while the man was struggling with the other officer. They called for Mexican authorities to make an arrest and bring emergency medical aid. Those authorities reported the suspect died of his wounds. In the investigation that followed, Rodriguez and all the other officers were absolved of any criminal blame, and Arizona's Governor Ernest McFarland, himself a former judge and U.S. Senator, signed the case off. No blemish was ever reported on Rodriguez's record.

When I asked Corbin why he was investigating this now, he answered that the FBI had given it to him out of a background check they were making on Rodriguez as one of the nominees for the post of Assistant Secretary of the Army for Installations and Logistics. Corbin said he had received the request in April 1986, more than nine months before, and never bothered to do anything about it.

The FBI had a different story about how Corbin had gotten this case from their files. What Corbin had told me about them contacting him was a complete fabrication. They told me that Corbin had asked them for all the old files they had on the case. Because the shooting had involved American police officers and a Mexican national, Corbin had known the FBI would have to have some kind of record of it. If there hadn't been any cause for prosecution 34 years ago, there probably wouldn't be now. But suddenly the AG, who never had enough time to investigate current crimes against the state, felt it was imperative to launch a full-scale investigation of a 34-year-old, previously closed homicide. I asked him how long it would take, and he said about two weeks.

In the meantime, Corbin informed the press that I'd been negligent in checking backgrounds through him. We were having the Department of Public Safety do background checks on all appointment candidates, which was the proper agency, not the Office of the Attorney General. However, the press handled his news release to make it look like we were appointing people without checking their background. As if on signal, the Senate announced that from now on they would conduct their own investigations of all my appointees, a step never before taken. Both the Senate and the press knew we were taking every precaution but they did all they could to make the public think just the opposite. A tribute to the quality of our appointments was that only one we considered for a position had any background problems, and that was one DWI citation.

Not wanting to dump a good man just because he was being smeared by the combined media and AG attack, I told Corbin I'd hold Rodriguez's nomination for the two weeks his investigation would take. Once Corbin had me on the line like this, he ignored the two-week limit and expanded his investigation to the point of absurdity. The same attorney general who hadn't been able to investigate the Bolles murder, supposedly because he was afraid he might not have the authority, now sent a team of investigators into Mexico to interview everyone still living who knew anything at all about the affair. He spent hundreds of thousands of dollars, even having the burglar's body exhumed. Whipped into a frenzy by the media, the Senate turned Al's nomination into a circus, the result of which could only be a defeat for him. I finally withdrew his name before the vote.

Corbin milked the publicity from this 'investigation" for months before having to admit he could not act on his own. Months later (not the two weeks he promised), he took it before Superior Court Judge Alice Truman, who immediately ruled that Corbin had no jurisdiction in the matter to begin with. He had spent hundreds of thousands of dollars of the taxpayers' money without first bothering to get such a preliminary ruling? Jurisdiction on a 34-year old case involving federal issues would look like an obvious stumbling block to even a first year law student. Corbin did accomplish what he was after. He injured Col. Rodriguez's reputation and got many negative press stories about me. *The Arizona Republic* sent multiple reports on the national Associated Press wire, which stated that among the many bad people I was appointing to office was a man under investigation for murder, who would head the Liquor Department.

In the private sector there are legal ways to seek redress from such an offender as Corbin, but not so in dealing with government officials. Some of the gravest injustices I have ever seen have been done by officials using their vast powers to injure, and sometimes destroy, innocent people. Attorney General Corbin was one of the worst.

Even after the Al Rodriguez incident, I attempted to give Corbin the benefit of the doubt. He responded with an unmistakable shot across our bow. It was in response to my desire to hire Fred Craft to do some things for me in Washington. Craft had graduated from ASU law school and worked on Governor Jack Williams' staff before moving to Washington to work for Senator Paul Fannin. He had later become counsel for one of the Senate committees and begun a private practice in DC. Because Fred had worked on Illinois' successful lobbying effort to land the Fermi Reactor Project, I thought he would do a good job heading up our bid for the upcoming $4.5 billion Super-Conducting Super Collider Project. And Craft had already been doing some *gratis* work on the Super Collider, as well as some general lobbying and representation.

Corbin said I could not hire Craft to represent us in the nation's capitol. To straighten out the problem, I told Colter to take all the information we had to Corbin and have him tell us how to hire Craft legally.

After three weeks, we got our answer, as usual, not from Corbin's office but by way of the newspapers. By this time we'd had to reimburse Craft for $1,900 in out of pocket expenses. The papers announced Corbin was demanding that money be paid back, and he was investigating Craft and me for violating the state's purchasing code. Since the only information Corbin had about any of this was what Colter had given him in his capacity as legal counsel for my office, I was completely aghast at his misrepresentation of events. Not only could the sole purpose of Corbin's actions have been to create negative press for me, but normally this kind of abuse of a working relationship would have been considered a violation of the Code of Ethics of the Bar Association. Colter wanted to report it to the Bar Association, but I said no. Whether we liked it or not, the law had us locked into depending on the attorney general for our legal matters. In hindsight, I was wrong in trying to get along. We were to later realize that Corbin was the key to the power brokers' plan for my early removal. In hindsight, it is easy to see that leaving Corbin unchallenged on his improper actions made it easier for him to proceed against me.

Despite his constant hostility and his refusal to investigate the possibility of really significant corruption and ties to organized crime in the racing industry, we still tried to work with Corbin. The Legislature was slightly more receptive to a working relationship, despite its enormous built-in hostility for the man who had defeated their patron saint of campaign handouts, Burton Barr. (See Tom Fitzpatrick article quoted in Chapter 3.)

All but two members of the Republican Legislature had signed letters of commitment to Burton Barr for his 1986 gubernatorial run. After I defeated Barr in the primary, some of these legislators had supported me as their party's candidate; others had not. While I was running in the general election, I met with the Republican legislative leadership to discuss future cooperation. A number of them felt I owed them apologies for characterizing the Legislature as spendthrift, or for attacking Barr's integrity. I didn't want to alienate them because I knew that if I won in the general election, we'd need each other's support to get anything accomplished in the state's government. At the same time, I didn't see how we could have a constructive working relationship if I simply mouthed platitudes and ignored the realities of the situation.

I explained that I didn't blame them personally for Arizona's having the nation's highest growth in taxing revenues over the past decade or for increasing the per capita cost of government by 250 percent during that same period, but that these things had nevertheless happened. The Legislature, led by Barr and Senate Minority Leader Alfredo Gutierrez, had followed the Phoenix 40 legislative agenda unfailingly during that period. Either the Republican legislators had been badly used by Barr, or they had actually desired that kind of spending. I told them I believed Barr had been the culprit, and I was anxious to work with them to set the state aright.

It was quite well known when Barr could not get his bills passed by the Republican majority, he would form a majority coalition of liberal Republicans and the Democrats to pass many of them. The price the Democrats usually demanded was higher spending and more liberal legislation. Thus, the Democrat minority often had more influence on the legislative results than did the Republican conservatives who put him in the position of Majority Leader.

The combo of Barr in the House, Gutierrez in the Senate, and Babbitt as governor following the orders of the Phoenix 40 power brokers, had a very costly effect on Arizona State government during the nine years Babbitt was governor. The price demanded by the Democrats for their cooperation was their own pet bills that increased spending and increased the expansion of government. By the end of our meeting, Senator Carl Kunasek and Rep. Jim Ratliff were at least considering my position.

After the general election, Kunasek became president of the Senate and Ratliff majority leader in the House. Joe Lane, who had been majority whip under Barr, became speaker of the House, and Barr supporters, Jane Hull and Bob Usdane, became House majority whip and Senate majority leader, respectively. Hal Runyan remained as majority whip in the Senate.

I had hoped that these leaders would come forward with their own agendas to compliment or even improve my administrative program so that when it came time to give the state of the state address on January 12th, we could advance some unified proposals. Several times I asked them for an outline of the programs they felt were important. I received none. I could not tell if they did not have any solid agenda to accomplish or if they just would not share it with me.

When we met with the legislative majority leadership, they would come to hear what I had to say and would comment on my proposals. The leaders provided a good sounding board and my assistants and I learned a lot from this, but they never suggested anything like a partnership agenda. Therefore we began to work with individual legislators who were interested in particular pieces of legislation.

A major mistake I made at this point was in assuming that these leaders were taking the information from our meetings and discussing it with the Republican legislators in caucus. This is how a large business organization works. Not only does a chain of command save time, but also the leaders supposedly know best how to communicate with their own legislators. Furthermore, their leadership positions are strengthened because they are functioning as a necessary and useful bridge between the Legislature and the governor's office. But, in fact, the legislative leaders rarely even informed their committee chairmen of what had transpired at our meetings. In business, leaders usually rise to their positions through performance. In politics, vote getting and performance are far from synonymous.

Committee chairmen hold a lot of legislative power because they determine which bills move through their committees and which do not. If the chairmen do not want a bill to move, they put it in the bottom drawer of their desks and there it stays. The chairmen really prefer the leaders of their body to be weak so they themselves can get what they want. It is sad but true that legislative leaders tend to hold their positions through their ability to compromise. Had I recognized this at first, I would have spent more time meeting with the committee chairmen and their members. When I finally made my address to the joint session on January 12th, the chairmen were already feeling that I had slighted them by not conferring.

Some legislators also seemed upset over what they perceived as my "interference" in state government. They were used to Governor Babbitt, who only occasionally became interested in particular pieces of legislation, and who allowed his department heads to cut deals directly with the Legislature. When they discovered that my department heads couldn't be used to promote pet legislation, the legislators often went directly to the press corps with their complaints. Since the press was willing to print virtually any criticism made of me, presumably these legislators were hoping I'd roll over for them just to avoid the bad publicity.

It is a natural phenomenon in state and federal government in the United States, for members of the legislative branch to want to run the executive branch when they choose to. Of course, none of them want the responsibility, they just want the advantage of doing it as a matter of choice. The 50 states vary greatly in the power and independence allowed by the chief executive. Arizona is perhaps in the middle ground, with ample power vested in the Office of Governor to accomplish what needs to be done. The actual amount of power rests with the ability of any given chief executive to exercise it in a strong leadership fashion. When this is not done, members of the Legislature will step into the vacuum, as happened so often with Babbitt.

Following him, a few of them resented the fact that I expected to use the powers of the office to run the executive branch. Although I expected to cooperate with the Legislature in every way possible, hoping that we could have a cooperative close-knit operation, when it came to making the decisions, according to the law, I expected to be the one to make them for the executive branch.

I suggested to the leadership of both parties to invite me to the caucus meetings of both parties in both Houses to express my desire to work closely with them and cooperate in every way possible. I assured them my door was always open and any time they wanted me to come and meet with them in the caucus to discuss any of the issues, I would be glad to do so. I instructed my secretary to interrupt me any time a legislator was calling on the phone, and I would take the call; I would interrupt my schedule to visit with them in the office. Likewise, I instructed my special assistants and chief of staff to do the same. It was ironic, after the efforts we made from the ninth floor, to see ourselves constantly criticized, and particularly myself in an often-venomous way, in a hostile press for being "uncooperative" with the Legislature. We did have some great supporters in both the House and the Senate, but their praise never got reported. A goodly number came to see me, or we talked by phone when they had something to discuss.

It was the constant harping from the Herstam-led group of the more liberal side of the GOP in the House and most of the Republicans from Tucson, except for Senator Jeff Hill, that kept the constant media fire burning brightly. Had I known that they were actually working a systematic plan, operated from outside by Barr and the power brokers, I wouldn't have been so surprised. The ones who were the most critical of me were the ones who never accepted my offer to visit over issues on a one-on-one basis.

Having been in the legislature myself, I knew a great deal about the legislative ego and worked hard to stroke those egos, while still maintaining the position of leadership. It was encouraging to see some of the legislators, who seemed somewhat cool at first, respond and the ones with honest intentions became a working coalition which helped us accomplish virtually all of our legislative programs in the first regular session and the three special sessions in 1987.

House Majority Leader Jim Ratliff summed up our first six months of 1987, at a speech he made in Sun City, in July. He stated that Governor Mecham had accomplished more in his first six months in office than any of the other four governors he worked with, had accomplished in their whole term. That is even more gratifying because he was a strong Barr supporter against me in the 1986 Republican primary.

Signs, reports, and rumors of organized opposition never stopped. Early on, Mark Dioguardi, a conservative Republican lawyer who had been a candidate for Congress and had a lot of contacts from his extensive activities in the party, informed me that Representative Chris Herstam had organized a group of the more liberal Republican legislators to watchdog my actions in the hope of finding some grounds for impeaching me. I knew that I had been investigated in detail, and I had no fear of what anyone would find in my background. Now to hear the word "impeachment" seemed far-fetched.

Even before Dioguardi's visit, Mrs. Burton Barr told my friend Dave Hall, deputy of the Department of Administration, that we would not be in office long. This was the same message that Steve Shadegg told my old friend, Jake Higgins, who had been in the House when I was in the state Senate. Bill Bowler from Tucson was told the same thing at the inaugural ball. Local television show host Rita Davenport saw me in the Dallas Airport and said she asked a prominent bank president how he thought I was doing. He answered "let's see how long he stays in office."

Herstam was close to Barr and worked for Jack Pfister at Salt River Project and was a venomous critic from the very first. Within the first few weeks of our administration, he wrote an article for a small weekly newspaper in North Phoenix that my appointments were terrible and everything else I was doing was very bad. Herstam never came to see me to tell me in person what his problems or suggestions were. He kept working to expand his influence and did affect a number of the House members. The group was the more liberal House Republicans and included Hull,

Herstam, Killian, Broughton, Hardigan, Hawke, Jewitt, Baker, Greene, Mundell, and Hermon. In the summer of 1987, they convinced Mark Killian to be their spokesman to publicly attack what they announced were the bad things being done by me and my administration.

Never were the attacks over issues or substance. It was always an attack on me personally. If my programs were so bad, why had we succeeded in getting almost our entire legislative program passed? And, why had many of these detractors voted for most of my legislative proposals? Jim Hardigan later came to my home and apologized for being part of the group.

Had I allowed myself to worry about the many threats and rumors, little else would have gotten accomplished. I considered the attacks part of the price you pay to be in the political arena. I was so busy doing what we had pledged to do for the people of Arizona, I had little time to worry about distractions.

One incident I did worry about was when our home was broken into and the police said it was done by a professional. Florence and I woke up one morning to find a ski mask on the floor just inside the front door. There were tracks all over the great room at the center of the house and down the hall near our bedroom, but the police found no fingerprints any place. The entrance was through a hole cut in the breakfast room ceiling adjacent to the kitchen. It was obvious that the one, or ones who did it knew how the house was constructed, cutting their way in so as not to trip the security system alarm. We were both asleep in our bedroom during the intruder's visit. Nothing had been taken and the exit of the intruder was back out the same hole he came in. Since then, we have used the motion detectors on the alarm system as well as the door and window detectors.

On another occasion, when I was out of the state on state business, our phone line and security system lines were cut to disable them. Something awakened Florence, and she picked up the phone to find the line dead. The feature on the security system that sends an alarm to the monitor center if the line is cut, worked. The police were called, and no physical break in had been attempted. The police had no information or solution.

Needless to say, I was very disturbed. To harass me was one thing, but to frighten my wife was entirely off limits. When the

150

press wanted to know what Florence was doing during the 20 minutes she waited for the police to arrive, I said she sat in the bedroom with her loaded revolver in hand. I purposely emphasized that she knew how to use it and if a break in had occurred, the intruder would have come off second best. I decided harassers needed to know that although we are not violent people, we are armed and know how to defend ourselves. Occasionally the press can be used for a good purpose.

The reason that I did not take the warnings of removal from office too seriously was because I thought they would have to catch me doing something illegal. I was sure we had done nothing illegal, nor would we. I also did not expect it to happen because I was getting such good reception from almost everyone I came in contact with. The rural counties were especially supportive. In fact, I could not come close to filling all of the invitations for speeches. The messages that came in from most of our people were very positive. The Republican Party workers always gave me an uplifting reception at party meetings and conventions. Our accomplishments were steadily winning us support.

In hindsight, it is easy to see that a conspiracy to remove me by impeachment was put in motion as soon as the election was over. The conspirators apparently recognized that they could make impeachment work because there is no standard of proof to convict for impeachment. All that is needed is to have the votes and the power brokers knew they owned that many legislators—provided they made a good enough show out of the proceedings to confuse the public.

The grand jury indictments and resulting criminal trial, the recall, and the push for resignation were all cleverly designed to create a steady avalanche of bad press. It was the best propaganda show in the history of Arizona and perhaps the nation. They were in such control that, from the very start, they made the impeachment work just the way they planned. The only place they did not succeed was that many people, maybe even the majority, were not fooled.

Chapter 11

LAW AND DISORDER

"I am for preserving to the states the powers not yielded by them to the Union, and to the legislature of the Union it's constitutional share in the division of powers; and am not for transferring all the power of government to the Executive branch."
Jefferson

During that first legislative session we introduced a variety of proposals through friendly legislators. Besides balancing the budget, the biggest immediate task we undertook was the war on drug smuggling and drug abuse that I'd promised during my campaign.

It was one of the most popular parts of my program and had strong public support. This support from the public was the reason we were able to get the legislative support to launch our Alliance for a Drug Free Arizona.

No one can really assess the damages being done to humanity by the scourge of drugs. But, occasionally, somebody does put an estimate on the amount of money being made from the production and sales of drugs. The figures are always astronomical. One of the key points of my campaign for governor was to lead a movement throughout the state to rid Arizona of drugs. To me, drugs were a foreign thing; straight out of stories I had read as a boy about the opium trade out of China, not something I ever expected to come face to face with.

When I went into the Arizona State Senate in 1961, I was given a crash course by the Arizona Alcohol and Narcotics Education Association on how weak our laws were. This association was a mixed group of ministers of most of the churches, and it was the backbone of the Blue Ribbon Committee appointed by then-Governor Fannin. They were given the task of coming up with a plan to strengthen Arizona's laws relating to drugs. I got a pretty good education working with that group; and the end result was that in the special session of 1961, we were able to get a much stiffer code of drug laws for Arizona. It was also a great lesson to me because of the opposition from some quarters to the passage of those laws.

As my children grew up and passed through the school system, we saw the growing presence of the drug trade in schools and throughout our society. I thought surely there would be enough push to eradicate this cancerous attack. Many speeches have been given about the fight against drugs and it had been used in many political campaigns, but still the avalanche continued to grow in size. My children reported to me that in the schools drugs were available to anyone who had the money. I could see the only safety and security was in our family, knowing how bad they were for them, and being committed to never touch them or experiment with them in any way.

The first step toward an Arizona program to stop the drug traffic was the Border Strike Force of the mid-1970s. It seemed like a good idea but later was abandoned as a waste of money. Since then, there has been an awful lot of talk, but neither much money nor much effort has been expended to translate the lip service into any kind of action. The drug trade thrived in Arizona, and our southern border became a virtual freeway, first for marijuana and then, in the mid-1970s, for Mexican brown heroin. Arizona is generally placed second only to Florida as an entry point for the flood of drugs engulfing America.

A large part of the problem was the complete lack of interest shown in the drug problem by the two top law enforcement officers in the state, Bob Corbin and Ralph Milstead. Milstead, head of the Department of Public Safety, the state police force, had done extraordinarily little about drug enforcement, despite having received healthy budgets from a friendly Legislature to pursue the problem. In fact, at the same time he was asking his friendly local Legislature for the money, he was telling people he didn't believe in the enforcement end of even the federal drug programs. Milstead flatly refused to cooperate with the federal "Operation Pipeline" program, which netted 2,843 pounds of marijuana in New Mexico and a million dollars in cash in California. Arizona's take: zilch. "What do I do when I intercept a load of narcotics?" he later asked a *New Times* reporter. "It will not make one whit of difference if I knock off a hundred pounds of cocaine or marijuana."

More to the point, strong initiatives in drug enforcement didn't make any difference to Milstead or Corbin. Having both built up their private armies "to fight the drug runners" at state expense, they no longer had anything to gain in the Legislature or from their other powerful friends by actually doing anything about drugs.

I recall one conversation in the early 1980's with a friend, who was then an assistant police chief for the City of Phoenix, about why law enforcement seemed so ineffectual in combating the drug problem in this state. He said, "Well, if you were a kingpin, someone well up in the drug cartel hierarchy, you'd probably want things just the way they are here now. Politicians placate the public by talking about the drug problem and making all kinds of minor, factional gestures. By creating this illusion of action, you prevent people from realizing just how little is actually being done about the situation. There are about 13 different agencies here, all saying that they're involved in drug enforcement. As soon as one starts to get on to something, it trips over another agency that's trying to get to the same place. There's so much confusion and back biting, nothing gets done. And, there are so many people trying to do it, that there's almost no chance of surprising anyone really big and well-connected in the drug trade."

Because drug abuse is clearly a social as well as a legal problem, we needed someone who could work with the business community, social groups, and educational organizations and coordinate their activities with all levels of government. Our plan was to mobilize every business, civic, social, church, and governmental group to wipe out drugs in their own spheres of influence. Our first move was to use people to coordinate the drug program from that portion of the governor's budget that Babbitt had used for a political section. I asked Lee Watkins to coordinate efforts among various members of my staff and to put together a comprehensive program. Unfortunately, as soon as Lee became a visible member of my staff, the newspapers released information about him that had not been uncovered by the Department of Public Safety's background check. As a teenager, Lee had pled guilty to an unarmed robbery charge. As is common with youthful crimes, when there are no subsequent violations, such matters are supposedly expunged from the record and hence from public scrutiny. But with the matter being ballyhooed by a press hostile to anyone in my administration, public tolerance seemed out of the question, so I accepted the resignation that Lee hurriedly offered.

To get back on track, I appointed Tim Murchison, a retired army colonel with a good deal of administrative experience, to head up my drug program. I also persuaded Rex Hogerson, the number two man at the federal Drug Enforcement Agency in Arizona to retire and come to work for me on this program. The two of them interviewed police agencies around the state, put together training programs, and planned the coordination of various local, state, and federal agencies. I asked the county attorneys, the State Attorney General's Office, and the Department of Public Safety to put together packages they thought they'd need to effectively combat drugs. The ultimate product of all this was called The Alliance for a Drug Free Arizona. U. S. Attorney General Ed Meese called it a model drug program for any state.

Our symbol was an umbrella, representative of both our means in enlisting the cooperation of every possible sector to combat drugs, and our goal was to completely shield the state from the evils of drug traffic. Arizona was already spending over $20 million annually on substance abuse treatment programs. We succeeded in getting some federal money to match our state funding for drug education programs in every school district in Arizona. We urged all the municipalities in the state to join our Alliance for a Drug Free Arizona, and had signed up about half of Arizona's communities before I left office.

As usual, the power brokers and the Phoenix press were much more interested in attacking me than in attacking the problem. Since they couldn't very well come out in favor of drugs just in order to criticize me, they decided to ridicule my enthusiasm instead. When I proposed that we throw all the resources at our disposal into the fight and set the goal of having a drug-free Arizona in two years' time, my opponents rolled their eyes and threw up their hands in exasperation. How could Mecham be so naive, when everyone knows what a complicated and deep-seated problem this is? Since the establishment had spent years convincing the public that they had, in fact, been doing everything possible to stop drug trafficking and abuse, many Arizonans were well conditioned to accept the idea of our collective helplessness. The obvious advantage of setting an immediate goal and striving to reach it is that even if you don't achieve everything you set out to do, you are still much better off than before. This was somehow made by the major media to seem completely quixotic.

I recognized the hazard of adopting an aggressive stance, and I was fairly sure that Pat Murphy would not abandon his war against me to help mobilize the public on this issue. I was not disappointed. I was right in thinking that the drug problem was so virulent and so obvious to the average citizen that we could be very successful in forcing a lot of action against it.

I knew we couldn't enforce the law without more funds. Initially, I hoped for sufficient funds to pay for a drug enforcement division in the city police departments and in sheriff's departments throughout the state. On the one hand, I believe that the community level is most appropriate for policing activities, since local law enforcers know their own communities the best. After studying the Department of Public Safety during my campaign, I had become extremely concerned about their waste of resources. Therefore, we decided to put together a comprehensive package for the Legislature that would finally enable us to mount an effective program.

Usually it takes several years to push a major program through the Legislature. The parties naturally have some differences of opinion on the means by which desirable ends are to be achieved. Politicians jockey for position on particular elements of this legislation as well as arranging trade-offs for votes on past and future legislation. Compromises have to be set up, backs scratched, fences mended, and egos massaged, before the public is belatedly served. In our original proposal to the Legislature, we asked for stronger penalties for drug possession and sales, and an additional appropriation of $7.5 million to add to $5 million federal dollars, principally for enforcement. I believed that spending in the area of drug abuse and trafficking would save the state money in the near future. While the social costs of drugs here can only be estimated, almost every authority assumes they're astronomical. About half of all crime is believed to be drug-related.

I wanted to set up five new Superior Courts to handle nothing but drug cases. I felt that if we had judges, investigators, and prosecutors who were real specialists in these laws, we could greatly accelerate the handling of drug cases and alleviate some of the pressures on the general court system that often resulted in mishandling of drug cases. In order to assure that we had judges who would really enforce the letter of the law, I hoped to appoint these judges myself. Some members of the House of Representatives, on the other hand, wanted to staff these courts with pro-tem judges to be appointed by the chief presiding judges of the county courts. Since that meant liberal Judge Michael Dann would be making all the appointments in Maricopa County, I could see the entire program being eviscerated. This led me to a confrontation with Chairman of the House Judiciary Committee Jim Skelly, a longtime lieutenant of Burton Barr and Bob Corbin. Since the House was willing to pass some drug legislation, Skelly couldn't see why I shouldn't accept his altered version of the bill, a version that would look like an attempt to solve the drug problem even if it didn't accomplish much in the courts. I told him I'd veto his "compromise" package if it came through with the presiding judges appointing the judges for the drug courts, and would keep sending it back down to the Legislature until it was done right.

Chairman Peter Kay of the Senate Judiciary Committee finally pulled the chestnuts out of the fire by formulating a compromise proposal. In it, the drug court judges would be chosen like other Superior Court judges, with the governor making the appointment from a list arrived at by the Judicial Selection Committee.

Even though we introduced our drug package bill fairly late in the first legislative session, we got a compromise form of the bill passed in that very first session. Although this bill didn't pass with enough votes to trigger the emergency clause we'd desired in order to allow its immediate implementation, it was nevertheless a landmark accomplishment to get an umbrella program through the Legislature in such record time.

Unfortunately, the bill didn't take effect until October, 1987, and funds wouldn't flow to enforcement until the following spring. When Mofford took over my office, she immediately discharged Murchison and his small staff, and eliminated the funds for continuing enforcement from her 1988-89 budget. As quickly as our Alliance for a Drug-Free Arizona had come into being, and despite the tremendous reception it had received in schools and businesses across the state, it was gutted and dismantled. The "establishment" simply had no use for a program that actually mobilized the citizenry against a common enemy. The drug industry celebrated my impeachment as the removal of another roadblock from the path of their continued prosperity, with no significant state program to impede them.

Under Babbitt, Colonel Ralph Milstead had literally turned the highway patrol into a state police, or as one newspaper put it, into his personal militia. What had been an exceptionally fine highway patrol bureau had been changed to a state police department called the Department of Public Safety. They now had a criminal investigation bureau which included a narcotics division, administration bureau, criminal justice support bureau and telecommunications support bureau, over 1,600 people with many officers doing clerical deskwork. It is managed like an elite police force in a banana republic. Instead of being a support for local law enforcement, Milstead had worked and schemed to impose it over all other law enforcement in the state.

While it had grown into a multi-tentacled monster, morale and efficiency had deteriorated considerably over the past six years. The specially trained narcotics officers from the old strike force told me they had next to nothing to do because the DPS narcotics division was largely a facade. Milstead gave members of the strike force only menial tasks but wouldn't let them really get into meaningful drug work. Gradually the force had become almost meaningless in the field of narcotics enforcement.

Whenever Milstead fired an employee with whom he'd had personal contact, and he fired a great many of them, he ordered complete criminal and civil investigations of the individual. It appeared to many of us that Milstead was using the information gathered in this way to protect himself from any disgruntled employee who was inclined to 'kiss and tell' about his administration. In one instance, Milstead spent over $250,000 of the taxpayers' money on legal fees defending himself for firing Bob Ayers, a DPS officer who had given Milstead's former wife, Debbie, a poor review for the way she handled her employees in the department's radio room. Ayers came to my home and personally told me what was going on. Milstead knew of our visit. My removal from the Governor's Office saved Milstead from being fired, and he never stopped prosecuting Ayers and others until he broke them and got them out of DPS and out of law enforcement. They couldn't meet the price of legal defense for themselves against his generous budget of taxpayers' money. This type of action was the rule, not the exception.

Misappropriation of state resources and general corruption within the DPS were legendary, with Milstead responding to charges against him by dismissing the officers who had made the allegations, accusing them of similar crimes, and then providing his own internal investigations to substantiate his position. Milstead and the DPS, in turn, were never investigated by anyone. In its 20-year history, the DPS has never once been audited by the Auditor General's Office. Such an audit can only be conducted at the request of the Legislature, and they have no stomach for that.

Many of the legislators are great friends with Ralph Milstead, and not merely because his DPS officers are always ready to chauffeur them around town. As his former girlfriend, Christina Johnston, later testified under oath, Milstead believed himself impervious to any real scrutiny because he had friends in all the right places, and in many of the wrong ones. Not only did he have a well-documented "working relationship" with much of the Legislature, he also claimed he was in touch with professional criminals as well, who would be glad to kill her if she made problems for him. Johnston said Milstead had named Bob Corbin as one of the men who frequently accompanied him on his hiking trips and on cruises to Tucson, where Milstead liked to womanize at restaurants and in hotel rooms at the state's expense.

When it became evident that not enough new drug enforcement money would be available from the Legislature to add the estimated 300 necessary officers to local police forces, I intended to proceed with the program through a reorganization of the DPS. Had I not been impeached, we would have been able to re-direct the efforts to beef up the highway patrol and field a drug force of about 250 officers without any additional money.

I wanted Milstead out from the beginning, but he had done his homework. He apparently had used his police empire to get the goods on dozens of state officials and then sequestered the information in his private files. When I began discussing his replacement, I was suddenly deluged by protests from various legislators. I literally was threatened by Pat Murphy in *The Arizona Republic*, and by Senator Tony West. I would have replaced Milstead anyway, but he had insured himself of tenure by having Babbitt grant an employment contract that ran until 1990. The only way I could replace him without paying off the contract in full was to prove cause for dismissal. Senate President Kunasek told me that the Legislature would not appropriate the money to buy out his contract.

Having an honest man as head of DPS would have enabled me to start cleaning up corruption activities. Instead, they used these same resources against me.

By August, 1987, I had enough information to prove Milstead should be dismissed for cause. In September, I planned to remove him from DPS, and also Sam Lewis as head of the Corrections Department. As I have stated before, I asked my legislative liaison, Donna Carlson, for the list of legislators I needed to brief before taking this action. She reported to Milstead and Corbin what my plans were and they moved in concert against me with the state grand jury to "investigate" my campaign finance report.

The public must have been very confused about what was going on in my administration because the reporters, critics, the columnists and editorials seemed to be mixed as to whether I was trying to do too much or too little. I was accused of doing both. Phoenix Newspaper Publisher, Pat Murphy, always enjoyed saying that I had no vision and no comprehension of state government. Yet upon entering the office, I found no evidence that my predecessor, who he always acclaimed as having great vision, had left the place with no advance planning. We started with a mismanaged government, with no set of road maps for its future course.

During the first legislative session, we had several major changes that needed to be made and we set out to do them in an orderly manner. To set long term plans in order, we wanted a 50-year plan for the growth of our transportation system. The director of the Department of Transportation put his planning staff on it.

I requested a 50-year plan from our Water Resources Department to do what would need to be done to guarantee an ample supply of water. Factors to consider were conservation, additional dams, buying more water out of the Colorado River to recharge our underground aquifers in times of surplus, and new water sources not being used at present. The Central Arizona Project still had some details to finish. Although the federal government controlled most of the CAP, it was rather touchy keeping things on track.

No spot on earth has a better opportunity for the development of solar energy than Arizona, and we wanted to move toward eventually providing 50 percent of our electrical energy generation from the sun. We became very active in promoting private sector involvement in this area. We looked into making all or part of the new state courts building a demonstration project for the use of solar energy.

Tourism is the second largest industry, exceeded only by manufacturing in Arizona, and with the beauties of our state it is obvious we have a great deal more opportunity to develop that vital and very clean industry, so that was to be emphasized. Arizona is not well known in the Pacific Basin, so we felt it necessary to establish a presence in that part of the world and open up a trade office to assist our medium and small-sized businesses. Through the office, we worked toward establishing contacts for export of Arizona products and to find markets for products than can be grown and manufactured in Arizona.

We knew that our citizens were not being protected by any enforcement in our Department of Weights and Measures. As a result, consumers were losing approximately $200 million a year on short weights and measures in the products they bought and in shoddy merchandise itself, whose quality did not meet the labeling on the packages.

I also was committed to repealing the last one cent sales tax that had been levied in the early '80's, first as a temporary tax, and then made permanent the following year to feed the expensive spending habits of the Babbitt administration.

These, along with the drug program as previously discussed, were the focal points of most of our planning activities and the things we were working on with the Legislature.

In each one we succeeded where legislation was needed except in the case of repealing the one cent sales tax. It was too much to expect of a Legislature that had been used to increasing spending almost at will, to suddenly curb that appetite and accept a budgeting process that appropriated the amount of money needed by state government rather than the amount of money wanted.

The best estimate of state revenue by the Executive Budget Office for fiscal 1987-88, was $2.6 billion. The Joint Legislative Budget Office estimated revenue to be at least the $2.7 billion to support what they wanted to spend. I wanted to reduce spending to $2.45 billion and reduce taxes. It became apparent that I could not prevail on my desired figure. I finally agreed to spend the $2.6 billion my budget office projected for revenue, providing it included a small appropriation to set up a Commission for Efficiency and Cost Reduction in State Government. With this Mini-Grace type commission, we would have the tools to prove to the legislators the overhead cost of government could be reduced enough to repeal the one cent "temporary" sales tax in subsequent years.

To effect compromise, I called a face-to-face meeting with Appropriation Committee leadership to convince them I would veto any budget bill that called for spending more than the $2.6 billion expected revenue. They fumed and argued and tried to justify the almost $2.7 billion they wanted to spend. That night they found ways to reduce the budget bill to my compromise amount and they had it on my desk the next day.

The ensuing Mini-Grace Commission, composed of professional consultants and loaned executives from the private sector, turned in their report after I was removed from office. It showed that $250 million per year could be saved in the operations of state government. With me gone, there was no interest in anyone implementing the suggestions of that report.

The secret to the value of our Mini-Grace program was how we structured it. I had talked with some of the CEOs of the larger companies in Arizona to see how they kept their expenses in line to stay competitive. Most have almost autonomous mid-management groups that have that responsibility. I recruited a number of these company heads to serve, without pay, on our Mini-Grace committee to run the project. We also secured the volunteer service from enough of the large companies' people in the expense control departments, to do the work with outside people. We knew it would not work to use in-house state government employees to do it. The Legislature appropriated a small fund for the project, part of which we used to hire Arthur Young, one of the "Big Eight" national accounting firms to do the computer work and provide the professional directions needed. Ray Roles did a very good job as managing director of the project. It took a solid six months of his life and he did it without pay. In the end, part of the money appropriated for the project by the Legislature, was returned to the state general fund.

Few taxpayers in Arizona know that each of the next three annual budgets were passed with a big increase in spending. To cover that increased spending, state taxes were raised by an average of over $165 million each year. By the end of what would have been my first term in office, these additional taxes added up to more than $500 million each year. None of these taxes would have been levied had I stayed in office.

We got our new Weights and Measures Department with proper enforcement, so the people of Arizona now are more nearly getting their money's worth in the products they buy.

We were the first state to open up a trade office in the World Trade Center in Taipei, Taiwan and, during two different trips I made, we established very valuable connections both there and in Japan. The first was in August, 1987, when I was invited, at their expense, to be one of the speakers to the World Anti-Communist League Convention at the Grand Hotel in Taipei. While there, I spent three very active days meeting with numerous business and government officials and their import and export trade associations. In October, I led an 18-party trade mission to Taiwan where we opened up the state office. I also was the guest of the President of the Republic of China at the "Double Ten," as they call the October 10th, Chinese Independence celebration. There I cemented more relationships with their trade and business people to open up more two-way trade with Arizona. It had the direct effect of adding more than $100 million in the export of American products, particularly cotton, for 1987, alone.

We also had a successful short visit to Tokyo, and Osaka, Japan. There we met with prominent leaders of business, banking, and trade, and made them substantially more aware of Arizona as a tourist Mecca, and as a state anxious to export more of our own products to their markets as well as welcome joint venture capital to our state.

Not only is it the governor's responsibility to propose and provide leadership, it is also his responsibility to communicate and help create and focus enthusiasm for things we are trying to accomplish among all the people throughout the state. I could feel the return of a feeling of optimism throughout the state, and I think that was responsible for receiving far more invitations to speak to various groups throughout the state than I could meet, although I did average at least 10 speeches a week.

Of course, it was impossible to make all the changes needed immediately, but one of them we did make was to stop the unauthorized use by state employees of over 1,000 state government cars for personal transportation to and from their homes. That unauthorized use of state cars was costing the taxpayers at least $3 million per year. Some departments cooperated very well while others grumbled and complied reluctantly.

This ban on using state cars for personal use is an example of how resistant bureaucracy can be to reform and consider that which would save taxpayer's money. The presidents of the three state universities were driving three of the cars. I later found out, after the restriction of their car privileges, the Board of Regents gave each one $7,200 annually for their personal car allowance.

Law And Disorder

Prior to the ban, DPS Col. Ralph Milstead had not owned a personal car. He was not happy about having to buy one because only people on 24-hour emergency call could legally drive a state car home. Most of the time, I furnished my own personal car for my official travelling.

Throughout all this, about the only contact between the Legislature and myself that seemed to attract any media attention concerned the Senate confirmation of some of my appointments. As long as the stories were negative, that is. When Senate Majority Leader Usdane, normally a vocal critic, quietly announced that the Senate overall had much less trouble with my appointments than with those of previous governors he had worked with, the remark was buried on a back page. Because they involved personalities and life stories, the nominations lent themselves only too well to sensationalistic journalism. Appointees with even a single enemy in the Legislature could count on a thorough bashing by the press, "objectively" quoting the one critic to the exclusion of everyone else. Sometimes simply to gain publicity, the legislators quickly became addicted to this extraordinary media attention. Where some legislators had once had to leave public meetings every few minutes for cigarette breaks, now they could be seen running to the press room to stoke up on self-importance.

Chapter **12**

THEIR PROPAGANDA MACHINE AT WORK

"This above all —-to thine own self be true; And it must follow, as the night the day, Thou canst not be false to any man."
Shakespeare

In March, 1988, I was introduced to Ed Hiner who had been recommended to me as one of the best business lawyers in the city. I was preparing to sell my Pontiac dealership and needed an experienced lawyer in this field to handle it. He told me he would be able to do the work I needed, but hesitantly added that he had a confession to make first. He had signed the recall petition against me and thought I wouldn't want to hire him after all.

"I wouldn't blame you if you were angry," he said.

"I'm not," I said. "Lots of people seem to have done the same thing. But would you mind telling me why you signed it. What did I do that made you believe I should be recalled from office?"

"Well," he said, and stopped there for a moment. "All I knew about you was what I read in the newspaper, and I thought you needed to be removed. Now I know more about you and regret signing it."

This man was known in his profession for being highly articulate and was an expert who could analyze complicated issues during the heat of a trial and explain difficult legal questions to a jury of laymen in a few words. He sat there, a little uncomfortable, because he was realizing for the first time that all he had behind his negative impression of me were a lot of unsubstantiated attacks by the Phoenix press.

When he came to know me, he admitted that he had been misled. In terms of basic principles and moral values, we were actually very much alike. When he came to know me, it was as if he'd been released from some kind of hypnosis and could finally see what was going on around him.

I grew up when the Nazi's held sway in Europe, and recall discussions in which people tried to explain how a nation as sophisticated as Germany could possibly be so enamored of a madman like Hitler. They always emphasized the role played by Joseph Goebbels, Hitler's minister of propaganda. As a newspaper editor, Goebbels almost single-handedly created Hitler's Berlin organization and, after the Nazi takeover, was instrumental in the public's acceptance of the Nazi's increasingly vicious and insane policies. After the war, when the Germans were questioned about their concentration camps, most dazedly replied they hadn't known. How is that possible? Goebbels had fooled them through the press and kept them looking in a different direction.

Brainwashing isn't something that requires laboratory headsets and electric transformers. It is simply indoctrination so intense and so thorough that it results in a radical transformation of beliefs and mental attitudes. The communists used it to great effect in Korea to transform the thinking and values of some of their American prisoners so they would do their bidding.

Explanations of hypnotism and brain-washing probably seem shockingly melodramatic to some, but that kind of magical-sounding concept is the only available way to explain behavior so far beyond what seemed to us to be reasonable. For very similar reasons, I have trouble avoiding those words in describing what the power brokers in Arizona were able to achieve through their control of the media and various lobbying and special interest groups. *The Arizona Republic* and the *Phoenix Gazette* are not informational organs; they are dangerous weapons wielded with considerable political purpose.

Because the movement to recall me from office began before I moved onto the ninth floor, it seems incredible that so many people have been able to maintain with straight faces that the recall was born of my misconduct in office. Clearly, while many factors may have contributed to its later signature gathering efforts, the recall was started virtually as soon as I was elected, in order to undo the consequences of my election.

Even commentators who were often critics of mine have pointed out that this is something of an abuse of the democratic process. The only logic ever propounded in support of the premature recall effort was that I had not been elected by a majority of the state's voters. Forget for a moment that Abraham Lincoln, who also ran in a three-way race, was not elected president by a majority of the voters. Or that our neighboring state of Utah had a three-way gubernatorial race in 1988, in which Governor Bangerter, with 40 percent of the vote, beat out his closest rival by less than two percent—all without any thought of recall. Put aside for a moment the fact that CBS's exit poll indicated that, without the third candidate in the race, I would have beaten Carolyn Warner 55 percent to 45 percent. If voters really are uncomfortable with plurality victories, the solution is not a recall but a change in the election laws to require a majority. If three candidates with substantial backing are going to be allowed to run for office, a winner based on a plurality, instead of a majority, of the vote is the most likely outcome.

To demand a recall immediately after the votes are in is no more credible than the loser of a supposedly definitive battle suddenly shouting out for a retroactive rule change: "How about the best two out of three?" To avoid this very eventuality, Arizona has a law preventing a recall election for the first 180 days any elected official is in office. For the good of the state government, losers are supposed to allow the winner of an election at least this minimum opportunity for performance, so that there is some objective measure of his abilities for the electorate to consider. Since my performance was not going to be an issue in this recall, no such period was deemed necessary in my case.

The recall movement was led by a determined young man named Ed Buck. He had campaigned for Warner, and, as soon as the votes were counted, started handing out bumper stickers at the Capitol demanding my removal from office. Previous to that newsworthy occasion, he had made the news twice before. The first time was when he was arrested on a morals charge and shortly thereafter on a drug charge.

Buck claimed to be a self-made millionaire and a Republican, neither of which was true. He registered as a Republican after the election, when he'd already started the recall, in order to give his hysterical unhappiness with me some sort of objective appearance. The hallmark of the recall movement was most noted for how well-packaged and financed it was and for how much favorable coverage it received from a never-skeptical press.

Buck's obsessive urgency with the derailment of my administration was startlingly vague at first, involving my general unfitness for an office in which the state's voters thought I would do a pretty good job. Not until others publicly disclosed that Buck was a homosexual, did it become evident that his hatred was motivated by his fears that I might crack down on homosexuals in Arizona. Exposed, Buck embraced this fiction as a rallying point for other "oppressed minorities."

Certainly Buck's outspoken advocacy of a package of moral and public policy issues that have come to be known as "gay rights" and my own, equally outspoken, advocacy of traditional family values, were in opposition. Certainly, I would never have appointed him to any governor's commission. But prior to Buck's invention of the recall movement, I don't recall ever having made a public statement relating to homosexuals.

The first time it came up was during a call-in radio program I was doing early in 1987, called "Talk to the Governor." For some reason I still can't fathom, a young man called in claiming to be one of many homosexuals who were members of my particular church. He wanted me to publicly validate their "rights." I was rather taken aback, and told him that in my church it was well-established doctrine that homosexuality was not an acceptable lifestyle. The papers were immediately full of news about my "homosexual bashing." The next time I was on the radio show, another caller identified himself as a homosexual and asked that I state my public acceptance of the "many homosexuals" who occupied positions in

Arizona as teachers and government employees. I said I wouldn't do that because homosexual acts are against the law in Arizona, and I don't condone having law-breakers in government and teaching.

According to the press, there was a hue and cry of biblical proportions across the land. In any event, the National Gay Rights Liberation Movement mobilized their battalions in Arizona and put a good deal of their resources into the recall movement. Remarkably, the press managed to use even homosexuality against me. They saw it as a sign of my ubiquitous "insensitivity," without crediting it as an issue. Likewise, Buck was always careful to posture himself as the personality of the recall movement, when there was any question of its rationale for existing. Yet even when discovery of his prior arrests for public lewdness and falsifying prescriptions to purchase narcotics forced him to resign as its official head, Buck was always in the foreground, always being quoted in the newspapers and appearing on radio and television interviews as a spokesman for the recall. A former model, Buck is photogenic, aggressive and articulate. He received a tremendous amount of positive press and had quite an impact through the massive amount of publicity. At the same time, his great weaknesses were nearly invisible to the media; it was my behavior, not Ed Buck's, that was at issue, they pointed out.

As I've said before, if only my actual behavior had been the issue, it would have been fine with me. I was criticized, however, for my alleged lack of sensitivity and other intangible qualities. When State GOP Chairman Burt Kruglick brushed off questions about the recall movement in July, 1987, with assurances that it was only "a band of homosexuals and a few dissident Democrats," his remark was treated as a more important indicator of the quality of my governorship than the anti-drug program I'd pushed through the legislature, with hardly a word of substantive interest from the press. On the other hand, when Buck called my appointee, Chief of Capitol Security Lee Limbs, a "G— D—— black baboon," Buck's insensitive racist remark was immediately forgiven and forgotten by the press. After all, the recall had put a terrible strain on Mr. Buck. And, as he pointed out in his own defense, "I've slept with more black men than most [whites] have shaken hands with."

Their Propaganda Machine At Work

Publisher Murphy publicly acclaimed Buck as one of the most outstanding political finds and one of the most powerful men In Arizona. Senator John McCain and later to be Governor Fife Symington supported Murphy's laudatory remarks about Buck. Not surprisingly, Buck quickly disappeared from the Arizona scene in any public way soon after the signatures were filed.

Although the state Democratic Party leadership professed they were taking no part in the obvious conspiracy to remove me from office, they were uncovered as the sponsoring agents of a massive telephone campaign to discredit me and raise money. We traced it to a telephone solicitation business in California that had been used by the Democratic Party to raise funds. This time they were calling all registered Democratic homes in the state, making slanderous accusations about me, and then asking for money to support the recall effort against me. When Democratic Chairman Sam Goddard publicly denied any connection with the telephone operation, we traced it directly to Glen Davis, the executive director of the Arizona Democratic Party housed in the law offices of Goddard and Goddard. Later one of the telephone solicitors who was working for the California company quit in disgust and came to Arizona. He showed us the written message of lies the phone solicitors were paid to say about me in order to shock the Democrats into making contributions to the Democrat Party, presumably to get me out of office.

I displayed little concern over the recall during the 180 days of its incubation, and the first squalling months after its official birth. I believed there were no substantial issues behind it. Although on a daily basis the newspapers were still covering me with dirty ink about the King Day and my alleged "insensitivity" to the group of the day, there had not been a single bit of hard news concerning mismanagement in my office. Since voters had elected me because they wanted certain issues dealt with, and I was dealing with those issues as I'd promised, I reasoned that the electorate would continue to support me if the time came for a recall. I often repeated that I had confidence in the people and that they would judge me by what I did, not by what my critics and the news media said about me.

Dealing with the media became more and more difficult as it became clearer to me that no matter what I did, they weren't going to like it. I didn't want simply to abandon press conferences since I could see no other way to inform the public. But, the public just wasn't being informed. If I held a press conference to discuss the drug program or our lobbying efforts for the federal Super Collider project, I could absolutely make book that certain reporters would only raise their hands to ask questions to support the personal attack on me they wanted to write about, regardless of the subject I brought them together to discuss. After the reoccurrence of these events, I insisted that reporters raise their hands before I would respond to their questions. This allowed me to ignore the hands of the *Republic* and *Gazette* reporters much of the time and made my press conferences more orderly affairs. When I controlled the conferences in this way, the results that were reported, particularly by the radio and TV people, seemed fairer.

I tried dealing with press in about every way I could think of, including responding with humor to the adversity they created for me. When they asked for a portrait of me to hang in the pressroom at the Capitol, I offered to have one made of cork so that they could throw darts at it. When I arrived on the ninth floor on April 1st, our telephones were ringing off the hook with inquiries from people trying to obtain jobs in a big movie production that was allegedly going to be shot in Arizona. Clint Eastwood and Bruce Springsteen were two of the lesser stars that were going to appear in this one. We soon discovered the inky fingers of the *New Times* all over this April Fool's joke. So I instructed our receptionists to insure all the callers that our number had been printed by mistake, and that the correct number and address where applications could be made in person, were those of the *New Times*. I then went out to meet the press for the morning.

They seemed rather surprised that I knew how to take a joke, and how to hand one out. In light of that, I said I was calling a press conference for 2:00 p.m. When they showed up, we put on a complete spoof of a press conference. I announced I was going on world tour as a soloist with the rock band U2, and that we were opening in San Francisco in three days. That Bill Hueisler and Associated Press Reporter Larry Lopez were opening a new furniture moving business. (Earlier Bill had threatened to break a chair over Larry's head.) I also said that I was declaring April 1st to be "Press Corpse Appreciation Day." (It wasn't a paid public holiday, so I had that authority.) It was one of the few times I got the press to loosen up and abandon their grim determination to misconstrue everything I said. Some even reported that I had a sense of humor.

The press virtually screamed that I was hurting tourism. In Tucson, where the press was far less hysterical, convention business was up 42 percent in the first half of 1987. In Phoenix, where Murphy's staffers were staging a sabotage effort, convention business was up only 10 percent over the previous year. We have later found an interesting statistic concerning the convention center in downtown Phoenix. Bookings there had been declining for the past several years. Their finger pointing at me and the King holiday as the basis for the loss was a shameful act on their part, but I suppose all is fair in politics and governor bashing. The mock horrified wringing of hands and rending of newsprint over the national humiliation I was causing the state never abated, despite the fact that the only real damage being done to Arizona was being caused by the furor created by the media. Of course, since the attention allowed the local reporters to reap national bylines, they wouldn't have had it any other way; perish the thought of my principles, the state's needs, or the electorate's desires interfering with their livelihoods.

A classic example of a national controversy created out of local mis-reporting was when Morely Safer interviewed me for *60 Minutes*. Like much of the national press coverage, Safer's interest in me was generated by the outrageous characterization of me made by the local press reports, and so the "story concept" his interview was designed to fill out was "Cro-Magnon Mecham The Racist Threat." Safer interviewed me for an hour and a half in order to create five minutes of tape that could be taken out of context and used for that purpose. Rather than ask me what I was doing in Arizona, he told me: "You've made so many racial and insensitive remarks that people have turned against you." I interrupted him at that point and asked him to quit the generalizations and give a specific example of my insensitivity.

"You called Black children pickaninnies," he stated.

I told him he was wrong. I had never called anybody a pickaninny. Stating that I had done so was a pure fiction manufactured by the press. What had happened was that, during a meeting of the Arizona Bicentennial Commission, someone had mentioned a particular book, *The Making Of America*, written by the well-known constitutional scholar and historian, W. Cleon Skousen, for possible program use. As a whole, I thought Dr. Skousen's book was an excellent history of constitutional issues; but another member of the commission thought it should be automatically barred because it contained an essay written in the early 1930's that used the word "pickaninny" in an isolated reference to black children. Although I personally never used the term myself, it was often used in those days without apparent derogatory intent. *Uncle Tom's Cabin*, *Gone with the Wind*, Harry Truman's favorite waltz, and the Disney film *Song of the South* all use it. One of the main characters in Huckleberry Finn is called "Nigger Jim." In itself, this didn't seem to me to be an adequate reason for dismissing any of these works.

Of course, Safer did not then respond, "Oh, I see, you were misquoted and you actually are not a bigot." Safer, of course, was not interested in the truth, but only in filming the information his producers had scripted for him. I asked him what other examples of my "famous" racial insensitivity he could recall. Instead of answering, he changed the subject. As far as he was concerned, my only asset as a media attraction was my reputation as a racial bigot; without that he had no show.

Ted Koppel pursued me for two weeks to appear on *Nightline*. I finally agreed to do so when he swore that all he was interested in was letting his viewers see what was actually happening in Arizona. I told him I was not interested in being on his show to argue. He said there would just be the two of us to discuss what was really happening.

He broke his word from the first by coming on with an attack of what I was accused of doing by the local news sources, principally the *Republic & Gazette*.

I was in a small studio at Channel 3 in Phoenix, looking into one small monitor at Koppel in New York. The press was in an adjoining room apart from us, watching live monitors. My lawyer Murray Miller and Press Secretary Ken Smith were off camera, but still in the studio with me. Their wives were in the room with the press, who obviously did not know who they were. Sam Stanton from the *Republic* was bragging about being on the phone a lot of the day with Koppel to give him information on how to pepper me with accusations to try to make me look bad.

When it was obvious that Koppel wasn't keeping his word to let me tell the facts, I simply listened to his attacking questions. Then when he paused for my answers, I ignored his questions and gave some of the true facts on what my administration was doing. As the show went on, I gained a lot out of ignoring his accusatory questions and making my own points. Stanton went ballistic about how easy Koppel was being on me; Koppel was not using the material on me they had given him. One good thing about being on live TV—they cannot edit it before showing.

Koppel finally got so angry that he blurted out on the air, "Governor we are not here to show the good things you are doing."

One of the most amusing parts was when Koppel used the statistics the local media had provided to show that I was destroying tourism. The statistics he used showed conventions were boycotting Arizona for not having a MLK paid state holiday. I asked him where he got his statistics, and he answered from my own state Department of Tourism. I said no, he was using Phoenix Convention Center statistics, which had been going down for years because they did not have competitive facilities. Then I gave him the true tourism figures, based on hotel rooms filled. Phoenix area was up 10 percent and Tucson was up 42 percent year to date. The next business day his producer called my press secretary to pass on to me Koppel's apology for using the wrong figures. He had checked them out and found I was correct. Of course he did not make that correction on the air where the mistake was made. I had a similar experience with Jim Lehrer, but he became much fairer when I called his hand early on the program.

Leslie Stahl wanted to interview me on tape, but I refused. Television news often can change the meaning of what you say through clever editing. She then agreed to interview me live. I went to the local CBS affiliate Channel 10, and we had the interview. It was then that I found she had not been truthful with me; it was taped instead of live. When I watched it later, it was heavily edited to put their own "spin" on what I said.

If I had gone into office with any respect for the press, either local or national, I sure lost it in my experience of their coverage of my administration and me. If the accusations of any of the media people, the local ones in particular, had been founded on a sincere fear that I was a racist, there would have been some actual discussion of whether or not there was any evidence one way or the other. There was none.

In the meantime, Corbin and the establishment were as busy behind the scenes as they were posturing in front of them. The first request I had made of the attorney general back in January of 1987, was for a meaningful investigation of Turf Paradise, the state's largest privately owned horse track. The State Racing Commission had been suspected of allowing racetrack owners to break practically every regulation it was supposed to control. Among other things, there was no state supervision of pari-mutuel wagering at the track, as mandated by state law. On at least one documented occasion, a betting window remained open until after the horses crossed the finish line. The Investigative Reporters and Editors exposé on crime and corruption in Arizona had alleged multiple ties between some of the track owners, some of the leading families in the state, and organized crime. They claimed to have documented the track's laundering of Mafia money from Las Vegas skimming operations.

We had been interested in finding out how and why the Arizona Legislature had been persuaded to pass a racing bill in 1978. It was supposed to "quickly increase the money going to the state" by pouring millions of dollars of the state's share of the pari-mutuel revenues into improving the privately owned facilities of Turf Paradise. In addition to this, in a series of legislative bills, the state's share of the pari-mutuel handle was reduced, step by step, from seven percent to one percent. As you might expect, the amount of money going to the track owners skyrocketed while the state's revenue from pari-mutuel wagering at the track plummeted from $25,000 to less than $5,000 per race day. Where the state had formerly received one dollar for every two dollars of pari-mutuel money retained by the track, the state now receives only one dollar for every 20 dollars received by the owners of Turf Paradise. (The state has yet to see any of the $14,000,000 it gave to the owners of the track to improve their privately owned facilities.)

All of this we believed to be just the tip of the iceberg. We turned over documentary evidence to Corbin, indicating bribes had been made to get the bills through the legislature. Two special investigators from the AG's office went with one of my assistants to hear testimony concerning the bribing of a key legislator. Following this, the special investigators were pulled off the case and the investigation was quietly buried in the Attorney General's Office.

In the meantime, I had managed to replace a majority of the racing commission and had appointed an honest director of the Department of Racing, who was starting a real clean up. After several months, when we launched inquires to find out what Corbin was doing about the investigation, he had promised faithfully to carry out, we discovered that he had been much too busy to take any further action whatsoever in looking into the race track cesspool. Some of his time was spent helping Representative Jim Skelly kill a legal action taken by the Department of Racing against Skelly's partner in the ownership of several racehorses.

When the story became public, Skelly was quick to point out that he didn't have any personal ownership in the fast horse his partner had attempted to enter in a race at Prescott Downs under the name of a horse that had never won a race. No, Skelly didn't own any of that particular horse, but he did just happen to be at the track the day that the "ringer" was to run against heavy betting odds. Skelly claimed that the wrong horse had been brought to the paddock at the racetrack through an "honest mistake." However, it turned out that the "ringer," under a false identity, had been delivered, after the closing of the racing season at Turf Paradise, into the care and training of an unsuspecting "trainer of record" six weeks prior to the race at Prescott Downs. A few minutes before post time, the state identifier discovered that the horse scheduled to race that day did not match the papers on file in the race track office. Only then did the trainer of record learn that the horse he had been training a month and a half as "J.B.'s Joy" was a faster horse named "The Officer."

Skelly's partner, Frank Cavello, the horse's regular trainer at Turf Paradise, delivered the papers on J.B.'s Joy directly to the Prescott track, without disclosing to the unwitting trainer of record that he was training a different horse. One of the oldest scams in racing almost worked, and probably would have before we changed directors at the racing department. Naturally enough, under Tex Barron, the new director I had appointed, Cavello was fined and legal action was being taken to have him banned from racing. That is, until Skelly got together with some of his buddies in the Attorney General's Office. They instructed the Racing Department to refund the fine and drop the action against Cavello. It was their contention that the hearing by the Racing Department was held improperly, even though Skelly, Chairman of the House Judiciary Committee, had been present at the hearing to testify on behalf of his partner, without indicating any such impropriety.

Suddenly, trouble with Corbin began to surface everywhere. The first really deadly sign of trouble was when rumors began circulating around the Capitol that I had mishandled the inaugural ball funds.

I had appointed Bill Long chairman of a committee to put on the inaugural ball. We had a great group of volunteers for the event, and it was an elegant and memorable affair. Ralph Watkins, chairman of my campaign finance committee worked with them. It was anticipated that our inaugural ball, like those of previous governors, would take in far more money than it would cost to produce. And like the previous governors, we needed this surplus money to help pay off some of the $350,000 still outstanding on loans the campaign committee had taken out to pay campaign expenses. Because I was so busy putting together my administration, I left all the details to others and took in only an occasional briefing to keep abreast of what was taking place. Long and Watkins had queried the Attorney General's Office and the Secretary of State's Office to make sure all the proper procedures were being followed.

To make sure that all funds relating to the Ball were handled according to the law, the inaugural committee asked the Attorney General's Office for advice. I am told that Steve Twist, the chief

178

assistant AG and John Shadegg, the number three man in the AG's office, came and told them how to handle the money.

The money donated by corporations to pay inaugural ball costs was put in a special bank account so it could not be used for anything but ball expenses. In Arizona, corporations cannot legally contribute to political campaigns but can donate money for events that are not a part of a campaign.

The tickets to the ball were sold to individuals, and they clearly stated that all money left over from expenses would go to pay my campaign debts. The corporate donations were expensed first. The balance of the ball expenses was paid for out of the separate ticket sales bank account. After all costs were paid, the ticket sales bank account had a $92,000 balance, which we expected to apply to outstanding campaign notes.

Over the next few months, while Watkins reported that he was working out an occasional snag, things seemed to be going according to plan. Suddenly in mid-spring, Ralph said there was some concern over whether Proposition 200, the new law relating to campaign finances applied to my campaign. It had been approved by voters in the November election, so it did not become law until after our campaign was legally over. All the lawyers I talked to thought this was ridiculous. The Arizona Revised Statutes (Section 1-244) states that no law is retroactive unless it contains a special provision declaring it to be so, and Proposition 200 had contained no such provision.

Even if Prop. 200 did apply, the ticket price was far less than the amount allowed to be contributed under its provisions. I was told that a special action suit before the State Supreme Court was considered by some of the lawyers being consulted. It was dropped as not needed and unnecessary spending. I told Finance Chairman Ralph Watkins to make sure everything was done properly, and if there were any questions about anything the inaugural committee had done, to give the money back to the people who had paid it.

The tickets had been clearly stamped to the effect that their money, over and above what was needed to pay ball expenses, was going to be used to pay back my campaign debts, and I wasn't going to spend it on anything other than what I had promised.

The attack on the inaugural ball funds was started publicly by a January 8, 1997 article by Sam Stanton in the *Republic*. In it he wrote: "Gov. Evan Mecham's inaugural celebration raised about $100,000 to help reduce his campaign debt, but the money was raised by having some of Arizona's largest firms pay for most of the festivities. Arizona Public Service Co., Mountain Bell, Circle K Corp. and others were 'inaugural sponsors' and contributed thousands of dollars apiece to pay for Mecham's inaugural ball and private reception. These contributions allowed Mecham's fund-raisers to keep most of the proceeds from the tickets to the events to help pay off part of the campaign debt Mecham still faces. The use of corporate funds for such events is legal and has been done with other governors, Mecham' fund-raisers say. They say they took great care to stay within the state's tough new campaign-spending law. [Even though it did not pertain to our campaign.]

"Legally, I had this checked out from toe to toe,' fund-raiser Ralph Watkins Jr. said: 'I had this checked out by counsel, and I have no concern in my mind.'

"However, John Anderson, executive director of Common Cause in Arizona, said that the practice raises questions and that the state attorney general should look at the matter." This is another of those strange things that suddenly had a life of its own. If the new law they were concerned about did affect my inaugural events, then the provision that someone must file an official complaint before an investigation can be launched must be followed. It was not. There is no record of anyone ever filing a complaint about the handling of the inaugural funds. But that did not stop Sam Stanton and Mr. Corbin from proceeding to try to find something. It was not the first nor would it be the last time Mr. Corbin started a well-publicized investigation into something pertaining to me without a legal basis for doing it.

To my surprise, a month or so later, I was informed that Corbin's office considered the funds to be proscribed by Proposition 200, although specifically why that could be true, no one could tell me. On the other hand, our committee people informed me that nothing had been done that violated the new law, so we were not concerned.

In late May, Long and Joyce Downey, who had been handling the money, brought all of their records and the bank account materials to me with instructions that I could use the money for anything I wanted, as long as it didn't go directly toward campaign or personal living expenses.

I again asked the Attorney General's Office for clarification, only to be told that they could not now advise me on these matters because of a professed "conflict of interest." That is, they had told us how to handle the funds in the first place, and now it appeared they were planning a suit against me for following the instructions that assistant attorneys general Twist and Shadegg had given the inaugural committee. Calling this a "conflict of interest" is like calling the Kennedy assassination a "change in policy."

Former Governor Jack Williams had told me to prepare to spend about $25,000 per year in office for expenses that would not be paid by the state. Some examples were air travel costs for my wife when she accompanied me on trips, gifts to visiting officials from foreign countries, dinners for legislators, and some meetings that were more political than state business, etc. In most states, groups of supporters contribute to a fund for the governor to pay for what otherwise would be paid by him/her with private money.

I turned the records over to my chief of staff, Jim Colter, and told him and Edith Richardson to look after the account. Choosing not to challenge the conclusion that the money couldn't be used to pay campaign debts, we concluded that the account would last throughout my term of office.

Colter had informed me that the money was in a money market account for the duration and was earning a little over four percent. In July, I asked Colter whether we couldn't do better, since I knew that my own business was paying nine to 10 percent at the time. He said he didn't know of any place specific it could be invested at that rate. I called my son, Dennis, who was managing my automobile business, and told him to draw up some papers assigning our real estate as collateral, and we would lend him $80,000 of the money at nine percent interest, with the stipulation that it would be repaid in part or in full whenever we requested it.

Considering the way the media was treating us, Colter had some doubts about the appearance of the thing. But he had no question that it was legal. It was private, and I resented the idea that we should settle for 4.5 percent money market interest from the Valley National Bank when we could double that rate from Mecham Pontiac and keep it both safe and available.

In late September, Colter came into my office and told me people were saying the loan hadn't been a wise thing to do. He didn't tell me how anyone else could have come into that knowledge, but I was getting used to the whole world knowing almost my every thought.

He assured me again that the transaction was legal, but he was clearly upset about the whole thing, so I told him to go ahead and have Dennis return the money, including the nine percent interest while it was at the dealership. Shortly thereafter, Colter put the funds back into the inaugural ball account with the Valley National Bank where the balance of the funds had always been kept on deposit.

Throughout this first year, we were plagued by constant leaks of information from the ninth floor. Ralph Milstead, the attorney general, and numerous legislators seemed to know relatively intimate details of our conversations. We had our phone system checked, and found that Lieutenant Beau Johnson, head of my DPS security detachment, had been spending a good deal of time in an office on the eighth floor. This room had been equipped with not one phone, but several, all with multiple connections. After toying with the possibility for a while, I finally had one of my staff go check it out. Johnson had moved out, taking every scrap of phone equipment with him.

One of the main reasons I had picked Jim Colter as my chief of staff was because I had believed that, as a lawyer, Jim would understand the legal intricacies of our job, which I didn't. Jim was totally trustworthy and had a good knowledge of the political scene. I was sure that he could learn the necessary administrative skills. Unfortunately, that never happened. Jim wanted to get along with everybody, to have everybody like him. He wasn't a strong enough administrator to keep the other strong personalities we had in line and focused on working in the direction we had initially mapped out. My own management style relies heavily on delegating responsibility. If an assistant doesn't come back to me and ask questions, I assume he knows what he is doing. I wanted him to put together the agenda for our staff and cabinet meetings, with all my special assistants channeling their ideas and needs through him. But, he never did this well on his own. Consequently, I had to reach out and take things back to do myself what I had expected him to do. I am sure this only made him feel even less sure of himself.

Jim Colter worked his heart out, and it probably was clear to others long before it was to me that he was under too much strain, and in the end just wasn't functioning properly. By October, he came unraveled. We had a quiet talk in my office, and he left. A high profile casualty of the power brokers propaganda machine.

In varying degrees the power brokers propaganda machine probably worked on everyone. Twenty months of unprecedented daily negative news media attacks, with almost nothing positive, is enough to sink everyone who does not have a very strong competitive spirit.

In my own case, I believe I was sustained by the following facts:

1. I knew we were making excellent progress on doing what the people elected me to do. This kept me busy twelve hours per day, six days per week, and I had little time to reflect on the negative attacks.
2. I paid little attention to the negative news media.
3. I paid little attention to critics and enemies.
4. I knew we had done nothing legally, ethically, or morally wrong.
5. I thought I could out last the power brokers propaganda machine.

As it turned out, I erred in my reliance on the power brokers being law-abiding citizens. The numbers of people in high places they controlled, many of whom broke the law to impeach me out of office, totally surprised me. I was out of my league in that state of lawlessness.

**State Senator Evan Mecham and Secretary Ione
Simonson. 1961 in the Senate Chambers.**

Lt. Evan Mecham - October 1944

Aviation Cadet Mecham at Primary Flight School, Wickenburg, Arizona in October 1943.

Mecham Receives Pilot Wings and Commissioned a 2nd Lt. Williams Field, Arizona - June 1944

**Governor Evan Mecham and First Lady
Florence L. Mecham. Inaugural on
January 5, 1987**

**Gov. Mecham
Sworn in By Chief
Justice Gordon in
Front of Capitol
Building in Phoenix**

**Gov. Mecham -
Inaugural Address -
January 5, 1987**

**Gov. Mecham Addressing A.S.U. Commencement
May 1987**

**Official
Campaign
Photograph
1986**

**President Ronald Reagan Meets With Governor
Mecham in The Oval Office**

Vice President Bush Welcomes Gov. Mecham to his Office

Senator Barry Goldwater Greets Gov. Mecham

Rep. John McCain, Evan Mecham, Rep. Bob Stump, Rep. Eldon Rudd Meet in Washington - October 1986

U.S. Secretary of Education Bill Bennett and Gov. Evan Mecham

Gov. Evan Mecham Visits U.S. Secretary of The Interior Don Hodel

Gov. Evan Mecham and U.S. Senate Majority Leader Bob Dole

**Gov. Evan Mecham Addresses World Anti Communist
Convention in Taipei, Taiwan - August 1987**

**Sonora Mexico Gov. Felix Valdez and Arizona Gov.
Mecham have a laugh at the Arizona/Sonora
Commission Conference in Hermosillo**

Gov. Mecham and Chairman Chang of The Republic
of China Trade Association Cut the ribbon to Open
the Arizona Trade Office, The World Trade Center
in Taipei on October 9, 1987

Arizona State Commerce Department Director Tom Caldwell,
R.O.C. Trade Association Chairman Chang, and Arizona
Governor Mecham at Opening of The Arizona State Trade
Office in Taipei October 9, 1987

Gov. Mecham, Chairman Chang and Ray Russell (Special Assistant to Gov. Mecham) with Arizona and R.O.C. Trade Delegations at Trade Office Opening, October 9, 1987

Gov. Mecham Places a Wreath at The Tomb of the Unknown Soldier at Arlington Cemetery on December 7, 1987

Gov. and Mrs. Mecham and Central America Trip
Companions Have Lunch with the U.S. Ambassador to
Nicaragua at the Embassy in Managua

A Nicaragua Truck
(horse cart) Hauling
Produce to Market
in Managua

Arrival at Panama

Panama, 1st Stop on Tour of 5 Central American Nations Relating to Arizona National Guard Units Doing Summer Training Assignments in Central America. Accompanying Gov. and Mrs. Mecham (center-standing) are Standing L to R: Ron Bellus, Fred Craft, Rep. Eldon Rudd, Burt Kruglick and Ralph Watkins. Kneeling in Front: Mrs. Likus, Joe Smith, Ivan Sidney and Dave Udall.

Pope John Paul II is Welcomed to Arizona by Governor Mecham, on the Pope's Historic Visit to Arizona.

Gov. Mecham and the Pontiac Bonneville He Furnished the State, at No Cost, for His Own Transportation While Governor.

Gov. Ev and First Lady Florence at Home in 1987.

**Ground Breaking for Confederate Air Force
Hangar at Falcon Field in Mesa**

Chapter 13

THE OCTOBER ASSAULT
FROM FOUR FRONTS

"I leave them, therefore, to the reproof of their own consciences. If these do not condemn them, there will yet come a day when false witness will meet a Judge who has not slept over his slanders."

Jefferson

There's an old Doris Day movie called *Lover Come Back,* in which Rock Hudson plays an unscrupulous advertising executive who accidentally launches a really effective advertising campaign for a product called "Vip." People are lined up around Central Park to buy Vip. They sincerely believe that they need Vip. Some of them think there's a high-level government conspiracy to deprive them of it when, in actuality, it doesn't exist. Vip was merely a name Rock Hudson concocted in order to talk a model into going to bed with him.

By the anniversary of my victory in the general election, *Republic* and *Gazette* Publisher Murphy, and Attorney General Corbin and company, had done nearly that good a job in selling many Arizonans on the need to get me out of office. Generally sober-minded citizens were persuaded that I was the worst thing to happen in Arizona since the invention of cattle rustling. They just didn't know specifically why, but the constant daily news media barrage against me made the uninformed majority feel that there must be something bad about me. I had no way to get the truth out to the general public so they had nothing else to go on.

Author Sammy Jenkins, in his well researched book *Arizona's Fighting Governor*, wrote: "The evidence shows that there may be no parallel in history where the media made such a blatant and prolonged attack on a public official, as has been made on Governor Evan Mecham . . As research continued through interviews, study of over four thousand clippings from the Arizona scene and study of the facts in the story, objectivity became very elusive. When taken in the broad perspective, a clear pattern emerged. A conspiracy was in progress to drive Mecham from his constitutionally elected office as Governor of Arizona."

Jenkins further reported: "This writer's study of press clippings of the two dailies of which Murphy is publisher revealed that during the calendar period of twelve months, beginning January, 1987, the Phoenix Newspapers published approximately 2,000 pieces with reference to Mecham. These pieces included "news," straw polls, surveys, commentary, opinion and letters to the editor. From January, 1987, through mid-February, 1988, the Phoenix Newspapers had published in excess of 350 editorials and personal opinion columns, taking on the appearance of editorial, news or commentary with reference to Mecham. Most of the pieces ranged from negative connotation to savage degradation. In addition, over forty cartoons appeared in these two dailies, all in negative light to Mecham; ranging from an attack on his wife's personal dress standards, to making his religion an issue. As a media comparison, the dailies (2) in Tucson, Mesa, and Scottsdale, Arizona, ran a combined total of around 1,100 pieces on, or with reference to, the Mecham story, in the calendar year of 1987.

"To attempt some show of even handedness, the *Republic* ran some letters favorable to Mecham, like the following from Peter J. Watt of Glendale: 'As the saga unfolds, Governor Evan Mecham is emerging as a man of intestinal fortitude and courage. He has a noose around his neck, a gun to his head and is dangling over a pit of hungry crocodiles, but he won't say "uncle." With a pack of political wolves at this heels and accused of bigotry, theft, misconduct, lying, cheating and any number of malicious deeds, and facing a triple threat of trial, impeachment and recall election, Mecham still refuses to run. All the odds are stacked against this man. The press hounds him, while television broadcasts a special prosecution by William French featuring the Department of Public Safety and former aides. Even Chrysler and General Motors are threatening his financial future, and still Mecham will not fold his hand. A guilty man would look for a deal, and a guilty man would fade out with as little loss as possible. Mecham's refusal to submit to overwhelming odds suggests that all these charges may be inflated out of proportion, and the paranoia may be on the part of his opposition. So much overkill. It's hang Mecham by public lynching or whatever means. Why all the rush and hysteria? Is there something about Mecham's values and ideals causing all this fear in his opponents? If he overcomes the first two hurdles, I'm voting for a courageous, unyielding man who stands firm in the face of adversity. Mecham is not perfect by any definition, but he's one hell of a man who has earned support.'"

The power brokers had created an enormous appetite for my lynching, but they still had nothing real to sell to the court. The moment for their action had arrived. Their personal need for my impeachment was imminent, but they needed the appearance of a legal tree limb to hang their rope from. They hadn't been worried before, because practically anyone in public life can be accused of something, but now they were looking into the bottom of the barrel and really didn't see much. I have often thought how ironic it was for them to spend so much money, time, and attention to try to get something on me and have to settle for the manufactured case they used. Corbin had known about our use of the inaugural fund since before its inception. After all, we'd asked his office how we should handle the inaugural ball contributions so we could legally use them as the people who gave them intended. Most lawyers I've talked to seem to think that Proposition 200, which was not yet law when I incurred my campaign expenses, did not really apply to those expenses. Furthermore, the $25 for tickets to the Ball, and even the $250 cost of each ticket for the special reception that preceded the Ball, were well below the contribution limit of Proposition 200. If there had been any real legal questions about the fund, Corbin had ample opportunity to address them, but steadfastly refused to do so. They were always available for his inspection.

Even in October, 1987, when the press made a big expose of the fact that $80,000 of the Inaugural Fund had been taken from the money market account at the Valley National Bank at 4.5 percent and loaned to my automobile dealership at nine percent, it seemed like no big deal. I had not "used" the money but just transferred it from one corporation paying 4.5 percent and loaned it to another for nine percent. The money had been returned from Mecham Pontiac and put back in the VNB money market account again when some thought it did not look good. It made good business sense but bad political sense, so we followed the political sense. Even Corbin stated to my *Arizona Republic* shadow, Stanton, that there was no legal basis for any charge against me concerning the fund because it was private, not state money. Had it been state money, Corbin would have quickly had me indicted for misuse of state funds. That is what French did because in the impeachment, he did not need any proof. The accusation was sufficient. It enabled the news media to proclaim that I had misused state funds. It has been printed in hundreds of articles ever since, and even as late as April of 1998, *The Arizona Republic* printed that total falsehood in an article by Mike McCloy.

In early October, Corbin's office had gone over our campaign reports with Chief of Staff Jim Colter and attorney Bob L'Ecuyer, and told them that while there appeared to be a few early mistakes, we had obviously made good faith efforts and could clear up everything. That is the way every question has been settled with the many dozens of candidates where questions about campaign reports have been raised. Mine was the single exception, right on down to the present spring of 1998.

Corbin decided to center his attack on me on campaign finance reporting. He had to know that he had no real hope of convicting me on any count. The only thing that made sense was that there was a master plan by the power brokers, and he was their coordinator. The minimum goal was to remove me from office so they could again run Arizona state government. The hoped for goal was to break me financially and put me in prison so that neither I, nor anyone else, would rise up again and challenge their supremacy in Arizona.

As a result of Corbin's mid-October meeting with House Speaker Joe Lane, House Majority Whip Jane Hull, and Lane's Chief of Staff Rick Collins, Lane let it be known that Corbin said he would indict me on at least 12 felony counts, stating further that the House should get started on Impeachment Hearings right away. With me facing a certain recall election in late spring, and with Corbin's widely publicized "secret" grand jury investigation a "certainty" to produce 12 felony count indictments, no one has yet come up with a sensible reason to start looking into impeachment. It was soon to become clear why.

Their plan was to attack me from four directions at the same time:

1. Recall Election

Early on, the recall movement had little success because the effort was based mostly on paying professional petition circulators to get the signatures, and the recall organizers did not have much money. Not many people were willing to contribute because they did not want their name on the contributors' list that had to be filed with the reports to the Secretary of State's Office. To correct this problem, the recall committee took their request to be exempt from reporting before the state Supreme Court and their request was granted. They had no requirements to report contributions or expenditures.

Fife Symington held a joint press conference with Ed Buck and, with a public flourish, handed Buck a $2,000 check and urged all the business people to join him to help get rid of Governor Mecham. The money began to flow; busloads of people came from as far as California to join the professional army of signature gatherers.

By furnishing plenty of money to buy signatures on the recall election petitions, they felt secure they could subject me to a recall election in the spring. We received a number of reports that many of their signatures were not valid. One person told us that many signatures were secured by having 15 people surround a table. Each would have a list of registered voters. Each petition had 15 signature spaces and each person signed one registered voter's name on each petition that passed so they completed lots of forged petitions. Our informant did not want to get involved, but wanted us to know the law was being broken. We expected the county recorders to check the petition signatures against the voter registration forms to see if they matched. The county recorders failed to do that, so there was no way to catch what our reports said were widespread forgeries. When we discovered this, it was too late to check them ourselves.

They knew they had accomplished the recall, but they had no comfort level that I would not win the recall election. In spite of their concern that I was the favorite to win the recall, they got lots of good out of it in daily negative publication benefits. It was accomplishing its goal without the recall ever taking place.

2. Corbin's Grand Jury Investigation

Corbin was to indict me on as many felony counts as he could possibly dream up. To indict a sitting governor who is already weakened by 15 months of negative press is a devastating blow. Even then, Corbin could not get the 23rd Grand Jury to indict me. They had been sitting for several months, and by then they were on to the sneaky ways of the AG prosecutors. By impaneling a green 24th Grand Jury and spoon feeding them only what Corbin wanted them to hear, Corbin was able to get six felony indictments against me and three against my brother, Willard. This is the method by which governors in the United States have been removed from office, if found guilty.

3. Impeachment

If they had had confidence that they could remove me from office by either of the previous two, they would have stopped there. But even in the summer of 1987, when they first hatched the plan, they knew impeachment was the only way they could absolutely control the process and succeed. They needed no election to overturn the people's elected choice. They did not have to prove any wrongdoing. All they had to do was to put on a good show to confuse the people and be able to control enough votes in the Legislature to get the desired results. It was a totally political tribunal. Had they had to conduct it according to any rules of evidence and abide by criminal court procedures, the result would have been different.

The senators had their own rules made up without any input from my defense. In effect, they ran the prosecution and then made the judgement. The prosecution lawyers had been preparing their case since October, but they refused to share their evidence with the defense, as they must in a court of law. An unbiased jury is the foundation of our justice system. In the Senate Impeachment Trial they started with enough votes to convict before even starting the trial.

4. Resignation

Early in October, Tony West was spreading the rumor that I would resign by the end of the month. Joe Lane was engaged in that effort to get some friends and my family to get me to resign. It was one of the regular questions being asked of me by the news media. My own new Chief of Staff, Dick Burke, made regular suggestions that he thought he could get everything dropped if I would resign. All but Representative Stump of our Washington delegation piled on. Then the most disgusting and hypocritical suggestion of resignation came from Rep. Jon Kyle and Senator John McCain in an early January meeting, the details of which will be covered later in this book. The key thing about resigning was that none of my family or friends ever suggested I should resign. Innocent people do not resign!

It was no surprise when we heard that the grand jury had been called and was in full swing. It was November 2nd, when the attorney general's prosecutors started presenting evidence to the 23rd Grand Jury. Stories suggesting that I had committed serious felonies had been regularly leaked to the press for about three weeks. The stories claimed that the boiler plate confidentiality letter I had signed for Wolfson was a "smoking gun," which implied a secret agreement to hide Wolfson's assistance to my campaign. Speaker of the House Joe Lane kept alive his story that Corbin told him I would be indicted on at least 12 felony counts and that the Legislature should get going on their Impeachment hearings, now. Corbin later denied this, since this revealed their entire strategy, or would have, if the press had cared to report it.

Arizona law provides that any high official convicted of a felony is automatically removed from office, and it also provides that Impeachment hearings are used only when that procedure is the only way to "reach" a high public official. According to Corbin, I was about "reached" by indictments from his second (24th) grand jury. This meant that I had to defend myself against the impeachment charges of the Legislature at the same time I was defending myself in criminal court. And had I been convicted, I would automatically have been removed as governor and could possibly even have been sent to jail. Not only was I being "reached" through the regular court proceedings, the recall election had already been certified so that the voters could have voted me out of office if they so desired. According to Arizona law, there was no legal basis for the Legislature to proceed with impeachment proceedings. Francis X. Gordon, Chief Justice of the Arizona Supreme Court, who presided over the Senate Impeachment Trial, said the same thing over radio station KTAR just a few days after the Senate trial. A word from him would have stopped the delicately balanced impeachment. The only explanation that makes sense is that he had his orders from the power brokers. Why he went ahead and presided over an impeachment instead of leaving any charge of law breaking to the Superior Court trial already scheduled, has no other sensible answer.

Wrongful Impeachment

There was only one reason why the impeachment hearings were rushed through the legislature. The "establishment" knew the criminal charges Corbin brought against me would not hold up in front of a jury. They also feared the voters would give me the victory in the recall election scheduled for May. The one sure way to get me out of office was a political trial in the Legislature, where conviction is not determined by the evidence but on the number of votes controlled by the power structure.

On October 22nd, House Speaker Joe Lane told one legislator that he was in no hurry to do anything, but he had to go uptown to talk to the "big boys" about it. Within four days, Lane, House Majority Whip Jane Hull, and Rick Collins (Collins was Burton Barr's Chief of Staff and is now the same for Lane), without consulting the rest of the Legislature, had hired a liberal Democrat, William French, to "advise" the House as to how to handle an Impeachment hearing, if one should become necessary. It was clear that Lane had received his marching orders from the power brokers.

What really worried me about French was his former membership on the corruption-riddled state Racing Commission. He had served one term on the Commission as a Babbitt appointee and was undoubtedly cognizant of numerous activities that we had been trying unsuccessfully to get Corbin to investigate. He had been re-appointed to a second term by Babbitt, before the latter left office, but had not yet been confirmed by the Senate when I took office. Since our investigations had convinced me that French must have known what was going on in the Racing Department, I appointed another person, instead, whose honesty I could count on.

In official transcripts of some of the meetings of the Racing Commission on which French (a former judge) sat, the Director of Racing Tim Barrow, admitted to violating state law. Barrow said he illegally transmitted racing results to gambling houses in Nevada and delayed post times to change betting odds at a dog track in Tucson "in the best interests" of the betting public, but promised that "it would never happen again."

French, as well as others on the commission, closed his eyes to these illegal activities, and now, as a darling of the establishment, was going to prosecute me. He was also publicly vocal about the fact that he had signed a recall petition against me.

It proves how corrupt Arizona had become. For the Republican Speaker of the House to hire a liberal Democrat, with his Racing Commission ties, to set up an illegal impeachment to remove the Republican Governor, could not have happened in any other state. Justice, fairness, and even party political considerations were swept aside to give the control of the state government back to the power brokers. It was a disgrace that Arizona would never live down when future generations read about this raw use of political power by Arizona's un-elected rulers.

Lane hired French for a reported $150,000, supposedly to prepare a set of procedures for the Legislature to follow "just in case" Corbin came up with some kind of charge against me. This didn't make sense because if Corbin came up with a charge, it would entail a trial in criminal court, not a House impeachment hearing. Instead, with what the Phoenix papers perceived as "his zeal for objectivity," French immediately went to work as a prosecutor, determined to get a conviction at any cost. The power brokers weren't taking any chances.

While still on retainer to the House for procedural guidance, French was really working under Corbin's control. Early on, Corbin gave him a list of 25 possible criminal indictments. He spent his time trying to make a criminal case while the legislative staff lawyers did the impeachment procedural research and preparation that French was supposedly hired for.

An author friend of mine doing research for a book he is writing, recently talked to one of the House staff lawyers about who was doing the House research and preparations, that Lane said French was hired to do. He told my friend that I had been badly treated and agreed to talk at length on what really happened. Then he cancelled the appointment. Even now, ten years later, he is afraid to talk, for fear of retribution. What retribution? He no longer works for the state.

French added two new charges of his own to Corbin's. Corbin could not use them in criminal court because there was no real evidence to support a charge of mis-using state funds or obstruction of justice. But, since French was also designing the procedures to be used for my prosecution in the Legislature, he could establish the rules by which he could virtually make anything of his choosing instantly legal in the House proceedings. In effect, he became judge, jury, and prosecutor, limiting the defense to only those rules that he himself established. I repeat again, he knew he did not have to prove anything for a conviction in the Senate. He knew he had the votes to convict before the senate trial even started.

The press continued to massage the grand jury announcement, and the recall committee was overjoyed. The general objective of all this seemed to be to force my resignation before they had to make good on any of their accusations.

The newspapers helped out by announcing that just about everyone they could think of wanted me to resign, whether or not they had actually spoken to these people about it. When Dave Becker, from the *Mesa Tribune*, called up Wolfson and asked him if he didn't think Mecham would have trouble being effective with the Legislature under these condition, Wolfson simply replied, "That's possible." Next day, the *Tribune* announced that Wolfson had called for my resignation.

Lane tried to apply as much personal pressure as he could to get me to resign. Early in October, he called Glenda Orr, chairman of the Graham Country GOP, and told her he had bad news. He told her that Attorney General Corbin said they had a sure 12-count indictment coming out of the grand jury. (Mind you, this assurance was made in October, even though the grand jury did not take any evidence until after November 3rd, 1987.) Lane said they would have to impeach Mecham, and it would be ugly and dirty. He asked her to come over to the Capitol with others in eight or ten days to get me to resign. He said he understood that I had a nice family, and by resigning it would save the family from the disgrace of impeachment for generations.

Lane then called a friend of my eldest son's wife, Linda, to try to talk her into convincing my family to pressure me in the same way. If I didn't resign, Lane said, the disgrace I would bring them would hurt everyone in the Mecham family for generations to come.

Lane obviously didn't know much about my family. And despite his loudly acclaimed concern for their welfare, he absolutely refused to sit down with anyone representing me to discuss what he was doing. He said his lawyers had warned him against it. He had to remain "impartial," in case he had to go ahead and conduct the Impeachment Hearing.

Publisher, Pat Murphy, offered further logic for my resignation: I should save the state money by making the recall election unnecessary. Apparently he didn't see the irony in giving a rationale like this. He was one of the very people who helped create the expense of the recall election and the many millions more spent in prosecuting me in the Legislature and the courts.

A parade of my usual legislative critics began calling for my resignation. Because, like everyone else, they knew that Corbin would end up charging me with something, it was hardly important that I hadn't yet even been accused of anything. Congressman Kolbe was the first of Arizona's Washington delegates to announce that I should resign for the good of the party and the state. He was joined by McCain, and all the others except Rep. Bob Stump. State Senator Tony West announced that I would probably resign before the end of October.

The voters, however, failed to line up so easily. The GOP District 18 state representatives and senator called a sort of press "non-conference" for the October meeting of this old home district of Burton Barr. Here they planned to announce the complete defection of public support for me. Senator Tony West, House Majority Whip Jane Hull, and Rep. George Weisz, the district's legislators, were to break the champagne bottle over the establishment's steamroller by being the first local Republicans to officially call for my resignation "for the good of the party and the state."

They seemed enormously surprised when the grass-roots party machine at first refused to budge, and then started to back over them. Like nearly all politicians whose real allegiance is to the establishment rather than to the people, they were too eager to believe that the people didn't care about what was really happening in the government. The precinct committeemen saw that I'd been keeping my campaign promises and had been doing my best to advance a truly conservative agenda, so they were solidly behind me. Instead of leading my funeral parade before appreciative reporters (who had attended the meeting en masse on a tip from Jane Hull about what they were going to do), the three legislators suddenly found themselves confronted by an angry crowd of Republican foot soldiers. They wanted to know why the politicians were betraying the first governor in over a decade who had really advanced the people's interests. Still visibly shaken a few days later, Hull confided to another House member that she might just be seeing the end of her own political career. Neither Senator West nor the other House member, Weisz, even bothered to run for their seats in the primary election the following year.

How could elected Republicans who really believed in the expressed tenets of the Republican Party, whose first concern was really the good governing of the state, never once in their "agony" speak about the likely consequences of my resignation? One has to conclude that far too many legislators' first loyalty was to the power brokers, not the Republican Party nor the best interests of the State. What about the really serious political considerations at stake here? For instance, what about the fact that my resignation would result in the ascendancy of a Democrat to the governor's office and the consequent waste of millions of dollars through excessive government spending that would result? What about the loss of Republican appointees, not only to the executive part of state government but also to the judiciary? In the spending category, it was obvious that too many Republican legislators wanted more spending and wanted to get me out of their way in doing so.

The appointments to the bench made by Babbitt over the past nine years had radically changed the course of state law. When these legislators, who claimed to be so selflessly concerned for the good of the party, discussed the need for my resignation, why were they never willing to discuss those consequences? Well, you can bet they were discussed at the precinct level, where workers were primarily concerned about how government affected their lives.

The grand finale to the resignation routine didn't come for several more months. Just after the New Year, Senator McCain and Congressman Jon Kyl asked to meet with me in private. I think their "visit" was sparked by recollection that it had been two Arizona Republicans, Barry Goldwater and John Rhodes, who had finally convinced Nixon to resign, and McCain and Kyl liked to envision themselves in a similar role with me. The difference was that I hadn't lied to anybody, no buildings had been broken into, no crime had been committed. I saw no similarity between Nixon's plight and my own, however much the editorial writers and cartoonists of the Phoenix press seemed to relish the comparison.

McCain and Kyl insisted no one else would know about the meeting, but before it occurred, they met with all the other Republicans, except Stump, to plan their strategy, and I heard about it. So that they wouldn't be able to misconstrue this "private meeting" for the press, I insisted on having my own witnesses present. The meeting was held at the office of Murray Miller, my lawyer at that time. They said they hadn't come to ask me to resign, but thought I ought to consider it so that I could devote my energies to my defense in the upcoming criminal trial. They also professed concern about how the state government could operate effectively under the circumstances. Since none of this was new, I knew that the whole meeting had been a press set-up all along, and was glad for my witnesses. As they were leaving, they again assured me that the entire conversation would remain private. Within minutes of their exit, the press was reporting exactly what they'd said to me and calling on me for a response.

As far as I could follow, the reasoning of McCain, Kyl, Rhodes, Kolbe, Udall and DeConcini was that since they had to keep berating me in the press, I was creating a lot of bad publicity for our state. Because my political enemies were doing everything in their power to prevent me from doing the job I'd been elected to do, I ought to quit trying to do it. I was unconvinced. I still owed it to the people who had elected me to clean up the state to stay on and keep the power brokers from taking it back. It was very obvious that the power brokers were willing to pull out all the stops to get me out, so they could again control Arizona for their own benefit.

Looking back, I now question the relative honesty and integrity of McCain, Kyl, and Kolbe. While they took an aggressive lead in trying to bring about my resignation, they were noticeably silent when the federal prosecutors indicted Symington on 25 felony counts in 1996. In fact, they were all vocally supportive of Fife even though the accusations against him were much more serious than the ones against me. Even after his conviction on six of the counts forced his resignation, they were doing what they could to help him get a reduced sentence.

Perhaps it is worthwhile to mention that when Symington was indicted, the news media descended on me to get my response to his plight. They invited and expected me to repay him in kind for his strong and vocal call for my resignation or impeachment in 1987-88.

To their surprise and dismay, I refused to join the many who were calling for his resignation or impeachment. I told them that two wrongs do not make one right. I pointed out, if we want Arizona to be respected as a state governed by laws we must adhere to our laws. Now that he had been indicted, we should let the legal system work. He should be given the presumption of innocence until the court came to a trial and a decision. Once that decision was made, then we should all abide by it. If he were convicted, he would be removed from office. If he were acquitted, he would remain as governor. I reminded them that I would like to have been treated that way. In fact, I'm convinced had I been given the same courtesy, I would probably still be governor.

Although Senator DeConcini and I have been on opposite sides of some political issues, we have always been personally friendly. He was the only one publicly calling for my resignation that surprised and disappointed me. I had thought of him as being more honest and having more integrity than to join in with the power broker's minions in their well-orchestrated call for me to resign. On a recent occasion I phoned him and, to my surprise, the first thing he said was how sorry he was that he had called for my resignation in early 1988. He said the reason he had done so was only because Attorney General Corbin told him he had me indicted and was sure of a conviction on enough counts to put me in prison for many years. He knew he should not have trusted Corbin and asked me to accept his apology, which I did.

At the State Republican Annual Convention, the party workers again made their opinions clear. Of all the high office holders, only Representative Stump, my sole supporter in the congressional delegation, and I received a warm welcome when we spoke. I was enthusiastically received and wildly applauded. McCain, Rhodes, and Kyl, appearing to be sticking to their statement that they wouldn't presume to call on me to resign, just looked around and waited for the convention to end. That very afternoon, the three of them, along with Congressman Kolbe, assembled a press conference before the state Capitol and publicly called for my resignation. The party workers were livid. But since the convention was over, their reaction and accusations that the McCain group was destroying the party, wasn't entitled to any kind of press coverage.

It was obvious they were following the orders of the power brokers. I had not broken my word to anyone, nor lied, nor broken any law. No lawyer with any knowledge thought Corbin's flimsy indictments would stand up in court. They all knew that if I resigned, it would turn the governorship over to a Democrat and yet these Republican office holders were doing all they could to bring that about. Then they had the audacity to say they wanted it done for the good of the party.

Throughout the resignation fiasco, the press kept asking me what it was that would make me want to resign. So I told them that I would resign when the "good people of Arizona" asked me to. They weren't reporting anything said by anyone without power and position, so they were skeptical that I could be talking about much of anybody. The "good people" part brought on a lot of derision from those who weren't, so I explained myself as simply as possible. As far as I was concerned, the good people were the ones with traditional moral and family values, who followed constitutional principles and what some of us thought were Republican principles of effective and economical government. They were the ones who wanted to get rid of drugs, pornography, and the corruption in our state government. Although they weren't being heard in the press, I was hearing from them by the thousands, by phone calls and letters and word of mouth. They were telling me that they were praying for the welfare of my family and me. They were telling me to "Hang in there!" They had elected me. I wasn't going to let them down, to tell them their votes meant nothing by me resigning.

My refusal to resign only made the power brokers more determined than ever not to let the issue of my administration be settled by Arizona's voters. I had naturally been upset by the recall movement, by their personal attacks on me and by the prospect of having to run for governor twice in two years. But, by this time I'd come to welcome the idea of a real plebiscite that would allow the people to determine whether or not my administration was accomplishing what they, the majority of the voters wanted. Ironically, the recall had become my best chance of forcing the establishment to back off and let me govern.

The October Assault From Four Fronts

Chapter 14

INNOCENT PEOPLE
DO NOT RESIGN

"So that we may boldly say, the Lord is my helper, and I will not fear what man shall do unto me."
Hebrews 13:6

The AG's lawyers got into their three point stances in front of Corbin and prepared for his call. They had known about the Wolfson loan for a year. Donna Carlson had been one of the co-signers and had been telling Corbin and Milstead everything she could think of about us all along. But there were obvious weaknesses to this line of attack. For one thing, Wolfson had never received anything except the 10 percent interest in return for the loan, so there was no way of implying an unsavory motive on his part for making it. He had been getting seven percent from the bank where he had previously kept the money, now he was getting 10 percent. For another, I had no need to mis-report the loan in order to hide it. If that had ever been my intention, I could simply have had my business borrow the money from Wolfson and then have the business lend it to me personally. And why would I report a $30,000 contribution from Wolfson and Gregan at the same time I was hiding the loan? Why not just hide the whole $380,000? Or, why not delay the contribution until after the pre-election reporting deadline? The accusation that I had tried to hide the loan simply made no sense. I had no motive to hide it.

Furthermore, no one in Arizona history had ever been criminally accused, let alone convicted, of a campaign reporting violation. Corbin had regularly whitewashed every campaign contribution investigation ever made into the affairs of his powerful friends. His "investigation" of illegal contributions made by a political action group called Two on Your Side, or "TOYS," during the 1986 campaign was typical. While Ted Humes was running for the Corporation Commission, his opponent, Renz Jennings falsely accused Humes of receiving money from the utility companies. Jennings hadn't a shred of proof, but the accusation was treated sympathetically by the media, even though receiving campaign contributions from a corporation under those conditions would have been a serious felony. Humes, a lawyer, decided to do some checking of his own, and discovered curious contributions to Jennings and one other candidate from TOYS.

Humes filed a complaint with the attorney general, documenting the fact that TOYS had never registered as a campaign committee as required by law. Its only address was a post office box that turned out to be rented by Arizona's premier Democratic campaign consultant, Rick DeGraw. Two days after the complaint was filed with the AG's Office, TOYS suddenly registered with the secretary of state, although the registration was unsigned and almost two years late. Four days later, Corbin told Humes he had looked into TOYS and couldn't find any wrong doing.

When Corbin reported this, he already knew that TOYS had been collecting and spending campaign funds over a two-year period without being legally registered. Humes' accusation had documented that much. He also knew that TOYS was made up of DeGraw (at that time busy on Babbitt's presidential campaign), Senator Dennis DeConcini, Phoenix Mayor Terry Goddard, and Paul Eckstein, the same lawyer who, along with William French, would prosecute me in my impeachment trial in the House and Senate.

So much for two-party politics. Here was a Republican attorney general protecting high profile Democrats (the group above). He then illegally abuses his office to coordinate the removal of a Republican governor who had broken no laws.

When Humes filed a formal complaint with Corbin against TOYS, alleging more than 20 serious violations of Arizona's campaign laws, the Attorney General's Office did not even bother to respond to it. Instead, Corbin merely told the press that there had never been any "intent" to violate the law. Never mind that three of the most sophisticated campaigners in the state must have known what they were doing when they hid this political action committee behind a post office box. DeGraw claimed the committee was two years late in filing because they had changed bookkeepers. Eckstein later accused my brother, Willard, neither an accountant nor a lawyer, of mistakenly filing the Wolfson loan when he followed instructions from the sec. of state. But in his own very flagrant case, he felt the matter was sufficiently explained as "neglect, pure neglect." DeConcini and Goddard wisely remained silent.

Then, a week later, it was Corbin who became silent when he received a follow-up letter that showed 10 corporate contributions to TOYS, each a Class 6 felony. Then, as ever, he was much too busy to investigate.

Errors and oversights occur all the time in election finance reports. In fact, every major candidate associated with the gubernatorial election of 1986, had made reporting errors. Perhaps because of that, the most rigorous enforcement ever sought by the AG's office (other than mine) had been merely a request that an amended report be filed. Leo Corbett, who won the GOP nomination for governor in 1982, had not even bothered to file his contributions and spending report by 1986. Neither had Duayne Pell, who ran in a Phoenix City Council race.

We didn't think we'd done anything wrong, but when the question of a possible impropriety was first raised, we filed an amended report without being asked to. No one had been hurt by the alleged error. We had not profited from it in any way, nor had anyone else.

Under any legitimate scenario, impaneling a grand jury at this point can only be seen as an unfounded and overtly murderous act. As a lawyer, Corbin knew that neither of these matters could produce a charge that would stand up in court, so he continued to hesitate. This no doubt frustrated his partners, who cared less for the substance and form of the law than he did. They had created a feeding frenzy, and had to do something quickly to feed the sharks.

Therefore, the attorney general pulled out his all-purpose weapon, the grand jury investigation.

Of course, Corbin couldn't just come out and say, "Hey, you know the loan documents that were purloined from your office by Donna Carlson can't be legally produced in court. And since we've known all along, it's not proof of anything. We're just gonna call it a smoking gun and use *that* allegation as an excuse to impeach you." Instead the AG's office gave the nod to Carlson to "leak" the story of the Wolfson loan to Sam Stanton at *The Arizona Republic*, along with a copy of the letter outlining the terms of the loan agreement that presumably she had taken from Colter's files. Corbin could then call up Stanton in mock-shock and demand to see the documents. Everything would be nice and tidy to state the accusations around, which they could perfect their impeachment, the only sure way to remove me from office

If Corbin had any real hope of finding me guilty of some crime here, even one never before enforced, he could simply have filed a complaint or an "information" against me in court and subpoenaed my campaign finance records. Under Arizona law (A.R.S. 16-903-B, to be exact), he was entitled to see them at any time, with or without a complaint being filed. But then he would have had to bring his accusations before a judge, who would probably have thrown him out for lack of evidence. We asked for an open hearing to no avail. We had nothing to hide and wanted the whole world to see and hear the facts.

A grand jury was more effective for Corbin for a number of reasons. First, the sound of a "grand jury investigation" is extraordinarily ominous. (Most people don't realize that it is only called "grand" because more people sit on it than do on a normal jury.) Even if Corbin came up empty handed and the jury laughed him out of court, the fact that I had been the subject of a grand jury investigation was bound to weaken me in the recall election. Second, if the jury did laugh him out, no one would know about it because the proceedings are supposed to be kept secret. That is, they are secret to the extent he wants them to be. Corbin's staff regularly leaked negative information to the press throughout his investigation, to which I was prevented from responding because the proceedings were supposedly "secret." Third, the grand jury

---

has broad investigative powers. Corbin could call anyone he wanted into court, threaten him or her with contempt charges if they didn't tell him what he wanted to hear, and prevent me from putting up any kind of defense whatsoever. These investigative powers allowed him to go "fishing" for possible wrong-doing in ways that are forbidden in a trial court, where the prosecution supposedly knows what crimes were committed before the defendant is charged with being guilty of committing them.

Since there were no dirty secrets lurking under the surface of my administration, Corbin's fishing expedition turned up very little. With things looking so doubtful, he put out a call for help to his henchmen. Milstead, the self-styled macho man head of DPS, could be counted on to do anything in his power to get rid of me. Milstead felt the pressure to do something about me because he knew I was planning to replace him. If he were deposed, the enemies he had so ruthlessly dealt with over the years might finally have a chance to get even. If any of them had ever had the opportunity to dig into DPS business and document his transgressions, they certainly would have. He kept insisting to his friends that I was only scrutinizing him because Max Hawkins was out to even their old score. Milstead didn't want to understand my administration on any other terms.

In any event, he was ready to believe Donna Carlson when she came to him with her latest bit of hysteria. I had told her I was about to place him on administrative leave if he didn't voluntarily resign.

After I had Alberto Gutier, who I had appointed as director of personnel, make an initial investigation of Milstead, more charges against the DPS director by former employees had continued to find their way to my desk. Gutier found the DPS situation a mixed bag, but, all in all, quite a group of people were confused by poor leadership in the department.

This investigation led me to believe that Sam Lewis, director of the prison system, should also be replaced as well as Milstead. Lewis was building a big central office bureaucracy instead of putting his support into the prisons themselves. He had established a large internal investigation staff, which he used to keep every one in fear of him, much as Milstead had done in DPS.

Yet he seemed incapable of doing enough internal policing to find why assets were missing in the department. He told me he would come up with a plan to revive the farming operation at Florence, which had once produced much of the food consumed by the prisoners. He was to also suggest other means to get those who wanted to work and learn, an opportunity to do so. He had not done any of that. ARCOR, the prison industries division, was losing money in a big way with no improvement in sight. A federal prison inspection team had made a report to us at our invitation, and it showed a sub-standard administration of our corrections system.

By August, 1987, I had enough information to prove that both should be dismissed for cause. I planned to replace Lewis in September, and then move on Milstead a month later. But at that very moment, Sam Steiger, my assistant overseeing these departments, fell flat on his face into his own trouble.

Unfortunately, it came at the hands of a person he had befriended and enabled to keep his job on the parole board. We knew we had problems with the parole board, and reforming it was going to be part of our over-all program in straightening up the corrections department. But for the time being, the only reforming we could do would be in the opening for appointments on the board.

Ron Johnson, a former justice of the peace in South Phoenix, had been one of the parole board members long enough for his term to expire. The job was very desirable as it paid $44,000 a year and only took about 20 hours per week. Steiger suggested strongly that I re-appoint Ron Johnson. We had reports he had done a good job as a J.P. and Sam said he had interviewed him. He said Ron would work very closely with us in our desire to improve the functions and activities of the parole board.

Steiger had picked out Pat Costello, who had been on the campaign office staff and then had been my appointment secretary, to move into the executive directorship of the parole board. It looked like a good spot to have one of our own people to take, and Johnson pledged to support that move.

Internal problems developed at the parole board after a few months and Johnson changed his allegiance, siding with the group that wanted to remove Costello and return Theresa Gilbert to the position. Apparently Johnson also was waiting for an appointment to function as a part-time "pro-tem" justice of the peace in the Tempe area. Maricopa County Presiding Judge Michael Dan was making this appointment. Johnson's vote was the swing vote, and Steiger evidently put the pressure on Johnson. Steiger told Johnson that if he did not continue to support Pat Costello, that Steiger would see that he would not be appointed to function as a pro-tem J. P. in Tempe. All of this was without my knowledge.

Steiger should have known that he did not have any power to keep Johnson from functioning there, and neither did I for that matter. Johnson had been safely re-appointed to the parole board, and that was the extent of our power over him until his term came up. Johnson ignored Steiger's warning and voted to oust Costello. Then Johnson, after about three dry runs, was successful in going to the Attorney General's Office where they tape-recorded the telephone conversation of Steiger telling Johnson he was going to follow through and see that he didn't get the part-time J.P. job. Steiger found himself hauled into Superior Court and charged with a felony of "theft by extortion." Steiger was wrong in what he had tried to do. He did not seem to understand that staff people do not make executive decisions unless empowered to do so by the executive to whom they report.

Coincidentally, this happened only a week after Steiger, with my approval, had passed a questionnaire out to all the department heads to see if the Attorney General's Office was properly serving their needs for legal advice and representation. If not, we needed to ask the Legislature, in the next session, to give more of the departments their own, "in house" counsel.

Corbin had taken great umbrage at that and felt we were attacking his position. I assured him it was a matter of information we were seeking, and that everything would be reviewed with him before any suggestions were made to change anything. I thought that it might be beneficial to him to see what the departments thought of the service from his department. He seemed to be mollified, but obviously wasn't. Within two days, I saw a Section B headline saying that he and I were in an all-out war. Whether his phone trap of Steiger was in retribution or not, we will never know.

Because of Milstead's hold over the Legislature, I knew I had to move very cautiously to remove him, and I asked Donna

Carlson to provide me with a list of the legislators who were his strongest backers. Donna asked me what I would do if Milstead didn't resign, and I explained that, with the situation he'd created for himself at DPS, all I'd had to do would be to place him on administrative leave and let his own men convict him.

The last time I had asked Milstead to meet in my office, he was prepared in case I fired him. He stationed one of his men (unbeknownst to me at the time) with a radio in the ninth floor lobby. When Milstead came out from our visit, he told his man to send word everything was still okay, apparently alerting people at headquarters that he still had his job. Others with a working knowledge of the DPS Headquarters operation presumed that if he was suddenly fired, there were things to be done before anyone else came in. Files on key people were located both in the computer and in drawers. My information was that they were greatly relieved.

Donna Carlson apparently gave Milstead the list of legislators to be briefed before she gave it to me. He also knew that upon my return from Japan, I would be meeting with the legislators to brief them on the investigation I had made. It showed that I did indeed have cause to ask for his resignation. Losing Steiger's help as special assistant over DPS slowed me down, and the press of duties before going to Taiwan and Japan kept me from the planned briefing of legislators concerning Milstead's replacement, until after the trip. This advanced knowledge of my plans gave Milstead, Corbin, and their downtown bosses ample time to launch their October offensive on four fronts, before I could return home and remove Milstead.

An *Arizona Republic* article of October 2nd was the official start of the big offensive to force me to resign or be impeached. Stanton revealed much more of the conspiracy than was realized at the time. It showed the House leadership's part in my removal was planned and carried out for reasons known only to the insiders. The rest of the members did not know what was going on.

The lead-off item in that article was: "Key Republican and Democratic lawmakers, warning that the state is being 'shaken to its very foundation' by the troubles hounding Gov. Mecham, are quietly discussing plans to tighten their control over state government. Lawmakers from both parties have been meeting

informally to discuss how to fill what they see as a void of power .
. . . They are moving to form a bipartisan effort to give stability to
state government." Stanton then quoted House Majority Whip Jane
Hull: "I think it's time for us to make a major move that says we are
not going to put up with it . . . . There's got to be leadership, and I
think there's a vacuum of leadership."

As usual, there were no specifics on any part of government
that was not functioning properly. It would seem that if there were
any real concern, the first thing the legislative leaders should have
done was to confront me and demand action to correct
administration failures. How Mrs. Hull could again put herself in
such an outlandish position, as reflected in her statement, seems to
be proof that she was a willing pawn of the power brokers in
executing their plan for my removal.

Even Donna Carlson, the governor's legislative liaison who,
in a few days would be told by Corbin's deputy, Steve Twist, to
resign and attack the administration, couldn't stomach the
legislative hypocrisy in this instance. She gave the real answer to
the legislators' concerns in Stanton's article:

> Donna Carlson dismissed the charges of instability,
> saying that the lawmakers are not used to a governor
> exercising his legal authority. "I've heard some talk from
> the legislators, but I don't perceive that there's any
> instability in government," said Carlson who was also a
> former lawmaker. "They, obviously, have created some of
> the problems themselves . . . . They had a Republican
> majority under a Democratic governor for 12 years and they
> really exercised as much authority as they could. I think
> they were really shocked when a governor came into office
> who said, 'this is what the Legislature is supposed to do,
> and this is what the governor will do.' I think their fears are
> exaggerated."

Donna's October resignation while I was in Japan, and her
subsequent attacks on me and my administration were well
choreographed to help launch the October offensive for my removal
from office. Any bit of innuendo that could make Donna Carlson
seem important to others was ripe for inflation into a full-blown

fact. She said she took it upon herself to tell Milstead I was about to fire him because she, "felt the governor had made a very, very bad decision." She said she, "did not feel it would be in the best interest of the governor at that particular time to relieve Colonel Milstead of his duties."

Donna must have realized that I'd discover she had been spying for Milstead so, while I was in Japan, she resigned, announcing to the press that things had gotten so bad in the Governor's Office that she just couldn't function any more. I wasn't at all dismayed by her leaving, but I'd been hoping to smooth out the controversy rather than stir it up. I realized by the style of her departure that something was afoot. I expected at the very least that, in order to gain attention for herself, she would begin attacking my administration in the press, and I wasn't in much of a position to counter her from the Orient. Sure enough, Donna began making all sorts of accusations in the press.

Since I wasn't guilty of anything, the indictments didn't worry me much. The only pain my resignation would have avoided would be to all my opponents. If I would resign, they would never have to go on record with the voters as having done anything definite. My resignation could be then trumpeted as a confession of guilt and a vindication of Corbin, Milstead, Lane, Jane Hull and the power brokers who gave them their orders.

The press had never given Donna any accolades as a quality member of my staff until she left. Suddenly, she became the most important person that was holding my administration together. Less than a month before, she had recorded a television statement extremely laudatory of my accomplishments. She said how well our administration was doing. Now she said she had come to "The despair of serving under someone who had isolated himself from state voters and whose actions had brought him to national attention in a most unfortunate way."

Barry Wolfson was flabbergasted at some of the untrue things Donna was saying about the loan from him. Barry Wolfson's letter to Donna Carlson dated February 17, 1988, responds better to her charges than anything I can say. He stated among other things:

"What kept running through my mind even as I read your 'don't blame me I just work there expose' was a pre-

---

Innocent People Do Not Resign

election Mecham Finance Committee meeting. You were seated to my left, as was Colter. Steiger was seated straight across from me and Pappas and Kruglick were there somewhere along with Gregan, Ralph Watkins, Richardson and other assorted political groupies, political heavies and would-be heavies. Someone with a higher up inside connection with the *Republic* abruptly left the room to telephone his *Republic* confederate. He came back and announced unequivocally that Murphy had already made up his mind to endorse Warner. This was well before the scheduled date of the debate between the three candidates for Governor in front of the *Republic's* editorial board. Even though the decision had already been made, the candidates were told that the debate would help them make their decision.

On another subject Wolfson continues:

"I would liked to have asked you about your utterly incredible (in the literal sense as well) statement that, 'Gosh, you honestly did not know Barry M. Wolfson was the lender.' But both KTAR and KFYI told me you would not take listener questions during either of your two recent radio interviews."

Donna truly had herself built up to a Mata Hari position, and her vivid imagination made her play it to the hilt. The second week in November she was called to testify before the grand jury concerning the supposedly "secret" Wolfson loan documents she had handed to Corbin and the press.

As usual, the press was running stories from bad to bizarre. One in particular that had worried some of my assistants, including Lee Watkins, was a full page in the *New Times* that ran a banner headline reading: "The Only Shocking Story Left."

Under it, in the center of the page, was a list of prominent Americans who had been assassinated, starting with President Lincoln and running through Garfield to Kennedy. Next to each name were the dates and places of the assassinations. At the bottom of the list was my name, with a question mark in the date column.

To clarify their editorial position, the newspaper ran a piece in the same edition saying, well, maybe the S.O.B shouldn't actually be shot, but just taken out in an alley and pistol whipped.

When I returned from Taiwan, we were met at the airport by reporters who didn't want to hear a word about the new trade package we had arranged and the meetings we held with banking and business leaders to encourage Japanese and Taiwanese investment in Arizona. They only wanted responses to the activities and allegations of Carlson and Joe Lane.

It was in this setting that, on Wednesday morning, November 11th, Lee Watkins expressed his understandable displeasure with Donna Carlson. As he was walking through a parking lot with Peggy Griffith, a former co-worker of Donna's, Lee unloaded his feelings. He himself claims this as a quote:

> "Boy, your friend has a real big mouth. Doesn't she know there are nuts on both sides of the deal? She ought to be looking for ways to smooth the waters like all of us are trying to do, not stirring up trouble."

Lee says after that he walked away. Then, an hour later, when he was up on the eighth floor, Griffith approached him and said she needed to talk to him.

"I had already blown off my steam," Watkins recalled. "But I said okay, and we went into the little conference room they were using for her office. She said, 'I want you to know that Donna is no longer my friend. We don't even talk to each other any more. This has really created bad blood.'"

Watkins continued "Peggy, let me tell you something. The truth is this. There are nuts on both sides of this. There are people out there saying someone should shoot the governor or at least drag him into an alley and pistol whip him. That's right in the public. That guy went on TV and said it. Yet Donna's trying to stir up trouble. Donna knew about the loan. Peggy, you were there."

Watkins recalled Griffith saying "Yeah, but Donna has a tendency to forget."

To which he replied, "Forget, my foot, Donna knew. Just like there are nuts over here trying to get rid of the governor, there are nuts that are going to try to protect the governor. There are people out there who have the capacity to give Donna a long walk from a short pier. Doesn't she understand it? It's time for cooler heads to prevail. We've got to get with the cooler heads."

Griffith then asked him "You don't really think there are those kind of nuts out there?"

Watkins said, "Yes, I do. Donna needs to shut up because this thing is getting all out of proportion."

Griffith said, "Oh my God. None of us realized it was that serious."

Watkins said, "Sure it's that serious when publishers are out trying to get the governor shot. I walked away again and forgot about it until Max Hawkins asked me about it on Friday afternoon."

Most people who know Lee realize he behaves occasionally as if he's in some B movie, and Peggy knew it as well. She said nothing Thursday and, according to her own story, she attended a meeting Thursday night where some people allegedly told her Lee can lose his temper and get violent. Friday morning she told DPS Officer Martinez that Lee had threatened Donna. Martinez told Lt. Beau Johnson, head of the Governor's Security Detachment on the ninth floor, and Johnson told Lt. Col. Chilcoat, who told Lt. Col. Phelps, who told Milstead when he came back late Friday afternoon. Phelps also told Corbin's chief assistant Steve Twist. All this happened within a matter of hours. After he reported it to the DPS, Johnson finally told Fred Craft and my new Chief of Staff Dick Burke, and all three informed me, just before noon on Friday.

Johnson merely said there had been an altercation between Peggy Griffith and Lee Watkins the day before (though actually it had been two days). I couldn't figure out why a simple matter like a spat between two employees was being brought to me. Since Lee Watkins was an assistant director of the Department of Administration, I told Johnson to give the matter to his boss, Max Hawkins, to look into. My total meeting time with Johnson was almost 90 seconds. Johnson said fine, and went ahead and told Hawkins about the so-called threat, but did not tell any of us that he had already reported it to DPS headquarters and through them to the Attorney General's Office.

Hawkins promptly interviewed both Lee and Peggy. Both told the same story, with the single exception that Peggy claimed

Lee had referred to Donna Carlson as "whore." On reflection, Lee said, he had probably said that, as it seemed appropriate to him.

Around 5:00 p.m., Max reported back to me that he felt there had been no serious threat, that it was a lot of "hot air" and that it would disappear on its own. He said that Peggy had told him that she was going to file an affidavit with DPS and take a polygraph there so that the matter would be on file in case they felt further investigation was warranted. I thanked him for his prompt attention to the matter and asked him to let me know if anything else came up. It didn't seem important, so I dismissed it from my mind.

That night Peggy called me at home about the matter, and she agreed that this was an internal matter for us to work out. She said she was upset that the AG's office and DPS were both trying to interview her, and that she didn't want to talk to them about anything. She was very emotional and said her husband could protect her. I was at a loss as to why she was so upset and told her not to worry about it, that we'd take care of any problem on Monday. I was puzzled as to why the AG's office and DPS were involved. Lt. Johnson hadn't told me that he had informed them, so I had no way of knowing they were cultivating this tiny sprout to make it into a man-eating plant.

Of course, that took a little time. It was almost noon the following Sunday when Chief Milstead called me at my home, ostensibly to inform me that the Attorney General's Office was conducting an investigation into this matter as an attempt to intimidate one of its witnesses in the grand jury proceeding. I was totally surprised. He had never called me at my home before about anything. Since I knew he taped all of the calls he made to me, I was relatively careful in what I said. The fact that no tape ever turned up at the hearing is a pretty good indication that I never said anything that could have been seen as incriminating.

Milstead professed that he had merely called to inform me that Corbin wanted Martinez down at the AG's office for questioning about the Watkins affair.

It would have been a waste of time to ask Milstead why he was bothering to call me about this. He had already taken the matter to the AG's office through Chilcoat and Phelps and didn't

214

need any authorization from me to have his men talk to the AG. In fact, he knew I had no authority to prevent it. I wondered what else he wanted from me. If it was my permission to order a man to go to the Attorney General's Office for questioning on a trivial matter on a Sunday, he didn't have it. I assumed at the time that he was trying to create the impression that I took the alleged death threat seriously enough so that the papers would be justified in blowing the thing up into enormous proportions.

I told him that we had already taken care of the matter with Max's investigation and determined there was nothing to it. I could see that Corbin would want to blow this verbal exchange between Lee and Peggy out of proportion in order to "prove" to a grand jury that we had something dangerous to hide on our campaign finance reports. Pat Murphy probably already had the *Republic's* headlines written.

Corbin, Milstead, Phelps, Chilcoat, Martinez and Johnson worked all Sunday afternoon, and by that evening the subpoenas were being delivered so that the grand jury could add this "death threat cover-up" to their investigation. And of course, this latest "leak" from the secret grand jury was the lead story in Monday morning's *Republic*.

Peggy had lied to Max when she said she was going directly to DPS to make a report. She later told Lt. Johnson that she'd lied to Hawkins because she didn't think he had taken her seriously enough. It wasn't ever made clear why, if DPS did in fact regard this as a serious matter, they never even took a statement from Watkins or Griffith about it—or even bothered to inform Donna Carlson until Saturday night. If Watkins was considered dangerous, as they later tried to claim, why didn't they make a single move to restrain him or protect Carlson? At first the DPS said it was investigating, but later they claimed it was the attorney general who was investigating. The evidence suggests there never was any investigation of the supposed death threat at all.

In fact, the illusion of an investigation served their purposes far better. An actual investigation would have had to conclude something, in this case that there had been no such death threat. But an "ongoing investigation" that wasn't actually proceeding to investigate anything in particular, could be used as a weapon against anyone who was willing to come forward to support me. Again and again we'd seen that Corbin's "ongoing" investigations usually went in the direction of anyone that stood in his way. In this manner, Watkins was prevented from making any statement on my behalf and from testifying at the impeachment or trial. Because charges against him were forever "pending" but never filed, his attorney saw no choice but to keep him from saying anything at all about the event.

When I first took office, Hawkins had advised me not to use DPS for my security detail because he had seen the way they treated Governor Castro. I had allowed myself to be led by my desire to be fair to Col. Milstead in those first days, and by my belief that, so long as I did nothing wrong, what my enemies knew about my operations wouldn't matter. I had allowed Milstead to persuade me that his men would be loyal to me, and would never be asked to report to DPS, much less to anyone else. He had assured me that everything happening on the ninth floor was confidential.

But it didn't happen that way. In fact, when Beau Johnson later took the stand at my Impeachment Hearing in the House, he turned our 90-second interview into an episode of "Most Wanted." In this version, he had informed the three of us that a "possible felony" needed investigating. Since both Craft and Burke had been federal prosecutors, they would certainly have seized on the implications of a "felony" had Johnson ever actually mentioned it in our interview. But French proclaimed that his testimony outweighed the three of ours.

Carlson testified she had made the phone call to Sam Stanton of the *Republic* to arrange his Monday morning headline of the new development in the Mecham case. It's of little importance to know who actually called. I knew when Milstead called me Sunday, what the Monday story would be. All the players, Carlson, Corbin and his key minions, and the DPS worked long and hard to learn their lines for this to become another big chance to get me to go away.

While Donna and the DPS were waving and shouting about the terrible threat, by the way, neither of those parties took it seriously enough to do anything about it. About 36 hours after he heard about the threat and had thought out his own moves, Milstead finally told Donna about the threat and recommended that she accept DPS police protection to pad the record, but she promptly declined it.

On the other hand, she later reported that she was so frightened that she had stayed "locked up" with Steve Twist until 11:00 p.m. Saturday.

The grand jury investigation on my campaign finances was sidetracked to try to develop something on Watkins for the alleged threat and on me for allegedly attempting to obstruct an investigation. They started it Monday morning, but it turned into another dud. Had Corbin the slightest chance to tie me to a charge of obstructing justice he would have made me a co-target in the Watkins grand jury sessions. I wasn't, and appeared only as a witness. Apparently that experienced grand jury saw through it all and found no basis to indict Watkins. However, Corbin never had the decency to ever announce that Watkins was cleared.

Several months later, Bud Roberts and Lee Watkins were at a service club meeting in Tempe where Corbin was the speaker. After the meeting, Bud asked Corbin why he had gone after Lee so hard and why had he not cleared him after all of this time. Bob's reply, as repeated to me by Lee, was that "we never cared about Lee. We got the man we were after." Of course he was referring to me, and my acquittal in his criminal trial meant he was admitting his part in coordinating the October assault on four fronts to remove me.

The Watkins grand jury sessions probably did exactly what Corbin had planned. Because of the secrecy oath all are required to take when called before the grand jury, the sessions kept Watkins from coming to my defense throughout the impeachment process. Although his testimony would not have changed the end result of the impeachment (that was already settled before it started), it would have enabled the live TV audience of the impeachment happenings to see and hear the truth from Lee, that there was no death threat. It would also have proved that Lee's boss, Hawkins, had made the investigation I asked him to make of the conversation between Lee and Peggy Griffith. It would also have brought out that Hawkins made the only actual investigation of the conversation between Griffith and Watkins.

Chapter 15

THE GRAND JURY

"I know of no safe depository of the ultimate powers of the society but the people themselves; and if we think them not enlightened enough to exercise their control with a wholesome discretion, the remedy is not to take it from them, but to inform their discretion by education."
Jefferson

All that the attorney general has to do to get an indictment is to persuade his panel of laymen that, if everything he maintains is true and every reasonable explanation anyone else might offer is false, the defendant might be convicted of something in a court of law. No defense or cross-examination of witnesses by the defense is permitted. Since the attorney general is interpreting the law for laymen who know little about the law, it is easy to see why grand juries almost always return an indictment. If they are hesitant, the prosecutor has only to tell them they are not making a judgement of the case, they are only signing an accusation that will give the accused his or her day in court to prove their innocence.

Corbin failed even under these circumstances in his first attempt before the 23rd Grand Jury to get an indictment on me. It is a tribute to the fairness of experienced grand jurors, as well as the lack of any real basis for his charge. When my brother, Willard, testified before them, the members of the jury were attentive to what he said and wary of the prosecutor's attempts to distort his testimony. Despite all the hype they had been fed about the governor who needed to be impeached, the jury still couldn't buy

218

even a completely one-sided version of my guilt, and so Corbin allowed their term to expire on December 3, 1987.

One of the Jurors in the 23rd Grand Jury met me on the street in 1997 and told me that they were very angry about being dismissed, after spending more than a month hearing the AG's witnesses on his investigation of me. He said the reason they were dismissed was because they knew the tricks of the AG's prosecutors and didn't see enough evidence against Willard and me to indict.

Even though the first jury had heard every witness but me, and there was plenty of time to finish, Corbin claimed his move was necessary because he didn't know how much longer the process would take. Since it would have taken two days at most, the truth is, this jury had become suspicious of the prosecutors after watching their tactics for months. The new jurors were green and could be spoon-fed only the portions of the testimony the prosecutors wanted them to hear in order to guarantee the proper reaction.

This time, the prosecutors called only four witnesses, and three of them were myself, Willard, and Secretary of State Jim Shumway, who would turn out to be one of our key defense witnesses in the criminal trial. The fourth witness was a CPA doing contract work for the Corporation Commission. To present the AG's one-sided story to the jurors, they brought in George Graham, a special agent from the AG's Office. Although the prosecutors cannot give evidence themselves, they were able to have one of their own tell the jurors only the parts of the evidence and witnesses' testimony from the 23rd Grand Jury that would make us look guilty. They controlled Shumway's testimony by asking him only about the parts of the law they wanted read. They were able to avoid the part of the law (ARS 16-901-4) that defines "itemized" as a class of like expenditures or contributions that is stated under one item, and that separate classes of expenditures are stated separately. That is what Willard did on the loans after being told by the Secretary of State's Office that was the way to do it. Since the notes being reported under one entry were the whole basis of the AG's accusation, even the green juror's of the 24th would probably not have returned an indictment, and there would not have been any criminal trial.

In the later criminal trial Secretary of State Shumway told the court that his office instructed people to handle reports just the way it is explained above. That, plus Wolfson's testimony, showed the jury that the prosecution had no case. Without the indictments as an excuse for the impeachment—it may not have happened either.

Attorney General Corbin, prosecutors French and Eckstein, House leaders, Joe Lane and Jane Hull, and the "big boys," as Lane called his downtown bosses, all were guilty of well-planned, gross abuse of our system at great cost to the taxpayers and myself. I was the one punished for doing what the people elected me to do.

By the time I came before the grand jury, I could almost cut their hostility with a knife. They had been treated to more than a year of media propaganda about what an evil man I was. They had been poisoned with half-truths and distortions by the attorney general, without ever hearing the real facts. If I'd been sitting where they were, I probably would have felt the same way about the accused. You have to credit an attorney general with knowing something about the law and about juries. In his second attempt he was able to impanel the new 24th Grand Jury and didn't have to call any witness he didn't want them to hear. Although the jurors can ask to hear witnesses other than those called by the prosecution, being new, they seemed reluctant to do so.

Like so many things in our society that start out with stated good intentions, the grand jury system has become a dangerous thing. It has become a terrible weapon when put into the hands of unscrupulous prosecutors who give lip service to justice but are concerned only with getting convictions. They say that the reason for the secrecy is to protect the reputation of the targets of their investigations. Inasmuch as the press always knows when a high profile person is the target if a grand jury proceeding, the target is muzzled and the press somehow gets what it wants from leaks. The target cannot defend himself or herself inside or outside of the courtroom. I believe that grand juries should be disbanded and all proceedings held in the open air of evidentiary hearings. That is what we requested but, for obvious reasons, we were not allowed that choice. In the bright light of an open court hearing, the public eventually would rebel against the star chamber-like atmosphere of the grand jury activities. No one who has ever experienced it will ever forget how helpless and frustrating it is to be locked in a room where the prosecutors have total control and the only right the target or the witness has is to plead the 5th Amendment and not answer. Even so, that is not much of a right because the assumption then is that you are guilty. I of course did not take the 5th.

The target of a grand jury investigation can have his attorney sit in the room with him, but the attorney can't say anything except to whisper in his client's ear when the client specifically asks him for advice. The defense counsel can't object to anything the prosecutor says or asks, even to verbal abuse and brow beating. A clever prosecutor can have a field day under these circumstances. He can push the accused around at will and try to make the accused seem combative by his reactions to improperly phrased questions. Prosecutors ask multiple questions in such a way that they cannot be answered "yes" or "no." They then demand yes or no answers and berate the accused in front of the jurors because he hasn't answered yes or no. Of all the things I've witnessed in our criminal justice system, this one-sided kangaroo court called a grand jury is the most criminal.

We were told that when the prosecutors were through with their questions and accusations, they would almost have to ask us if we had anything more to say. When Willard had appeared before the first grand jury, he had read them a prepared statement at the end of his testimony. It was reported that Willard's statement had been well received by the jurors, too.

The prosecutors took no chances with the second jury. They ridiculed and vilified Willard's statement, even before he had a chance to make it. Then the prosecutors got the presiding judge to edit my statement, taking out more than half the content before I was allowed to present it to the jury. After all, I wasn't allowed to present any evidence and they were fearful that I would present some proof in my summary statement, thus the censorship. This exercise took almost an entire day, and I might as well have saved my energy. Between the ironclad hostility of the jury and the emasculated version of what I was allowed to say, I could see that I had no hope of escaping indictment.

My defense lawyer in the criminal case, Mike Scott, told me that if this had been an ordinary case, it would have been thrown out because of the way the grand jury was handled. But this wasn't an ordinary case because Evan Mecham was involved.

The AG's, on the other hand, repeatedly told the press about how they had bent over backward to give us a special break by letting us make statements before the jury. I do have to pay tribute to their planning and the execution of those plans. I knew I hadn't committed a crime, but I totally underestimated their ability to compensate in the indictment for that little shortcoming.

After presenting their "case," the prosecutors, Lotstein and Cudahay, told the new grand jury there was no time for a more thorough investigation, they had to have an indictment immediately. Of course they didn't tell them why. First, they had no thorough case to present. Secondly, on Monday, the following business day, I was due to make my state of the state address to the Legislature. Anything I said would thus be discredited in advance.

Friday afternoon about 4 p.m., my attorney, Murray Miller, called and said he needed to see me right away. He arrived a few minutes later and told me the grand jury had voted to indict me on six felony counts; Willard on three. We needed to prepare for the onslaught of the press that would follow the AG's 4:30 p.m. release of this news. They had timed it carefully to give it a full weekend to grow before my address to the Legislature on the following Monday. Apparently, the indictments were expected to frighten me into resigning, particularly when they included Willard. I told the press I'd have a press conference the following day.

The press conference in the west rotunda of the Capitol was rather informal, with everyone including myself standing. We had a lot of national press there, but I did not expect to be there long. I gave a quick summary of what was going on and expressed my confidence that I would be acquitted of the criminal indictments from the day before. Some seemed surprised that I was not acting hostile and angry. The local press knew I usually remained calm, but the out-of-state people had been fed a distorted description over the AP wire by *The Arizona Republic*. I must have been quite a contrast to what they expected. One of them asked if I was angry toward Attorney General Corbin and how I planned to get even with him. I pointed out that I did not have to get even with anyone, nor did I intend to try. That was reserved for our maker when we

222

receive our judgement from him in the next step in our eternal life. I then ended with quoting part of Hebrews 10:30--"Vengeance belongeth unto me, I will recompense, saith the Lord."

Chapter 16

FRENCH AND ECKSTEIN ESTABLISH A NEW LOW TO WIN AT ANY COST

"Woe unto them that call evil good, and good evil; that put darkness for light, and light for darkness; that put bitter for sweet, and sweet for bitter."
Isaiah 5: 20

Republican Speaker Lane's hiring of a liberal Democrat such as William French, apparently to investigate my investigation by the grand jury, should have seemed at least mildly suspicious to Republican legislators. When I asked Majority Leader Jim Ratliff what was going on, he told me Lane was handling the entire thing by himself. He said that none of the other legislative leaders were even being called in for discussion. I later found that Majority Whip Jane Hull was just as much a part of it as Lane. Ratliff told me he knew they were having meetings with Barr quite often. Ratliff was the only member of the House leadership who had said anything good about me and our administration, so they may not have trusted him to know what they were doing.

Senate President Carl Kunasek pled with Lane to await the outcome of either the recall and my criminal trial, since either one would save the Legislature the unnecessary time and expense of an impeachment hearing in the House. After all, why be in such a hurry. If I won acquittal in the criminal trial and the people voted to retain me in the recall election, the Legislature would not have dared to hold an impeachment trial. Logic was to no avail to anyone. Though French was being paid by the Legislature, it became evident Lane was taking his orders directly from the "big boys" as he called them, on this one.

Lane did not have to hire French to tell them how to proceed with a House hearing to decide if there was a need to hold impeachment hearings. Lane's own staff attorneys needed to only go back to the precedent set in 1964, with the impeachment hearing against state tax commissioners, Thad Moore and Bill Stanford.

That hearing was handled by assigning the logical choice, the Judiciary Committee, to conduct the hearings. That is the proper procedure for impeachment, on either the state or federal level. In 1964, there was no high-profile counsel to try to make a criminal case out of it amidst a daily hoopla from the press. For more than a month, they conducted the hearings and gave everyone who could shed any light on the accusation of misconduct in office a chance to be heard. The rest of the Legislature continued on with their normal functions.

After the full hearings were complete in the Moore-Stanford case, the Judiciary Committee voted just as they would on any legislation or proposition before them. In that case, the Committee voted to pass out a bill of impeachment for the vote of the whole House. It passed and was sent over to the Senate for the trial. The Senate voted not to convict.

Lane told one of his many lies when he said he hired French to give the House advice and instructions on conducting an impeachment hearing. That was done by the House staff attorneys, as one of them told my author friend in the previous chapter.

It quickly became evident that the reason French was hired was much bigger than advising the House on how to proceed. French and staff went into action to make their own investigation, which we could quickly see was running in sync with the attorney general's grand jury investigation. It was easy to see that the House prosecutor could go on any kind of fishing expedition into anything they could think of. Word seeped out that they were going to look into anything and everything I had done, and they were not necessarily concerned with breaking the laws. They could call anything they chose malfeasance in office.

Lane stated that they would have everything looked into, and French would report before the legislative session started. At one time, he said it would have to be done that way or wait because they couldn't let it interfere with the regular session. It was obvious someone else was telling him what to do because it kept changing—almost daily.

Because it was clear that French was coordinating his activities with Corbin, my attorney, Murray Miller, advised extreme caution in dealing with French's people. When French wanted to question me under oath without providing any of the protections of a legitimate courtroom procedure, we wanted to know ahead of time what we were getting into.

Since French's design was never to solicit information, but only to trick me into some ambiguous response that could later be used against me, Miller told him that I would respond only to written questions. French immediately dropped his request.

French used a similar strategy to explain why he never interviewed Lee Watkins or offered any testimony of any sort from Peggy Griffith concerning the "death threat" Watkins had allegedly made. These were the only two people at their second meeting. Their conversation was the entire foundation of the obstruction of justice charge. You would figure that whether Watkins had ever made such a threat, how, or when, or what he had told me about it would have some bearing on whether or not I had thought I was interfering in the investigation. Likewise, French, without any excuse at all, refused to bring in Max Hawkins for testimony, though he was the only public official who had interviewed both parties in the "death threat" fiasco. Hawkins has written and signed an affidavit attesting to the fact that I asked him to investigate, that he did so, and that he had reported to me that there was no threat.

Ironically, Watkins was never brought before any court on any charges. The only time he was even interviewed by anyone besides Hawkins was during the secret grand jury investigation, so no one ever heard publicly what he had to say. None of my prosecutors ever wanted anyone to hear what he had to say because the charge was silly to begin with. The "French Report" does not even mention the Hawkins investigation into the alleged threat. French never even asked Hawkins for his findings.

French And Eckstein Establish A New Low To Win At Any Cost

226

French knew that Lane had enough power to run over any legislator who would object to anything he did. But, impeaching a governor over a death threat that never occurred might have raised some eyebrows outside of the Legislature, and he did, after all, want to preserve a sense of legitimacy for the folks at home. So, again, French reported to the media that legal technicalities would have made it difficult for him to interrogate Watkins under the conditions he most desired. But then, the 14th Amendment assuring defendants a fair trial would have interfered with many of Mr. French's preferred conditions, most of the time.

In the House Impeachment Hearings, he didn't have to abide by "due process" or any of those other Constitutional limitations, so he had a field day. Paul Eckstein, another liberal Democrat who was reputedly going to be the manager in Carolyn Warner's campaign if there was a recall election, joined the fray announcing he would represent the Democratic House Minority without charge. The Democratic Minority already had fully paid staff attorneys, but they claimed French was aloof, arrogant, and wouldn't let them know what was going on. As could be easily predicted, Eckstein soon was engaged at a high hourly rate to join French in the prosecution.

A number of House members were very angry at the secrecy surrounding the investigation and its escalating costs that Lane and Jane Hull had approved without any apparent agreement or approval by other House members. Lane claimed he had the authority to do what he wanted, and showed them the truth of that statement by simply doing it. -

When I questioned House Majority Leader Ratliff about Lane's actions, he just shook his head and said he was in the dark and seemed to be powerless to do anything about it. He knew that Lane was listening to people outside the Legislature on this matter, and reconfirmed that he knew that Lane was in communication with Burton Barr quite often.

From the very first inkling of the possibility of a House hearing, Lane would not talk to me, my staff or party leadership. He said that his lawyers had told him if he had to conduct a hearing, he should not have any conversations with anyone about it in advance. That was a sure way for his masters to keep him on their leash. He only had to do what they told him without thinking for himself in any conversations with others. It stopped anyone from showing him what his actions were going to do to the party, and the state. If he persisted in being the point man, he would replace the sitting Republican governor with the Democratic secretary of state who was standing next in the line of succession.

At first I wasn't so worried about the House hearing because I knew if they followed the Arizona precedent of 1964, the Judiciary Committee would hear it. I knew that I had at least four good friends on that committee who would insist on fairness. Lane and his bosses apparently knew the same thing, so they took care of that with a bypass of their own precedent. Without any input from the House members, they set up a "Select Committee" to handle the hearing. Not only did the Republican House leaders Lane and Hull hire big time, high priced, Washington trained liberal Democrat special counsel, but they also chose a Washington named "Select Committee" to justify the large amount of tax payer funds they spent to put on their show. This enabled Lane to appoint eight of the 11 members who were avowed enemies of mine. One member, Jack Brown of Apache County, was a strong Democrat but proved he wanted to see fair play and ended up voting against the bill of impeachment. Republican Mark Killian had been one of the Herstam-led group of House Mecham bashers, and he at least tried to appear fair. Gary Giordano was the only strong Republican friend I had on the Committee.

From the tone of their questions and statements, Chairman Skelly and the other seven members wanted to replace me at all costs. This left Judiciary Committee members Burns, Denny, Steffey and Johnson, all Mecham supporters, on the sidelines, and made the results of the Select Committee report a foregone conclusion.

In frustration, Representative Leslie Johnson published "The Johnson Report," a January 26th summary of how the whole thing had been handled. It's text follows:

I will try to avoid biased, flamboyant or inflammatory language and attempt to merely present the facts as I found them:
1. Speaker Joe Lane hired "Special House Counsel," William P. French, without the consultation or approval

French And Eckstein Establish A New Low To Win At Any Cost

of the Members of the House. Rumors of House actions geared toward impeachment were rampant in the newspapers.

2. When questioned as to the purpose for the Special House Counsel, Speaker Lane explained Mr. French was going to "track the proceedings of the Grand Jury."

3. Later, when questioned as to Mr. French's purpose, Speaker Lane explained the Special House Counsel was now investigating, independent of the Grand Jury, allegations of wrongdoing by the Governor of Arizona.

4. Impeachment proceedings were formally announced.

5. The French Report, which presented a prosecutorial view of the Governor's alleged wrongdoing, was presented to the House with national media coverage. No questions were permitted from House Members by the Speaker, but he promised they could ask all the questions they wanted of Mr. French on the following Monday.

6. The following Monday, the "Select Committee" was announced chaired by the Chairman of the Judiciary Committee. Among those excluded from the Select Committee, who served on the standing Judiciary Committee, were: Representatives Brenda Burns, Bob Denny, Leslie Johnson, and Lela Steffey, all critics of the French Report and the impeachment proceedings to date.

7. Channel 5 News reported a secret meeting took place some weeks prior to its report between House Speaker Joe Lane, House Minority Leader Art Hamilton, and former House Majority Leader Burton Barr. (It should be noted, Burt Barr was the man Governor Mecham handily defeated in the 1986, Primary Election and has been rumored to be embittered and vengeful over his defeat.)

8. When requests were made of the Speaker for independent counsel to clarify points of law in dispute in the French Report, those members were told Mr. French is the House Counsel and will answer those questions.

9. At the opening meeting of the "Select Committee," Mr. French sat at the left hand of Chairman Skelly, a

position not occupied by committee counsel before this time.

10. Special rules for the Select Committee were formulated by Mr. French, Mr. Skelly, and others, which contradicted earlier assurances that House Members would conduct the meetings and question the witnesses. Under new rules, Mr. French would initiate interrogation and House Members would be permitted to pose questions afterward.

11. As of this report, House Members have yet to have the opportunity to put questions to Mr. French concerning his report.

(Author's note: Lane never kept his word on that and they never did get to ask questions.)

This can lead us to no other conclusion than to deduce that the impeachment proceedings in the Arizona House of Representatives against Governor Mecham are a railroad job on a fast track.

If there is any other conclusion to be reached, it cannot be clearly identified because there are the true facts and the perception is such that only one logical conclusion can result. The Johnson Report points to the need for a free, and truly unbiased, arena for the finding of the truth in a free trial in the courts. This was also under way, so why the impeachment?

If, as Representative Bob Denny has said, "We afford every extent of the law to a fair and unbiased trial to accused murderers, rapists, known racketeers and underworld figures, surely, we should accord the same privilege to the duly elected Governor of this State."

My attorneys appealed to the state Supreme Court in a special action aimed at forcing the House Select Committee to honor my civil rights, and give me due process in their deliberations. French and Eckstein, the House Special Counsel, argued that in the legislative venue, I had no rights whatsoever. They were entitled to run their proceedings like the ancient English Star Chamber Courts (where the accused had no rights), and there was nothing I could do about it. The Supreme Court agreed with them.

Lane had previously said that if the French Report, and any resulting action the House needed to take, couldn't be done before the legislative session, it would wait until after the session was through.

The master planners of the "Mecham Removal Project" saw two reasons that waiting for the impeachment trial would put it in jeopardy.

First, the recall election was scheduled for May 17th. The campaign would give me a good opportunity to get out to the people and focus on what my administration had accomplished so far, and emphasize what we planned to do for the future. We had made some important, progressive steps for Arizona, and I stood a good chance to win the recall. We had hired a statewide poll that showed over 80 percent of the voters agreed with me on the issues. But the hostile media kept most people from knowing what we were doing on those issues. I looked forward to an election campaign that would give me a chance to inform them.

Second, the criminal trial that resulted from Corbin's indictments was scheduled for March 22. My lawyer in the criminal trial, Mike Scott, told me their case was so weak that if my name weren't Mecham, he would be able to get it thrown out without a trial. It was because of who I was that we would stand trial, but he was as sure as he possibly could be that we would be acquitted.

Note my opposition's clever planning. The usual process that has removed most governors from office during their elected term, is conviction on a felony charge. No governor in the last 70 years has been subjected to an impeachment process and no governor in the history of this nation has ever been subjected to an impeachment process while also subject to a criminal trial on felony indictments. It was obvious that there was no crisis calling for this unprecedented action against me.

Logic says that I cannot be in two trials simultaneously. The criminal trial was scheduled and obviously was the more important event. Lane had said he would not start impeachment hearings if they could not be completed before the start of the legislative session. Therefore, we planned for the March criminal trial and the May recall election as the two legally mandated things we had to face. The criminal trial was projected to take two weeks or less, so it would be finished before the recall election. If they still wanted to have impeachment hearings in the House, they could start right after the end of the session in May or June. But the Power Broker's master planners were not about to let anything under their control operate in a reasonable way.

The power brokers directed Lane to reverse himself, choose the Select Committee, instruct it to get to work immediately on the hearings, and suspend all House activity on anything but the Select Committee Hearings (supposedly so House members could sit in and observe and hear for themselves). There was no place we could turn to for a sane decision that would make the House comply with reason and justice. We had no choice but to ask the Superior Court to postpone the criminal trial and proceed with the Arizona House of Representatives' special model of a kangaroo court. The Senate was able to conduct some business but soon had to suspend work themselves and wait for the House.

One thing the Senate could and should have done, but didn't, was hold hearings and confirm or reject my appointments. We had them all ready for their consideration when the senators came back to work in January. We also had our budget waiting on them for consideration. They sat on their hands and then sent them all back to Governor Mofford to be replaced with her choices. They also replaced my budget with their own model that was 10 percent higher, and then passed a big tax increase to pay for the increased spending. If the government was at a standstill, as Hull and others were charging, it was because the Legislature brought their work to a standstill to get rid of me. Nothing in the governor's office was holding anything up.

In contrast to the announced way that the hearings would be conducted, Skelly was chairman in name only. He was literally a Charlie McCarthy dummy doll for French and Eckstein, who actually ran the House hearings. Instead of the members asking the questions of the witnesses, it was French and Eckstein who asked the questions of the carefully selected witnesses to elicit the exact answers they wanted. It was only after the prosecutors were through with their questions that the members of the Select Committee could ask questions of the witnesses.

Again, the whole affair was very much like a grand jury investigation, except that it was held in the open. No defense

French And Eckstein Establish A New Low To Win At Any Cost

attorney was allowed to be in the hearing, question any of the witnesses or in any way test the veracity of the testimony being given. From my perspective, the conduct of the hearings was totally a prosecutor's show and considerably belittled the stature of the members of the Select Committee and the other House members. All but a few members of the House of Representatives looked like a herd of sheep, rather than elected representatives of the people. It was a tremendous embarrassment and disappointment to see that outside interests led by the key power brokers could so completely and brazenly flaunt their control of the Legislature of this state. An honest and truthful news media could have easily brought this to the attention of the majority of the citizens. Had they done so, it may have triggered enough response to take back the power of the Legislature for the people. But rather than being part of the solution, the press was a large part of the means by which the power brokers kept the truth from the people.

Neither Peggy Griffith nor Lee Watkins was called as witnesses for the House members to determine if there ever was a threat to Carlson's life. Although Giordano asked repeatedly that these witnesses be called, Chairman Skelly turned a deaf ear to the request.

When Corbin started his 23rd Grand Jury investigation, I engaged attorney Bob L'Ecuyer to make an exhaustive investigation on the whole matter of the inaugural funds. We presented his findings and all of the back-up analysis of the law, etc., to show there was no basis to ever consider the inaugural funds to be state funds. Had they been looking for honest information, Bob's report, Murray Miller's papers, H. Jay Platt's letter and my testimony, left all House members without an excuse for voting to pass the bill of impeachment.

The French Report was the basis of the House hearings and the Senate trial. Inasmuch as French was so egregious in his misstatements of the law and the facts, I have deemed it easier for the reader to get the truth about the law and the facts from an honest attorney named H. Jay Platt.

Attorney and Apache County rancher, H. Jay Platt, sent the House members his carefully researched review of the mistakes and what appears to be intentionally misleading parts of the French Report. The following excerpts are from Platt's letter to the House:

> I have recently studied the "French Report," the "Miller Report" and reviewed the pertinent statuary provisions. My conclusions may be summed up thusly, with due respect to Winston Churchill: "Never have so many made so much of so little."
>
> The flimsy nature of the "evidence," the overall tone of the questions presented by the members of the Select Committee, and the dogmatic approach of the "French Report" and the current spectacle of the impeachment hearing are simply an exercise in working back from the predetermined desired result of impeachment.
>
> Article 8 of the Arizona Constitution specifically provides that the governor is only "liable to impeachment for high crimes, misdemeanors, or malfeasance in office." There has simply not been an impeachable offense committed by the governor, even viewing the "evidence" and testimony in the most damaging light.
>
> (i) The Republican House Majority "counsel" has signed a recall petition and was dismissed from the Arizona Racing Commission while his Democratic House Minority counterpart is the campaign chairman for the governor's chief rival, Carolyn Warner. That the Legislature selected and labeled these two lawyers as independent "counsel" is absolutely shocking.
>
> (ii) The French Report's misrepresentation of the State ex rel DeConcinni v. Sullivan, 66 Ariz. 348 P. 2nd 592 (1948). Specifically, Mr. French purportedly quotes the following sentence: "The object of the removal 'by impeachment' of a public officer for official misconduct is not to punish the officer but to improve the public service. Id."

Mr. French has inserted the words "by impeachment" into the above quotation. The original quote, at 359, does not contain the words "by impeachment" but is otherwise the same. Mr. French asserts that the above quote indicated that impeachment "is to ensure that state government can continue while normal criminal processes are at work." French Report, p.1.

This is a flagrant, inexcusable and deliberate misrepresentation of the Sullivan case.

Sullivan, the Arizona Attorney General, was convicted of conspiracy to violate gambling laws. A.R.S. 12-404 provided that an "office shall be deemed vacant from and after the happening of his conviction of a felony, or any offense including violation of his official duties . . . ." Accordingly, the governor advised Mr. Sullivan that he considered the office of Attorney General to be vacant and that he therefore had appointed Evo DeConcini to such office.

Mr. Sullivan, however, refused to recognize the appointment, contending that the impeachment provisions contained in Article 8 of the Arizona Constitution were the sole means of removing him from office.

Such issues required that the Arizona Supreme Court consider the purpose of the impeachment provisions of the Constitution...the Court observed that: the object of prosecutions of impeachment in England and the United States "is to reach high and potent offenders, such as might be presumed to escape punishment in the ordinary tribunals, either from their extraordinary influence, or from the imperfect organization and powers of those tribunals..."

The Court stated that the purpose of impeachment is to serve as an added protection to the public against those officers who may be so powerful as to effectively block court action against themselves.

This issue was disposed of by the Court's observation that a vacancy is created the moment a judgement of conviction is entered against a public officer.

Immediately after making the above statement, the Court...made the following comment which Mr. French altered by inserting the word "impeachment": the object of the removal of a public officer for official misconduct is not to punish the officer, but to improve the public service. The public interest demands that public affairs be administrated by officers upon whom rests no stigma of conviction of a felony or any other offense involving a violation of their official duties.

The insertion by Mr. French of the word "impeachment" into the above quotation significantly alters its meaning. Absent such alteration, there is absolutely no language in the Sullivan case to support Mr. French's contention that the impeachment process "is to ensure that the state government can continue while the normal criminal processes are at work. (In the past 75 years a number of governors have been removed from office when proven guilty of committing felonies. In no case has their Legislatures moved into any action to impeach until 1988 in Arizona.)

Mr. French again misled the members of the Legislature by his omission of A.R.S. 16-901 (4) from his list of pertinent statuary provisions relating to the Wolfson loan. The "pertinent statues" of financial disclosure statements are listed at page 76 (B-17) of the French Report, while A.R.S. 16-913 and 16-915 are not. A.R.S. 16-901 (4) is conspicuously absent. In light of the importance of the word "itemized" as used in 16-915, surely its statuary definition as contained in 16-910 (4) is highly relevant and ought to have been called to the attention of the Legislature by its "special counsel."

In short, Mr. French's glaring errors of addition and omission in his report, coupled with his sophomoric conclusions and his leading questions written out for Representative Weisz and King to question and cross examine him (Mecham) in his appearance before the House Select Committee clearly demonstrates that Mr. French is not merely rendering legal advice on the impeachment process to the House of Representatives as the members thereof and the public were originally told.

The report at p. 62 (B-3) lists the critical finding on the question of disclosure as follows: The Wolfson Loan was kept confidential and not disclosed as an itemized matter on campaign statements, but rather included in a lump sum contribution from Evan Mecham.

The above conclusion completely ignores the statutory definition of "itemized" contained in A.R.S. 1-901 (40). The Mecham letter to Barry Wolfson simply states what the governor testified was its intent. That letter confirms an "agreement" by Barry Wolfson to "advance up to $600,000...upon certain terms and conditions." After detailing those terms and conditions, the governor states: "I am relying upon your agreement to advance the funds. Your agreement will remain confidential."

Query: What was to remain confidential? The "agreement" was to remain confidential. What was the "confidential agreement?" It was an "agreement to advance funds." There was no indication that the governor was representing that the actual receipt of the funds would not be disclosed in accordance with the law. When A.R.S. 16-915 and 16-901 are read in tandem, it is most difficult to conclude that the governor knowingly failed to "itemize" or otherwise properly disclose the Wolfson loan. Like the issue of campaign disclosure, this is a creature of statute. A.R.S. 13-2409 requires a knowing attempt to "obstruct, delay or prevent the communication of information or testimony relating to a violation of any criminal statute..." by "means of bribery, misrepresentation, intimidation of force or threats of force."

The "criminal statute" at issue is A.R.S. 13-2802 whereunder a "threat" of itself is not particularly relevant. What is relevant is that the threat issue with intent to:

1 - Influence the testimony of that person or
2 - Induce that person to avoid legal process summoning him to testify or
3 - Induce that person to absent himself from any official proceeding to which he has been legally summoned.

Mr. French, however, focuses not on "intent" but solely on the fact of the alleged threat. Thus, when examining the pertinent statutes, it is apparent that the Legislature, to impeach the governor on an obstruction of justice theory, would first have to conclude that Lee Watkins not only made the threats but that he did so with the intent of influencing Donna Carlson. Secondly, the Legislature would have to conclude that the governor with knowledge of Mr. Watkins intent, sought to delay or prevent the communication of Mr. Watkins' statutory violation and that such attempt be made by means of "bribery, misrepresentation, intimidation or force of threats of force." There is not a scintilla of evidence presented in the French Report nor in the hearings which could possibly lead to the conclusion that the governor violated A.R.S. 13-2409.

PROTOCOL FUND

Perhaps the most troublesome area is the so-called "protocol fund." However, a close examination of the facts reveals that there was certainly no crime committed. No one could seriously contend that the protocol fund is now a public fund.

The key on this issue is that N. Warner Lee letter, signed by William Long and sent to Tom Collins (county attorney). The letter contains assurances that the fund would not be expended in violation of Proposition 200, thereby obviating the "time and expense which would be necessary to obtain a judicial determination of the question." This was all that was needed to resolve the dispute. Unfortunately, N. Warner Lee added additional gratuitous language to the effect that the fund would be "expended, at the governor's discretion solely..." for purposes set forth in A.R.S 41-1105...(Note: The letter Long signed was dated June 26. Long had turned the records and bank account over to Governor Mecham on May 17 and was no longer in any authority to make such an agreement.)

While admittedly troublesome language, several observations are in order. First, while there was a statement that the funds would be expended only for the purposes described in A.R.S. 41-1105, there is no basis for assertion that there was a gift within the context of 41-1105. In other words, the funds would be expended "pursuant to the provisions and the spirit ..." of 41-1105 but the money did not become a 41-1105 fund.

Secondly, an expenditure is not at issue but rather a loan. Clearly, there has not been a violation of any statute. At best, it may only be argued that the loan was contrary to the letter agreement between Tom Collins and the Inaugural Committee. While there may be questions of contract law presented by such an agreement (and also that County Attorney Tom Collins was practicing law in violation of A.R.S. 11-403 (B), there was certainly no crime committed.

In summary, far more is at issue in the impeachment proceedings than Mr. Mecham. The integrity of the election and impeachment processes are at issue. I would implore, hope and indeed pray that members of the Legislature would put aside personal feelings regarding Governor Mecham and personal party agendas and dwell upon the importance of preserving the integrity of our system and process of government.

There is a criminal trial pending and if convicted the Governor's office is statutorily vacated, as indeed it should be. However, from what I have read and observed, the impeachment proceedings are a sham, should be discontinued, and the criminal proceedings allowed to run their course.

Signed H. Jay Platt

According to French, the impeachment hearing was just a counterpart to the grand jury indictment process. Following his display of half truths, he informed the legislators that if they felt there was a reasonable chance that I had broken the law in any way, it was their duty to vote for impeachment. (Here French is not acting like an "independent counsel" but rather he is assuming the position of a judge instructing the jury after the evidence has been presented by both sides.) Under these conditions, he could have convicted Mahatma Ghandi of gluttony. French misquoted DeConcini v. Sullivan (Arizona Supreme Court, 66 Ariz 348, 188 p. 2nd 592 (1948) to change it's meaning. French informed the Legislature that actually he was being too hard on himself when he asked for even this much; since the stated object of an impeachment is not to punish the impeached official but to "improve public service." It was his opinion that the Legislature should impeach me simply if they felt it would be in the public interest. In other words, if they didn't like the conservative spending measures I was trying to implement, that would be sufficient grounds for an impeachment. Yet in the beginning of his report, as I previously quoted, he had said I had to have broken the law. (Judge Gordon recognized how confusing this was and felt it necessary to tell the Senate that the framers of the constitution did not intend the term high crimes and misdemeanors to be tied to violation of the criminal law.)

I thought surely there were enough honest legislators to stop this blatant insult to everyone's intelligence, especially theirs. But I was wrong. The majority was only interested in finding ways to justify what they were already committed to do.

French left out the part of DeConcini v. Sullivan that says impeachment is proper only when the official cannot be reached by normal criminal process. Since I had already been indicted by Corbin, the DeConcini standard was totally ignored in my case. But then, this wasn't a court of law, so we were not allowed to raise that objection.

The simple truth is that French's charge of misuse of state funds was an utter and total fabrication from beginning to end. The transformation of inaugural ball ticket funds into state money is impossible.

Corbin's statement to Sam Stanton was that the inaugural funds were private and there was nothing wrong with what I had done. That wiped out any contention by French that I had misused state funds. That should have been a major breakthrough for us in the hearings and in the press. Instead it was a one-day story in the *Republic* buried where few would see it.

Every legislator should have known the facts about the handling of money by the Governor's Office. The only state funds under the governor's direct control were the office budget. It was appropriated by the Legislature and handled by the office manager who paid the expenses for running the office. There was no "Protocol Fund" in the governor's budget as passed by the

Legislature. That was a name French and Company cleverly put on the inaugural funds to make it sound like they were state funds. The only funds a governor could spend for things envisioned for a Protocol Fund were his own private funds, or those raised from private sources to keep him from having to spend his own funds.

Facts were overpowered by the day after day drum beat accusation that I had misused state or public funds. There were never any valid charges on any of the counts proposed by William French. None can stand up to point by point scrutiny, as the Platt letter has proven.

French was held to no standard of accountability as is necessary in a civil or criminal court. I've tried only to show that whatever French claimed, even if some of his fantasies had been fact, there was never any basis for any sort of criminal charges against me, and he and Corbin knew this. That is why the only way to remove me from office was by impeachment, where nothing needs to be proven and where all they need is the votes of two-thirds of the Senators. Proof of that was the fact that Corbin was able to get indictments from his grand jury on only one of French's three basic impeachment charges. And that one, the Wolfson loan, was dismissed by the Senate in the impeachment trial. In the criminal trial that followed my removal from office by impeachment, the jury gave us a quick acquittal on June 16th. But by then, I had already been removed from office by impeachment. Their well-planned four-front assault succeeded on the one front they were sure of.

Their concern was never to see justice done. Rather, it was to create an excuse for a lynching: strip a man of his rights and of his ability to protect himself, and then, under cover of darkness, open the cell door for his enemies to finish him off. The next morning, everybody's a little embarrassed and nobody seems to remember much. But since so many solid citizens were in on it, most of them can agree that the whole thing is best forgotten as quickly as possible. Reproaches and recriminations are in the worst possible taste. Let's get this behind us now and enjoy our recovery of our control of the government Arizona. When it is mentioned, blame it all on the victim for getting in the way.

Chapter 17

STAFF CHANGES ON THE RUN

"Men are qualified for civil liberty in exact proportion to their disposition to put moral chains upon their own appetites — in proportion as their love of justice is above their rapacity; —-in proportion as they are more disposed to listen to the counsels of the wise and good, in preference to the flattery of knaves.s."
Edmund Burke

It was at this time that I wished I could back up and start all over with my staff because I now realized that I had very little real support. Instead of having people I knew were loyal and committed to the same principles I was, I found myself with five staff changes that were designed to help us get along with those who were shooting at me the hardest, but to no avail.

The first change I had made was to replace Ron Bellus as press secretary. None of us in my administration was actually equipped for the full-scale war that had erupted with the press. We thought we were living in a normal, civilized society where rules of decency allowed for differences of opinion. Nothing prepared any of us for the vicious hatred that was directed at us on a daily basis. We never dreamed that once the election was won, fair and square, that there were elements in our society that decided from the beginning that they were determined to undo the election by whatever means it took.

Ron Bellus would have done fine in any administration before mine, or since. Under the constant attack it began to look like he was too defensive and argumentative to be effective. The truth is, it would not have mattered who was there. Ken Smith, the man I appointed in place of Ron, was no better than Ron and he had no understanding of the political situation in Arizona.

My belief in the public's right to know the true facts about what is happening in their government, made progress with the few journalists who had some standards for truth and decency. But most of the journalists we dealt with had none and, even worse, very few were qualified for front line reporting. I felt that my openness would gradually win them over; they would see that I was not the double-talking type of person they often covered in the political arena. The bottom line is that the qualities of honesty, decency, and journalistic excellence that should be present in reporting on government were generally missing.

With a full and constant attack on us, we could hardly afford to give them legitimate fuel for their fires. Even worse for Ron, when the press corps saw that they could get under his skin, they were like a pack of bloodhounds after a wounded prey. Ron became the object of their attacks as well as myself. That had some of the staff and outside supporters advising me that Ron should be replaced for someone with better relations. I refused to replace him until I thought I had no other choice. He and I talked, and we decided he should go back to his old advertising business. I believe he was one of the most relieved people in the state. As a very decent, moral, honest and loyal person, he had really wanted to be a high-profile part of the administration, but when the parting came, I believe he was glad to be out of it.

Although I appointed people already residing in Arizona in all positions up to that time, I decided I should bring in a press secretary from out of the state who, I was led to believe, was more suited for the battlefield which the office had become. One applicant from Washington D.C. was what I wanted, but he would only come for a salary that was out of the question. I settled for Ken Smith, from Sacramento, in September of 1988. Ken made little or no difference. He too wanted to be my spokesman, often without authorization. He too was to get into heated arguments with the press, but by now I was not concerned with winning the press over. I reduced my exposure to them; didn't answer questions from them after speaking appearances and made "no comment" my most frequent response to their queries. Had I done this from the first, we would not have been so easy to attack.

Steiger, too, was a casualty in the same time frame, as explained in the previous chapter.

In November, when it appeared there would be a recall election, I moved Edith Richardson from the governor's staff to my campaign staff and payroll and had her begin setting up a campaign organization from my Glendale office building

Jim Colter was the next change made. When I came back from Japan in October, I found that Jim appeared to be suffering from near exhaustion, which could possibly have ended up in a nervous breakdown if he had stayed on. He had done the very best he could, and I believe that the real trial for him was in his realization that I needed talents in the position of chief of staff that he did not possess. Early in life, he had been a small rancher, schoolteacher, and principal in Apache County. Then he went back to the University of Arizona, attended law school, and practiced law for more than 20 years in Phoenix. He had done legal work for me very satisfactorily. He and Liz had been friends with Florence and myself over the years. He had served a term as GOP State Chairman and was very informed and acquainted in political circles. His agreement with me on principles and issues was almost 100 percent, and his personal loyalty and honesty was unquestionable. He had seemed like the perfect choice, but Jim lacked a key ingredient. He was far too trusting, far too eager to please everyone, and was just not tough enough for the jungle in which I chose him to serve. Like Ron, Jim would have been fine in a society where decency prevailed.

Jim and I had a private visit, and we jointly decided he should leave for his own good. It seemed to bother the press to no end that we said little about it, except that we jointly agreed he was leaving and that we were parting professionally but remained longtime friends. The press wanted something more interesting, like a firing or leaving in a huff, but that was not the case.

With Carlson replaced by Randy Thomas as legislative liaison; Bellus replaced by Smith as press secretary; and Colter, Steiger, and Richardson gone, only Ray Russell, Sam Udall,

Mac Matheson and the secretaries were left as the original key staffers in the Governor's Office.

Fred Craft came from Washington for the purpose of helping to carry some of the load while we were looking for a new chief of staff. When we had realized we were in a full-scale war and that its purpose was to force me to resign, or try to remove me if I didn't, we decided to hire Dr. Richard Burke to take Colter's place. Burke had assured me he could build a lot of bridges with the establishment and the legislative leaders. He was sure he could get House Speaker Joe Lane to listen to reason, but needless to say, Burke never was effective on any of the things I brought him on board to accomplish. Probably no one else could have done it either. The establishment, the power brokers, and my political enemies would be satisfied with nothing but my scalp. As I was to realize later, they knew they had the troops in the Legislature to wield the scalping tomahawk.

I'd known Dick Burke many years before, when he had run for Congress in 1962. He'd had a distinguished career as dean of the law school at the University of South Dakota, as a law professor, and as a federal prosecutor and high-ranking official in the Justice Department. Because he also was a very amiable man, he seemed to be just the person to help rebuild our relationships with some of the hostile factions in the state. He also thought he could bring reason into Speaker Lane's thinking and perhaps head off the impeachment drive in the House.

As my new chief of staff, Burke spent too much time trying to persuade me to let him discharge three of my top people: Max Hawkins, head of the Department of Administration; Lee Watkins, supervisor in that department and in charge of prison construction; and Mac Matheson, who was in charge of constituent mail. I viewed this as an attempt to please my critics and to show them I had completely capitulated. I refused, but Dick never quit trying.

It was soon evident that Burke was not going to be able to fight the kind of fight we needed. Instead of turning Lane around or negotiating with the AG's Office to drop their inane indictments, Burke was soon reporting to me that by his count the House was sure to vote out a bill of impeachment and that there were already enough votes in the Senate to convict me. All of this before any evidence had been presented to the House. Throughout the coming months, his primary advice to me was to resign. Maybe, he would say, Corbin would agree to drop the indictments if I resigned. Rather than gaining strength, I got weakness from Burke. From a lawyer's standpoint, he was probably doing what he thought needed to be done.

It is probable that Burke was completely bowled over by the onslaught from four fronts. He told me soon after he came on board, that from his close observation as a member of the Justice Department during the Nixon Administration, that the press attacks on me made the press treatment of Nixon look like a Sunday school picnic.

At that time, I was just hoping I could weather the storm of threatened impeachment, win the recall election, and win acquittal from the AG's indictments and then rebuild my staff with those who were capable, loyal, and akin to me on principles and issues.

I really knew what was needed when, to my surprise, Burke took most of an executive staff meeting trying to convince me it was in my own best interests to bow before the onslaught and resign before the House hearings got started. I will never know if that was his own idea, or if he was following someone else's instructions.

The logic was that I should agree to resign and retire from the scene without having to spend from $500,000 to $1,000,000 in legal fees to defend myself. But I said "No!" The resignation quadrant of the attacks would never work with me. That would be agreeing to totally abandon the field to the corrupt forces that had been running the state for so long and give it up to them for the foreseeable future.

I don't think I was successful in convincing Burke of the correctness of my position because he suggested to me several more times that resignation was still an option until the Senate voted to convict on the bill of impeachment. Strangely, or maybe not so strangely, it was the last thing we talked about as we parted company.

I had the comfortable feeling that in the battle, the majority of the people would finally become aware of what was going on in the real world of corrupt political control over the state. That was the reason I entered the political arena in the first place. I knew I had broken no laws and had worked harder than anyone in the history of the state to get its many problems solved and head the state in the right direction. Both Florence and our family felt that we were fighting a crucial battle to make Arizona the kind of place where we wanted to live out our lives. We also felt the great need not to disappoint the thousands who had expressed their prayers, support and confidence on an almost daily basis. It puts one in a position where you almost owe your life to the people who have faith in you when the stakes affect their lives and future, as well as your own.

I also knew the power brokers would love to be able to use me as an example of what happens to those who refuse to conform to the old political adage that one has to "go along to get along."

Chapter 18

THEY DON'T HAVE THE PROOF BUT THEY HAVE THE VOTES

"A false witness shall not be unpunished, and he that speaketh lies shall not escape."
Proverbs 19: 5

In the House Hearing, Milstead, for once, told the truth when Representative Giordano, unlike the other members of the House, actually bothered to question him. He admitted that when he called me at my home on Sunday, I had told him that I had asked Max Hawkins to look into the Watkins - Griffith squabble and that the whole thing was just a lot of hot air.

Milstead reported that I had not threatened him, nor had I tried to stop him from ordering his men to go to the Attorney General's Office on Sunday. He didn't need my permission to do so, and I never attempted any retaliatory action for his having done so. On the other hand, he did not mention in his testimony that he had already taken the entire matter to the attorney general before calling me. That would have made the reason for calling me seem a little strange and puzzling to those anxious to believe William French's theory.

This was a finesse performance. Milstead knew he had no reason to call me in the first place. He had never called me at home before. The entire phone call had been meaningless, except for French. It was his whole case in trying to prove that I interfered with a criminal investigation. Even people who found it hard to take the whole obstruction of justice business seriously weren't going to see anything by looking in Milstead's direction.

Representative Giordano's questioning of Col. Milstead brought out answers that completely exonerated me of interfering in an investigation or obstructing justice. Giordano asked the Colonel, "Did you go to the statute books and look up that statute to see if Watkins statement conformed with the statutory definition of a threatening conversation?"

Col. Milstead's answer, "I did not go to the statute books, I was not ready to arrest anyone. I was simply investigating at that time."

Yet at another point in his testimony he stated that it was the attorney general making the investigation. He then admitted under questioning that I did nothing to stop him from going to the Attorney General's Office, and that I made no direct or indirect threats of any punishment if he did. He twice admitted when he called me he was not asking for my permission, and admitted that, "No I do not think I needed his permission to do that," meaning going to the attorney general. He also answered, "His (meaning me) conversation did not influence what I did if that answers your question." And then he said later, "I did not tell the governor it was a violation of the law. I just did not want him to be blind sided."

When Milstead had hung up, I felt quite sure he had recorded the conversation. I was told by those who had worked for him a long time, that he always recorded his phone calls. I was not concerned because I said nothing wrong. When Giordano asked him if he recorded the conversation, he did not answer until the next day. Then he said he did not tape it. I hoped he would admit it because I knew there was nothing incriminating on it. Had they played it to the House Select Committee, it would have put an additional dagger in French's case. I was sure that was why they told him to deny he had taped it. Had we been able to defend ourselves with regular court procedures, we could have brought in Milstead's girlfriend and, under oath, she would probably have had to testify that he did record it. He made the call to me from her house. He would then have had to produce the tape and prove I said nothing incriminating.

The only basis of any accusation of my obstruction of justice was Milstead's testimony that I had told him not to take Martinez and Johnson to the Attorney General's Office on Sunday. There was no crisis to demand they go Sunday, instead of normal hours on Monday. Milstead's answers proved that I did nothing to constitute obstruction of any investigation, which to my knowledge had already been taken care of by Hawkins the previous Friday.

Milstead's answers to Giordano in the House hearing completely wiped out any chance for French to legitimize his obstruction of justice charge. French was not deterred because he knew the Senate would vote to impeach without any proof to the accusation.

The only time I was allowed to testify in my own behalf was a brief appearance before the House Special Hearing Committee in which I gave a 20-minute statement of my version of events. I then agreed to answer any questions from the members of the House, but, since none of my attorneys had been allowed to cross-examine any of French's witnesses, I refused to be cross-examined by French and Eckstein. They were furious. Chairman Skelly was furious. French had assured him that they made all the rules here; they could do whatever they wanted with me; and were obviously looking forward to doing it. Skelly threatened to have me subpoenaed and held in contempt if I refused to answer. He got so confused that he was almost irrational and out of control. French had him call a recess to try to regain control of the situation.

You must remember that we were on live television at the time. Every minute of the House hearing, the Senate trial, and the criminal trial was broadcast live on television. I was to later find out that was a great benefit to me. Many people watched and saw a much different scene than was reported by the news media. Even today, ten years later, I still have people come up to me in public and say that they thought I was a bad guy until they saw the actual proceedings on TV. When they saw it for themselves, they changed their mind about me. Never before nor since has any trial been broadcast on live TV in Arizona.

Skelly knew that he had to at least try to maintain a pretense of fairness, because so many were now able to watch for themselves. All I was objecting to was the impropriety of French and Eckstein doing the questioning in a House hearing where by now they had dropped any pretext that it was an impartial House conducted hearing. It was now becoming obvious to most people watching that it was really a political "grand jury" being conducted by French and Eckstein as prosecutors, determined to get their indictments in the form of a bill of impeachment. I kept thinking that enough members of the House would revolt against this prostitution of the integrity of the institution of the House of Representatives. The few who protested were quickly and loudly shouted down in caucus and smaller meetings.

Until then, everything had gone according to French's and Eckstein's carefully laid plans; they were in total control of every detail. Only those they chose as witnesses were called. They ignored the request of at least one member of the Committee to call Griffith and Watkins as the two people who participated in the so-called "death threat." Their witnesses had been carefully questioned and in the case of the DPS witnesses, Milstead and Beau Johnson, they had been coached for hours on just what to say and even how to act as they said it. Most members of the House Select Committee were well-rehearsed in downtown legal offices. Later, a lot of the Senators were given the same treatment, including being coached on what questions to ask.

In my refusal to go along with French's and Eckstein's questioning, I said I would be glad to answer any question put to me by any member of the House, not just members of the Select Committee. Most of the House members were present as observers. Supposedly the reason no other House business was being conducted was so they could observe and acquaint themselves with the facts of the case. My refusal to let French and Eckstein cross-examine me was their first roadblock, and it threw them all into confusion. Upon having Skelly call the recess, French immediately called Steve Twist, Corbin's chief assistant AG, and asked him how to proceed. This certainly made the lie out of the declarations repeated often by French and Corbin that the House investigation was not an extension of the AG's grand jury investigation.

Word was being passed that they were preparing to serve a subpoena that would compel me to submit to the French-Eckstein brand of prosecutorial cross examination or face jail for contempt of the House. Apparently they couldn't decide on that action quickly, so they came back and Chairman Skelly acted on his instructions from the AG and House prosecutors to recess the Select Committee Hearings for two days.

We knew that the two days were to give them time to school some of the Committee members on how to cross-examine me since French and Eckstein could not do it in person.

The two puppets chosen were Rep. John King and George Weisz. King was a lawyer and more acquainted than most with the skills of examining witnesses. Weisz had been an investigator for the Attorney General's Office before his election to the House. He too was somewhat skilled in interrogation and questioning along a prosecutorial vein. Most thought Weisz was still Corbin's complete lackey, along with Jim Skelly in the House. That opinion gained more credibility with Weisz's return to the AG's employ when he didn't seek re-election in 1988.

We knew that neither the AG nor the House prosecutors had any proof that I had violated any law. However, we had to be cautious to avoid their carefully laid trap, set to trick me into contradicting myself. With clever and experienced interrogators, it can be difficult to answer the multiple questions couched in very different ways with answers that sound the same. We felt certain that Corbin was counting heavily on French and Eckstein to be able in some way to get me to answer questions in such a way that he could use them to bolster his case in criminal court. The danger of this happening is the reason almost all lawyers will have their client take the 5th Amendment right not to answer any questions on grounds that what is said under some tricky questioning might be used against the client. In this way they avoid the multiple questioning and make the prosecutors settle for a one-time cross-examination in front of the jury.

Had I been trying to manufacture answers at any time, I would have really been trapped because I had spoken freely to the press about all details of the accusations. I had discussed the charges and answered questions by the dozens in public speeches and in statements on TV. Channel 12, and their same network affiliate in Tucson set up a full hour live broadcast in Tucson on

November 4th, preceding the hearings. Both stations had their news anchor people there to ask the questions, and I gave the answers. We knew that French and Eckstein had video tapes of every news conference, every interview I had made in order to try to comb out some indication where I may have said something to which they could point to as contradicting something I had said at another time. In the end, when they found nothing, they invented contradictions to try to destroy my credibility.

During the two-day recess, my lawyers were certain that if they did try to subpoena me and force me to submit to French and Eckstein, that the Supreme Court would quash the subpoena. Apparently the AG, French and Eckstein felt the same way because nothing would have made them happier than to win that battle instead of having to back down from their threat.

By Friday, when the Hearings reconvened, their players had been well coached. They asked generalized questions, two or three at a time, and tried to demand yes or no answers to make it appear that I was contradicting myself. In order to avoid playing into their hands, I insisted on qualifying my answers and asking them to be more careful to define what they meant by some of their questions.

The sessions went on for 13 hours. It was quite a frustrating experience for both sides, and I'm sure that my determination in putting up a fight wouldn't have mattered anyway, except to satisfy my sense of dignity. But I think something else started happening that pointed out the biggest long-run mistake my executioners could have made, short of giving me fair treatment. When they opened the entire proceedings to live broadcast television, it created a new large audience whose interest had been piqued by the year-long onslaught of newspaper misrepresentation of my actions and my administration. It was an overpowering volume never before, or since, experienced in Arizona. I believe the high rate of viewer interest was brought on by a lot of people wanting to see for themselves, without news commentators' interpretations. Vast numbers began to see for themselves what was really going on in the political and governmental arena, and we saw a wave of sentiment start to turn in my favor.

During the House Hearings and the Senate trial enough people watched to cause retail merchants to complain about their business being off noticeably. Throughout that time and for months later we received stacks of letters and lots of phone calls saying they were unsure until they looked at the proceedings. That convinced them that I was being "railroaded" and gave many more colorful descriptions of the events.

Of course it was far too late to do much about the impeachment. The votes had been counted before the hearings. We were told that the House would not vote out the bill of impeachment unless they were assured in advance of a guilty verdict in the Senate. The proceedings were only a formality.

Suddenly, people who had been stuck reading phony newspaper accounts saw a brief glimpse of reality. People from all over the political spectrum, some of whom had never had much use for me and my particular views, sat up and saw the railroad job whistle through their living rooms. And some of them must have scratched their heads and wondered, if I was so darn bad, and guilty of everything I was accused of, why couldn't I be afforded a fair trial before the hanging?

Even though I knew the House vote on the bill of impeachment would be coming in as soon as I left the Legislature on February 7th, I decided to keep a speaking engagement I had made for that evening at Lake Havasu City. It was their Lincoln Day Dinner and there was something good about honoring that great man in a small city with folks that really cared about him. The people who took time off to think about Lincoln had my appreciation. I was told that the approximately 300 at the dinner was the biggest crowd ever to attend a dinner in Lake Havasu City. It meant a lot to Florence and me. It was a great outpouring of support, and I knew that in the end it would have to be these people that counted, and not the power brokers and their minions in the Capitol.

I listened to the vote on the radio while we were driving to the airport. Unable to convince even themselves that I had actually done anything wrong, most of the legislators were busy explaining that their votes to impeach didn't necessarily mean that they thought I was guilty. They just thought the matter ought to go to the Senate for a real trial. We knew we'd lose, but I was a little saddened by the lopsided vote, 46-14. I had hoped that there were more than 12 honest and courageous Republicans and two honest and courageous Democrats in the House.

Representative Gary Giordano, one of the few who stood up for truth and justice put the best summary of what the House actions should have been as he explained his vote:

"It is unfortunate that a decision was initially made to proceed with an impeachment since Arizona case law clearly spells out, 'The purpose of impeachment is to serve as an added protection to the public against those officers who may be so powerful as to effectively block court action against themselves.'

"The governor is presently before a court of law concerning his campaign disclosure forms. The governor's use of the protocol fund has been investigated by the attorney general and there has been no indictment. The governor's alleged obstruction of justice has not ever been the subject of an Attorney General's investigation. Yet we are proceeding with a resolution that removes the Governor of the State of Arizona from his duly elected office.

"I had hoped that our Select Committee could have helped us determine if conclusions reached in the investigative report were true. Instead, it provided a forum for those who assembled the report to serve as prosecutor to further prove that conclusion. For all of us that is most unfortunate.

"Our vote today should have nothing to do with our feelings about the governor or because of any outside pressures but because of clear and convincing evidence. I vote nay."

This had to be the very lowest point in the history of the Arizona State House of Representatives. The majority of the members, by their inaction, allowed the operation of their House to literally be taken over by two prosecutors hired by their speaker, without their input or permission.

By the majority's inaction, they allowed "the big boys" (Lane's words) to direct their Republican speaker to hire two high profile liberal Democrats who were known enemies of mine, and cast aside any pretense of truth and justice.

By the majority's inaction, they allowed the Judiciary Committee (which previously handled impeachment hearings) to be replaced by a "Select Committee" made up of mostly members who wanted the target of the impeachment removed, regardless of the facts.

By the majority's inaction, they allowed the prosecutors to run the Hearings like an open, one-sided grand jury seeking an indictment, instead of the members holding unhurried Committee sessions looking for the truth.

By the majority's inaction, they allowed a weak and pliant speaker of the House to be used as a puppet in doing the will of the downtown power brokers to remove a legally elected Republican governor and replace him with an unelected Democrat.

By the majority's inaction, they allowed their speaker to lie and break promises without taking any action to force him to change his ways or be replaced.

By the majority's inaction, they allowed their institution be used to bring about a disgraceful, illegal, political execution named by the *Wall Street Journal* as "a coup d'etat more akin to a banana republic...than a state of the American Union."

Chapter 19

PREPARATION FOR
THE SENATE TRIAL

"I love to see honest and honorable men at the helm,
men who will not bend their politics to their purses,
nor pursue measures by which they may profit."
Jefferson

The rumor mill repeatedly brought us word that the votes in the Senate to convict me on the bill of impeachment were assured. Although we didn't want to believe that so many were so controlled, it was easy to see that the big House vote against me would not have been there if they had not been assured the Senate would do likewise. Very few would have had the courage to vote against the sitting governor if they had not known for certain that he would be removed. Even the ones who were totally "owned" by the power brokers would have begged their masters not to force them to commit political suicide. Had there been any risk that the Senate would not convict, and leave the House standing alone against me still in power, common sense tells you that many House members would not have voted for the bill of impeachment. One House member, Nancy Wessel, a liberal Republican from my own district 19, verified this when she expressed surprise at the anger toward her in the district GOP meeting. She unthinkingly replied that she had been assured that there would be no retribution against those who voted to oust me.

In light of the opposition received from the rank and file party workers, some representatives tried to justify their vote to turn over the Governor's Office to the Democrats by telling the party workers how bad I was as a governor. This didn't wash well with the G.O.P precinct workers, many of whom knew me personally. Others had watched TV and felt differently. It was very evident that the combination of forces that planned my removal convinced the majority in the Republican caucuses in both houses of the Legislature, that I would go out in disgrace and they would be viewed as heroes. They were assured that I would have no more influence on politics in Arizona ever again. Corbin was constantly assuring all political players that he had an airtight case against me on the six felony counts in his indictment. With the daily attacks on me from four fronts, it appeared they might be successful. However, they misjudged the power of the people. They also misjudged the power of honest jurors to see through corrupt prosecutors.

After the display in the House, the Senate knew it could get away with just about anything. While a few votes were uncertain, the establishment could already count between 21 and 26 votes, and they only needed 20. There was no need to pretend the trial was anything but a formality. The number of senators who had declared how they would vote even before any evidence was shown, made a mockery of the Senate trial. I thought that perhaps we could change this if we got the criminal trial out of the way first and broke their momentum. It also would give us sufficient time to really work on preparing a defense. Murray Miller, my chief attorney at that point, also wanted to prepare for the criminal trial, first.

Although there was a constitutional question as to whether or not I could still legally act as governor prior to the vote of the Senate, we knew we would have to go to the Arizona Supreme Court for an opinion, and that any decision from the Court was preordained. Likewise, Secretary of State Mofford initially indicated, through our mutual friend Bob Stump, that she would act as governor from her offices on the seventh floor while my staff and I stayed on the ninth floor during the Senate trial. I was still governor after all. But almost immediately after the House vote on the bill of impeachment, the press started circulating a story that Mofford wanted me, and all of my people, to move out as soon as possible.

Bob assured me this was a fabrication, and the two of us went to see her about it on a Monday following the House vote. Sitting next to her was her new "volunteer" chief of staff, Andy Hurwitz, formerly a key man on Babbitt's team. The whole time we were there, as Bob and I would talk to her, she would look to Hurwitz and he would answer all the questions. "It would be good if we could have everybody off the ninth floor by Wednesday," he told me. "Yes, Wednesday would be fine, at the latest." The power brokers were back in the saddle again!

Ray Russell and his secretary moved to a vacant office on the first floor of the capitol building, which had been vacated by the Department of Revenue when it moved into it's new building. The remainder of my staff, along with my reduced security detail, moved into a building I owned in Glendale. We used it as our interim headquarters.

Initially, Mofford announced she didn't want to disrupt the administration any more than necessary, but immediately removed Max Hawkins as director of the Department of Administration to please his critics. I believe Mrs. Mofford's first statements were her own, but when she became surrounded by former Babbitt advisors, they took over.

Within a week she had replaced virtually everyone who had worked for me, except those remaining on my immediate staff. Then she complained that we had taken everything with us. By "everything," I guess she meant all that belonged to us because we left the governor's offices exactly as Babbitt had left them to us. But I don't recall any newspaper stories about that. Or maybe the establishment folks were so used to reading all our files and memos, that they just couldn't get used to the idea that the paper work wasn't actually theirs. We even left behind a file containing photocopies of checks that had been given to Babbitt's political campaigns. It had been left, stashed away in a closet where bottles for the water cooler were kept!

Also left behind were the Governor's Official Proclamations including the one I issued creating the third Sunday in January as "Martin Luther King Jr. Civil Rights Day." Unfortunately, sometime after Mofford and her new staff took over the ninth floor, that particular proclamation mysteriously disappeared from the files and, to my knowledge, has never been seen since.

The criminal trial was set for March 22, only six weeks away from the House vote, and it seemed reasonable to assume that we'd be granted some kind of extension by the Senate until that had been settled. But French and Eckstein were well aware of the situation, and immediately advised Senate President Carl Kunasek that neither he nor any of the other Senate members should be entertaining any kind of communication with me. It was my tough luck that I'd have to prepare for two major trials at once.

How Kunasek, normally a fair-minded man, ever reconciled his action to schedule the Senate trial for the end of February with a promise that it would be a fair proceeding, I'll never know for sure. Kunasek told a friend of mine that he was invited to a meeting at Barry Goldwater's house over the weekend and that the decision to go ahead with the impeachment trial in the Senate immediately, was arrived at there. Perhaps that explains why Kunasek told me on Friday he would have to talk to the leadership about my request to hold off on the impeachment trial until the criminal trial was finished. That also would have allowed them to finish their legislative session work. By Monday things had changed. Kunasek said the Senate would not wait

This crunch had a snowball effect. It was soon evident that Murray Miller wasn't able to do nearly enough preparation for the Senate trial. Initially, Miller's strategy was to bring a Constitutional challenge to the authority of the Senate to, in effect, try me in two places at once. Whether or not we won this point, we hoped we could get the criminal trial out of the way in the meantime. We were very certain we would be quickly acquitted in the criminal case and that would guarantee the Senate wouldn't dare vote to convict on the House bill. Our enemies knew the same thing and made sure that didn't happen.

As soon as Miller began to research the point and we made a preliminary motion in the state Supreme Court, it became apparent that the position of the Court would be that I had no civil rights whatsoever in the Senate trial. Because of their interpretation of the constitutional doctrine of separation of powers, the Court told me they could not interfere in any internal legislative process and that, as far as they were concerned, the Senate trial could employ any inquisitorial means the Senate wanted.

Miller had not had time to have a backup plan. Fred Craft and Roy Dunton, a friend of mine from Kingman, told me that I better bring in some outside legal help. Roy told me he thought he could raise a lot of the estimated $500,000 needed for legal fees if we found a "name" attorney in whom those supporting me could have confidence.

Having never been around a serious trial in my life, I had little realization of the amount of work that lawyers had to go through in research, talking to witnesses, and getting ready for a trial. Now that I was starting to see the mass of details that Murray was working with, and what a tremendous amount of work preparing for both the Senate and the criminal trial was going to be, it was obvious he was going to need a great deal of help.

Miller has a good track record as a criminal defense lawyer, and I personally liked him and enjoyed working with him. He had worked more as a loner and didn't seem to be amenable to open the circle up to a substantial amount of additional help. Already we had hired Mike Scott, another well-known criminal defense lawyer in Phoenix, to represent Willard in the upcoming criminal trial in Superior Court, but Murray had used Mike very little, which caused me some concern.

I told Craft to go ahead and see who was available on this short notice. I also gave Roy Dunton the go ahead to do all within his power to raise legal defense funds. Shortly thereafter, Fred told me he had a lawyer who had been successful defending three different governors from many indictments that had been secured against them. He thought that my case should be easy and simple for him. He agreed to have lunch with us while he was in Phoenix on some other business. After hearing the outline of my case he, in effect, said that my case seemed very simple, and what he considered easy. He said it appeared obvious I was not guilty of any criminal act and he had gotten others off from much heavier accusations like bribes, kickbacks, etc. He was afraid his time schedule would not allow him to handle the case. After returning to his home office, he shortly verified he could not handle it.

Next, Craft called me from Washington. He said he had tried to talk to number of high profile lawyers to no avail, but he finally had one whom he thought was just what the doctor had ordered. His name was Jeris Leonard. Fred had worked with him before and assured me he was very well qualified and experienced in this sort of thing. As a further benefit, Leonard had spent quite a number of years in the Wisconsin Legislature, and had ended up holding the office equivalent to what we in Arizona call the President of the Senate. Fred felt his political knowledge and experience would be a decided asset in the impeachment trial. He was ready to bring him out for a conference to see if we could agree to allow him to join the impeachment trial. I approved.

We had a get-acquainted meeting with Jeris, and he decided he needed at least a day to get acquainted with others on my defense team: Mike Scott and his partner Tom Crowe; Col. Lavern Hutchins, who was working on research; Bob L'Ecuyer, who had done a lot of the legal research as well; and Murray Miller. The idea was that he would meet them and then would determine what he thought about assisting in the case. We had our meeting, and Leonard changed from just being here to take a look, to an enthusiastic participant. He formally outlined how he could bring together the whole team of Scott & Crowe and add another attorney, Norbert Settle, doing research. He would have Fred Craft and hopefully Murray Miller. He would get a Dr. Fishman to do legal research in Washington. But, he would be the quarterback of the team and organize the legal talent so that the criminal case for Willard and me, as well as the impeachment trial, could go on almost simultaneously. Yes, they could give me good legal representation.

Leonard was a tall, thin, dark-complexioned man with a somewhat commanding personality. He gave me confidence that he could be the leader needed. He moved with obvious difficulty from the crippling effects of a head-on automobile crash that had almost taken his life some years ago. I faced the Senate impeachment trial which, if I lost, would remove me from office. Willard and I faced the criminal trial in less than a month, which could take away our freedom. And, I faced the recall election that was set for May 15th, for which I would have to organize a complete campaign and work very hard to win. It was not a time where decisions could be made at our leisure. I was comforted by Leonard and Craft's assurance that this was a quality team and that they could give me good legal representation. I agreed to appoint Leonard as the quarterback of the team and immediately bring in the added legal reinforcements.

Roy Dunton had felt confident that he had already seen some success in setting up a Legal Defense Fund Account in all the Valley National Bank branches across the state. Already funds were starting to come into the account in a surprising number. John Thomas felt he could have a huge rally in the ASU Activity Center and raise a quarter of a million dollars. Roy felt that we could raise the half million dollars that Jeris said we might possible need for the total legal defense. I also was quite encouraged by the assurance that everything would be researched and tracked, so that if we didn't get fair treatment in the Senate trial, we could appeal it to the state Supreme Court or to the federal court if necessary. Thus began the three-and-a-half months that would be the most tense and trying period of my entire life.

As oftentimes happens, things did not work out quite as smoothly as the picture was drawn in the first place. In retrospect, there is little value in pointing fingers toward anyone in saying why it didn't happen that way. The prosecutors had unlimited money and resources to plan every move and almost every word they said. We, on the other hand, were never able in the impeachment trial to even hope to be prepared. The appeal to the Supreme Court to postpone the Senate trial until after the criminal trial met with no success. At the urging of the chief justice, who was designated as the presiding officer of the Senate trial, the Senate did agree to wait one week to start the trial. This gave my lawyers only enough time to set up their organization, start the research, and talk to some witnesses. Leonard told me he had to tell them he was ready when he was in only at 10 percent of readiness and preparation. I was not happy with his representation of being ready when we weren't, but when he told me it was too late to say anything. This was according to the careful plans of the prosecution team. In addition, the prosecuting attorneys withheld vital information that in a criminal or civil court they would have had to turn over to the defense.

Senate Majority Leader Usdane made a public accusation that I was bringing in the new lawyers in an attempt to try to delay the trial. It showed that he was totally unsympathetic in giving us an opportunity to prepare. They seemed to almost be in a panic to start for at least two good reasons. First, they needed to get the impeachment trial finished before the recall election scheduled for May 15th. If the trial were to extend beyond the recall election, which I might have won, they would then be hard pressed to find reasons to convict me in the face of the voters' wishes that I stay. And secondly, both French and Eckstein knew their case was based on accusations without legal proof. Since October, they had been working in close collaboration with Corbin to prepare a case. Their biggest ally was their ability to keep my lawyers from being prepared. Had this been a criminal trial, they would have had to grant a continuance to give my defense counsel time to prepare. But it was a political trial, so all bets were off. The Senate was making the rules and, inasmuch as it was only my political life at stake, their rules were supreme. Due process and the protection of any reasonable rights of the accused were thrown out the window.

Our concern was continually heightened with the recurring word we received that they had enough votes to convict me. This they stated even before any evidence was presented. That gave us some additional apprehension that a guilty vote in the impeachment trial might prejudice the outcome of the following criminal trial. We knew that Corbin was hoping it would.

To further complicate matters, Leonard approached Murray Miller in what Murray considered a rather high-handed attitude and said he was now in charge of the defense. Things were happening so rapidly, and I had so many other things to attend to, that I couldn't be there to see that every detail was handled with diplomacy. Leonard had arrived in town on Sunday, and by the following Wednesday was appearing with Murray and Tom Crowe to have the Senate accept him as counsel assisting on the case. I had expected Leonard to get each one working on the part of the case they were best suited for and to have the team work in a harmonious unit. Murray felt like Leonard was coming on in a high-handed way, ordering him around like an intern attorney. The result was that there would be no harmony between those two—always an undercurrent of hostility.

Leonard told me that Murray had refused to work with him and had pulled off the case. He said that he would go settle up with Murray and get all the materials. I said no, I would talk with Murray and handle that part of it. I liked Murray and, although I was disappointed he was pulling off the case, I didn't want him to leave with hurt feelings. We paid him in full, and Col. Hutchins got all of the material and moved down to the office of Crowe and Scott, which the legal team used as their headquarters.

It was not until many months later when Murray and I were talking, that I discovered his total surprise at me coming. He took what I said as my desire to terminate his service, when, in reality, I was just doing what I considered was acquiescing to the decision he had already made to leave the case. Whether Leonard tricked me into dismissing Murray because he wanted him out of the way, I will never know. We needed more lawyers, not less and I was disappointed to lose Murray's services. However, I knew that it wouldn't work if it was not harmonious.

It's common practice for civil and criminal courts to grant reasonable extensions for new lawyers to prepare to defend a case. When I asked the Senate for just a few additional days so that my new counsel could familiarize himself with the case, I was flatly refused. It was as if I was being reminded that, since my defense couldn't possibly matter, bringing in a new attorney was just the equivalent of stalling.

Chapter **20**

THE SENATE TRIAL

"Never does the human soul appear so strong and noble as when it foregoes revenge, and forgives an injury."
Chapin

By the time we were required to start the Senate trial, we realized the well-planned four-front assault was being executed to perfection by the power brokers and their minions. That is easy when they controlled the whole system. We knew we had no level playing field. The state Supreme Court had said I had no constitutional rights, no civil rights, and no due process. The prosecutors could conduct the court like a Star Chamber of ancient England. Our defense was not allowed adequate time to prepare for the trial, nor were the prosecutors made to share witness and evidence information with our defense as is standard in any civil or criminal suit. The prosecution was allowed to bring up almost everything they wished, whether or not it pertained directly to the three Articles of Impeachment passed by the House.

Any thought that we were living in a normal, civilized society where rules of decency allowed for differences of opinion and the rule of law was ever-present, had been driven from our minds. We now knew that once I had won the election fair and square, that certain elements in our society decided immediately that they would do anything it took to get me out of office. They

---

266

wanted to stop me from dismantling their money-making machine that depended on their control of state government. French was allowed to go through my business records, bank accounts, property information, etc., to find some place where I had done something wrong that he could charge me with. They even checked my property and dealings in Tacoma, Washington, and found nothing. It was truly a witch hunt, a desperate search to find anything to back up their pre-determined goal to remove me from office and jail me if possible. Their abuse of power was where the crimes were really committed, but who was there to call them to account? They controlled the system.

It is almost amusing now to read the preliminary remarks by Judge Gordon of the Arizona Supreme Court who was the presiding officer of the Impeachment Court. Excerpts follow, along with my comments:

Judge Gordon: "Impeachment is a political, rather than a criminal proceeding."
My comment: That was always the justification given for handling the impeachment like a kangaroo court. * (Webster's Dictionary meaning: . . . an unauthorized, irregular court, usually disregarding normal procedures, as an irregular court in a frontier region or a mock court . . .) Because it was political, there was absolutely no appeal to a higher state or federal court. Conviction took only 20 votes, regardless of any standard of proof or how the Senators had conducted themselves as both the judges and the jury.

Judge Gordon: "Impeachment thwarts the will of the voters who elected the impeached official."
My comment: "Gordon said over KTAR radio shortly after the impeachment that it should not have been used because I was already subject to a recall election and a criminal indictment. If Gordon was sincere, he was duty bound to use his high judicial position to try to stop it. Ten years later, in April of 1998, Senate President Kunasek also said the same thing as Judge Gordon about impeachment being wrong. That was over Channel 8 TV.
Together they could have stopped the impeachment. Had they been committed to justice, they would have left the verdict on my future

to the recall election and the criminal trial as precedent nationally has followed.

Judge Gordon: "My role as presiding officer will be to keep the proceedings moving on track, in an orderly fashion, and in compliance with the rules adopted by the Court of Impeachment. These rules, and to 'some extent' the Arizona Constitution and Statutes, the Arizona Rules of Evidence, and certain provisions of the United States Constitution, should greatly help and guide us."

My Comment: The only rules followed were the Senate's own Court of Impeachment rules. All others were ignored. The protections afforded by the State and Federal constitutions for an accused were ignored as well as the Arizona Rules of Evidence. Perhaps in this case "some extent" meant "not really."

Judge Gordon: "These senators, who will be referred to as Judges of the Court of Impeachment, are 'in a sense' really both Judges and Jurors. They are bound by the Constitution to do justice according to the law and evidence."

My comment: The 'in a sense' phrase, above, is typical of the whole impeachment process. It seems designed to signal that anything goes, nothing is really set in cement, and there is nothing indicating the Senate had to feel constitutionally bound to do justice according to the law and the evidence. How can anything be presented as constitutional in this nation when the judge and the jury are the same people, and most of them are taking their orders from the unelected power brokers? Judge Gordon would have been much more honest if he would have said the only rule in this trial is that it takes 20 votes to convict.

Judge Gordon: " . . . the senators will ask whether the charges have been proven by clear and convincing evidence. This standard of proof is more demanding than the preponderance of evidence standard used in ordinary civil litigation. The clear and convincing standard is reserved for cases where substantial interests at stake require an extra measure of confidence by the fact finders in the correctness of their judgement, though not to such degree as is required to convict of a crime."

My comment: The senators certainly failed on the standard of proof test. When the state grand jury failed to indict Lee Watkins, it proved there was no death threat. Corbin called me as a witness on the Watkins question but I was not a target and, as bad as Corbin wanted to convict me of something, he would have included the obstruction of justice charge if there had been one scintilla of evidence to support it. In addition, Milstead said in his House testimony that I did nothing to interfere with him or his officers. That made it impossible for the senators to come up with clear and convincing evidence that I obstructed a criminal investigation when the one who I was to have obstructed said I had not.

Neither House Hearings nor the Senate trial produced any evidence that could change the status of the inaugural funds from private to state or public funds.

The other article in the House bill of impeachment was on the subject of the Wolfson Loan, and it was dismissed and left to the criminal court. Where were the senators looking to find clear and convincing evidence on which to convict? They certainly ignored any standard of clear and convincing evidence as described by Judge Gordon.

Judge Gordon: "It is up to all of us as citizens to let the system work. Pressuring your senator to vote based on anything other than his evaluation of the law and evidence is in effect pressuring your senator to violate the oath to uphold the Constitution."

My Comment: I think that the Judge was part of the orchestrated campaign to keep the voters from trying to stop the Senate from an old-fashioned political lynching. No one has the right to tell the public they cannot contact their elected officers at any time on any issue. Two cases of the many senators who were pressured by the power brokers to violate their oath and convict me are as follows:

Gene Hall of Show Low contacted Senator Bill Hardt from Globe about the trial. Senator Hardt assured Gene that Governor Mecham was not guilty of anything impeachable and not to worry. Then Hardt voted to convict. When Hall contacted him for an explanation for his big switch, Hardt said: "You just don't realize how much pressure they put us under." I wonder if the "pressure" he was put under made it legal for Senator Hardt to violate his oath?

The other was Senator John Hays, who assured his constituents there was nothing impeachable on Governor Mecham—not to worry. I was told that he was called down to the Valley National Bank shortly before the vote was taken. It may only have been to discuss the mortgages the VNB was reputed to have on his property, who knows? He then voted to convict. Hays was not re-elected in 1990, but was rewarded with a much higher paying state government job. The high paying jobs also greatly increased his retirement pay amount. Make your own judgement about whether he was, or was not pressured to impeach.

While Judge Gordon's preliminary speech may have recited words that had the trappings of legitimate due process and fairness, the actual procedure employed was just the opposite. The system was bent and changed to produce the result planned by the power brokers, right from the first. Judge Gordon assisted in making sure it worked that way. Had the system been allowed to work there would not have been an impeachment trial.

Our system calls for two ways to replace a governor, aside from regular elections:

1. A recall election is part of our system, and I was facing that election with the anticipation that I could have won it. Had I not won, I would have been peacefully removed from office.
2. A criminal trial is the other, which I also was facing on the questionable indictments the attorney general secured from the grand jury. I was quickly acquitted of any wrongdoing in that. Had I been convicted, I would have been out of office immediately.

Removal by impeachment is not legally an option of our system unless the officer in question is so powerful he or she cannot be "reached" in normal legal procedures when suspected of being involved in illegal activities. That is why it is never used except in my case. As I have pointed out above, I was already "reached" by both of the above methods. The Chief Supreme Court Judge knew this, as is reflected in his comment on KTAR that impeachment should not have been used. As I have said before, had he and

Senate President Kunasek acted according to their later stated beliefs against the impeachment, their words would not ring so hollow.

The Senate trial could have been handled in half of the time, had not French kept trying to help Corbin strengthen his weak criminal case. Apparently, he also liked the added time at the high hourly legal fees he was charging, and he liked the publicity. From the information we were getting, French knew the votes were there for conviction before the trial started. The charges were fairly simple when stripped of French's theatrics and misinformation.

There were only three Articles of Impeachment. Article I was the obstruction of justice. In plain words, it charged me with trying to keep Col. Milstead from cooperating with the attorney general in the investigation of the alleged death threat made by Lee Watkins to Peggy Griffith about Donna Carlson.

Article II charged me with hiding the $350,000 loan to the campaign by Wolfson & Gregan. The Senate Court of Impeachment dismissed it.

Article III accused me of misuse of state funds. The "state funds" they referred to were the $80,000 of the inaugural ball ticket funds. The misuse referred to was our removal of $80,000 of the inaugural funds from a money market account at 4.5 percent interest and depositing (loaning) it to Mecham Pontiac at nine percent interest.

Since the Court dropped Article II, the trial was based on Articles I and III.

Please Note: My objective throughout this book is to provide factual information with as little use of legal language as possible. The third person excerpts that follow are from Hutchins manuscript. (For those who want the legal proof of every point pertaining to this wrongful impeachment, a scholarly book called, *Arizona's Big Lie: The Removal of Governor Evan Mecham,* by Col. LaVerne Hutchins, is scheduled for publication in 1999).

Article I - Obstruction of Justice

On Thursday, November 12, 1987, Peggy Griffith and her secretary Terri Fields met Lee Watkins crossing the parking lot west of the Capitol. After greetings were exchanged, Watkins commented, "Your friend Donna Carlson is a bad girl." Mrs.

Griffith's light answer: "So what else is new?" Both went on their separate ways.

At 1:30 p.m. the same day, they were both on the eighth floor when Mrs. Griffith asked Watkins to come into a conference room and tell her what he meant earlier about Donna being a bad girl. Both Watkins' and Griffith's reports agree essentially that the following conversation took place: Watkins— "I told her that she ought to tell Donna to keep her mouth shut and quit running the governor down in the press and making the statements that she has been making. That there's a lot of people out there who are excitable and she could have harm come to her."

That night Mrs. Griffith talked to some friends in Mesa and to her husband about the conversation. She was advised to take her story to the governor. She set up an appointment to talk with me but I was forced to cancel. Mrs. Griffith decided to see Lt. Johnson, head of my security. He was not there so she gave Officer Martinez a brief overview and asked him to get her in to see me to give me the complete story.

Lt. Johnson, in his report, said he came back and listened to Martinez, then called Lt. Col. Chilcoat at DPS and requested that he listen to Martinez' explanation of his talk with Griffith. Johnson said Chilcoat agreed with him that a crime may have been committed and "we decided the governor should be informed immediately." (Johnson made two cardinal mistakes here. Instead of making his report to me or my chief of staff, he called Chilcoat at DPS. Johnson then made no move to inform me at that time, 9:40 a.m.)

At 11:30 a.m., Mrs. Griffith returned to the ninth-floor security office and asked Lt. Johnson to get her in to see me so she could tell me her whole conversation with Watkins. Johnson told her to wait and he would try to do so. But instead of getting Mrs. Griffith in to see me, Johnson began to tell Chief of Staff Dr. Richard Burke what he knew. Burke told Johnson to see Fred Craft, my Washington representative who was in Phoenix to assist Burke who was new on the job. Craft, assuming it was a threat to the governor, stopped Johnson short and said they should tell him. Craft and Burke accompanied Johnson to the governor's office where, instead of trying to get Griffith to tell what she heard,

Johnson gave his version of what Martinez had told him about the altercation between Griffith and Watkins in the parking lot.

Craft described the meeting with the governor in his written report: "Lt. Johnson said it had been reported to him that Mr. Watkins engaged in a verbal altercation with Mrs. Griffith and the upshot was that Mrs. Griffith considered his remarks to be a threat against Donna Carlson, a former employee of the governor. This report was very preliminary and third or fourth hand. The matter had not been investigated. There was no discussion as to what laws, if any, may have been violated.

"The governor heard Johnson out and instructed that the matter be turned over to the director of administration for investigation. That concluded the meeting, which lasted less than two minutes.

"The report was sketchy, details were not known. Nothing said by Johnson alerted anyone to the need for taking steps other than those ordered by the governor. The governor handled the problem in the only appropriate way possible, given the information presented."

Dr. Burke said basically the same in his report: "There was no extended conversation about the matter. The governor told Lt. Johnson simply to take her over to Max Hawkins, who was Watkins' supervisor, and report the incident. I was advised Lt. Johnson did arrange for her to see Mr. Hawkins later that day."

The following is the governor's testimony to the House Committee: "Lt. Johnson accepted the assignment to turn the probe over to Hawkins without a word to anyone that he had already reported it to Lt. Col. Chilcoat at DPS who, in turn, had reported it to Lt. Col. Phelps (deputy director) who had reported it to Attorney General Bob Corbin more than two hours earlier. Nor did Johnson tell Hawkins. He didn't tell Griffith that he hadn't tried to get her in to see the governor although he led her to believe he had. He said he had carried her message."

That Friday afternoon, Hawkins interviewed both Watkins and Griffith. He was to be the only one who investigated the matter by talking to both participants. Hawkins reported: "I interviewed Lee and Peggy. Their story was very similar with one remembered exception. Peggy said the word 'whore' was used. I asked Lee if he had used the word 'whore' and he said he probably had used it. I reported to the governor about 5 or 6 that evening, Friday, Nov. 13th. I told him I had heard no serious threat and that the matter would disappear on its own. He said thanks and let me know if anything else comes up, or keep your eye on it."

The discrepancies in Lt. Johnson's statement and his testimony before the House Select Committee and the Senate impeachment trial are so numerous as to lead one to believe he was carefully coached on what to say, but could not always remember what he had said earlier. Some examples:

1. His reason for going to see the governor was because Mrs. Griffith asked for his assistance in getting in to see him. Instead of pursuing that objective, he saw Chief of Staff Burke who sent him to Craft and they both took him to see the governor. He reported back to Mrs. Griffith that he had delivered her message, which he had not! Her message was to get an appointment. He gave what sketchy account he knew of the event instead and never relayed Griffith's desire to tell the story to the governor in person.

2. Contrary to the agreement on how the ninth-floor security detail was to work, Johnson immediately reported to Lt. Col. Chilcoat at DPS headquarters who, in turn reported it to Phelps, who turned it over to Corbin. This was done secretly without ever informing the governor or his staff, which by agreement were to be reported to first.

3. Johnson said, "Mr. Craft advised the governor that the he should be distanced from these events and that this should be a matter that Mr. Max Hawkins should handle." Both Craft and Mecham said the matter should not have been brought to the governor, but to Hawkins as a personnel matter, and it was the governor, not Craft, who instructed Johnson and Burke to see that this was done.

4. Johnson said he realized a felony may have been committed (but this is not what his written report said) when Martinez told him at first, so he called his superior, Lt. Col. Chilcoat. (Remember at this point Johnson only had Martinez' oral report which Mrs. Griffith said was a brief overview)

5. To the House Select Committee Johnson testified: "... and then I explained after that it was a felony to tamper or influence a grand jury witness. That was the whole reason of coming in and seeing him." (He had forgotten that the reason to see the governor was to get an appointment for Peggy Griffith. Johnson had never mentioned to Burke, Craft, or Mecham anything about "a felony or grand jury witness.") Peggy said she never told Johnson the full details of her conversation with Watkins because she expected to talk with the governor and the only reason she talked with Johnson was to secure his help in getting an appointment with the governor.

6. In the Senate Court of Impeachment, Lt. Johnson's first testimony did not mention any felony. Later he was recalled by French to add to his testimony, . . . "I said it is a possible felony to tamper or influence a grand jury witness." Johnson had to be brought back to the stand and receive promptings from the prosecutors before he added that statement to his testimony before the Senate.

7. On another subject, Lt. Johnson was asked in the House Select Committee Hearing if he thought it was unusual that the investigation of this incident was turned over to the Department of Administration. His answer: "I found it unusual. I didn't treat it as a personnel matter . . ." But during his Senate testimony he was asked, "Did you tell Max Hawkins that you had already informed the Department of Public Safety of the relevant facts as you were relating them to him?" Johnson answered, "No!" Another question: "Is there any reason you didn't?" Johnson: " I didn't see any need to tell him that I informed my department. I didn't see any need. I

assumed that this investigation was going to be an administration investigation and at the time I didn't see any need to tell him." Question: "You thought it was a personnel matter, didn't you?" Johnson: "I did. I thought I was treating it, yes, that way. (While testifying in the Senate, Johnson apparently forgot what he had said in the House and totally reversed himself.)

When Lt. Johnson testified earlier before the House, the words "death threat" were used on numerous occasions. Mr. Weisz asked: " Lt. Johnson, there are a number of statements made in that tape by the governor. He talked - the governor mentioned that it was - and I am paraphrasing because I don't have a transcript, but you saw it, ...it was never portrayed to his consciousness that there was a death threat. Did you express that there was a death threat, that you were concerned about the governor?"

Lt. Johnson's answer: "Yes, I did. I again explained to him the conversation that Mr. Watkins had with Mrs. Griffith, and that if she didn't keep her mouth shut something could happen to her, maybe not now but next spring."

During Lt. Johnson's first appearance before the Senate he was asked: "Again, for the purposes of the record, because the senators need to know, please explain to the Court exactly what you told the governor."

Johnson replied: "Again, walked in, Mr. Craft said that 'Beau has something to tell you Governor.' Proceeded with my story. Peggy Griffith had been stopped in the parking lot a couple of days ago by Lee Watkins. According to Peggy, Lee told Peggy to tell her friend who's been a whore, that she better keep her mouth shut. That if she does not, that something could happen to her, maybe in the spring, that she could take a long boat ride."

(There is nothing in this exact rendition of what Johnson allegedly told the governor about possible felony, grand jury, tampering with or influencing a witness, or death threat.)

Johnson was then asked: "There's been a term used and coined, and it is floating around in these hearings, and I think we ought to try and get it straight. In describing the situation to the governor, did you ever use the term "death threat?"

Johnson answered: "I never did."

He was then asked: So if the term has come about, it was not through your conversation with the governor?"

Johnson's answer: "I never said that, Mr. French."

In responding to the question, "Did you express that there was a 'death threat' that you were concerned about to the governor?" Johnson testified before the House, "Yes, I did." Then, later, in the Senate, to the question, "Did you ever use the term death threat to the governor?" he answered, "I never did." Both times he was under a sworn oath to tell the truth. One answer was a lie and to lie under oath is a clear case of perjury.

Johnson's written statement as well as his testimony are riddled with inconsistencies and contradiction. The truth is that Johnson did not know enough about the alleged threat to brief anyone on it. He testified before both the House and the Senate that he wanted Peggy Griffith to brief the governor because he didn't have the story; and he wasn't even certain that Martinez did. Johnson did not brief Chilcoat; he asked Martinez to get on the phone and relay the information to Chilcoat. That was when the words about finding Donna Carlson in the bottom of the river were created. Chilcoat, Phelps, and Milstead were the only ones to ever use those words.

FRENCH INVENTED THE 'DEATH THREAT'

French wanted to make it look like Governor Mecham was lying on television when he said that he knew little about a "death threat." Nothing since has ever proven that Watkins had issued a death threat. The words 'death threat' were never used before being introduced by French when he had Milstead as a witness in the House Hearings. The words never appeared in the written statements of Officer Martinez or Lt. Johnson that were taken at the AG's office on Sunday. Fred Craft, Dr. Burke, and Mecham all testified that Johnson never used the words in his report to the governor. Mrs. Griffith's statement never said anything about a death threat and Lee Watkins never used the words. It is obvious French planned to make the conversation into a death threat in order to give substance where there was none.

Since the governor was not allowed to be represented by a lawyer in the House proceedings, it was easy for French to slyly introduce the words as a given fact by his questions to Milstead: "Do you consider the director of administration, Mr. Hawkins, to have the experience, training or expertise to conduct an investigation of a death threat? The answer from Milstead: "No, sir."

A scene had been carefully created in this hearing that would never have been permitted in a criminal hearing. French was establishing a mind set with the words, "death threat." Milstead used those words on two more occasions during his testimony. French worked desperately to destroy the credibility of Hawkins' probe and report to the governor that Griffith and Watkins conversation was "hot air" and would blow over.

Hawkins oversaw Capitol Security, and had he seen anything serious in this threat, he would have summoned the Commander of Capital Security Lee Limbs, who has the law enforcement detail to protect the Capitol Complex. Milstead knowingly lied when he testified that the Department of Administration did not have the authority, the expertise, or jurisdiction to investigate a death threat.

The bottom line on the French-designated "death threat" is that Hawkins' investigation was proper, legal, and the only real investigation into the altercation between Watkins and Griffith. Furthermore, there was no death threat by Watkins against Carlson. It was a crime manufactured by Mr. French to give the Senate an excuse for my impeachment. It also gave the press a new ominous buzz word to liven up their stories.

History will record that the only crimes committed were those perpetrated against me by my accusers. (Refer to Platt letter on page 187)

Even though Milstead's answer to Representative Giordano and Representative Killian in the House Hearing wiped out any hope French had in proving I did anything to obstruct a criminal investigation, it was the only horse he could ride on that charge in the Senate trial. Milstead was the star witness, and a review of his testimony is valuable:

Giordano asked the colonel; "Did you go to the statute books and look up that statute to see if Watkins' statement conformed with the statutory definition of a threatening conversation?"

Col. Milstead's answer: "I did not go to the statute books; I was not ready to arrest anyone. I was simply investigating at that time."

Yet at another point in his testimony he stated that it was the attorney general making the investigation. He then admitted under questioning that I did nothing to stop him from going to the Attorney General's Office, and that I made no direct or indirect threats of any punishment if he did. He twice admitted when he called me he was not asking for my permission, and admitted that, "No I do not think I needed his permission to do that," meaning going to the attorney general. He also answered, "Mr. Killian, his [the governor's] conversation that day did not influence what I did, if that answers your question."

No prosecutor in his right mind would ever have put Milstead on the stand as his star witness in a court of law because of the ease by which the defense could impugn his testimony. French was not deterred by that in the Senate impeachment trial because he had it set up that we could not question his character, or even question his actual illegal intimidation of our witnesses in the account that follows.

Every time we attempted to introduce evidence concerning Milstead's motives into the Senate trial, it was deemed "inadmissible". (The chief judge finally said Milstead had the motive of knowing I planned to dismiss him.) The fact that Milstead's massive abuse of DPS resources and his conduct in office, hiring and firing on a personal basis (sometimes for sexual favors); charging his romantic adventures to the department's budget; using his private police force to harass anyone who objected; and my desire to remove him from office because of this, which provided him with a motive for lying, was deemed "irrelevant" under French's rules of procedure. Although Milstead was the prosecution's star witness, his character and credibility, we were told, was not an issue here.

That is entirely at odds with the bottom line that we could and should have been allowed to impugn his testimony. We had 21 different items that could have been used to do so. In a court of law we would have had him easily discredited, but in this political court he was given complete protection. One senator who voted for impeachment admitted to a mutual friend, several months after the Senate impeachment trial, that he and others knew that Milstead was lying through his teeth. (So much for the character of that senator.)

It was even harder to accept that Milstead and the DPS were allowed to get away with what, in normal circumstances, would have been serious criminal witness tampering.

When Terri Fields, an assistant to Peggy Griffith, was due to testify in the impeachment trial, Milstead ordered her arrest. Terri was with Peggy when she talked with Lee in the parking lot and Milstead knew her testimony, that there was no threat from Lee, would hurt the prosecutions case. The Milstead and DPS action was designed to keep her from testifying or, failing that, to discredit her testimony. This was criminal witness tampering in the worst form. But, of course, there was no action taken, even though my lawyers went to the Feds with it.

The crime Fields was accused of committing was missing a court-ordered meeting of Alcoholics Anonymous. Of course, a single unpaid parking ticket could have done just as well. Otherwise the DPS probably would have had to arrest her as a suspected accessory to something so they could have continued to investigate until my trial was over.

Milstead had attempted to insulate himself from the action during the Senate trial by having a DPS officer, posing as a *New Times* reporter, telephone Fields and ask to meet her at a hotel to interview her. Milstead then planned to have Mesa traffic police officers arrest her as she drove to the meeting. In this scenario, they could run a computer check on her driver's license that would have turned up the outstanding warrant for missing the AA meeting, and the Mesa cops would jail Fields without even having to wipe Ralph Milstead's fingerprints from the scene of his real crime.

When Fields refused to go to the hotel to meet the "reporter," Milstead just said, what the heck, and had her arrested at her home. Then the DPS issued a statement that they were investigating the possibility that Fields was wanted in Florida for child abandonment and cocaine abuse. Later, of course, Florida authorities reported there never had been any substance to these charges, but the accusation and its prominent reverberations through the news media had its desired effect. The Senate, in their own eyes, was then justified in disregarding the testimony of the only witness to the "death threat" conversation between Lee Watkins and Peggy Griffith.

Sergeant Alan Schmidt, Milstead's spokesman, claimed all this was just standard procedure and had nothing to do with intimidating or discrediting Fields as a witness. Milstead had never spoken to anyone at all about Fields, Schmidt stated. (When reporters learned that the order for Fields' arrest had come from Lieutenant Colonel Gary Phelps, Milstead's second in command, and hardly the man to be chasing down misdemeanor warrants, the DPS simply failed to react to the reporters' questions, and everyone including the press dropped the subject.) Schmidt said that while watching Fields testify in my trial, a DPS officer had recognized her as the subject of one of the state's 250,000 outstanding warrants. (If only the FBI could have that kind of luck with their post office wanted posters!) DPS's elaborate plot to lure Fields out of her home so that someone else could arrest her for them was meant to effect her capture on "neutral ground." Apparently they feared this single mother who had once missed an AA meeting.

More amazing than Milstead's story was the fact that the *Republic* and *Gazette* gave them full credence, and then followed that up with editorial support. Only the *New Times* found any of this either preposterous or objectionable.

Milstead then went after another witness. Electronics expert, Antonio Corio, worked for the Dept. of Administration and had come to us with evidence that my office had been bugged, and that the Attorney General's Office was using high tech eavesdropping equipment as well. Corio proved Corbin lied when he said they had no such devices when he showed us the invoices for the purchase of a van full of eavesdropping equipment made for the AG's office. But when Corio took the stand for us in the Senate, he told a very different story. Upon investigating, my attorney discovered that DPS officers admitted having paid a visit to Corio prior to his testimony, but only to encourage him to tell the truth, they said. After he was observed being let out of Col. Milstead's car in front of the Capitol Tower, Corio became a different person. If they had threatened him, they were very effective.

Corio totally forgot the Saturday morning in early 1988, when he, along with Capitol Security Chief, Lee Limbs, and Deputy Director of the Department of Administration Dave Hall, met in the governor's office to test for listening devices. Corio was sure they were being used to listen to my conversations, and with the equipment he had, he picked up a beam and called the FBI. Three of their agents came over and identified the frequency of the beam being used to eavesdrop on my office as that assigned to DPS. The beam then quit and the FBI agents said that DPS now knew that they had been discovered and would probably not resume their clandestine eavesdropping. The FBI agents said they would keep a quiet look out, but didn't want any of this made public.

Another bit of purely circumstantial evidence, which tends to substantiate this type of activity by DPS, was the discovery of an empty room on the third floor of the new Water Resources building. It was situated in such a location as to allow line-of-sight electronic transmission between that room and the governor's office on the ninth floor of the state Capitol. Most of the windows in the room were covered with wall-board, but in front of one was a chair surrounded by empty coke cans and cigarette butts. It indicated someone had used this as a post for electronic surveillance of the governor's ninth floor office.

Corio had a change of heart from the time Craft first interviewed him. When he was called to the witness stand, he completely changed his story. In frustration, Craft tried to get the judge to declare him a hostile witness, which would have given Craft the opportunity to bring out the testimony we knew we had, but to no avail. Presiding Judge Gordon refused Craft's motion and Milstead's police power thwarted us again.

At about this same time, DPS Intelligence Officer Jerry Dodd called Maricopa County Sheriff's Detective R. S. Ploeg for a favor. He wanted another of our witnesses, Christina Johnston, arrested on a six-month old charge of misrepresenting herself while trying to repossess a car. Ploeg pointed out that if DPS had nothing better to do, he had 25,000 outstanding warrants of his own they could help with. Dodd dropped the issue and instead leaked a story about Johnston's " criminal past" to the Phoenix papers, which promptly printed it. Again, the DPS wanted our witnesses harassed, but not so it could be traceable to them.

Although the AP story about DPS's witness tampering appeared the next day in the news media all over the rest of the country, the local papers never ran it. Instead, the *Republic* continued to feature unsubstantiated stories that other DPS officers, who began coming forward with stories about Milstead, were actually mentally ill.

When Lt. Coy Johnston (no relation to Christina) testified that Peggy Griffith had lied to Max Hawkins during Hawkins' investigation of the "death threat," Milstead immediately released a story that Johnston, the head of the DPS Merit Review Board, was mentally unbalanced.

When we pointed out in the impeachment proceedings that Col. Milstead was using DPS officers and, where possible, city police to harass and falsely discredit defense witnesses, we were told not to worry, someone would look into it. The "someone," of course, turned out to be Milstead himself. The AG's office couldn't "investigate" its witness, because that would be a "conflict of interest." (In fact, Corbin found he had a conflict of interest investigating virtually anyone in government except me, the person whom his office had been responsible for advising all along.) The feds couldn't investigate the witness tampering charges against Milstead because that is not a federal issue. Acting governor Mofford appointed her special assistant, Andy Hurwitz to "look into it." Hurwitz, formerly Milstead's personal attorney, promptly turned the investigation back over to the DPS, which managed to report, with a perfectly straight face, that it found no improprieties in its own actions.

Fortunately, the Associated Press went national with a lot of news items, including accounts of the DPS witness tampering and witness intimidation. *In The Arizona Republic* and the *Phoenix Gazette* these stories either were ignored or printed with a reverse spin to show that I was now completely paranoid. The factual happenings, when mentioned, were twisted to look like they were only a figment of my imagination. Now, ten years later, when Arizona media and my political enemies still continue to repeat that

I was an embarrassment to the state, many out of state people know that it was the almost unbelievable treatment I received that was the embarrassment to our state. I am still surprised how many people from other states are aware of what was brought about to remove me from office. It's difficult for them to believe this could happen in modern America.

The feared length of the impeachment was apparently behind the move to have the Senate drop Article II on March 30th, at 4:30 p.m.

Article II had not been taken up as yet and appeared to be the one that would take the most time. It was rumored that the prosecution feared that the defense lawyers could probably prolong it past the recall election time. To solve this concern, another illegal step was taken.

Dr. Heinz Hink, one of the House Board of Managers, remarked that they could not dismiss any of the charges without hearing the evidence and voting on the law and the evidence. Unfortunately, Hink did not have the courage to protest the wrongdoing.

Each senator took the following oath as part of the requirements of the impeachment process: "Do you, and each of you, solemnly swear or affirm that you will truly and impartially hear, try and determine the impeachment adopted by the House of Representatives of the State of Arizona, and the Articles of Impeachment presented by the Managers elected by the said House of Representatives, against Evan Mecham, as Governor of the State of Arizona, and do justice according to the law and evidence, and a true judgement render therein, so help you God?"

This oath required them to vote on the whole bill of impeachment sent over by the House. Had this been a trial based on the law and the evidence, and where each senator felt bound by the oath they had taken, Article II could not have been dismissed. Again the kangaroo court was in progress. Anything goes as long as they reach the right conclusion, which was to get me out.

As I watched them dismiss Article II and then get ready to vote on articles I and III, I was very glad that my upcoming criminal trial would be in a court where the jury of my peers would be called on to make the decision on the law and the evidence. Of the 30 senators sitting in judgement of me, I do not believe that even one-third of them would have passed the jury selection process of a formal Superior Court case. If for no other reason, many would have been rejected because of a pre-trial bias against me.

The Senate Court was a very confusing mess, and I am quite sure it was planned that way. First of all, the House bill of impeachment was so full of confusing language and far-reaching charges it made one think that they were throwing a lot of mud on a wall in hopes that some of it would stick, so I could be removed from office.

The House bill had a long list of charges contained in 20 subsections listed in three articles. There was no set procedure for the voting except that it was to be done by roll call. There was a disagreement on whether each of the charges/subsections should be voted on separately, or just the three articles as a whole. Had they voted on each charge, each senator would have had to declare himself or herself, on each charge and it was obvious that there was a lot of difference of opinion among them. Had the majority of them not owed their soul to the power brokers, I doubt that there would have been a two-thirds convicting vote on any one charge. Perhaps that is why they went into secret caucus to decide behind closed doors what to do. They came out with the decision to vote on the two articles instead of by subsection, as is done in Superior Court.

Those who explained their vote proved there was real confusion and not a lot of substantive thinking to their reasons for voting to impeach me. This would have made a great case for an appeal, but French and Eckstein knew there would be no appeal to pick apart the garbage they had assembled for a case. Had their handiwork had to stand up to appeal inspection, they would both have been hanging their heads for their shameless antics masquerading as law and justice. But in this venue, there is absolutely no appeal. The senators' votes were final, and they had one vote more than needed to convict.

The one explanation that was worth repeating here is by Senator Sossaman. First, please note that Senator Sossaman had been an ardent Burton Barr supporter in the 1986, Primary when I defeated Barr for the nomination. He was then serving in the House as Speaker. It was to him that Hawkins and myself appealed to have an Ethics Committee hearing on important charges that Barr violated their conflict of interest rules. He quickly refused. He never supported me in any political race. He has always been an establishment Republican who moved from the House to the Senate in the 1986 election and was from District 30 where I had very strong support. He is a fair and decent man, but some of his speech was dictated by the district he represented.

Sossaman's explanation of his vote is by far the most informative of any:

> I envy all of you that have come to a decision and you feel comfortable about it. I am not sure I will ever have that peace of mind.
>
> Each of us has our own blending of ideas together to come to a decision, and these include our understanding of the facts in a case like this, politics involved, what is consistent with our own personal philosophy and how we perceive the voters in our district feel on a subject. At the same time, we have to evaluate how it affects the state as a whole. I am sure you, here on this floor, have other ideas that you put into this decision-making, and I am sure at times I do also.
>
> I would like to go back to the beginning for just a moment, because I think that reflects on what my decision had to be.
>
> In the beginning of this trial I want to remind you that I was one of six senators that voted to delay the impeachment process until the criminal court trial and the recall election had a chance to take place. Those mechanisms were already set in motion, and that vote, at least in my case, was based on four main reasons.
>
> Number one, why should we interrupt a particularly difficult legislative session for what could be as long as 10 or 12 weeks when the other methods of resolving this issue were taking place. Especially when we consider the cost and time and money that would be involved in this impeachment trial.
>
> Second reason, I was convinced that justice could be better served if the governor was tried in a court of law for

the criminal allegations against him rather than an impeachment, which is a political trial.

I have to certainly agree that we had the legal right to hold this trial and understand completely why many of you felt we had an obligation to do so.

But let's be honest. We here on this floor carry a lot of baggage and biases that would not be tolerated in a court of law. This is not to say we haven't been fair, but if I were on trial for a serious criminal offense, I believe I would prefer to take my chances before a jury selected by the court rather then by my fellow senators.

The third reason that I had been concerned if we were to convict the Governor prior to the recall election there could be some real legal ramifications that could prevent him from serving, thereby circumventing the will of the people.

In addition, as a Republican, I have been concerned over the possibility of simply handing over the office of Governor to a Democrat, personable though she may be. That is not the way I play politics. And that was a distinct possibility, if the person being recalled is no longer in office.

The fourth and final reason was that in my entire time in the Legislature, setting this trial in motion has to be one of the most serious political mistakes that the Republican majority has ever made. Setting up a forum before the entire state to uncover all the dirty linen of the Republican governor and his administration. [Note: I still do not know what "dirty linen" he was talking about.]

I understand that some of you, and you remarked that to me, that felt a responsibility to clean our own house, but in my opinion, that point is valid only if you felt there was no other way to accomplish that cleaning.

But there were other ways, and they were in progress. If those failed or were not accomplished to our satisfaction, we always had the option of coming back after our regular work was done and taking up the issues of impeachment.

But I realize that is in the past. We can't go back. Senator Mawhinney, my Humpty-Dumpty was broken early on and I didn't get it fixed, but I would like to at least share with you where I started in this process.

Because now, no matter how we vote here today, many of the voters in our district will feel that we have betrayed them. People who have been our friends and political allies will no longer support us. Precinct committeemen will refuse to carry our petitions. It will be some time before my party will totally recover. And some of us will not be back again, raising a possibility of losing the majority that we the Republicans have enjoyed in the House and Senate. In short, this has been a no-win situation.

Now, in every controversy like this, there are a few positives that come out of it. I think our secretaries have done yeoman's work in handling all these phone calls. Why they haven't quit is beyond me.

It has already been mentioned that you, Judge Gordon, have done an excellent job. I think we have created a greater awareness by the public of what state government is all about, which should translate into a better participation in future elections. A great number of people know who their legislators are, and they know that we can be contacted, and they know how to contact us. And we here on this floor have a better understanding of what judges and juries are faced with as they perform their duties.

I have been characterized by some reporters as a staunch, ardent supporter of Governor Mecham. Let me assure you that that is not the case. Reporters like to put everybody in nice, neat little boxes. And sometimes even they make mistakes.

I would be the first to stand here on this floor and admit the Governor has made a number of politically embarrassing mistakes; some members of his administration have proven to be incapable of running state government. I certainly do not want to hold his administration up as a model for future governors to follow. It is apparent that there were many lapses of good judgement, not only on his part but on the part of others on his staff.

And although I am uncomfortable with these and other actions of the governor, I am even more uncomfortable with the idea that I would in any way negate what the voters of this state have done.

The right to vote is a privilege that I hold sacred, and to negate an election by the people requires great reflection on my part. I am still convinced the best and most Democratic way out of this morass is to let the people of this state resolve this issue by their vote May 17.

I can wait 44 days. Therefore I vote no.

On Article I all 11 Democrats and 10 Republicans made up the 21 yes votes to convict. The remaining 9 Republicans voted NO.

On Article III the 11 Democrats voted yes. They were joined by the same 10 Republicans that voted yes on Article I plus Sossaman, Kunasek, Kay, Steiner, and Usdane who had voted NO on Article I switched to vote YES on Article III. Their explanation was that, inasmuch as I was already removed from office on the first vote, it did not matter on the second one. Why not pile on and prove to the power brokers they were still safely under their control.

Sossaman was right about some of them not returning because of their actions in the impeachment. Senate President Kunasek and Speaker Lane were among the largest group of legislators ever to lose their seats in the next election. Never before had the speaker of the House and the president of the Senate both lost their seats in their party's primary election.

Then the presiding officer called for the vote on whether I should be barred from ever holding office in Arizona again. By a margin of 17 Yes and 13 No votes, I was not disqualified from holding office again. Apparently, there were a few with a guilty conscience who felt this would give them some relief from what they had already done.

The court recessed for a day and then came back to finish up the business. My lawyers then made a motion for payment by the state for my legal fees. The debate over that was most amusing. Some wanted to allow me to keep my inaugural fund as payment. Finally the vote was carried with 16 votes to pay and 13 against.

Runyan was not there for that vote, but his vote against paying me would not have changed the outcome. He was too ill to attend and, in fact, was confined to the hospital most of the 18 days he did not attend out of the 26 days of the trial, but he showed up to vote to convict in a wheel chair.

Col. Hutchins, who did investigative work on my trial defenses is a retired Air Force colonel and had served with Senator

Runyan, also a retired Air Force colonel. He talked with Senator Runyan and indicated he did not feel that Runyan, due to his illness, had the mental alertness to have qualified as a juror in any court of law. Runyan's absence for 70 percent of the trial days also caused him to miss many important votes on motions throughout the trial.

Senator Lunn also was absent seven days, or 27 percent of the trial days. Neither should have been allowed to vote in the final outcome. Had he and Runyan been disqualified from voting because of lack of attendance, as would have been the case in any other court in the land, I would not have been convicted. Both had been very vocal critics of me and were known yes votes for conviction before the trial started. Their being allowed to vote certainly made a mockery of the oath they had taken which included "...and do justice according to the law and evidence, and a true judgement render therein, so help you God." This merely adds to the total of many illegal acts perpetrated in this most famous kangaroo court.

It is worth noting that the "stalwart" senators who made up the Court of Impeachment and who so often questioned my integrity, proved to have little integrity themselves. They became the biggest deadbeats in my life. They would not pay the legal fees that they voted to pay. I had to file a lawsuit and then, finally, in 1994, they paid me part of what I had coming and I agreed to withdraw the lawsuit.

As I left the Senate chambers where I had just been removed from office, I had a hard time getting through the mass of members of the press. All were anxious to make the most of this once-in-their-lifetime opportunity to question a governor removed from office by impeachment.

Although I had been told many times that the votes for the senators to impeach were assured before the House bill of impeachment was voted on, I still had a hard time accepting the fact that, even for political considerations, the majority of the Legislators could act so much like mindless robots. Now I knew they could and did.

I have observed that having a political office seems to make too many people feel important and too often willing to trade their souls for furtherance of their political careers.

The Senate Trial

I had maintained an optimistic attitude throughout the impeachment trial. Now it had arrived at its well-planned goal of my removal, the press seemed sure that I would lose my pleasant demeanor and finally explode with some colorful quotes. But I did not feel like exploding on anyone. I only felt a deep disappointment in people who could take oaths in the name of God, say such things as truth, integrity, and justice while doing all the things that political corruption has brought into our system of government by those who want to continue to control it. I told the press that I was fine, and I could live at peace with myself without being governor. I had done my best and kept my word with the people of Arizona. But the real tragedy brought on this day was not with me, but with the majority of the senators. They had violated their oath, betrayed the people of Arizona, and would have to live with that on their conscience the rest of their lives.

With that I left a subdued press and went down to the first floor where my DPS security detail seemed anxious to get me in the car and leave. There were about 150 of my supporters assembled there but unknown to me, they had become concerned about a young man in a "Mecham for Ex-Governor" shirt who was shouting that he was going to "kill the governor." Instead of being arrested by the DPS, or Capitol Police, or the Phoenix City Police, he was allowed, to the disgust of my supporters, to simply disappear with nothing said. Sort of ironic, considering one of the articles on which I was impeached was in relationship to a death threat that never happened. This one happened in public with law enforcement people in attendance with no action was taken.

I knew I had a ride home because I furnished my own car instead of using a state car for my transportation, for most of the time I was governor. The DPS security detail insisted driving me home safely, and there we said our good byes. We had become good friends. According to what some of them told other people, I had treated them as equals, which they were not used to from other governors. I preferred to ride in the front seat with them and saw to it that they always had meals when I went to an event where food was served. Except for Lt. Johnson, they served me well.

Chapter 21

THE RECALL ELECTION

"The end of law is not to abolish or restrain, but to preserve and enlarge freedom. For in all the states of created beings, capable of laws, where there is no law there is no freedom."
John Locke

We had one more chance to see if there was to be anything resembling honesty, legality, and justice in the actions of those controlling government in Arizona. We had the recall election, legally qualified and certified by the secretary of state to be held on May 17, 1988. It was to be an interim election for the balance of my term.

My name as the target of the recall, was automatically put on the ballot. This was called for by the Arizona Constitution when I refused to resign within the five-day window after the signatures on the recall petitions were approved. Carolyn Warner, 1986, Democrat nominee; retired Congressman John Rhodes; and Jack Londen had all announced their intentions to run. They had set up organizations and, by the time of my impeachment, they had spent a lot of money on the race, as had I. Mrs. Mofford had not as yet announced her intentions to run.

I had looked forward to this election as a great opportunity to inform the people of all the things we had accomplished and how well the government was responding to my administration's leadership.

All of the other candidates running were tuned into the Power Broker circles and all started their campaign activities in early February, shortly after the February 1 announcement of the recall to be held May 17th. The House bill of impeachment was not passed until February 8, 1988, so the other candidates must have had assurance from their inside sources that the votes to impeach were already counted, even before any votes were taken in the House and two months before the Senate vote.

The only thing that they appeared to be concerned about was whether or not the recall election would be held if or when I was impeached out of office. On January 21st, Corbin issued an opinion that it would be held regardless of the outcome of the impeachment proceedings. He said there was no provision in the Arizona Constitution whereby a recall election could be canceled, once it had been certified by the secretary of state. That seemed to settle that question, but it left a big problem for the power brokers. Even though their attacks on me had been unrelenting and vicious, their saturation point seemed to have been reached, and it seemed some backlash against them, and in my favor, was under way. That was aided by the live television broadcasts of the proceedings that allowed the people to see for themselves what was going on.

With at least four candidates to divide up the vote, it was generally believed that I would end up with the largest number of votes, and win back the office. They had assumed that the impeachment would include the Dracula Clause to disable me from holding any office again. That motion failed for lack of votes, so I was free to run again.

Again we see that the power broker's dilemma was being solved by the Supreme Court's violation of the state Constitution, when they cancelled the recall election on April 12th. It stated the reason for the cancellation of a legal election was that the new Governor Mofford could not be recalled because she had not served for the necessary six months before an officer can be recalled.

The members of the Court surely knew that Governor Mofford's time in office had nothing to do with the recall election. She was never subject to recall regardless of how long she served because she succeeded to the office. The Arizona Constitution does not provide that office holders are subject to recall unless they have been elected or appointed to the office. Mrs. Mofford succeeded to the office. She was neither elected nor appointed thereto.

The Arizona Constitution, Art. VIII, pt.1, Section 7, reads: "Every public officer in the state of Arizona, holding an elective office, either by election or appointment, is subject to recall from such office by the qualified electors of the electoral district from which candidates are elected to such office. Such electoral district may include the whole state..." Thus the major reason given by the Supreme Court for canceling the recall election is invalid. This eliminated what the Court alleged was a contradiction in the Arizona Constitutional provisions. This means that the attorney general was correct on the fact that there is nothing in Arizona's Constitution that allows a cancellation of a recall election once it has been scheduled.

Justice Cameron dissented from the majority opinion of the Court and made the following vital points:

"Ariz. Const. Art. 8 pt. 1 Sec. 3 provides: If he (the officer being recalled) shall not resign within five days after a Recall Petition is filed as provided by law, a special election shall be ordered to be held as provided by law, to determine whether such office shall be recalled. The duty to order a recall election is based upon the determination of the sufficiency of the recall petitions and is mandatory .... In this case, Governor Evan Mecham did not resign and an election was properly called.

The recall provisions in the Constitution under Art. 8 pt. 1 Secs. 1, 2, 3, 4, 5 and 6 set up the procedures not only for the removal of public officers, but also for the election of their successors. The Constitution contemplates that a recall election will be held even if the officer being recalled has his name removed from the ballot...In this case, Arizona law required the position of Governor be filled by the designated line of succession as found in Ariz. Const. Art. 5 Sec. 6 ONLY if the candidate who has won the recall election fails to qualify..

The Constitution does not require that the recall election is cancelled or the officer subject to recall is removed from office, or otherwise had his name removed from the ballot.

Art. 8 pt. 1 Sec. 4 is consistent with Art. 5 Sec. 6 which states: In the event of the death of the Governor, or his removal from office…, the Secretary of State, if holding by election, shall SUCCEED to the office of Governor until his successor shall be elected and shall qualify."

Justice Cameron also points out that Governor Mofford was to hold the office only temporarily until my successor was elected. He asserts that in this case, "the recall election is merely a special midterm election which would fill the vacancy created by Evan Mecham's removal from office."

Justice Cameron takes his fellow jurists to task as he quotes from their decision and then shows their fallacy: "There is no purpose to be served by the recall election. This 'finding' (decision) by the majority is not a justification for this Court to DEVIATE FROM THE CLEAR MANDATE OF OUR Constitution. Once the recall process has properly begun, this Court has no power to stop such election regardless of whether we believe 'no purpose will be served' by such an election. The recall provision in our constitution is intended as a reservation in the people of the power to recall any official without judicial interference…"

Our Judiciary all too often seem that they are entitled to act confused by clear statements in the Constitution, whether state or federal, and then proceed to change it by their own decisions as the majority of four did in 1988.

To solve the power brokers' fear that I would win the recall, Corbin instructed the secretary of state to remove my name from the ballot. Had the Supreme Court majority not cancelled the election, they would have had to replace my name on the ballot because there was no restriction to my being in the race and finishing my term if I had won.

I saw a parallel to this in the 1998, NBA basketball finals. It was the sixth game with the Chicago Bulls leading the Utah Jazz three games to two. The Jazz had to win to take the series to the seventh and deciding game. If Chicago won, they had won the series. In the realm of basketball, the world championship is the pinnacle of success so everything is at stake.

Late in the game, Utah had the ball and was leading by 4 points. As the 24-second clock wound down, Utah guard, Howard Eisley, launched a shot from beyond the 3-point line and it went in giving the Jazz a seven-point lead. But wait a minute! Even though the shot clock still had one-tenth of a second showing on the face, when the ball left Eisley's hands the referee ruled that the shot clock had expired and took the points away. The replay run repeatedly by the TV broadcasters showed that the call was wrong.

A few minutes later, Ron Harper of the Bulls launched a jump shot with the shot clock clearly showing no time before it left his hands, but the referee ruled the two points counted.

The sum total to Utah of those points was a loss of 3 points they earned and Chicago got 2 points they did not earn. When the game ended, Chicago was ahead by 1 point. In the actual score they were behind Utah by 4, but that is not how the NBA calls it.

Did the four of the five Supreme Court justices know they were violating the rules of the game we were in by violating the state constitution? In the case of the NBA referee, he had the excuse that it was a split second call. The jurists had no such excuse! They had plenty of time to read the sections of the state constitution that clearly show that they violated the rights of the people to choose the governor for the next 32 months by their vote, not by the Court's wrong decree. It was a clear betrayal of the people's right to choose who will govern.

In Chapter 24, I will cover some of what that decision has probably cost the people of the State of Arizona since April 4, 1988.

Chapter 22

THE CRIMINAL TRIAL--
CORBIN'S FRIVOLOUS SUIT

"In questions of power, then, let no more be heard of confidence in man, but bind him down from mischief by the chains of the Constitution."
Jefferson

After the Senate trial, Craft and Leonard assumed that Corbin and the establishment would drop their criminal charges against me. They knew as well as we did that those charges were rubbish, and they had gotten what they wanted out of them, which was to create the appearance that I was guilty of something throughout the impeachment trial. Furthermore, all their talk about the need to "bury the hatchet" and heal the state's wounds would have given them a perfect alibi to drop their charges without having to admit they were groundless.

Based on that logic and, I suppose, acting like any good defense attorney would, Craft and Leonard went to the AG's office to see if the charges in the criminal trial could be dropped. They were amazed to learn that the AG's idea of a plea bargain was for me to plead guilty to a Class 6 felony and take my chances on whether the judge made me serve time or not. It was an amazing display of overconfidence by the prosecution since it wasn't even clear that any of the charges made were felonies, even if I had been guilty of them. I can only surmise that they had been lying to the public for so long that they'd come to believe their own propaganda.

Between the announcement of the grand jury investigation in October and the actual start of my criminal trial, which had been postponed until June 6th, there had been a constant, unrelenting barrage of publicity, all of which was presented in a way that assumed I was guilty. Practically every day for five months, the residents of Phoenix, where my trial was to be held, heard stories repeatedly saying that the six indictments against me could put me in jail for up to 22 years. As far as the press was concerned, I was already tried and convicted. While this was certainly wearing on my nerves, it also quickly became a matter of concern to my lawyers. They feared that I might not be able to get a fair trial within the domain of the Pulliam press.

Therefore, my lawyers requested a change of venue so that I could be tried anywhere else in the state. Like the other 23 of the 24 motions made to Superior Court Judge Ryan, it too was turned down. Initially Mike Scott, who had appeared before Ryan on other cases, was rather shocked. Eventually he got used to the idea, as I had, that no matter how good a case we presented, the Court was likely to rule against us whenever the possibility presented itself.

It was like being held in a vise-grip and being unable to move enough to save yourself. We had felt confident from the first that, given an honest jury, we would get a quick acquittal. Now, being tried without even that benefit loomed as a possibility. Scott, who had never worked with a psychologist on jury selection before, suggested we call in a noted expert from San Jose, Howard Varenski, who had been involved in a number of high-profile cases.

Varenski was skeptical that Willard and I could ever get a fair trial in Phoenix, but he promised to do his best. He suggested we put on a mock trial for ourselves, using a cross section of the local population as jurors to determine their reactions to various strategies. We hired 16 "jurors" to fit his list of what was needed for a random sample to represent our possible jury. Craft became the prosecutor and Willard's lawyer, Joe Keilp, and Mike Scott, my attorney, took their actual roles as defense lawyers.

With Varenski's help, we learned quite a bit. Among other things, we discovered that it wouldn't help us to embarrass Donna Carlson in front of the jury, although she would have been particularly easy to discredit.

Varenski left from this first visit very concerned about our ability to get an honest jury. After having lost on most of the motions we made, not only in the Superior Court but the Appellate Court and Supreme Court, we were extremely delighted to win on a very important request: that we be allowed to question the jurors as they were chosen by the judge.

Initially, a panel of 100 was chosen from which to pick the jury. The 100 people were then called in and asked to fill out a 100-question questionnaire that was made up jointly by the prosecution, defense, and judge. Varenski had assisted Scott and Kelp in submitting the questions that we wanted to ask and, naturally, these questions were designed to let us find who would be prejudiced against me and have a foregone decision to convict me in advance of the evidence. I had already had too much of that in the impeachment trial with the legislators.

The prosecution, of course, would pose questions that would do just the opposite. The answers to those questions eliminated 48 of the list that were struck for inability to be impartial as interpreted from the answer to the questions. Then we sat for an almost two-day-long session as the judge, the prosecution, and the defense all questioned each juror individually in the courtroom. Varenski sat between Scott and Kelp and weighted each juror on a scale of one through five, according to their answers to all the questions. One was the best and five the worst.

Willard and I sat on a bench behind, and I also set up my own rating system and made notes relative to the disposition of each according to their answers. If a person were obviously not equipped to be an impartial juror, the judge would excuse him or her. For those who fitted what the defense lawyers thought showed an obvious bias against myself or Willard as determined by their questions, they moved to get the judge to strike them for cause, and the prosecution did the same in reverse. The objective was to choose a panel of potential jurors that the judge certified as being able to be impartial jurors. The prosecution and the defense each was given the opportunity to strike six of the 24 from the list, leaving 12 jurors that would be impaneled as the official jury for the trial. Afterward, we had a session at Scott's office and determined the six that we wanted to strike and also knew that the prosecution would be putting in the names to strike a number we would love to see stay on.

Older men are the least likely to vote to convict and older women are the next best for the defendant. That changes in proportion to age, right down to young women who are most apt to vote to convict and young men next. Family, background, business, profession, etc., all have a statistical bearing that Varenski uses. A juror was dismissed if either side could establish a reason why he or she should be "struck for cause," that is, eliminated because of clear evidence of the possibility of bias, such as personal acquaintance with me or Bob Corbin. If the judge did not agree with the attorneys' claims, the jurors remained in the pool.

After interviewing 42 prospective jurors, the judge had 24 of them, men and women, certified to serve. Then the prosecution and the defense were allowed to eliminate six of the final 24, resulting in the final jury of 12 citizens. Varenski was much more optimistic than he had been initially, believing that we had succeeded in seating 11 who would listen to the evidence before making a decision.

When we were through, Varenski was much happier. We all felt that with a decent jury we could win an acquittal, and we were all pleased with the overall quality of the people chosen. As Varenski left, he said to let him know when the victory celebration would be after the acquittal because he wanted to come. And true to his word, he did.

Despite the absence of any positive signs, Scott went to the usual pre-trial meeting with Corbin's chief assistant, and some say, the man who really runs the AG's Office, Steve Twist. Again Twist was adamant on my pleading guilty to a felony. It was obvious they wanted me in prison as a means to remove me from the political scene in Arizona forever. We could see that he had gotten used to having his way and felt that pretty much anything was possible. Besides that, he had no compunction about spending millions of taxpayers' dollars in his prosecution, knowing that I would have to deplete my own personal funds to defend against their onslaught.

Then, suddenly, two days before trial, Scott called to tell me he'd been getting feelers from the AG about a settlement. He said he'd never seen such a reversal in attitude before, and that he could only assume that they'd finally realized they didn't have a case. I really wanted to go to trial to vindicate myself. I could see their overconfidence had finally created an opportunity for me to prove to any of the public still willing to listen, just what had been going on all along. I was really tapped from paying attorneys' fees and other trial costs like Varenski's fee, and I suppose that, in the back of my mind, there was still some fear that however innocent I was, the establishment would somehow own one more hammer to use against me.

In the evening before the start of the trial, Mike Scott called and in between profane descriptive references about Corbin and his staff, he said they were making a last minute plea offer. The AG's new offer was for me to plead guilty to three Class 1 misdemeanor counts and Willard to one. Probably sensing that the AG was indeed panicking, Scott told me he was confident we could win the case, but it was my decision. But even with five empty chambers, I didn't want to play "Russian Roulette" with my brother's life. I told Mike that, if all charges against Willard were dropped, I would consider a plea of *no lo contendre* to one misdemeanor. That was like saying to a traffic policeman that I believe I can prove I am not guilty of the traffic ticket you have written. But I will sign it because it is much cheaper and less trouble to pay that small fine, than go to court to prove my innocence. The AG's prosecutors insisted on the three misdemeanors for me and one for Willard, so they made it easy to say no deal. Mike concurred and reminded me that while we could probably trust a jury made up of Arizona citizens, Superior Court Judge Ryan, appointed to the bench by Governor Babbitt, had not proven any more reliable than the Legislature, in his treatment of our motions for dismissal.

After using a dozen lawyers to prepare their case, the AG's Office had decided to go with Michael Cudahy and Bernard Lotstein for the trial itself. Lotstein seemed to have been angry for so much of this life that it had cast his features into an unpleasant countenance. Looking at him reminded me of President Lincoln's saying: "By the time a man reaches age 40, he's responsible for his own face." Maybe that was part of the price Lotstein paid for being one of Corbin's minions.

Judge Ryan made the trial itself about as difficult as we were afraid he would, despite the presence of television cameras that we had hoped would restrain any out-and-out favoritism. Time and time again, the prosecution was allowed to introduce virtually anyone or anything they wanted into the courtroom. They had so few witnesses of any substance, they had to bring in everyone they could create an excuse for calling, so it would look like they had a real case to present. In reality, they had a frivolous case and they knew it. They were allowed to bring in a handwriting expert to testify that Willard had signed my name on a document, even though we would have been glad to stipulate that to have been the case. Their sole object was clearly to create the impression that Willard was some kind of cunning forger, when, in fact, the judge was aware that half the documents presented by the prosecuting attorneys had probably been signed in a like manner by their secretaries.

In order to create the impression that Wolfson was some kind of crook, the prosecution flew in a Philadelphia bond expert to "explain," in highly pejorative terms, where Wolfson had gotten the money to lend to us. Wolfson had done nothing either illegal or unethical. We had stipulated that Wolfson had in fact loaned us the money. Where he had it invested before, had nothing to do with us. We began to see that the real reason he was brought in at great cost, was an attempt to cover up the fact that they had no credible witnesses. We were hoping the jurors saw through it, and we were to later find out they did.

Despite what we perceived was the partiality of the bench, it seemed to us that when the prosecution rested, they had utterly failed to state a case against us. We couldn't see how on earth any jury could convict us, even without our presenting a defense. However, when we moved for a summary judgment for acquittal, it was automatically rejected by Judge Ryan. We discussed asking for the verdict without putting defense witnesses on the stand, but with so much at stake we decided not to take a chance.

When we tried to introduce evidence that the attorney general had refused to take action in every case of at least 50 campaign financial filing improprieties at least as severe as what he claimed we made, that information was deemed inadmissible. When attorneys Robert L'Ecuyer and Michael Greene, both experts on campaign finance reporting, were scheduled to testify for us concerning the actual construction and the confusing inconsistencies in the finance reporting laws, Judge Ryan refused to let either of them take the stand. I began to worry that again we might be prevented from getting crucial information to the people so that a fair judgment could be rendered.

We had at least two key witnesses that Judge Ryan had to permit. One of those was Jim Shumway, who had taken over as secretary of state when Mofford became governor. Jim had been in charge of the election records at the Secretary of State's Office when our campaign statements were filed, and he had been a witness for the prosecution in the grand jury hearing. However, the prosecutors knew that Shumway was honest and that his testimony had only served so well in the grand jury setting because the prosecutors had been able to selectively ask him leading questions with no cross-examination or clarification for the defense allowed. They had to call someone from the Secretary of State's Office in order to introduce the documents to the jury and it should have been Jim Shumway. But, to prevent him from taking the stand in a real trial, the prosecution had called a new clerk who knew nothing at all about the documents, so we called Shumway ourselves.

The prosecution no doubt had felt, by not calling Shumway as their witness, they would eliminate our ability to cross-examine him. When an attorney calls his own witness, I was to find out, he cannot cross-examine or lead the witness in his examination. Our attorney solved that by having my attorney Mike Scott call him as my witness and then Joe Keilp on behalf of Willard did the cross-examination of Shumway. We got far more than we could have even hoped for out of that cross-examination. Throughout the trial, Lotstein would pop up and object to almost everything we would try to do to get our case laid out in front of the jury. To his credit on this witness, Judge Ryan made Lotstein sit down and shut up and let Kelp bring the answers from Shumway we needed to prove our case.

First was the provision in the law that said we could lump like sums of money together, which was what Willard had done on our finance report. Then Shumway was asked what he told people who inquired about how to list different categories of money on the report. He quoted that portion of the law about lumping like kinds of money and gave that as his instructions. That is exactly what had happened when Willard called the Elections Division of the Secretary Of State's Office to get clarification of the instructions on how to fill out the forms. Willard followed those instructions when he lumped the loans together on the single line for loans. He listed my name on the loan line because I had loaned part of the money personally and I had taken personal responsibility to pay all loans if the campaign could not raise the money to pay them all. Western Savings had loaned me $300,000, Wolfson had offered $600,000, of which we actually used $350,000, and the other loans for smaller amounts made up the total.

After the election was over, I did personally pay the balance of the loans that the campaign did not raise enough money to pay.

Our second crucial witness was Barry Wolfson. On the one hand, Wolfson was able to convincingly explain to the jury what the prosecution had been calling a thoroughly incriminating letter. My campaign manager, Jim Colter was an attorney and he worked with Wolfson, also an attorney, to put the papers together for the loan. Wolfson did not want to be known to the political community as a lender of large sums, for fear other candidates would pester him to help them in this election. To cover this requirement, he requested a standard commercial business "boilerplate" provision that his loan must remain confidential. He wrote us a letter covering this and the other provisions we had agreed upon for the loan, including my blanket personal guarantee of repayment. Wolfson and ourselves knew that all the money that came into the campaign had to be reported, and nothing in the letter gave any indication that the loan was not to be reported.

Perhaps most important, however, was Wolfson's presence before the television cameras. The logic of the prosecution's argument depicted Wolfson as an evil person who had given me secret funds with some subversive purpose in mind. They had first accused me of promising him appointments as the lure to make the loan. What he got was his money back plus 10-percent interest, and nothing else.

Since the prosecution had never been able to show the faintest outline of any other purpose, their only chance was to make

Wolfson appear so vile that the jurors would somehow imagine a motive where the prosecution had been unable to convincingly provide one. To this end, the AG's office had continued to harass Wolfson with a variety of groundless civil accusations that, one by one, were being thrown out of court. They never tried to charge him criminally, but they did create the appearance that Wolfson had been involved in illegal bond transactions and that his loan to me made me look like I was doing something less than honest. They apparently figured as long as they could keep at least one accusation against him alive, they'd be able to have him perceived as a criminal, just as they had tried to do to me. The fact that the AG used the power of the state to utterly destroy the career of a once-prominent bond attorney was, of course, no concern of Corbin's.

Again and again Lotstein attempted unsuccessfully to trick Wolfson into making apparent contradictions by misquoting the testimony Wolfson had given previously. Wolfson would first correct the misquote and then answer the question. Lotstein finally realized he had no chance to trip up Wolfson. It was a typical example of the prosecutors trying to make a case without any facts to back it up. The jury seemed to enjoy watching Wolfson make a fool out of Lotstein in a good-natured way.

Throughout the trial, the press badgered me incessantly about how I felt and how I thought things were going. Because, to a certain extent, they had helped put me on trial, I was hardly inclined to favor them with thoughtful answers. I always replied "no comment." But, as we were leaving the courthouse the day of Wolfson's performance, and I was asked how I thought the prosecutors cross-examination of Wolfson was going, I couldn't help smiling and commenting that I thought Lotstein had more than met his match today. As I expected they would, the press printed that quote and I knew egocentric Lotstein would read it also and explode. I'll confess it gave me a slight taste of satisfaction.

The last strategic decision we had to make was whether or not Willard and I should take the stand. We had plenty to say about the way the Attorney General's Office had tried to twist reality into a hangman's noose of lies, but we doubted that Judge Ryan would let any of it go on record. Instead, considering the Judge's performance to that point, we figured that taking the stand would probably just offer Lotstein a chance to try to verbally assassinate me in front of the jury, under the guise of cross-examination. The press was speculating that I would not dare to take the stand, but if my ego were such that I had to have my say, Lotstein would make mince meat out of me and cause me to lose the case. I had watched Wolfson make a fool out of Lotstein, just by making him state the questions properly and then giving an honest answer. The press knew that I had talked openly, well before the actual trial, about every part of the real facts of the things I was accused of. I have always found that decent people prefer a truthful, straightforward answer, and I was sure this jury would do the same. Personally, I would have liked nothing better than to have had it out with Lotstein verbally, but it was easy to see that this would accomplish nothing for our cause.

Just as we had done with all the questions that came up, we again talked about Willard and I taking the stand. We analyzed the prosecutor's case and our defense. We felt that we had covered all aspects of our case and that Willard and I would not bring anything additional to the jury that they did not already have. We finally concluded that the only reason for either one, or both of us to take the stand would be just for personal satisfaction, and that was not worth it. Scott left it up to Willard and me. He and Joe Keilp thought we had won the case and suggested we close it up now and let the jury acquit us. That is what we did, and that is what the jury did.

I was quite surprised and disappointed in the unprofessional statement Judge Ryan made about our decision not to take the stand. The time and occasion was the death of Mike Scott, in 1997. Scott was being recognized for his legal feats by the press and much attention was turned to his two most high-profile cases, both of which he won against Attorney General Corbin. One was the acquittal of Richard Kleindienst and the other one was the acquittal of Willard and me. Ryan said the smartest thing Scott ever did was to keep me from testifying because if I had testified we would have lost the case. That statement proved the arrogance of Ryan and most of the legal profession in their attitude toward non-legally trained citizens. They seem to think that straight facts and total truth have no place in the modern world of their sophistication. I had already told the whole world every true fact regarding this case, before it got to court. Ryan's statement could only mean that he thought I was so dim-witted that Lotstein could tie me up in knots on the witness stand, and make me change these facts in answering his cleverly worded questions in cross-examination.

Had there not been so much at stake, I could have actually enjoyed the lawyers' performances in the trial. We knew going in that the prosecution had very little confidence in their case, and as they presented their witnesses, we also saw no witnesses of any substance to back up their allegations.

Throughout my life, I have always tried to adopt the idea of not disliking anyone, although I have often said I like some people more than others. The AG's prosecutors' actions in this trial severely tested me on this point. Both Lotstein and his co-counsel, Michael Cudahy, were absolutely grim throughout the trial. Cudahy would often watch our reactions as Lotstein would be examining a witness or making his many violent, venomous verbal attacks upon Willard and me. Apparently Cudahy wanted to see whether any of the points were telling, and see what emotions we would respond with that would perhaps be of benefit to them in presenting their case.

Having never even sat in a criminal trial prior to this one, let alone be the accused, I will say that no one can fully relate to this unless they have been there. It certainly showed me that there was nothing in my previous life that allowed me to actually relate to others in this same predicament, until I found myself in this court.

To we laymen, the most onerous thing about our justice system is that justice does not usually seem to be the object. It is somewhat akin to watching a theatrical production. The prosecutor's success is gauged by his or her conviction percentage. The defense lawyer is engaged to prove the accused innocent. They are both given wide latitude in what they do and say in the courtroom to sway the jury. Slander and libel against a defendant are accepted practice, and the prosecutors are immune to suit for what they say in court about the defendants.

The judge is almost deified in the courtroom and is the authority in charge.

The salvation of the system is the jury. It is the only part of the system that is not trained in the legal profession and is the part of the system that gives an accused a hope of getting true justice.

Lotstein, with his attempt at being pompous and his obvious overgrown ego, provided a good deal of comic relief for us between sessions, and sometimes in the court itself. It is obvious his key stock in trade is to try to intimidate the other lawyers, the witnesses, and, for that matter, the judge. And I am sure, in some cases, he succeeds.

There is a cushioned bench that runs in front of the rail separating the spectator section from the rest of the courtroom, and just behind the tables where the respective members of the defense and prosecution sit during the course of the trial. It is used by members of the defense or prosecution and messengers coming into the courtroom, etc. At the beginning of the trial, I asked Scott to ask the bailiff if he would ask the judge if he would let our wives sit on that bench. It was cushioned and would be much more pleasant during the long hours in court. The judge gave his permission. Unknown to me, this really irritated Lotstein. When the lawyers would approach the bench to discuss some points quietly with the judge, and this occurred quite often, I would go back and sit on the bench with Florence and chat. I recognized how heavy the tension was for her and Willard's wife, May. They could only sit and watch and say nothing, knowing how our futures hung in the balance. Apparently, Lotstein didn't like that appearance to the jury and kept continually complaining to the judge. One morning, Michael Scott came in and, with a few words of profanity to give vent to his anger, said I would have to ask May and Florence to sit behind the rail on the hard benches because Lotstein's continual complaining finally got the Judge to give him his way. Knowing how thin-skinned Lotstein was and how uptight he was, I concluded that we would make this work to our own advantage by letting everyone know how petty he was. I told Scott I would do it before things started. I waited, however, until the press had all filed in and the jury was filing in. Then stepped back to tell Florence in words loud enough to be heard by all the press, and perhaps the jury, that she and May would have to move back behind the rail. All eyes turned in that direction and I knew full well that Florence would ask why, which she did. This gave me the opportunity to also say reasonably loudly, "Because Lotstein has complained to Judge Ryan and he has said you have to do it." Lotstein jumped to his feet and pranced liked a wooden soldier in front of the Judge and said, "We want to approach the bench. We want to approach the bench." Of course our attorneys, Mike Scott and Joe Keilp, also approached the bench and had a little quiet talk.

Florence and May in the meantime had gone back. Although the courtroom was packed, our friends on the front row squeezed in and made room for them, so Willard and I could now sit back on the cushioned bench and talk to them over the rail when the lawyers were having their discussion with the judge. When Scott came back to the table, I asked him if it had worked that out all right or had it given him any trouble. His smiling answer was that it worked just right. And from the response of the press and others, it was an amusing little piece of drama where Lotstein in effect was 'hoisted on his own petard'.

Both Lotstein and Cudahy seemed to feel that if they could be cutting and venomous enough and strong enough in their accusatory tone of voice in what they said to the jury, that their accusations in themselves would make us guilty. And we could only hope, as we listened to the untruthful representations, that the jury would be able to clearly see through it.

It is not easy to find yourself being called names and being characterized as everything that is bad in society. I had almost gotten used to attacks on me, but in this trial, Willard, too, was brought in for the same type of character assassination. That hurt me worse than hearing those things said about myself. Willard is a person who has had few unkind thoughts ever cross his mind, and has certainly been the epitome of honesty and integrity. What really made it all endurable was the security we felt in knowing that we had done nothing illegal and nothing basically ethically or morally wrong in any way. We also knew that many tens of thousands of people were praying for us and for our families. We were virtually avalanched with letters and phone calls at the office, as was our family throughout the valley by well-wishers who would say "we are praying for you; you are in our prayers; our whole congregation is praying for you." It is a humbling experience to have that many people be that deeply concerned and that active in asking for God's assistance. Those were the great things that helped us endure and see the great things that can come out of adversity, if we would just endure in humility.

When people have said, "I don't how you could stand all the things you have had to endure," I would often assure them that I think they really did know how we stood it. The inner strength that comes from receiving answers to your prayers brings a quiet inner peace, comfort and security, knowing that when you have done all you can, the rest will be handled by a higher power. It gives strength that can come from no other source.

For being the most widely publicized trial in the history of the state and, to my knowledge, the first one broadcast gavel-to-gavel over live television, it had to be a totally "under-whelming" experience for those who were looking for real fireworks and great things to come out of it. Had the prosecution been willing to just settle for what the case was, principally accusations, and only presented witnesses that had something to give credence to their accusations, their side of the trial could have been compressed into half the time. Nothing new was brought out in accusations. They had been circulated by the news media around the world for many months. Finally, for the first time, we were getting to cross-examine their witnesses and present our own defense. I was grateful that it was being broadcast on live TV so the interested citizens could hear it, first-hand, and judge for themselves. It gave me a great hope that the people watching and listening to how empty the charges and accusations were, would finally start realizing what a clever conspiracy had been put in place to get me out of the Office of Governor. From what we have heard since, many did see that, but not nearly all.

Closing arguments were scheduled for the following Monday, which went into Tuesday, and then the judge gave the jury his instructions. Mike Scott had theorized that we could hope for a very quick verdict of not guilty, perhaps even that same day. If it didn't come then, we certainly didn't want to hear anything for at least two days because his experience led him to speculate that you get acquittal in hurry. You get a conviction if the time is medium, and if it's a long drawn out deliberation you get a hung jury. No word from the jury on Tuesday and Wednesday, and then we began to cross our fingers and hope we heard nothing until Friday. We tried to keep ourselves busy and our minds on other things. That was interrupted quite suddenly just before noon on Thursday, when we began to get press calls that the jury was ready to come out with a verdict. I called Scott to see if he had heard, and he just had. I asked him how he felt and he was extremely tense. It was the "middle time," which he had projected was the bad time to hear.

And that brings me to where I started in chapter one, waiting for the verdict.

"Has the jury reached a verdict?" the judge asked. The jury foreman responded with a sober "Yes." The judge asked the bailiff to hand the verdict forms to him. He quickly shuffles through them with no perceptible change in his sober expression and hands them to the clerk to read aloud. Thirty seconds seem like 30 torturous minutes, but at last the clerk reads, "Evan Mecham on Count 1. Not guilty. Willard Mecham on Count 1. Not guilty. "

Willard Mecham not guilty on Count 2. Evan Mecham not guilty on Count 2.

The suspense builds and the atmosphere in the courtroom becomes charged. Willard had been tried on three counts; I have been tried on six.

"Evan Mecham not guilty on Count 3. Willard Mecham not guilty on Count 3."

Willard Mecham is a free man. The jury had declared him not guilty on all three of the charges that had been brought against him by Attorney General Bob Corbin. The three additional counts against me relate to the Governor's Financial Disclosure Statement, and the verdict is also not guilty on these counts.

Bedlam breaks out in the courtroom in spite of the warning from the judge beforehand. Cheers, hugs, and tears wiped from many eyes and now, finally, there are smiles from the jury. A female voice from the crowd is heard to say, "Thank you, Jesus!" and that just about sums up the real feeling of most everyone there.

The two prosecutors stand with no one but a few members of the press to talk to. They seemed stunned, in a state of shock. This is the end of the most carefully laid plans in the history of Arizona politics for the destruction of one man who had dared to not "go along to get along." The man who defeated the candidates of the political power brokers wouldn't "play the political game," so he had to be removed from office, broken financially, and if possible, sent to prison, as a warning to everyone in the future that it is not healthy to try to clean up corruption in the state of Arizona.

As long as I could be captured in the vice-like grip and tight control of the legislators and the judiciary, they could guarantee the success of their plan. Seven months and a small fortune had gone into a fruitless defense in the battle to stop an impeachment and get a fair trial on the criminal indictments. The string of newspaper accounts of my continual losses in this arena made everything a foregone conclusion until the first time that I was given an opportunity to be judged by "a jury of his peers." Even corrupt Arizona was not so far gone as to tamper with the jury, and that jury found my brother, Willard, and me not guilty."

Only time will tell if this shameful chapter in Arizona history will awaken enough people to finally change the direction of a politically corrupt state. The attempt to crush one man who would not go along to get along has been the catalyst by which the awful truth has finally leaked out to some of the thinking people. But one man cannot change the course of events. He may provide leadership and direction, but it takes the work and support of the majority of the people to bring about the cleanup of corruption wherever it exists.

Some not-so-subtle bumper stickers appeared that tell the story: "38th LEGISLATURE - THE BEST THAT MONEY CAN BUY." People now realize a new governor cannot clean up a corrupt state in the face of a monopoly newspaper and a Legislature, the majority of whom are controlled by power brokers" who are bent on maintaining their control over state government. The people still have the power to take control by electing senators and representatives who will respond to the voters' wishes instead of taking orders from the elitists.

The first big step was taken in the 1988 election. The largest change in the Legislature's membership resulted from some retiring and many others being defeated in their bids for re-election. Both the president of the Senate and the speaker of the House were defeated by under-financed political unknowns in the Republican Primary in September of 1988.

Conservative Republicans increased to where they held almost equal membership with the liberals in the Republican majority in the House. The impeachment fallout in the Senate was extensive enough to give the Democrats control in the 1990 election.

Step number one, in 1988, was successful in making the biggest change in the makeup of the Legislature in memory, but the power brokers' control was re-established as solidly as ever with my removal. Many people have been awakened but are still powerless to make the needed changes without a truthful newspaper to give the voters the facts and a governor to serve the people instead of the power brokers.

Chapter 23

HOW THE INAUGURAL
FUND WAS STOLEN

"A popular Government, without popular information, or the means of acquiring it, is but a prologue to a farce or a tragedy; or perhaps, both. Knowledge will forever govern ignorance and a people who mean to be their own governors must arm themselves with the power which knowledge gives."
James Madison

    The four front final assault, launched against me in October of 1987, achieved its objective. It removed me from the Office of Governor by a wrongful impeachment on April 4, 1988. It worked just the way the power brokers planned it because they controlled the Attorney General, the County Attorney, the majority of the Legislators, and exercised great influence over the Judiciary of the county and the state. The key ingredient of their awesome power was the monopoly newspaper, *The Arizona Republic* and *The Phoenix Gazette*. The Publisher of the *R. & G.* made good on his promise to "crucify the little b-----d," meaning me, of course. Most people in the state had little knowledge of what was really going on because I had very limited opportunity to respond to the constant attacks.

    1st Front of Attack—Resignation! Their pressure to get me to resign didn't work. I was doing exactly what the voters elected me to do. I was not guilty of any infraction of the law or of any standard of ethics. There was no reason to resign.

2nd Front of Attack—Recall! The recall election furnished much of the fuel for the negative media blitz against me from the day I won the election. As the May 17, 1988, date for the recall election approached, it looked like I had a good chance to win it and resume my term as governor. To avoid any opportunity for that to happen, the recall election was illegally canceled by the Arizona State Supreme Court. They had no legal authority to cancel a duly certified election, as was covered in Chapter 21, but who can change the rule of man when the rule of law is cast aside by the very judges who are appointed to uphold the law.

3rd Front of Attack—Corbin's frivolous indictments! In June, the jury quickly returned a not guilty verdict on all six of Corbin's indictments against me. That showed how frivolous the charges were, but it served their purpose to cover me for six months of negative media on that subject. Through their control of events explained in the previous chapters, they were able to postpone the criminal trial until they had succeeded in my removal by impeachment.

4th Front of Attack—Impeachment! It is obvious that I could have survived all of the power broker coordinated attacks, except impeachment. A careful review of the House hearings and the Senate trial reveal that prosecutors French and Eckstein did not present a single item of proof that I had broken any law. Their whole procedure was to put on a good show, based on accusations only. They knew there is no rule of law to designate what constitutes guilt of an impeachable offense, and they knew they had the votes for impeachment before they started.

Now that was all behind us. The one thing left was the disposition of the inaugural fund. Parts of this subject have been covered in previous chapters, but this chapter will put the important facts about the Inaugural Ball Fund in its proper place for clarity.

The Inaugural Ball Committee Chairman was Bill Long and his top assistant was Joyce Downey. To make sure all funds were handled properly, they took the precaution to ask the attorney general to advise how the funds should be handled. Steve Twist and John Shadegg, the number two and three men from the AG's office,

---

met with the committee. The summary of the advice given was that corporate funds could be used, provided it was used only for ball expenses and not for anything to do with a campaign or campaign debts.

To comply with the advice given, the ball committee opened two separate bank accounts at the Valley National Bank. One was for corporate donations for the ball expenses. The other account was for the ticket sales.

The people who had bought tickets to the Inaugural Ball had done so for the purpose of helping pay off my campaign debts with the money left over after the costs of the ball were paid. This message was printed on all of the literature about the ball, including the tickets. We did what most of the governors before, and since, have done.

All of the money in the corporate funded account was spent for ball expenses. When that account was used up, $12,000 was paid from the ticket sales account for the balance of the costs of the ball.

The ball was a very nice social event. It was well supported, well attended, and well staged by the inaugural committee. It was handled very much like a number of previous governors had done. To our knowledge, no previous governor (the most recent being Babbitt) had been questioned when he used the surplus funds from his inaugural ball to pay outstanding campaign debts. But events revealed that there was a plan to keep me from using them for that purpose.

Arizona Republic reporter Sam Stanton wrote an article on January 8, 1987, designed to start the questioning. The headline, "Big Firms Paid for Most of Mecham's Inaugural Ball." The story starts, "Gov. Evan Mecham's inaugural celebration raised about $100,000 to help reduce his campaign debt, but the money was raised by having some of Arizona's largest firms pay for most of the festivities. Arizona Public Service Co., Mountain Bell, Circle K Corp., and others were "inaugural sponsors" and contributed thousands of dollars apiece to pay for Mecham's inaugural ball and private reception. Those contributions allowed Mecham's fund-raisers to keep most of the proceeds from tickets to the events to help pay off part of the campaign debt Mecham still faces."

The "negative spin" of this article was carefully done to look like I was becoming obligated to the big companies. It carefully avoided the facts that this was the way previous governors had handled this event.

There was an additional purpose in this article that I was to see so often during the next 14 months. The purpose was to have another quotable person, or persons, raise a question about the legality of what we had done. Note how Stanton continues:

> "However John Anderson, executive director of Common Cause in Arizona, said that the practice raises questions, and that the attorney general should look at the matter."

This was the standard method used by Stanton for the Republic and Murphy of the Gazette. They daily injected opinions and attacks on whatever issue they were using to create some controversy over something I was doing, or had done. They would call some one whom they could be sure would have a negative comment. Then they would build the story around what that quotable person, or persons, had said about me. They did not invent this tactic. It is common among "yellow journalists."

When Anderson states that the attorney general should investigate us, it was designed to raise a question in the minds of readers about whether or not we were doing something illegal. Had Anderson been really concerned, he would have backed up his words by filing a written official complaint, which is necessary by law to bring the attorney general, or the county attorney to the point of opening an investigation. That is generally true, but not if Mecham is the subject. Col. Hutchins, in his detailed investigation for his book, *The Big Lie*, found no record of any official complaint being made to Corbin on this subject. To launch an investigation without a written complaint is a violation of the law, but when you are the attorney general of this state the law is what you say it is.

Without an official complaint, Corbin illegally jumped in on January 10, 1987. According to Stanton in the *Republic:* "Arizona Attorney General Bob Corbin said Friday that he will launch a criminal investigation into how money was raised during Gov. Evan Mecham's inauguration to help pay off Mecham's campaign debt.

The move was sparked by comments from John Anderson, executive director of Common Cause in Arizona, that the fund-raising techniques used by the Mecham camp may have violated state campaign-financing laws."

I was rapidly getting used to finding out in the *Republic & Gazette* what Corbin had in mind for me. At no time did he ever call me before he made his accusations through the press.* Corbin also worked hard to clutter the landscape with confusion about Prop. 200. It was a campaign finance reform initiative that passed the same time I was elected. It did not have a clause to make it apply retroactively in its application, so it did not effect my campaign. But it was used often and effectively to raise questions of our possible violations. It was one of the 'straw men' that was raised to keep our inaugural committee from finishing up their work in a timely manner. Even if the change of the law brought on by Prop. 200 had applied to us, we were never in violation of its provisions.

Mr. B.G.Burke was assigned by Corbin to investigate. He made a few interviews with some of the inaugural committee members but there is no record of any conclusions having been made by the AG's office. Keep in mind, there still had been no official, written complaint, as is legally necessary before the attorney general or county attorney can launch an investigation. This law is on the books to stop these kinds of enforcement officers from misusing their offices for unfounded investigations.

On February 2, 1987, Steve Twist, Chief Assistant Attorney General, signed a letter to Tom Collins, Maricopa County Attorney, regarding the investigation of the Mecham Inaugural Committee's fund raising. From the letter, I quote: "I have enclosed the Attorney General's Office file relating to an investigation of an allegation that Governor Evan Mecham's Inaugural Committee may have violated A.R.S. Sec. 16-919 and recently enacted Proposition 200 because of the corporate nature and size of contributions received.

*(Note the insertion of "criminal" in Corbin's announcement of his investigation. That sounds much more ominous than just the word investigation. To my knowledge, I am the only one in Arizona before, or since, who has been the target of an attorney general criminal investigation on campaign finance or inaugural finance.)

I have decided that further participation in the investigation by this office would be inappropriate because one of our attorneys gave advice to persons associated with the Mecham Inaugural Committee." Twist could not even be honest enough to say that it was he and Shadegg who gave the advice to the inaugural committee. All they had to do to see that their advice had been followed was to look at the ball records.

Collins assigned Howard Schwartz of the county attorney's office to investigate the matter. On March 23, 1987, he met with Warner Lee and John Mangum, two attorney's representing Bill Long and the inaugural committee. Obviously, neither of these attorney's was representing me, so I was not informed on what was being done.

I was so busy with all of the organizing work and the legislative session that I did not have time to worry about things that did not compete for my attention on a daily basis. But as the months rolled by, I became concerned as to why the inaugural committee was not finished and the surplus money paid toward campaign debts. Ralph Watkins told me that there was a little trouble but they thought it would be settled soon. I told him that if there was any question about the use of the funds, to send the balance of the money back to the ticket purchasers on a pro-rata basis. That was the only input I had on the subject. I was assured that we had good lawyers handling everything so I relaxed. That was a big mistake. I have found that sometimes lawyers get you into more trouble than they can get you out of. This was one of those times. The assurances that we had broken no laws was totally correct, but I still was not given the information as to why the delay.

In late May, Bill Long and Joyce Downey came to my office with all of the records of the inaugural committee and turned them over to me. Bill was totally exasperated and said he was glad to get it out of his hands. He told me, "You can use them (the funds) for any damn thing you want to, as long as you don't use them to pay off campaign debts or (to) campaign and don't use them for personal living expenses." They gave me all the bank records, which proved both types of money had been kept separate. The corporate funds were all spent on the ball event itself plus $12,000 out of the ticket sales money.

I did not like this settlement, and I would have appreciated the courtesy of having had something to say about it before it was made. The county attorney was bluffing to help Corbin tie my hands on the use of the inaugural funds. Had Mangum and Lee been working in my behalf and told me what was going on, I would have had them call the bluff. The abuse of office by threats should have been taken away from Collins and Corbin. This would have been done by filing a declaratory action in Maricopa County Superior Court that would adjudicate all questions of the legality of what we were trying to do with inaugural funds. At that point in time and events, there is little doubt that the money would have been declared private funds, according to the law. We could have used the funds for their intended purpose, and there would have been no further questions about the use of the inaugural funds.

Keep in mind that the committee had not been accused of wrong doing. There was no basis to question or accuse. The money was handled just the way the committee had been advised by the AG's top assistants. The controversy was manufactured by press reports, innuendo and the threat of a criminal investigation— first, by the very public announcement by Attorney General Corbin; then by turning it over to County Attorney Collins, who assigned Schwartz to make a full investigation of it.

Schwartz, never presented a written report of his investigation, so we can only surmise that he did not make one. If you keep it verbal, it can keep changing; whereas, if it is written, it stays written. He kept saying we had violated A.R.S. Sec. 16-905 (the outcome of Prop. 200), but the only specific violation he claimed is that the inaugural committee had not been certified as a campaign committee by the Sec. of State. The ridiculous part of that is Prop. 200 passed in the same election that elected me, and it did not include a retroactive clause. It was signed by the Governor on December 16, 1986, which was past the 1986 election and would only apply to future elections. The second part of Schwartz assertion is that the inaugural committee was not a campaign committee. There was no way it could apply to the inaugural committee activities because the inaugural committee was organized to put on the inaugural ball event only. Nothing it did had any effect on any campaign for election, so Prop. 200 could not apply to it. But, facts never got in the way of the attorney general and the impeachment prosecutors.

If I did not accept it as a done deal, as explained by Long, I would have to refute what the inaugural committee had done, so I said I would abide by the rules Long stated. And, we did abide by those rules.

Corbin and the power brokers had achieved their goal of stopping me from using the funds for the purpose they were paid in for. It would mean that I had to personally pay $90,000 more than I had planned for campaign debts.

Former Governor Jack Williams had told me that it had cost him about $25,000 per year, personally, for expenses the state did not pay. Airfare for the governor's wife to conventions; presents for visiting dignitaries; dinners for legislators, etc. In many states, citizens groups raise the money and pay those state non-paid expenses for their governors. I concluded that I would use the inaugural fund for that purpose because it would save me from paying for those things out of my personal funds. Then someone in one of the meetings pertaining to the inaugural fund cleverly described it as a Governor's Protocol Fund. That name was used from then on to give it the connotation that it was state funds. The more I tried to correct this, the more my critics and the press called it by that name.

To my knowledge, the State of Arizona had never had a Protocol Fund. The Legislature appropriates the governor's budget to pay for all approved expenses of the Office of the Governor. These funds are disbursed by the office manager.

The inaugural fund was still in the Valley National Bank in the name of Mecham Inaugural Committee. When Long and Downey brought the records to me, they included new bank signature cards. I entrusted Jim Colter and Edith Richardson to sign the cards, look after the fund and pay what I approved out of the fund.

Bill Long and Joyce Downey had turned over the bank account and the records of the Mecham Inaugural Committee to me on May 25, 1987. That constituted their replacement as officers of the committee with myself. I turned it over to Colter and Richardson, who were now the governing authority of the committee. The inaugural committee was a private association. Its' fund was a private fund and was never in any way gifted to the state to make it state funds. Colter and Richardson were never approved to receive or spend state funds. By the same token, the office manager, who handles the state funds appropriated to the governor's office, had nothing to do with the inaugural funds.

There is a definite procedure, spelled out in detail in Arizona state law, that has to be followed to transfer private funds to the state before they can become state funds. The inaugural fund was never put through that process, so it was impossible for any honest person to ever think they were state funds. Every person who said they were state funds was either not informed, or a willful liar. The only people who had any legal right to a say in how the funds were expended, was the ticket purchasers. That would hold up in any court in the land.

On June 26, 1987, one month after Long and Downey gave up their authority over the committee, Warner Lee brought Long a letter to sign for the committee to comply with the request of the county attorney as to the disposition of the funds. Long was no longer head of the committee. He had no authority to negotiate nor sign for the committee after having turned everything over to me on May 25th. Had I known about this letter, with it's wording that was designed to make it look like state funds, I would have settled it then by sending the remaining funds back to the ticket buyers. Bill Long agreed with me. He testified at the impeachment trial that the funds were private and had he thought there was any plan to make them "public or state funds" he said he would have favored sending them back to the donors.

It was not until the impeachment investigation started that I knew there was a letter. When I finally saw a copy, I noted that it was dated 31 days after Long had turned the committee and it's funds over to me. Under all legal circumstances of which I am aware, the only signature that can bind an organization is the current managing officer, or officers. Long had no authority to sign anything for the inaugural committee after turning it over to me on May 25th. Inasmuch as the letter was the basis French used to say the inaugural funds had become state funds, I will include it in part:

"In order to avoid any risk on an unintentional violation of the law (or even the appearance thereof), or incurring the time and expense which would be necessary to obtain judicial determination of the question, we have determined that the funds remaining in the Ticket Sales Account should be held in a separately maintained account and "expended, at the Governor's discretion", solely for the purposes of promoting the interests of the state, or to promote and encourage citizen public service to the state, and comparable such purposes within the purview, and pursuant to the provisions and the spirit, of A.R.S. Sec. 41-1105. Accordingly, as has been publicly announced and reported, all funds remaining in the Ticket Sales Account (the Inaugural Expense Account has a zero balance) have been turned over to the "office of the Governor of Arizona" to be held and expended as stated above."

I repeat that this letter was designed by Collins and Corbin to make it appear that the Inaugural Funds became official state funds without going through the legal process that the state law sets up to receive funds for the state. They did not have the authority over the fund to attempt to gift it to the state. Their clever insertion of the words, "turned over to the office of the Governor of Arizona," was to give the appearance of having bridged that gap by this meaningless letter. In addition, there is no place in state law where the governor is given funds to expend at his sole discretion, as the letter directs. That point alone determines they could not be talking about handling "state funds" in that manner.

The funds were turned over by Long to me in my capacity as a private person who was also the Governor of Arizona. The Office of the Governor is a state institution. The person occupying that office does his/her official acts for the state in that state institution. The rest of his/her acts are as a private person and have the same effect as any other private person's acts. The inaugural ball was strictly a private event to celebrate my going into office and that The Office of the Governor had no part in it as a government event. The only part of the inaugural events that are officially government is the swearing in ceremony.

I had agreed to the conditions verbally given to me by Long when he brought the records. Those conditions were that I would not use the funds for campaign debts or personal living expenses. We had adhered to that. I knew that Long had no authority to further bind the committee after turning over control, so the letter was meaningless. In addition, the letter did not constitute the transformation of the funds from private to public funds.

In early July, I asked Colter how much interest the fund was earning in the money market account in the bank. He looked it up and reported they were earning slightly less than 4.5 percent. I told him, at that time the going rate of interest on loans from banks was in the area of 10 percent. My eldest son, Dennis, was general manager of my automobile dealership, and he told me we were currently paying the Valley National Bank 10 percent on loans from them. I suggested to Colter to look around and find a friend in business to whom we could loan most of the Inaugural Fund to earn closer to the going rate of 10 percent. It needed to be safe and available, on call as we used it. A few days later, I asked Colter if he had found anyone to place the funds with and he said "No." He did not know where to begin. I then told him to arrange with Dennis to give the fund a back up mortgage on our real estate and loan Mecham Pontiac $80,000 out of the Inaugural Fund at a rate of 9 percent per annum. That would earn the fund $300 more per month than the 4.5 percent at the bank. With a net worth of more than $4 million, Mecham Pontiac qualified as a safe place to put the money at interest.

Colter told me that this might look questionable to other people. I asked him why that was so if it was legal, safe, and handled as an "arm's length" transaction. He assured me that there was absolutely nothing legally questionable, so I said to go ahead on July 16, 1987.

It was not long until the rumor mill stated that I had done something wrong with the inaugural fund money. We were using it just like we had verbally agreed to do. Colter drew some of the money back from Mecham Pontiac to pay for things that we needed to do, but for which state funds were not provided. Uses were discussed among the staff, so it was not handled as a secret. No one said it was wrong, but some said it was politically stupid because it did not look good. I instructed Colter to get the remaining funds back from Mecham Pontiac. That was done, and the interest was also paid. This short stay of the $80,000 with Mecham Pontiac, for the sole purpose of getting double the interest on it, was spun into an accusation by French that I had committed a Class 4 felony. Corbin did not agree because in his criminal court case he had to prove his accusations. French did not have to prove anything, only accuse.

An article appeared in the *Republic* on November 3, 1987, that "Sources told the *Arizona Republic* that Mecham borrowed most of the $90,000 in the Governor's Protocol Fund earlier this year but recently repaid it at 10 percent interest. State Attorney General Bob Corbin said that he was given information last month that such a loan may have been made but that he was not investigating it because his investigators have been too busy.

Corbin said he does not think that such a loan would be improper because the protocol funds do not belong to the state." This was almost 30 days after French had been hired by Speaker Lane to start his House investigation into my alleged impeachable offenses. This was also about the time Corbin started his 23rd Grand Jury investigation of me. Note the reference to "Protocol Fund" by Stanton and Corbin in the story. The Inaugural Funds had now been turned into Protocol Funds as if by magic in this news story.

I readily told all questioners all the facts. I was amazed that this simple thing could take on a life of it's own and be the basis of an accusation that circulated world wide, that I had misused state funds. They knew it was a lie, but they have kept it going. It was repeated in an *Arizona Republic* story again in 1998.

The intentional use of the word "misused" shows the intent to injure me by using a word that accused me of an illegal act. Then to intentionally call the funds "state or public" funds is designed to convince the public that I had broken the law. The funds were not "used" by me when we substituted the car dealership for the bank as where the funds were put to earn interest. Had they been used, they would not have been available at any time we needed them. When we returned them to the lower interest bank account, that definitely showed they had not been "used".

During the House hearings Attorney Warner Lee was asked by Rep. Giordano: "Mr. Lee, in your cover letter of June 23rd, you stated very clearly to Mr. Long that our understanding is that the remaining funds will not be used to retire campaign debts. Was the intention, as had been implied, that the monies not only would not be used for campaign debts, but that they would be in some fashion turned over to the State of Arizona?

Lee's answer: The issue of whether or not these funds were going to be turned over into the State of Arizona in any way you may be using that phrase was never addressed by any of us, was never considered.

Question: So if I understand you, Mr. Lee, in all the discussions, and I will preface this question by saying including the County Attorney, that there was no discussion of the monies becoming public monies?

Lee's answer: No, this is where I must differ in recollection from Mr. Schwartz. (the county investigator) I recall the terms public funds, private funds, gift, none of those things to my recollection were ever discussed as to these funds.

Question: So the intention of the letter you drafted which was signed by Mr. Long was that the monies would go into a Protocol Fund, but that does not necessarily mean that they were becoming public funds.

Lee's answer: That issue was simply never addressed.

Question by Rep. Hawke: Mr. Lee, just to be clear, from your own personal knowledge, in terms of the negotiations, the proposed solution for settlement, the final settlement and the letters, communications, you never had any, or did you have any conversation or communication with Governor Mecham as to any of the aspects of this whole issue?

Lee's answer: That's correct, but to be totally candid with you, I have to explain that answer. At the meeting in Mr. Colter's office that I mentioned to you after we had described the agreement to Mr. Colter, Governor Mecham came in and sat down just very, very briefly. Mr. Colter said something to the effect that these gentlemen have been very helpful to us, or something like that, without any further definition that I can recall of what we had been helpful in the conversation, even though it was very brief, then turned to other subjects and that was it."

Colter knew the exact verbal agreement Long had expressed to me when he turned the committee and records to me, on May

326

25th. I am sure that if his discussion with Lee and Mangum had proposed any change in the status of the inaugural fund, he would have told me.

Colter was asked in the Senate trial:

Q. Did you ever consider the funds in the Mecham Inaugural Committee account to be public funds.

A. No.

Q. In the course of your discussions with Mr. Lee ——-

A. Matter of fact, I was told to the contrary, that it was not public funds and it was not pursuant to 41-1105, and that it was the Governor's fund just exactly of (sic) the letter of 26 June says, that was my understanding.

Here Colter is clearly stating that Lee and Mangum told him that it was my money to use however I choose as long as it was not for campaign debts or personal expenses.

Mangum expressed in the Senate trial that he did not perceive Long's June 26th letter to Tom Collins as an action by which the monies were "conveyed to the state."

Senator Steiner commented while questioning Mangum: "The case here has been built on the basis that they had to be public funds for the specific restrictions to apply. I believe". Steiner was correct. The only way French could have anything to accuse me of on Article III was to build his case around the inaugural funds being transformed into state funds. The catch there is that it was impossible for French to offer any proof that they were state or public funds. Attorney Lee who composed the June 26th letter said it was never even discussed. Attorney Mangum said the letter was not an action that conveyed the money to the state. Colter testified in the Senate trial that he was told that the funds were definitely not public or state funds.

Even Prosecutor Eckstein commented: "But even if it isn't public money, under 1105, it could not be used in the fashion it was…" That statement shows that Eckstein knew the money had not been put through the legal steps proscribed by law to make it state money.

The best summary of the law and the facts regarding the status of the inaugural funds comes from the testimony of Bob

L' Ecuyer. As an attorney who had served on a Congressional staff in Washington and also for the Arizona Legislature, he was one witness who really knew what he was talking about. He had spent over 200 hours of research on the effects of the passage of Prop. 200, which became A.R.S. Sec. 16-905. Although L'Ecuyer was called by our legal team as an expert witness, he was politically always, by his own statement, on the side of my political opponents. Eckstein tried to block his testimony and often objected to the content of his answers. But enough got on the record to make a clear summary of the truth of this matter which we quote in answers to questions by our attorney Leonard, as follows:

Q. Mr. L' Ecuyer, was asked if he had reviewed the affidavit and transcript of the testimony of William Long, which is in evidence? When he answered that he had, he was asked his opinion as to whether or not the letter of June 26th, 1987, was applicable to the funds held in the Mecham Inaugural Account in July of 1987?

A. The June 26th letter from William Long to the County Attorney was of absolutely no force or effect in relation to the Mecham Inaugural Committee funds.

Q. On June 26th, 1987, were any of the signatories to that letter in a position to bind or control the use of the funds on that date?

A. Mr. Long was the signatory, and he was no longer chairman, had no power to bind anything in relation to the Mecham Inaugural Committee or the funds.

Q. Did you, Mr. L' Ecuyer, in the course of your investigation and your involvement in the issues relating to this Article, do an analysis of what constitutes public funds in the State of Arizona?

A. I did. They were not public funds.

L'Ecuyer was then asked whether he reviewed "various statutory provisions of the State of Arizona" His reply: "I did."

Leonard proceeded through a series of Exhibits while posing questions to L'Ecuyer regarding applicability to the Mecham Inaugural Committee funds. A.R.S. Sec. 35-302, which dealt with receipt of money by various officers "in their official capacity' was addressed. L' Ecuyer was asked:

Q. How do you distinguish the monies held in the Mecham Inaugural Committee in July of '87, with respect to the thrust ...of that statute?

A. Well the account was a private checking account in the name of a private unincorporated association, not the State of Arizona, and the holder of the account was a committee, and control of that committee had been transferred to Evan Mecham, not in his official capacity, but as the ultimate beneficiary of the people who donated the funds.

Leonard next referred to Exhibit 92, which was A.R.S. 35-212. L'Ecuyer referred to Subsection B, read it , and declared that it was: "another indication that public monies are only monies received in official capacity, and therefore , the funds in the Mecham Inaugural Committee were not public funds."

L' Ecuyer then referred to Exhibit 93, which was A.R.S. Sec. 41-2501, and testified that he relied on that statutory provision in formulating his opinion that the Inaugural Committee funds were not public funds. He then referred to Subsection B and read the critical language, "this chapter applies to every expenditure of public monies, including federal assistance monies..."

We presented much more proof that the inaugural ball funds were private, not public, but it was to no avail. French's case was built on the basis that Legislators would vote for impeachment on Article III with accusations only. No basis can be found in the record of the House hearings or the Senate trial that gave the Legislators any excuse for their votes for impeachment. All members of both the House and the Senate had much evidence to show I was innocent of all of French's accusations and they had no evidence to the contrary. Even Senator Steiner voted for impeachment on Article III, after she recognized that it had to be state funds before I could have been wrong. As I have said before, it is they who have to live with what they did for the rest of their lives, and maybe farther.

Corbin's abuse of his office continued through the means he utilized to steal the inaugural fund for the state.

The funds were still in a private account in the bank in the account named Mecham Inaugural Committee. No proof had been presented, that could stand the scrutiny of an honest trial before a jury, that anything illegal had been done by me or the inaugural committee regarding the fund. The best proof is that as much as Corbin would have liked to charge me with some crime regarding the inaugural funds, he had no basis for filing criminal charges. My retention of the funds made a lie out of the contention of the impeachment trial that I had violated the law regarding the inaugural fund. If it was allowed to rest there, many more people would realize what a farce the impeachment was.

Remember that Corbin had said in early December that the funds were private. Now he was apparently ordered by his power broker bosses that he must get the funds, or the impeachment might unravel. As if on a signal, the healing process being called for by the new Governor Mofford and some members of the legislature, was replaced by a renewed stir about the inaugural fund. When Corbin was queried as to why he was threatening action on what he had said was a private fund of money, he replied that the Senate action had changed the private fund into a state fund. This was completely untruthful, and Corbin knew it. There was no action taken by the Senate trial that could change the status of private money into state funds.

I was hoping there would be an opportunity to try the question of the status of the inaugural fund before a jury. My lawyer and I felt certain we would prevail. We had overwhelming evidence on our side, as well as the law. In Superior Court, where they had to prove their allegations, Corbin had absolutely nothing to go on. The power brokers undoubtedly saw the same thing that I did. If we prevailed in a Superior Court case in front of an impartial jury, we would receive the Inaugural Funds back from the clerk of the court with no restrictions. That may, or may not have changed the effect of the impeachment, but it would certainly have made the whole event suspect in the eyes of most of the public. The power brokers did not want to take that chance, and they knew how to keep it in the hands of a judge who could be influenced by Corbin, instead of a jury who couldn't.

330

On August 5th the following letter was delivered to me:

ROSE MOFFORD
GOVERNOR

Office of the Governor
State Capitol, West Wing
Phoenix, Arizona 85007

𝔄ttorney 𝔊eneral
1275 WEST WASHINGTON
ℜhoenix, 𝔄rizona 85007

ℜobert ℜ. ℭorbin

August 5, 1988

HAND DELIVERED : 5.5.8 4:32 PM

Mr. Evan Mecham
8802 N. 61st Avenue
Glendale, AZ 85302

Dear Evan:

There has been considerable publicity recently regarding the remainder of the funds originally raised in connection with your Inaugural Ball. We would like to make a concerted effort to resolve the current dispute concerning these funds without the necessity of litigation.

As you indicated in your letter to an assistant attorney general on July 25, 1988, any solution should be "in accordance with justice, harmony, and equity for all." We believe we have a proposal that could accomplish those ends.

If you agree, those who originally contributed the funds could be contacted and given the option of having their pro rata shares either returned to them or donated to an agreed-upon state program for the benefit of children. This program could be the Crisis Nursery, Arizona School for the Deaf and Blind, the Council on Developmental Disabilities, or another similar program. Any funds that are unclaimed would also be donated to this program. We could devise mutually agreed upon procedures to ensure that all contributors are contacted and all monies are distributed in accordance with appropriate accounting practices.

Alternatively, the account in question could be turned over to the Office of the State Treasurer and the funds then made available for the exclusive use of the mutually agreed upon State program for the benefit of children.

Of course, under either alternative the funds would be presented to such agency with the public acknowledgment that the contributors to your Inaugural Ball Committee were the source of the funds.

Wrongful Impeachment

Mr. Evan Mecham
August 5, 1988
Page -2-

We feel that the use of these funds to benefit children would meet with the approval of all those who contributed toward the Inaugural Ball, whether through ticket purchases or otherwise. But, as was indicated, we would be agreeable to the contacting of those persons you believe have a say in the disposition of these funds and allowing return of their shares if requested.

If you are in accord with either of these proposals or would like to discuss them further, please let us know. We believe that a prompt and equitable resolution of this issue would be in everyone's best interest.

Upon your acceptance in principle to either of these alternatives, our respective representatives can meet to work out the details necessary for a formal agreement. We look forward to hearing from you shortly.

Sincerely,

ROSE MOFFORD
Governor

BOB CORBIN
Attorney General

RM/BC/sl

I was delighted to receive the letter because it proved that both Gov. Mofford and Corbin were recognizing that the funds were private. Their letter offers to have a representative from each of us meet and decide what to do with the funds. They even suggest the ones who contributed the money (the proper word should have been "bought tickets" so no confusion could be brought in about contributions) "could" be contacted and given the option of having their pro-rata shares either returned to them or given to some charity or state program for children. The key admission of the letter is that both Governor Mofford and Attorney General Corbin were admitting that the funds are not state funds. If they were state funds, then none of the three of us, the present governor, the former governor and the attorney general, had any authority to spend them or decide where they should be sent. Only the legislature had the power of directing and authorizing the spending of the state funds. In addition, if the fund was public money there was no legal basis to give "state funds" to the ticket purchasers. If they were state funds all three of us, plus the recipients, would have been in violation of the law. Inasmuch as they had stated in two different parts of the letter that they would be agreeable to let the ticket purchasers have their pro-rata share back, I went ahead and made checks to all ticket purchasers on a pro-rata share of the balance of the money. I mailed all of the checks and then informed Mofford and Corbin by the following letter on August 10th:

"I am pleased that in your letter of August 5th, you have both verified that the Inaugural Funds are private monies, and the decision for their use is up to the contributors who gave them for the purpose of paying Ball expenses and to retire my campaign debts.

To shorten the process of putting this issue to final rest, I am sending a check to each of the 687 contributors for their pro rata share that is left in the fund. It goes without saying, that you may contact any or all of the contributors to see if they would choose to donate this or any other part of their private funds to any of the state agencies you have suggested in your letter."

To my astonishment, without any notice, the checks were being returned unpaid. We then found that Corbin, with nothing more than a phone call to the Valley National Bank, had frozen the account. My lawyer called the bank and told them we had the basis for a suit if they did not release the funds. They invited us to go ahead and sue them because they were not going to release the funds. They feared the attorney general and they had no fear of me. More evidence of white-collar corruption in Arizona.

I had considered getting cashier checks to send out so they could not be stopped. I decided against it when they said it would cost me about $1,200 to do it. I also considered putting the funds in a different bank but thought that might make me look sneaky, so I decided to send regular checks out of the account.

I could also have waited a few days without telling them until the checks had cleared, but my lawyer said it would take Corbin a few days to go to court and file the necessary papers to freeze the account while we litigated it. In the end, I felt with Governor Moffords signature on the letter meant that they were happy to see the ticket purchasers get the money back. I was wrong on all counts. I have regretted many times that I didn't get the cashiers checks.

On August 11, 1988, Corbin filed suit to gain possession of the Inaugural Fund on a summary judgement. The quick timing of that suit may indicate that he sent me the other letter just to keep me occupied while he prepared his suit. It was a civil suit, which proves no laws were broken on our part regarding the funds. We responded and because of the many issues to be decided, and this being such an unusual case, we expected a trial by jury. I was pleased because there were many important issues to be settled in a court where we could present our case in front of a jury.

I was soon reminded that they are still in control of the whole system and justice was not in their plans. There were so many issues of law to be settled that we felt they would have to give us a jury trial. They did not! Instead, we were not even given a regular judge to hear the case. It was heard by a Judge Pro Tem (a lawyer who sometimes fills in for a regular judge). He gave the decision to the state just the way it appeared Corbin wrote it out. Not only did the decision give the state the money and accrued interest, he also awarded the state the excessive amount of $19,712 for attorney fees. If that was not enough punishment for us to handle, the state was awarded an additional $15,702 civil penalty against Florence and me.

We appealed to Division 1 of the State Court of Appeals, feeling that surely we could get the totally uncalled for $15,702 penalty reversed. Not so! They upheld the Pro Tem Judges ruling, instead of letting us have a trial. The State Supreme Court would not hear it.

As I have gone over the manuscript to prepare this book for publication, I have recalled how often the word "justice" has been used and abused in the course of these events. Our system of government, in fact the foundation of our whole society, is predicated upon each citizen being able to rely on receiving justice from his/her fellow citizens in any question that may arise in the handling of their affairs. The use, and misuse, of such a keyword as "justice" suggests it is wise to revisit what the word really means. According to Webster's Dictionary, the definition is: *The use of authority and power to uphold what is right, just, or lawful. The administration of law; procedure of a law court.*

Using the above definition, I received justice on only one occasion, which was the acquittal by the jury of my peers in the criminal trial. They were the only ones who played an important part in what transpired that were not connected with the legal system or the legislature of this state. All the rest, the Legislature; the Attorney General; the hired prosecutors in the House and Senate; all three levels of the courts, Superior, Court of Appeals, and the State Supreme Court; and the County Attorney made a mockery out of the word "justice" in the way and the frequency of times, **they broke the law** in order to remove me from office and punish me where ever they could.

Chapter 24

ARIZONA
A DECADE LATER

"Let us have faith that right makes might and in that faith let us, to the end, dare to do our duty as we understand it."
Abraham Lincoln

Countless times during this past ten years, people from all walks of life have approached me with almost the same greeting. Whether I am putting gas in my car at the service station; boarding an airliner; waiting in the line at the post office; buying groceries with my wife; etc. the first question usually is, "You are Governor Mecham aren't you?" As I say "Yes," they then put out their hand and usually say, "Well you don't know me, but I just wanted to shake your hand and tell you what a railroad job you got when you were governor." Many will add, "I thought you were doing a great job as governor and sure wish you were still there. I think you sure got treated badly."

To the many variations of the above, I usually answer that I faired much better personally than the people of the state did. It was hard on my family, it cost me a lot of money and personal time, it caused me to sell the business I had spent thirty-eight years building, but the damage to the state and it's people are much larger than anyone can imagine.

As the 10th anniversary of my impeachment approached, a number of media people interviewed me to bring their readers/viewers/listeners up to date on me and what I had done with myself for this past decade. In most interviews the question was asked, "What would have been the difference in Arizona if you had stayed in office as governor?" It would take a big book and lots of research to answer that question completely. In this final chapter, I believe I can answer in a condensed version, what most people would like to know.

Twenty years ago when Bruce Babbitt became governor of Arizona in 1978, the state population was 2.6 million and total state spending was approximately $1.2 billion. That amounted to $460 per person per year to fund the state government spending.

From 1978 to 1998, Arizona population has grown 80 percent (.80) to 4.6 million while state spending has increased 10 times (1,000 percent), to $12.84 billion. That amounts to approximately $2,800 per person to fund the state government spending this year. The fact that state annual spending has increased from $460 per person to $2,800 per person should be a wake-up call to every citizen.

It was this cycle of big annual increases in state spending that I promised the people I would break, when they elected me governor. I kept my word. The only state fiscal year general fund budget in this past 20 years to not have a big increase was the 1988 budget of $2.6 billion, passed while I was governor. Total state spending that year was $5 billion.

As soon as they removed me from office on April 4, 1988, my policy to keep spending increases to within inflation and population growth was brushed aside, and the wild spending era resumed. The records show that state government cost $1,470 per capita in 1988. The 1998, state spending is $2,800 per capita, for an increase per person of $1,330. Of great concern is that the state general fund spending increase for the 1998 year alone, grew $600 million, or more than a 10 percent increase over 1997. Arizona is one of the states where the annual state spending percentage increases are ahead of the extravagant federal annual increases.

The bottom line of this wild increase in government spending is that it now takes more than 50 percent of all income generated in the U.S. to pay these high costs of government on all levels.

The direct costs in taxes you personally pay are only part of your real tax bill. The taxes that business pays is passed on to the consumers as added costs of the goods and services sold. There are so many hidden federal taxes passed by Congress and state taxes added by the Legislature that there is no way most people can assess what their real tax costs are. We all feel the squeeze but can't identify all the sources, which is the intent. Tax creep is intentionally subtle. Need I point out what we can expect during the next decade, unless there is a definite change in the trend of government spending on both the state and federal levels?

Briefly, let us look at the first key change that was made in the operation of Arizona state government when I took office in early January of 1987. The state economy, like the national economy, was in a moderate recession. The Babbitt administration and the Burton Barr-led state Legislature had a steady string of years of raising taxes to pay for their spending increases in excess of the yearly increases in revenues. During the nine years of the Babbitt administration, state spending increased by three times it's starting figure. As I took office, I was faced with a mid-budget year of being over spent by $157 million. This had to be covered because the state constitution does not allow deficit spending.

Instead of raising taxes, as had been the habit before, I worked with the Legislature and secured the passage of a mid-year budget correction to reduce spending by the $157 million needed to balance spending and income. That set the tone of my administration and verified my campaign promise to have no tax increases in my term.

There were many things that needed to be changed, and during the fourteen months I was in the governor's office we accomplished an impressive list of very positive things that put Arizona on the proper path for the future. We will project what Arizona would be like now, if I could have had the opportunity to continue this past ten years, what we started in 1987-88.

1. SPENDING AND TAXES

Government spending, and the taxes and fees that are the result of that spending, are the largest and most important report card on any government; therefore, we will start our comparison with them. We will compare my projected record, based on the trends created by my actions as governor, with what actually has happened in the administrations of the three other governors who served from 1988 to 1999.

After my removal on April 4, 1988, the Mofford administration and the Republican controlled Legislature started a big spending and tax increase spree. That has taken Arizona from the lower ranks of the states, when comparing taxes and spending, to the higher ranks, in a hurry.

As soon as I was gone, they increased the general fund appropriations spending bill I proposed in January, by 10 percent and promptly passed a large tax increase to pay for the increase in spending. For three years in a row, starting with 1989, fiscal year ending June 30, they burdened us with a large annual tax and spending increase.

For comparison we will use my 1988 fiscal year budget as the starting benchmark:

State Population	State Tax Receipts	General Fund Spending	Total Spending
	To Pay General Fund spending	Appropriated by Legislature	
3,480,534	$2,580,534,000	$2,573,828,000	$5,105,468,128

My "projected budget" (below), would have kept all state spending at or below a four- percent annual increase that would have resulted in the (present) 1999, fiscal year totals as follows:

State Population	State Tax Receipts	General Fund Spending	Total Spending
	To Pay General Fund spending	Appropriated by Legislature	
4,615,700	$3,972,613,534	$3,962,289,956	$7,859,633,620
Amount Per Capita	$860	$860	$1,703

Instead, my removal from the office of governor put the reins of state management into the hands of Rose Mofford for fiscal years 1989-91; Fife Symington 1992-98, and Jane Hull for the fiscal year budget of 1999. The results of their spending and taxing records are told in the current budget below:

State Population	State Tax Receipts To Pay General Fund spending	General Fund Spending Appropriated by Legislature	Total Spending
4,615,700	$5,491,868,000	$5,874,195,000	$12,840,552,800
Amount Per Capita	$1,189	$1,272	$2,781

My budget would have Saved in this year alone:

	$1,519,254,466	$1,911,905,044	$4,980,919,180
Amount Per Capita	$329	$414	$1,079

My " projected budget" increases in the eleven fiscal year budgets comparison is approximately 54 percent. The other governors increased the state budgets for the eleven fiscal years, for a total of 128 percent

The record-setting tax increases of 1989-91, when applied to the population and economic growth of the 1990s, increased state tax collections so rapidly that Symington was able to make some modest state income tax reductions and still increase spending by record, or near record amounts each year. It was amusing to see the media cover up these big spending increases by putting the emphasis on the modest tax reductions. Many Arizonans were led to believe we had a conservative state government because there were some small tax reductions, even though we also had big spending increases.

I repeat that my projected budget would have had annual tax reductions. The yearly increases in tax revenues from the population and business growth would have paid for the projected four percent per year budget increases and allowed for the total phase out of all of the state personal income tax by the current fiscal year.

If sales tax reductions would have been more desirable, we could have cut them by 80 percent, which would be a savings in all taxpayers' hands every time they made a purchase. The bottom line is that the savings to Arizona taxpayers would now be over $2 billion each year. That is the equivalent of sending a check in the amount of more than $1,000 to every person who pays taxes in the state. Actually, the state would not have collected the money in the first place.

By following the financial plans we put in place in 1987-88, my administration would have saved the taxpayers of Arizona at least $11 billion dollars over the amount actually spent since I was removed. That amounts to approximately $5,500 average that each taxpayer could have spent or invested as they chose, instead of paying it to the state in taxes.

2. STOPPED THE VIOLATIONS OF STATE CONSTITUTIONAL DEBT LIMIT

In January, 1987, as we were preparing our 1988 (July 1, 1987 to June 30, 1988) budget to present to the Legislature, we were surprised to find the state debt limit of $350,000 being heavily violated. The early Arizonans, who authored the state constitution, did not give the Legislature the power to use deficit financing. That is why Article 9, Section 5 of the Arizona State Constitution states…"the aggregate amount of such debts…shall never exceed the sum of three hundred and fifty thousand dollars." Simply stated, the state founding fathers set a pay-as-you-go financial system in place so future generations could not mire the state in debt. The small debt limit was designed for occasional emergencies only.

The Babbitt administration and the Legislature had put together what they called a "lease purchase" plan. The state borrowed the cost of the building to be built by selling investors "certificates of participation." They were borrowing against the future of the state in order to spend money on current expenses that should have been spent to build the buildings.

The legislators told me that they had an attorney general's opinion that it was legal to ignore the $350,000 state debt limit if they obligated the state no farther than each year at the time. But, I saw no such provisions in the state constitution to legalize what they were doing.

I told the legislators that I thought it was an unconstitutional, unnecessarily expensive policy to put the state in debt for buildings. By the time interest and principal were paid to the investors on a 20 year pay-back schedule, the taxpayers will have paid approximately double the original cost of the building. I intended to go by what the constitution said instead of the AG's opinion.

A date had been set by the previous administration to let the contract to build the new state courts building with "lease purchase" borrowed funds. We cancelled the taking of bids for a year so we could get the first half of the $26 million cost of the building in our next year budget.

Almost every needed reform we instituted enabled the media to get some angry comments from the usual core of critical legislators. My cancellation of the illegal debt program brought an explosion. This time it was in the persons of State Supreme Court Judge Duke Cameron regarding the courts building, and Rep. Sterling Ridge about the ASU West campus.

I had known Judge Cameron for many years and his surprising demeanor bordered on anger. He showed little concern for my plan to save $26 million of taxpayer money that the long-term borrowing would add to the cost of the new courts building. I appealed to the sense of pride he and his fellow judges would feel when they moving into the completed building already paid for. He did not share my concern for what I considered the illegality of borrowing. The court's current facilities were only about twelve years old and still very comfortable. There was obviously no crisis to get into the new quarters.

Rep. Ridge came to challenge my decision to build the ASU West campus with appropriated funds in the budget, instead of the lease-purchase borrowing plan. The projected cost of $65 million over a ten-year period had been agreed on by the previous Legislature. My commitment to put $11 million in the budget each year to pay for the ASU West campus in place of the borrowing plan, should have given Ridge and others the assurance they wanted, but that was not the case. After I was removed from office, the lease-purchase debt financing was renewed immediately by Governor Mofford and the Legislature.

It has built up year by year to a total of twenty-two projects for state government and a number of projects at each of the three state universities. The total amount of money thus (in my opinion) illegally borrowed has totaled $541 million. The payments of principal and interest for this fiscal year are $50.21 million.

Governor Hull put in her executive budget $65 million more borrowing this year that is not in the totals above. In addition to the above, the three state universities have $800 million outstanding in what is labeled revenue bonds. This year's repayment on those is $58 million.

3. $2.2 BILLION WOULD HAVE BEEN SAVED BY OUR MINI-GRACE COMMISSION

Had the Commission of Cost Reduction and Efficiency in State Government been used, it would have saved a projected $2.2 billion in state government spending so far. We named it the Mini-Grace Commission in honor of the industrialist who did the same for the federal government under President Reagan. He gave me a lot of help in how to go about it.

We used "loaned" experts from the business world to make a plan to install business management practices to state government operation. The report on the findings listed changes to be made that would save between $200 million and $400 million per year. In addition, it would have resulted in more efficiency and better service. The report was finished at about the same time I was removed from office, so I was not able to install the changes that would produce the savings in state government operations. After I was gone it was never used. If I had stayed in office during this decade, we could quite safely have projected a savings of $200 million per year in the cost of running Arizona state government.

4. WE STOPPED THE ILLEGAL USE of 1,000 STATE AUTOMOBILES

State employees had been using state government automobiles for personal transportation to and from work for decades. My administration put a stop to that, and would have saved the taxpayers between $2 and $3 million per year. That was revoked as soon as I was out of sight. Had I remained in office, the savings to taxpayers would now add up to approximately $25 million.

5. THE BIG DIFFERENCE MY DRUG PROGRAM COULD HAVE MADE

In Chapter 10, you were introduced to our drug program, which we named the Alliance for A Drug Free Arizona. We knew that our goal to stop the sale and use of drugs completely in two years was very optimistic. To the critics who ridiculed our stated objective, I answered that it is entirely possible we may not accomplish all we plan in the first two years, but it would sure be a great improvement if we reached 50 to 80 percent. As it turned out, we accomplished a lot throughout the state with the voluntary support from various organizations, municipalities, schools, businesses, etc. Many did a lot of good in their effort to voluntarily use peer pressure to erase the blight of drugs in their areas of influence.

The tougher laws that were passed did not take effect until October, and the $13 million in additional funding was not available until the spring of 1988. We have no way to tell how successful we would have been with the entire program in operation because the impeachment took me out of the leadership position just as the funding was becoming available. The positive response from all but a few in law enforcement, as well as the voluntary side of our alliance, convinced us that they wanted to follow constructive leadership to solve this disastrous problem.

Had I been able to avoid the impeachment, we would have had a good start with the resources we had by the spring of 1988. It appeared there was much more federal money available for the next year, and our own state budget could have added more to that. Money from seizures of assets from drug criminals, in a successful program, could have added a huge amount of money to plow back into the enforcement program.

Our plan to reorganize the DPS and reallocate some resources to bring 250 more enforcement officers into the drug war, would have been very effective starting the following year, and that cost would have been minimal.

With a successful state program under way, we would then have been in position to sit down with the federal enforcement officials and force their hand into doing their part to stop the avalanche of drugs coming across our borders. I had an excellent working relationship with Governor Felix Valdez of our bordering state of Sonora, Mexico. He was trying to help, but it is the federal government, not the states who is responsible for guarding our borders from invasions of every type. The drug traffic is very definitely an invasion, and the federal government has been far too weak in meeting that challenge.

Instead of the big decrease in the sales and use of drugs that we felt we were on the way to achieving, it is very saddening to observe that in 1998, the sale and use of drugs in Arizona is from three to four times worse than it was in 1988, when I was removed from office. I do not want to disparage the valiant efforts being put forth by present-day law enforcement. But, it is essentially the way it was a decade ago. I have not seen nor heard any evidence that any law enforcement organization in Arizona has moved against the real power that operates the drug trade in Arizona. Until it becomes a war from the top down, by people who won't sell out or be intimidated, it will remain the biggest single blight on our whole society.

I am also concerned about the aura of inevitability that drugs now seem to carry. It is as if it cannot be controlled so why try. This points to the lack of concern and courage in our political leadership, both state and national. Drugs are the root cause of more than half of all of the crimes that are committed. The cost to society is astronomical, and the profits to those engaged in the drug trade are also astronomical. Big money can corrupt a lot of key people.

The thing we are certain about is that the Alliance for A Drug Free Arizona was quickly scrapped as soon as they got me out of office. A small amount of lip service was given to it so that the public would not be aware of its low priority in the plans of the power brokers. The news media certainly cooperated in allowing our war on drugs to have a very quiet funeral. The special drug courts, that we obtained legislative permission to set up, were never activated. The efficiency designed to expedite drug cases was never put into operation.

The small staff we had leading the volunteer program around the state was dismissed, and everyone who was in the very profitable business of importing and distributing drugs in Arizona must have had a celebration. The planned money and manpower we organized for this battle failed to arrive in the field, because the project was cancelled.

No battle, let alone a war, was ever won without a general to lead and an army to follow his lead into battle.

6. INTERNATIONAL JET PORT

The completion of the planning of the International Jetport near Coolidge, to serve as an air transportation hub for western America, Central America, and the Pacific Rim countries was quietly buried. That included the bullet train to connect Sky Harbor on the north and Tucson International on the south, with the new International Jetport in the middle. This ultra modern, speedy transportation system would have tied our two major cities together, creating a development corridor of more than 100 miles along this ideal route, for the future growth of Arizona.

We felt we had enough interest from passenger airlines and freight carriers to move ahead with a projected completion date of 1997.

7. FOREIGN TRADE OFFICES

We opened the first Arizona trade office in early October, 1987, in the World Trade Center in Taiwan. If this venture proved to be of assistance to small- and medium- sized Arizona business firms in their export business, we expected to follow it up with more offices in other important markets as needed.

8. SOLAR ENERGY ADVANCEMENT

Help for solar energy advancement in Arizona was another casualty of my removal from office. A budding industry was in the making here, and we gave it all the help and encouragement we could. We were in the process of changing the design of the new courts building to accommodate the use of solar for heating and cooling for part of the building, as a demonstration project. It would have gained worldwide attention and was thought to be a big leap for the industry in Arizona. When I was removed, the plans for partial solar were dropped.

346

9. HELP RESTORE THE CONSTITUTION

One of the more important reasons I wanted to be governor was to work with the governors of the other states to restore the United States Constitution. The most direct way to do this is for the states to force the federal government to reduce its activities back to the powers granted to it by the states when the Constitution was written and adopted.

In the Constitution, the states retained their sovereignty in all actions of government, except those limited few they delegated to the federal government to carry out its assigned responsibilities. The founders were fearful of an overpowering central government. That is why they carefully limited the actions of the federal government to only those powers clearly written in the Constitution. All other governing powers were reserved to the states and to the people.

Every elected official in the federal government and state governments take a solemn oath to protect and uphold the Constitution of the United States. In spite of this, at least 80 percent of what the federal government does is outside the power given to it in this document.

It is obvious that the power-hungry bureaucracy in Washington has overstepped its constitutional authority and will never restore the powers illegally taken from the states. The only other way to get the federal government back within the confines of the Constitution is for the majority of the states to join together and force their "creation," the federal government, to carefully disengage itself from those activities where it has no constitutional authority to be.

At my first national governor's convention, I got a feel for the potential the governors have if they would unite and confront the federal government in a step by step plan to take back their constitutional power.

For years, The Federal Department of Transportation has collected gasoline taxes in all of the states to use to build the interstate highway system. They then dictated most everything, including the speed the automobiles could travel on these highways.

There was a lot of desire throughout most of the nation to get the unrealistic 55 mph federal speed limit raised to a realistic speed of at least 65 mph. A move in the U.S. Senate to do so failed to pass, but it appeared some outside help might revive it.

I was appointed to the National Governors Association Transportation Committee and got a resolution passed at the convention to inform the Congress what the wishes of the governors were on this matter. Three-fourths of the governors voted for the resolution. It had enough power to get Congress to revive and pass the bill and allow the states to raise the limit to 65 mph.

My position was that no department of the federal government had any authority over the speeds we travel on the highways, all of which are within the boundaries of the states. That position was too much of a first step for governors who were too used to obeying the dictates of the feds, so I settled for what we were able to get at the time.

There were more Democratic governors than Republican ones, and if you attached a label of liberal or conservative on all of them, the liberals would have been in the majority. But, this resolution passed overwhelmingly because it became an issue of states' rights and "us against them." Party and political ideology labels will be secondary, if the governors ever wake up and organize to reclaim the states' sovereignty.

I came away from that first convention with the feeling that we had a good core of governors that could be organized to take more steps to reclaim the constitutional rights of the states. I had high hopes for what we could do in the future.

That hope, too, was dashed with my removal from office.

I could go on, but I believe the picture is very clear. A Republican-controlled Legislature teamed up with a Democrat as governor wrought very expensive havoc in place of the more efficient and much less expensive government for which my administration was leading the way. I could name a number of other areas in which I can show my projected administration would have been very beneficial for the people of Arizona, but I believe there are enough listed to make my case.

I believe I have also made the case that I was wrongfully removed from the Office of Governor by a conspiracy so desperate to regain control of the government of Arizona that nothing would stand in their way to remove the people's choice in the election

It was not party politics; it was power broker politics in its most greedy, power hungry, and "white collar" form.

Only when elected officials are ready to serve the people instead of themselves and special interests, will we have government at all levels operating without continually raising the people's tax burden. Growth can be embraced and all needs of government can be met, with the added revenue from a growing economy without raising the level of taxes per person if those voting for the appropriations will insist on proper government accountability. This will take a whole new mind-set in most legislative bodies in America. Certainly, it is true for Arizona. The inevitability of spending increases and raising taxes have been so well programmed that most lawmakers, and too many voters, have accepted the false premise that "it can't be done without raising taxes." That is why Speaker Lane told Jim Cooper (mentioned earlier) that they had to get me out because if they didn't get me out early they would have to put up with me for three more and possible seven more years. Having good, honest government, devoid of the control of the power brokers can be mighty pleasing to the voters, if they have a chance to enjoy it for a few years.

Perhaps Arizona will emerge from its embarrassing "political lynching of its governor" as a state that has been shocked into action. Hopefully, it will become one of the test-beds to prove that when the people become activated, they can insist on government that is responsive, efficient, and economical, and one that lives within the means of the people who must support it.

The growth of the share of the national income used to support government from 25 percent twenty years ago, to more than 50 percent now, must be reversed. The burden of too much government is crying for adjustment before it destroys the ability of any business to function economically.

The rapid decline of moral values and the erosion of the family as the foundation of our society are trends that also must be reversed. The idea that more government action is the answer to every problem must be replaced with the knowledge that individual freedom can only survive where individual initiative is not stifled by overpowering government intervention on all levels.

My wrongful impeachment is about a lot more than my removal from the Office of Governor of Arizona after serving fifteen months of a four-year term. It is about a breakdown of law and order. It is about allowing an elitist group to negate the votes of the people, which is the basic foundation of our American system of government. It is about whether we will return our government to the rule of law, or allow the power brokers to continue the rule of man.

My removal was definitely obtained by casting aside the rule of law. This should be a concern of the people in every state and in the national capital as well. The rule of man has been allowed to creep into many parts of the federal and state governments and freedom, as we have known it, is disappearing in the same proportion.

Epilogue

12 September 1998

Hon. Evan Mecham
Glendale, AZ.

Dear Governor Mecham:

As you know I am writing a book about your role in the history of western American political culture and over the past several months I have interviewed a few persons who served in the legislature or other offices in state government during your period as governor of Arizona. The results of these interviews will surprise many and, taken together, represent a dramatic change in position concerning your impeachment and removal from office.

Rose Mofford, your successor in the governor's chair, for example, indicated to me earlier this year that "Ev should never have been removed from office." Moreover, Gov. Mofford, perhaps to the surprise of political pundits, suggested that you treated her well, that she considered you "a man of integrity," and that you were a pleasure with whom to work. "Mecham," she put it succinctly, "should never have been impeached and removed from office."

In fact, one of the chief impeachment strategists in the State Senate at the time, Republican Tony West, suggested to me recently, that upon reflection, he probably would have changed his stance and voted against your removal from office. Two Democrat State Senators, Carolyn Walker and Bill Hardt, after reviewing the decade of Arizona's political history subsequent to the Mecham ouster, have indicated that there was no legal basis to remove you from office. Both of these former Senators agree that there was no impeachable offense committed during your time in office. In short, the impeachment process was a tool used by opponents of the Mecham administration to remove you from office, because, among other things, you would not submit to special interest and lobbyists pressures.

If these first interviews suggest anything it is that Members of the Arizona House and Senate, for a variety of reasons, may have rushed to judgement and helped to remove someone from office who did not commit an impeachable offense.

Sincerely

Jack L. August, Jr. Ph.D.

P.S. Although I have not yet interviewed him, I have on record that former State Senate President Carl Kunasek stated over Channel 8 TV in April of this year that you should not have been impeached.

Index

A

Adamson, John Harvey, 47
Akers, Stan, 85
Amigone, Tony, 47
Anderson,
    Albert, 21
    John, 179, 316-317
Anton, President, 122
Avery, Ben, 17
Ayers, Bob, 158,

B

Babbitt, Bruce, 46, 48, 53, 69, 111,
    157, 336
Bangerter, Governor, 167
Barkley, Bill, 13
Barr, Burton, 61, 70, 83, 87-88,
    90-91, 94,
Barron, Tex, 177
Barrow, Director of Racing Tim,
    191
Bellus, Ron, 116, 241
Bennett, Frank, 21
Benson,
    Ezra Taft, 124
    Steve, 123
Berger, Moise, 59-60
Blansett, Glen, 16
Bolin, Wesley, 45, 115
Bolles, Don, 45, 48, 64
Brown, Dr. Eddie, 109
Buck, Ed, 167, 169, 187
Burbacher, Ralph, 13
Burke,
    Edmund, 241
    Dr. Richard, 189, 212, 244, 271

Burns,
    Bob, 9, 228
    County Supervisor Barney, 17
    Representatives Brenda, 228
Bush, George, 77

C

Cameron, Duke, 293-294, 341
Carlson, Donna, 78, 208
Carpenter, Clarence, 19
Carson, Johnny, 69
Castro, Raul, 45, 215
Cavello, Frank, 177
Chanen, Herman, 47, 52
Conlan, John, 113
Cooper, Jim, 348
Cope, Lanny, 76
Corbet, Leo, 68, 115, 202
Corbin, Bob, 1, 2, 59, 86, 272,
    310, 316,
Corio, Antonio, 280
Costello, Pat, 205-206
Craft, Fred, 120, 215, 273, 275
Craig, Judge Walter T., 59
Crowe, Tom, 261, 263
Cudahy, Michael, 221, 300, 306

D

Dan, Michael, 156, 206
Davenport, Rita, 148
Davis, Glen, 170
DeBolske, Jack, 58
DeConcini, Dennis, 113, 121, 201
DeConcinni, Evo, 234
DeGraw, Rick, 201
Denny, Bob, 58, 228-229

Dioguardi, Mark, 148
Downey, Joyce, 135, 180, 314,
  318, 320
Dunton, Roy, 260, 262

E

Eckstein, Paul, 201, 219, 226, 326
Eisley, Howard, 295
Eller, Karl, 56-57, 69, 83, 179, 315
Elson, Roy, 24
Ewing, Reid, 63, 132

F

Fannin,
  Bob, 90
  Governor, 13, 15, 21, 39
  Paul, 12, 28, 113, 143
Ferguson, Jim, 103
Fields, Terri, 270, 279
Fitzpatrick, Tom, 82, 144
Fowler, George, 28
French, William P., 224, 227, 250
French-designated, 277
French-Eckstein, 250
Frohmiller, Anna, 10

G

Garrett, Roger, 83
Gasser, Vern, 100
Gilbert,
  Jack, 43
  Theresa, 205
Gillett, George, 84
Giordano,
  Gary, 227, 254
Giss, Harold, 15-16, 18, 43
Goddard,
  Sam, 170
  Terry, 96, 121-122, 210

Goebbels, Joseph, 166
Goff, Charlie, 16
Goldwater,
  Robert, 60
  Barry, 11, 30, 38, 115
Gordon, Francis X., 190, 281
Graham, George, 218
Greene, Michael, 301
Gregan, Hugh, 99
Griffith, Peggy, 232
Gutier, Alberto, 204
Gutierrez, Alfredo, 47, 70, 144

H

Haldiman, Joe, 14, 19
Hall,
  Dave, 148, 281
  Gene, 268
Hamilton, Art, 127, 130-131, 132,
  228
Hardigan, Jim, 149
Hardt, Senator Bill, 268
Harper, Ron, 295
Hart, Gary, 76
Hawkins, Max, 273
Hayden, Carl, 24, 30, 35
Hays, John, 269
Helmick, Ray, 86
Hensley, Cindy, 74
Hermon, Bev, 149
Herstam, Chris, 58, 127, 147-148,
  227
Hervey, Fred, 83
Heuisler, Bill, 117
Higgins, Jake, 148
Hill, Jeff, 147
Hiner, Ed, 165
Hink, Dr. Heinz, 283
Hodel, Interior Secretary Don, 120
Hogerson, Rex, 154
Hopkins, Harry, 80

Hull, Jane, 127, 130, 186, 191, 194, 208, 223
Hurwitz, Andy, 90, 258, 282
Hutchins, LaVerne, 261, 270

J

Jacques, John, 106
Jameson, Bill, 69, 97
Jefferson, Thomas, 80, 129
Jenkins, Sammy, 184
Jennings, Renz, 201
Johnson,
Beau, 181, 205, 212, 215, 250, 274-275
Leslie, 227-228
President Lyndon, 38
Ron, 205
Johnston,
Christina, 158, 281
Lt. Coy, 282

K

Karie, Jack, 32
Kay, Peter, 90, 156
Keilp, Joe, 297, 302, 305, 308
Kennedy, President, 25-26
Killian, Mark, 149, 227, 277-278
Kimball, Richard, 77
King,
John, 251
Martin Luther, 125-126, 127, 129-132, 258
Holiday, 125-135, 172
Kleindienst, Richard, 28, 30,305
Kolbe, Jim, 104, 194, 198
Koppel, Ted, 173
Kruglick, Burt, 91, 94, 96-97, 104, 169
Kunasek, Carl, 111, 145, 223, 259
Kyl, Jon, 104, 189, 195

L

Lambert, Florence, 8
Lamparter, Janice, 86
Lane, Joe, 111, 145, 186, 189-191, 211, 219, 223, 227-228, 244
LaSota, Jack, 84
Lee, Warner, 237, 318, 321, 324-326
Lehrer, Jim, 174
Leonard, Jeris, 261, 264
Lincoln, Abraham, 167, 210, 300, 335
Locke, John, 291
Londen, Jack, 67, 133, 291
Long, William, 237, 324-325, 327
Lotstein, Bernard, 72, 221, 300, 306-308
Lunn,
Bob, 111
Greg, 58

M

MacEachern, Doug, 88
Madison, James, 313
Mallery, Dick, 46, 53, 69
Mangum, John, 318, 326
Mardian, Sam, 17
Marley, Kemper, 64
Martinez, DPS Officer, 212, 271, 276
Mason, Tony, 55, 70, 78, 88, 91
Matheson, Mac, 26, 86, 117, 244
Mawhinney, Senator, 286
McCain, John, 73, 77, 105, 112, 170, 189
McCloy, Mike, 186
McFarland, Ernest, 10, 141
McGowan, John, 15
Mecham, Willard, 62, 310
Meese, Ed, 154

Milstead, Ralph, 152, 157-158, 164, 181, 213, 279

Mofford, Rose, 59, 62, 115, 257, 292, 329, 333, 338

Moore, Thad, 224

Moore-Stanford, 224

Mormons, 110

Morrison,Robert, 10, 12

Murchison, Tim, 154

Murphy, Frank, 14

Murray, J. Edward, 17

N

Nixon, Richard, 69, 195-196, 245

Norton, John, 51

O

Orr, Glenda, 193

P

Pappas, Tom, 101, 115

Pell, Duayne, 202

Pfister, Jack, 148

Phelps, Gary, 280

Platt, H. Jay, 232, 238

Pulliam, Eugene, 11, 15, 33, 51

Pyle, Howard, 10

Pyper, Bill, 13

Q

Quayle, Dan, 77

R

Rasse, Lorenz, 7

Rather, Dan, 103

Ratliff, Jim, 58, 111, 145, 148, 223

Reagan, President Ronald, 73-74, 342

Rhodes,
Jay, 44, 104, 112
John, 10, 56, 75, 195, 291

Richardson, Edith, 112-113, 119, 180, 243, 320

Ridge, Sterling, 341

Roberts, Bud, 216

Rodriguez, Al, 140, 143

Roles, Ray, 162

Rosenzweig, Harry, 30, 47, 60

Rottas, Ray, 71

Runyan, Hal, 57, 111, 145, 289

Russell,
Ray, 76, 112, 119, 243, 258
Richard, 25

Ryan, Superior Court Judge, 297, 300

S

Safer, Morely, 172

Schmidt, Sergeant Alan, 280

Schulz, Bill, 55, 62, 69-70, 96-98

Schuster, Bob, 90

Schwartz, Howard, 318, 325

Scott, Mike, 297, 307

Shadegg,
John, 72, 135, 178, 314
Steve, 11, 25, 28, 135, 148

Shover, Bill, 76

Shumway, Jim, 218, 302

Simmons, James, 51

Sinner, Rudolf, 7

Sitter, Al, 72

Skelly, Jim, 156, 176-177, 227-229, 232, 249, 251

Skousen, W. Cleon, 173

Smith,
John, 39

Snell,
  Dick, 51
  Frank, 52
Sossaman, James, 284
Spear, Ed, 8
Stahl, Leslie, 174
Stalin, Joseph, 11
Stanford, Bill, 224
Steffey, Lela, 227-228
Steiger, Sam, 207
Steiner, Senator, 326, 328
Stover, Henry, 131
Stulls, Bill, 136
Stump, Bob, 77, 104, 189, 194,
  197, 257
Symington, Fife, 170, 187, 339

T

Tanner, Maurice, 17
Teets, John, 56
Thomas,
  John, 262
  Randy, 243
Thompson, Ray, 17
Trial, Senate Impeachment, 189-
  190, 261, 273, 278-279
Truman, Harry, 173
Tully, Duke, 69, 71, 75-76
Turley, Keith, 53, 58, 69, 108
Twist, Steve, 135

U

Udall,
  Sam, 107, 109, 243
  Stewart, 26, 38
Usdane, Bob, 63, 109, 111, 145,
  164, 263

V

Valdez, Governor Felix, 344

W

Warner,
  Caroline, 70, 91, 97-98, 291
  Ron, 62
Warren, Ned, 60
Watkins, Ralph, 76, 99, 178-179,
  237, 271-272, 275
Webb, Del, 58
Webster, Daniel, 1
Weisz, George, 194, 235, 251, 275
Wendland, Michael, 46
Wessel, Nancy, 256
West, Tony, 159, 189, 194
Williams,
  Jack, 45, 67, 138, 143, 180, 320
  Russ, 28
  Susan, 111-112
  Ted, 109
Wine, Senator, 21
Wolfson, Barry M., 210
Wolfswinkel, Conley, 44
Wynn, Bernie, 27, 29

Y

Young, Arthur, 162